Tokyo TARAREBA GIRLS

5

AKIKO HIGASHIMURA

TODAY'S RECOMMENDATIONS

ACT 16 SLUDGE WOMEN

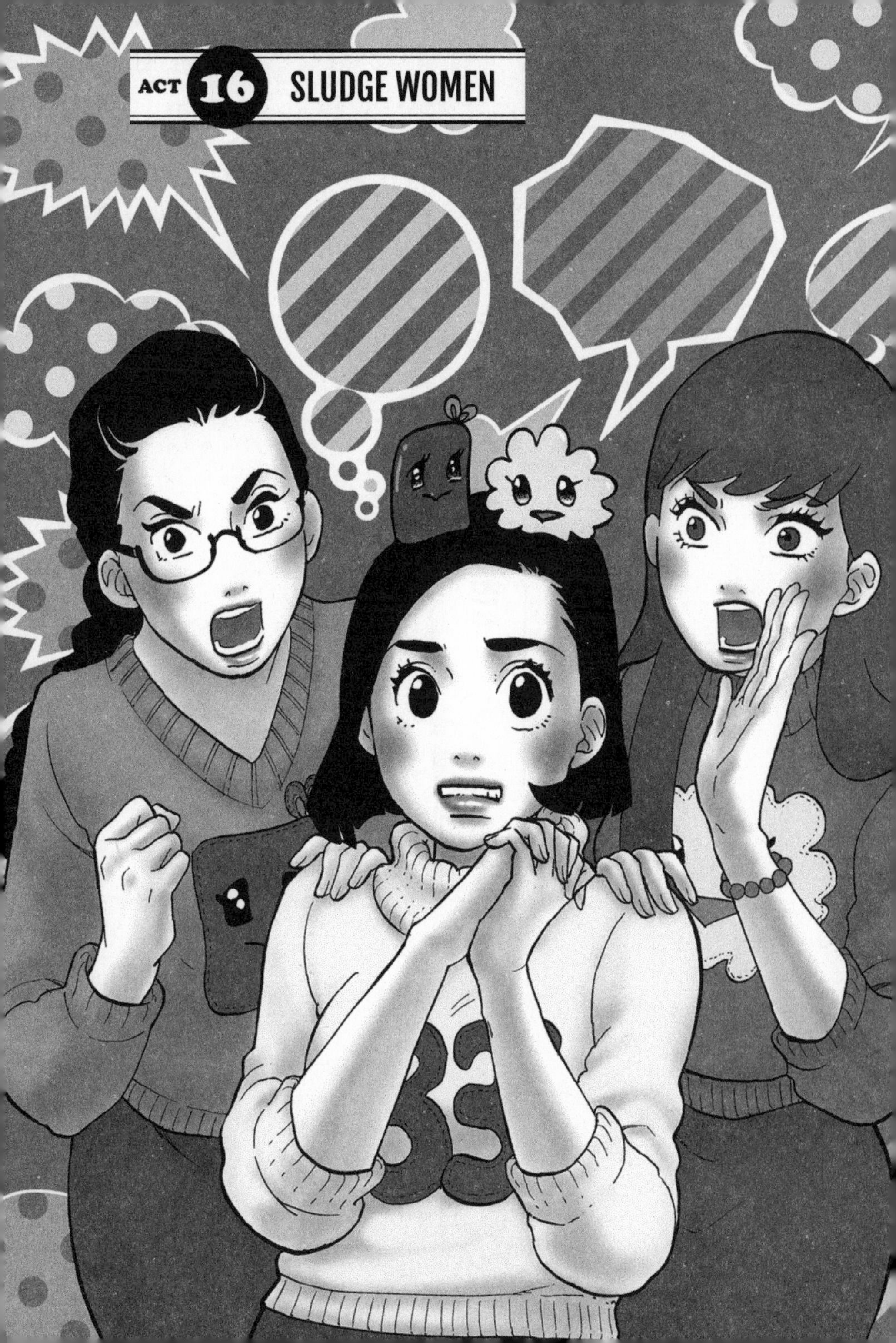

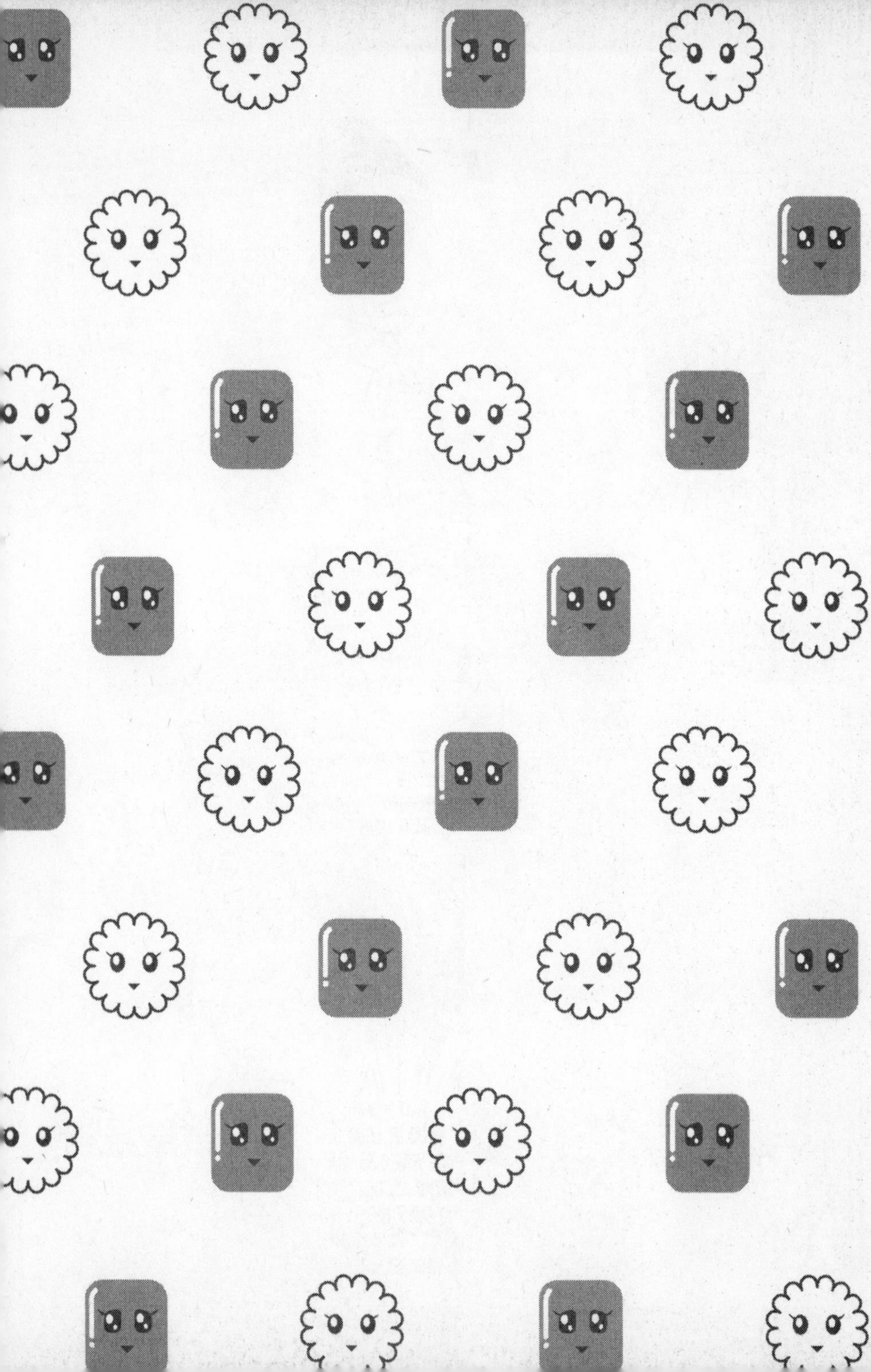

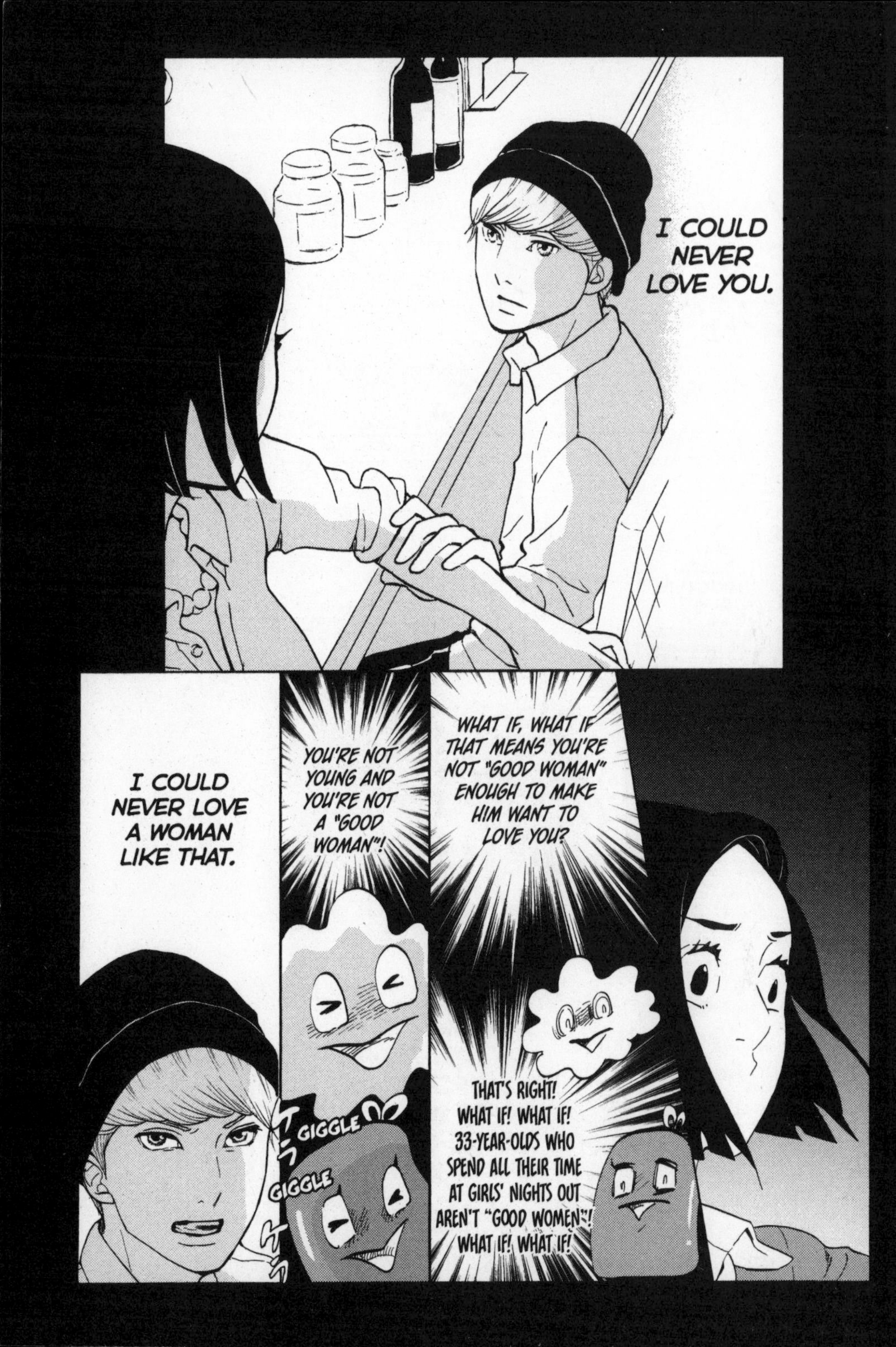
I COULD NEVER LOVE YOU.
WHAT IF, WHAT IF THAT MEANS YOU'RE NOT "GOOD WOMAN" ENOUGH TO MAKE HIM WANT TO LOVE YOU?
THAT'S RIGHT! WHAT IF! WHAT IF! 33-YEAR-OLDS WHO SPEND ALL THEIR TIME AT GIRLS' NIGHTS OUT AREN'T "GOOD WOMEN"! WHAT IF! WHAT IF!
YOU'RE NOT YOUNG AND YOU'RE NOT A "GOOD WOMAN"!
GIGGLE
GIGGLE
I COULD NEVER LOVE A WOMAN LIKE THAT.

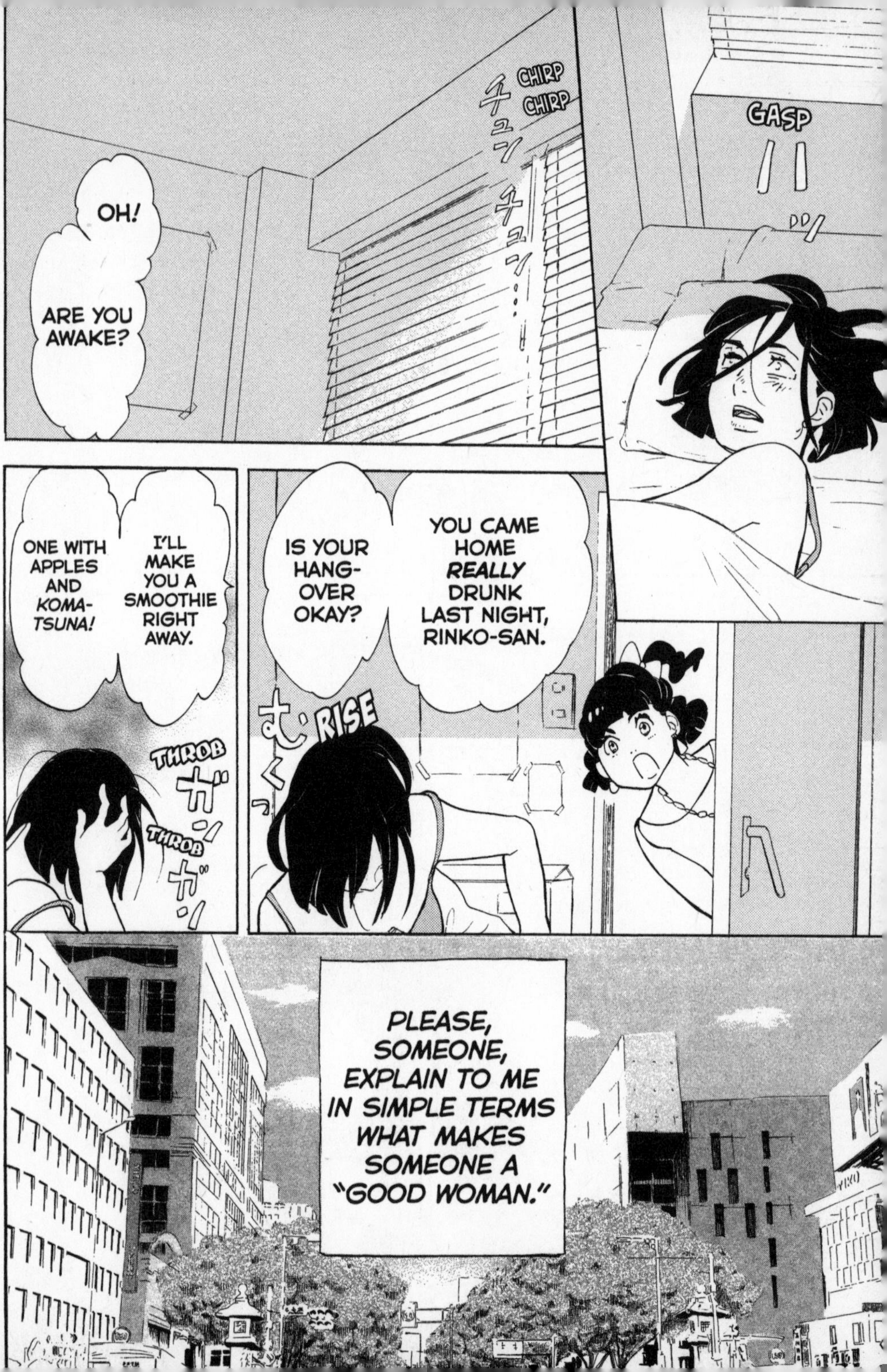
GASP
CHIRP CHIRP
OH!
ARE YOU AWAKE?
YOU CAME HOME *REALLY* DRUNK LAST NIGHT, RINKO-SAN.
IS YOUR HANG-OVER OKAY?
RISE
I'LL MAKE YOU A SMOOTHIE RIGHT AWAY.
ONE WITH APPLES AND *KOMA-TSUNA!*
THROB
THROB
PLEASE, SOMEONE, EXPLAIN TO ME IN SIMPLE TERMS WHAT MAKES SOMEONE A "GOOD WOMAN."

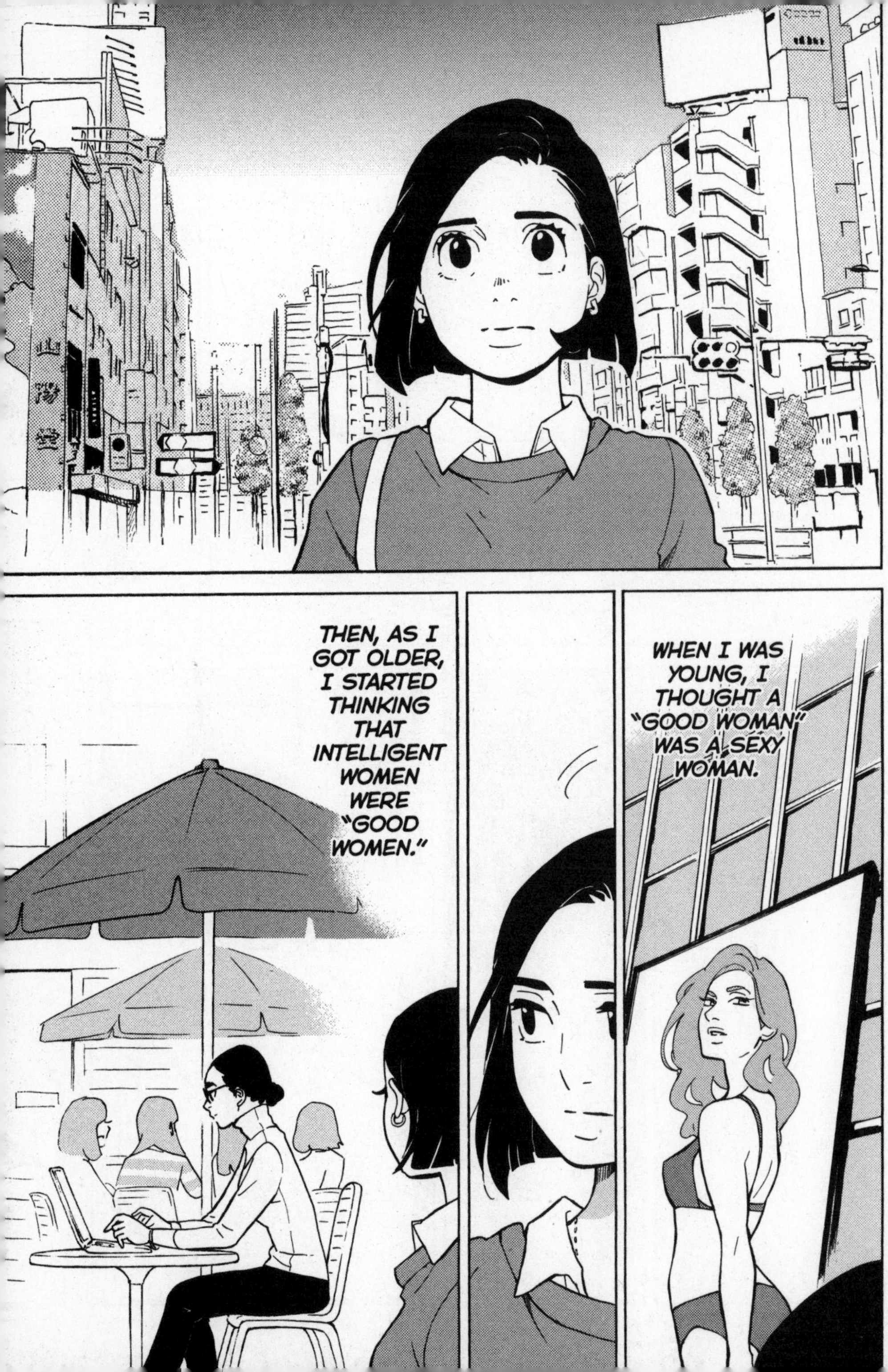
WHEN I WAS YOUNG, I THOUGHT A "GOOD WOMAN" WAS A SEXY WOMAN.
THEN, AS I GOT OLDER, I STARTED THINKING THAT INTELLIGENT WOMEN WERE "GOOD WOMEN."

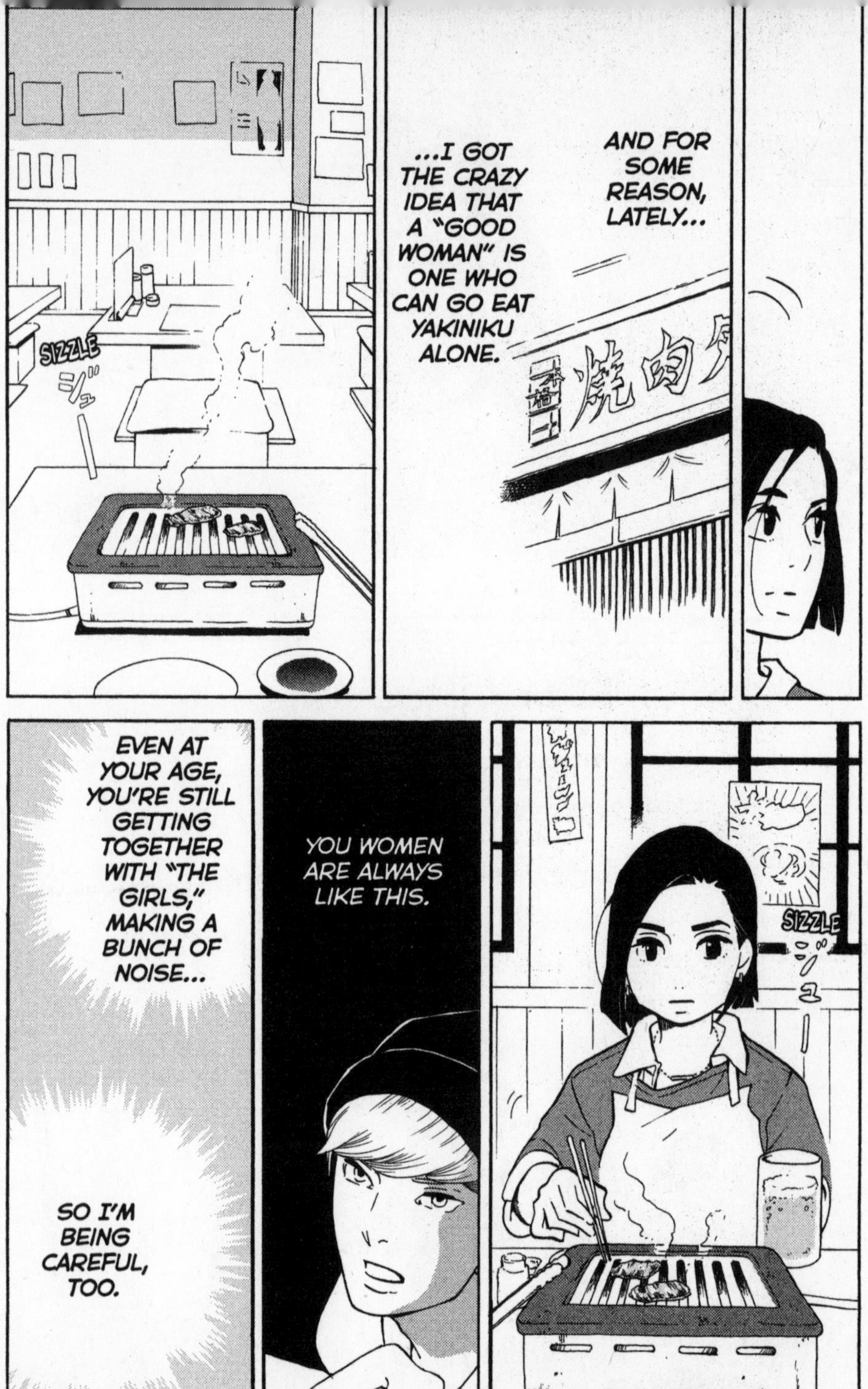
AND FOR SOME REASON, LATELY...
...I GOT THE CRAZY IDEA THAT A "GOOD WOMAN" IS ONE WHO CAN GO EAT YAKINIKU ALONE.
SIZZLE
ジュ
SIZZLE
ジュ
YOU WOMEN ARE ALWAYS LIKE THIS.
EVEN AT YOUR AGE, YOU'RE STILL GETTING TOGETHER WITH "THE GIRLS," MAKING A BUNCH OF NOISE...
SO I'M BEING CAREFUL, TOO.

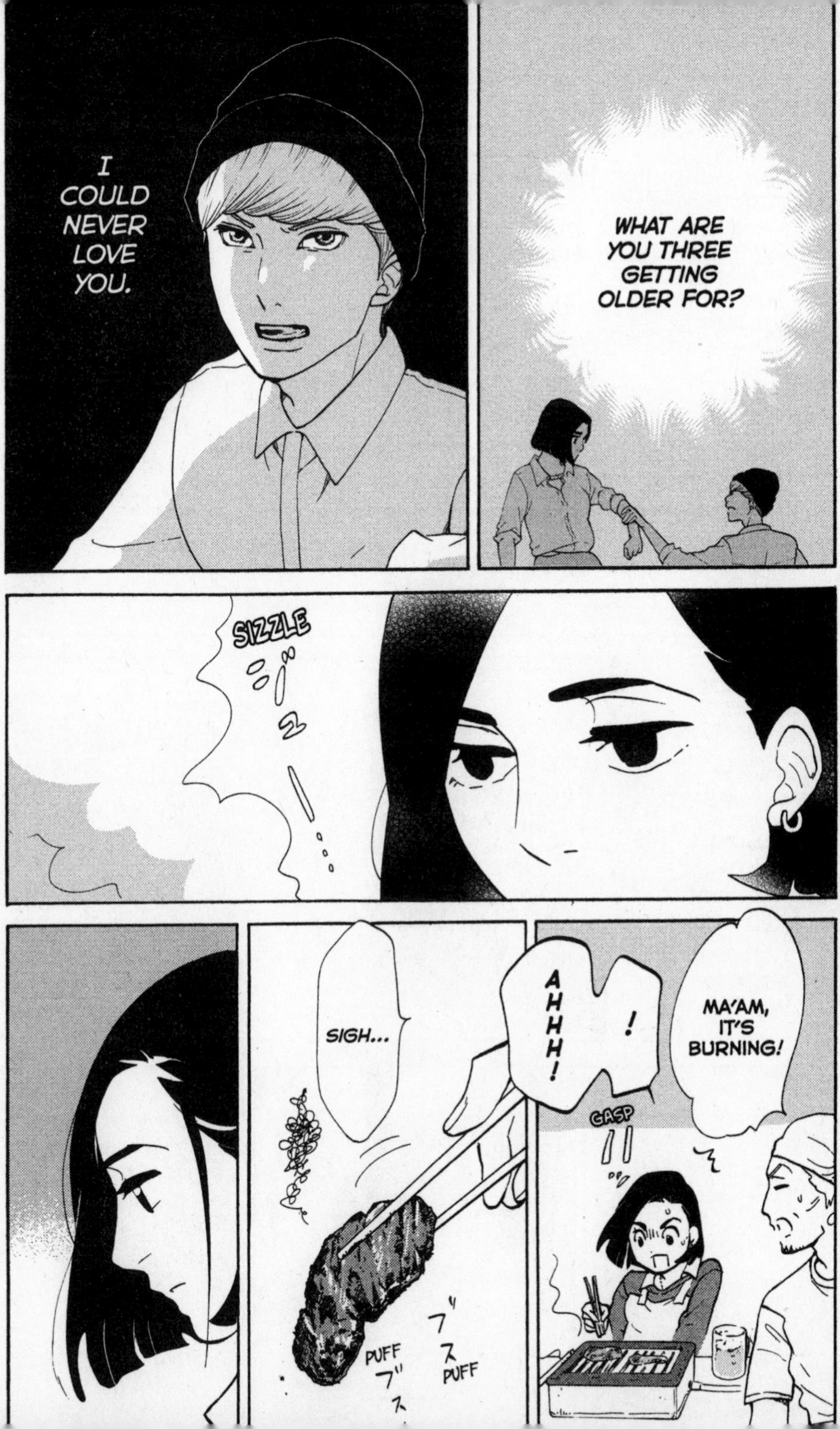
WHAT ARE YOU THREE GETTING OLDER FOR?
I COULD NEVER LOVE YOU.
SIZZLE
MA'AM, IT'S BURNING!
AHHH!!
GASP
SIGH...
ブス
PUFF
ブス
PUFF

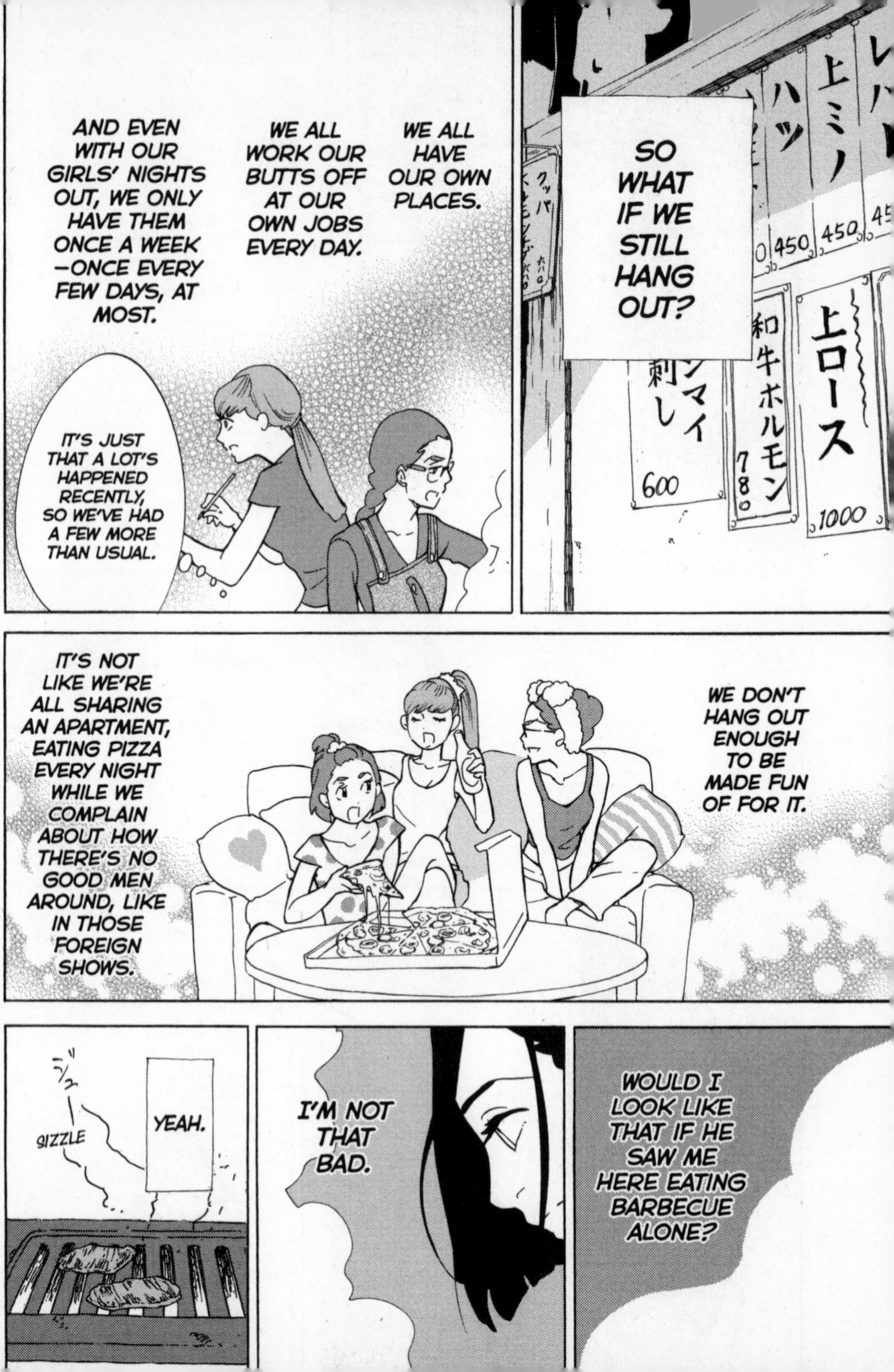
SO WHAT IF WE STILL HANG OUT?
上ミノ
ハツ
450
450
上ロース
1000
和牛ホルモン
780
刺し
600
WE ALL HAVE OUR OWN PLACES.
WE ALL WORK OUR BUTTS OFF AT OUR OWN JOBS EVERY DAY.
AND EVEN WITH OUR GIRLS' NIGHTS OUT, WE ONLY HAVE THEM ONCE A WEEK —ONCE EVERY FEW DAYS, AT MOST.
IT'S JUST THAT A LOT'S HAPPENED RECENTLY, SO WE'VE HAD A FEW MORE THAN USUAL.
WE DON'T HANG OUT ENOUGH TO BE MADE FUN OF FOR IT.
IT'S NOT LIKE WE'RE ALL SHARING AN APARTMENT, EATING PIZZA EVERY NIGHT WHILE WE COMPLAIN ABOUT HOW THERE'S NO GOOD MEN AROUND, LIKE IN THOSE FOREIGN SHOWS.
WOULD I LOOK LIKE THAT IF HE SAW ME HERE EATING BARBECUE ALONE?
I'M NOT THAT BAD.
YEAH.
ジュー
SIZZLE

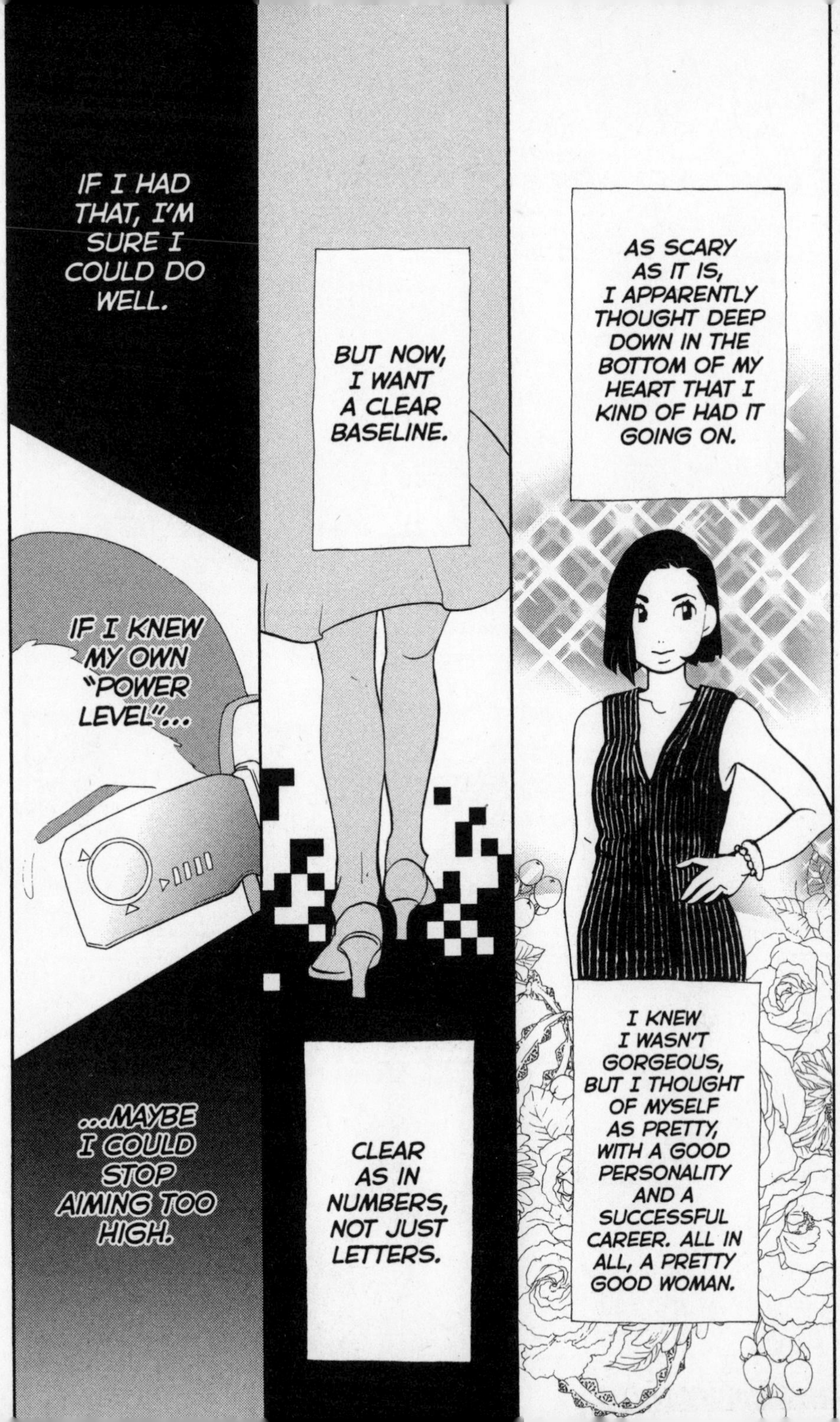
AS SCARY AS IT IS, I APPARENTLY THOUGHT DEEP DOWN IN THE BOTTOM OF MY HEART THAT I KIND OF HAD IT GOING ON.
I KNEW I WASN'T GORGEOUS, BUT I THOUGHT OF MYSELF AS PRETTY, WITH A GOOD PERSONALITY AND A SUCCESSFUL CAREER. ALL IN ALL, A PRETTY GOOD WOMAN.
BUT NOW, I WANT A CLEAR BASELINE.
CLEAR AS IN NUMBERS, NOT JUST LETTERS.
IF I HAD THAT, I'M SURE I COULD DO WELL.
IF I KNEW MY OWN "POWER LEVEL"...
...MAYBE I COULD STOP AIMING TOO HIGH.

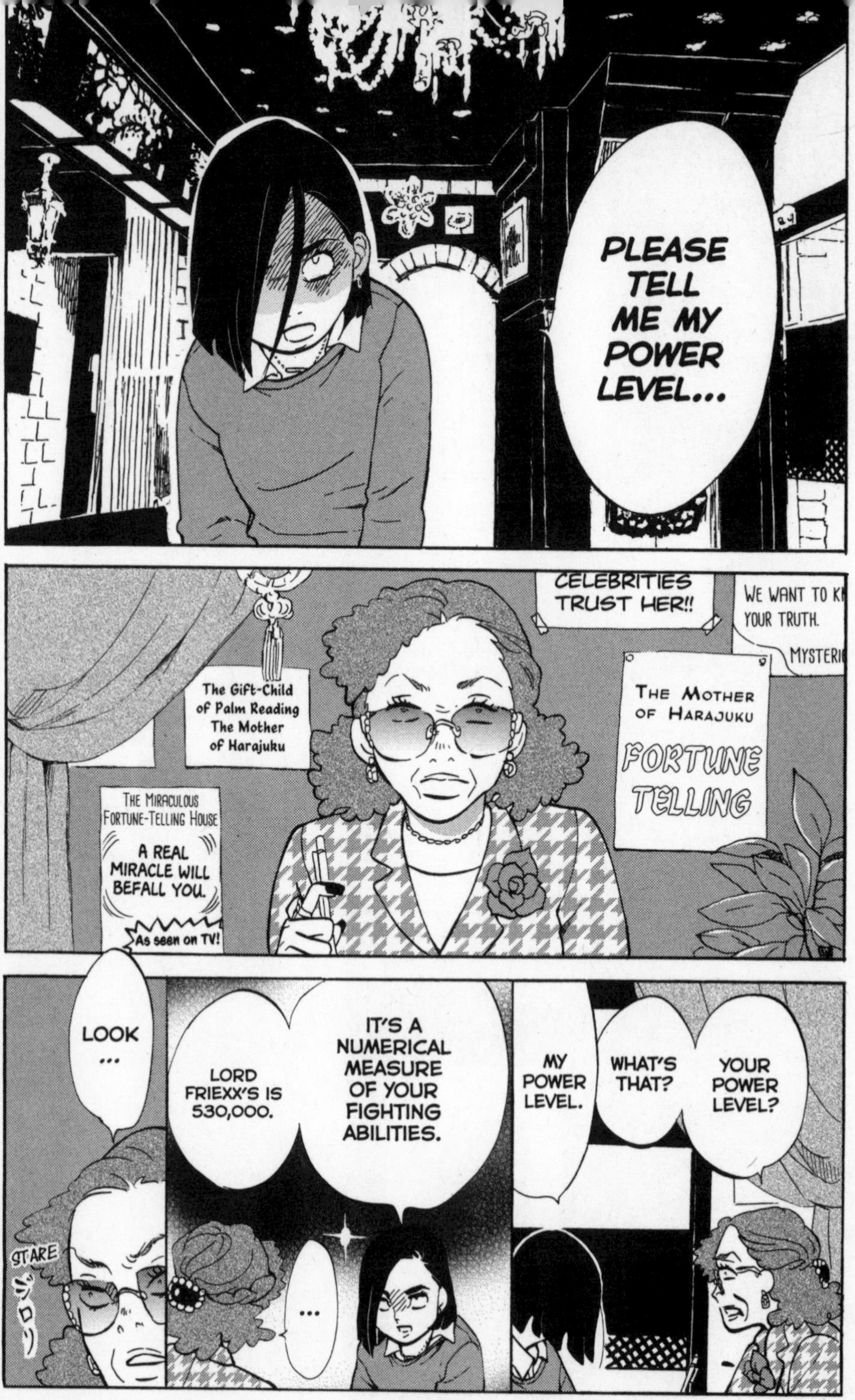
PLEASE TELL ME MY POWER LEVEL...
WE WANT TO
YOUR TRUTH.
CELEBRITIES TRUST HER!!
THE MOTHER OF HARAJUKU
FORTUNE TELLING
The Gift-Child of Palm Reading The Mother of Harajuku
THE MIRACULOUS FORTUNE-TELLING HOUSE
A REAL MIRACLE WILL BEFALL YOU.
As seen on TV!
YOUR POWER LEVEL?
WHAT'S THAT?
MY POWER LEVEL.
IT'S A NUMERICAL MEASURE OF YOUR FIGHTING ABILITIES.
LORD FRIEXX'S IS 530,000.
...
LOOK ...
STARE
ジロ

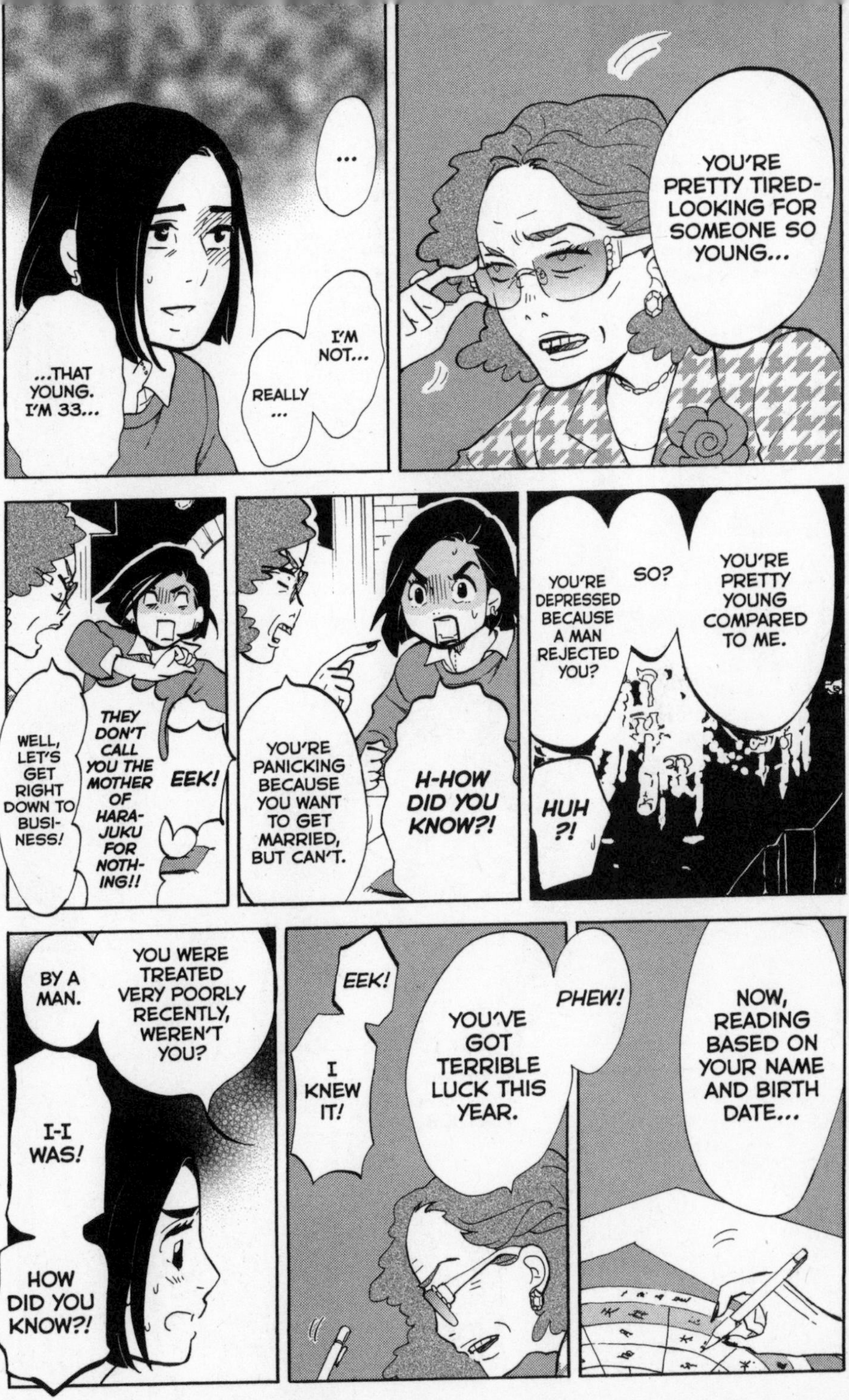
YOU'RE PRETTY TIRED-LOOKING FOR SOMEONE SO YOUNG...
...
I'M NOT...
REALLY...
...THAT YOUNG. I'M 33...
YOU'RE PRETTY YOUNG COMPARED TO ME.
SO?
YOU'RE DEPRESSED BECAUSE A MAN REJECTED YOU?
HUH?!
YOU'RE PANICKING BECAUSE YOU WANT TO GET MARRIED, BUT CAN'T.
H-HOW DID YOU KNOW?!
EEK!
THEY DON'T CALL YOU THE MOTHER OF HARAJUKU FOR NOTHING!!
WELL, LET'S GET RIGHT DOWN TO BUSINESS!
NOW, READING BASED ON YOUR NAME AND BIRTH DATE...
PHEW!
YOU'VE GOT TERRIBLE LUCK THIS YEAR.
EEK!
I KNEW IT!
YOU WERE TREATED VERY POORLY RECENTLY, WEREN'T YOU?
BY A MAN.
I-I WAS!
HOW DID YOU KNOW?!

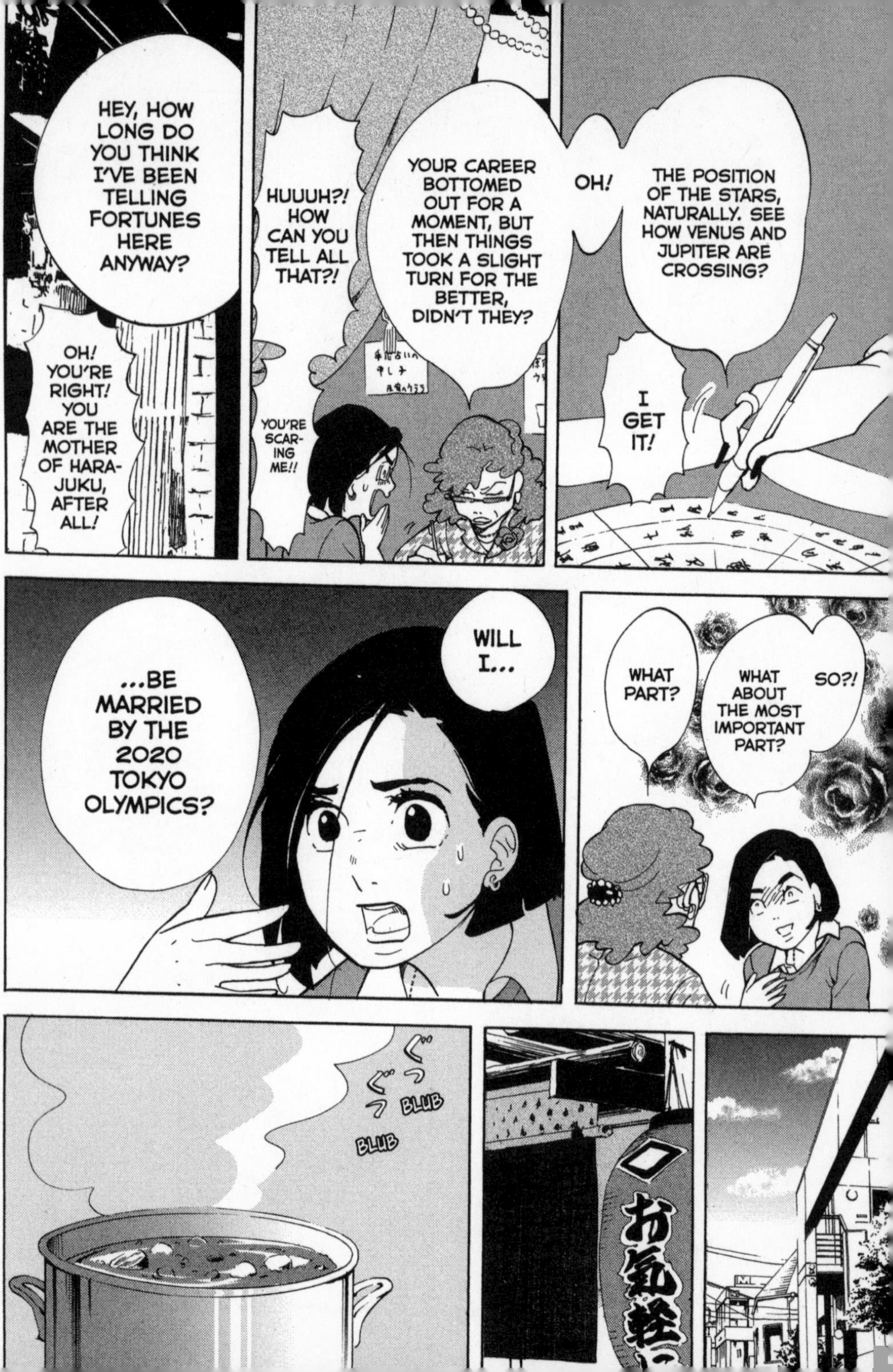
THE POSITION OF THE STARS, NATURALLY. SEE HOW VENUS AND JUPITER ARE CROSSING?
OH!
I GET IT!
YOUR CAREER BOTTOMED OUT FOR A MOMENT, BUT THEN THINGS TOOK A SLIGHT TURN FOR THE BETTER, DIDN'T THEY?
HUUUH?! HOW CAN YOU TELL ALL THAT?!
YOU'RE SCARING ME!!
HEY, HOW LONG DO YOU THINK I'VE BEEN TELLING FORTUNES HERE ANYWAY?
OH! YOU'RE RIGHT! YOU ARE THE MOTHER OF HARAJUKU, AFTER ALL!
SO?!
WHAT ABOUT THE MOST IMPORTANT PART?
WHAT PART?
WILL I...
...BE MARRIED BY THE 2020 TOKYO OLYMPICS?
お気軽
ぐつぐつ
BLUB
BLUB

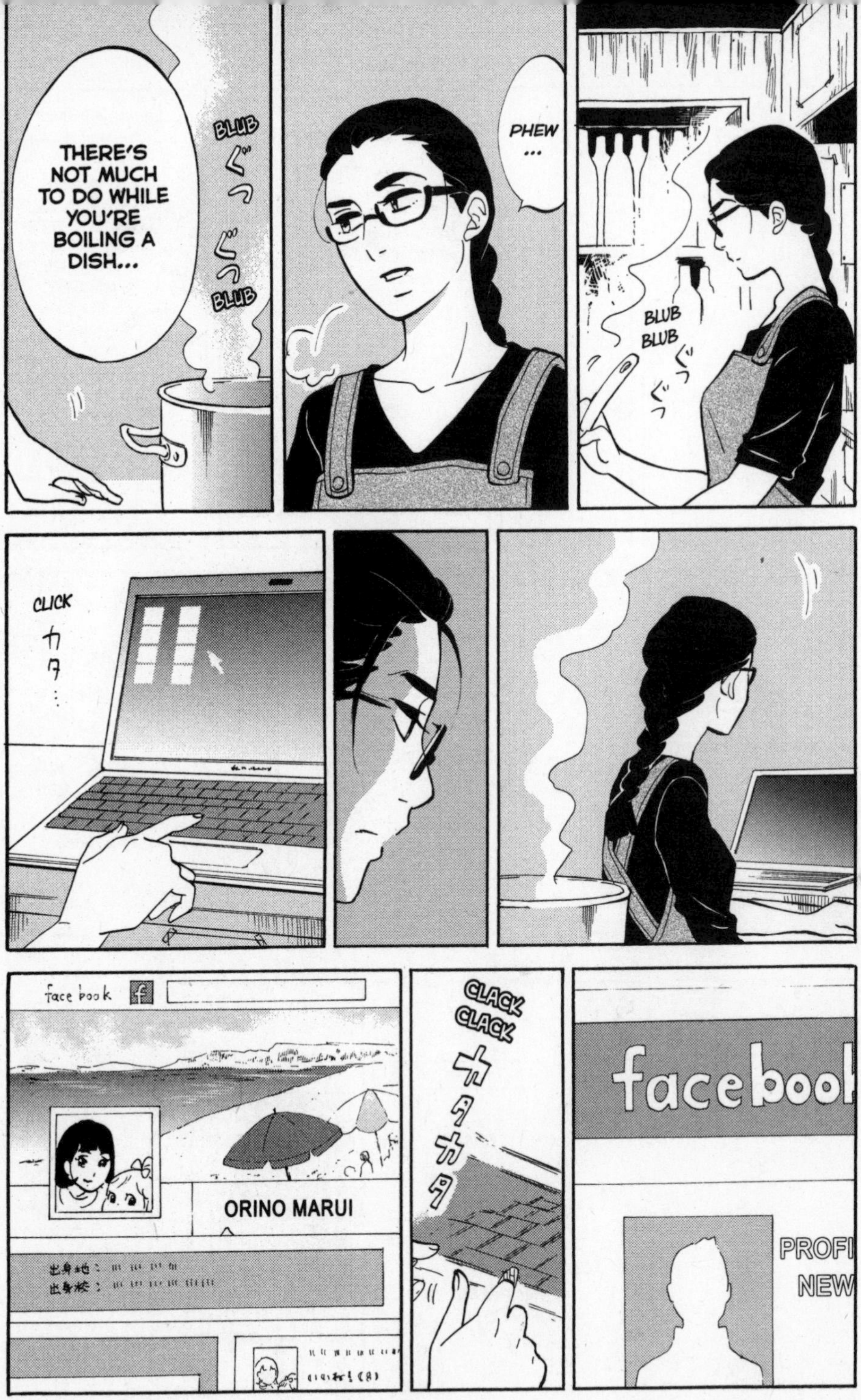
BLUB BLUB ぐつぐつ
PHEW ...
THERE'S NOT MUCH TO DO WHILE YOU'RE BOILING A DISH...
BLUB ぐつぐつ BLUB
CLICK カタ...
facebook
PROFI
NEW
CLACK CLACK カタカタ
face book
ORINO MARUI
出身地：
出身校：

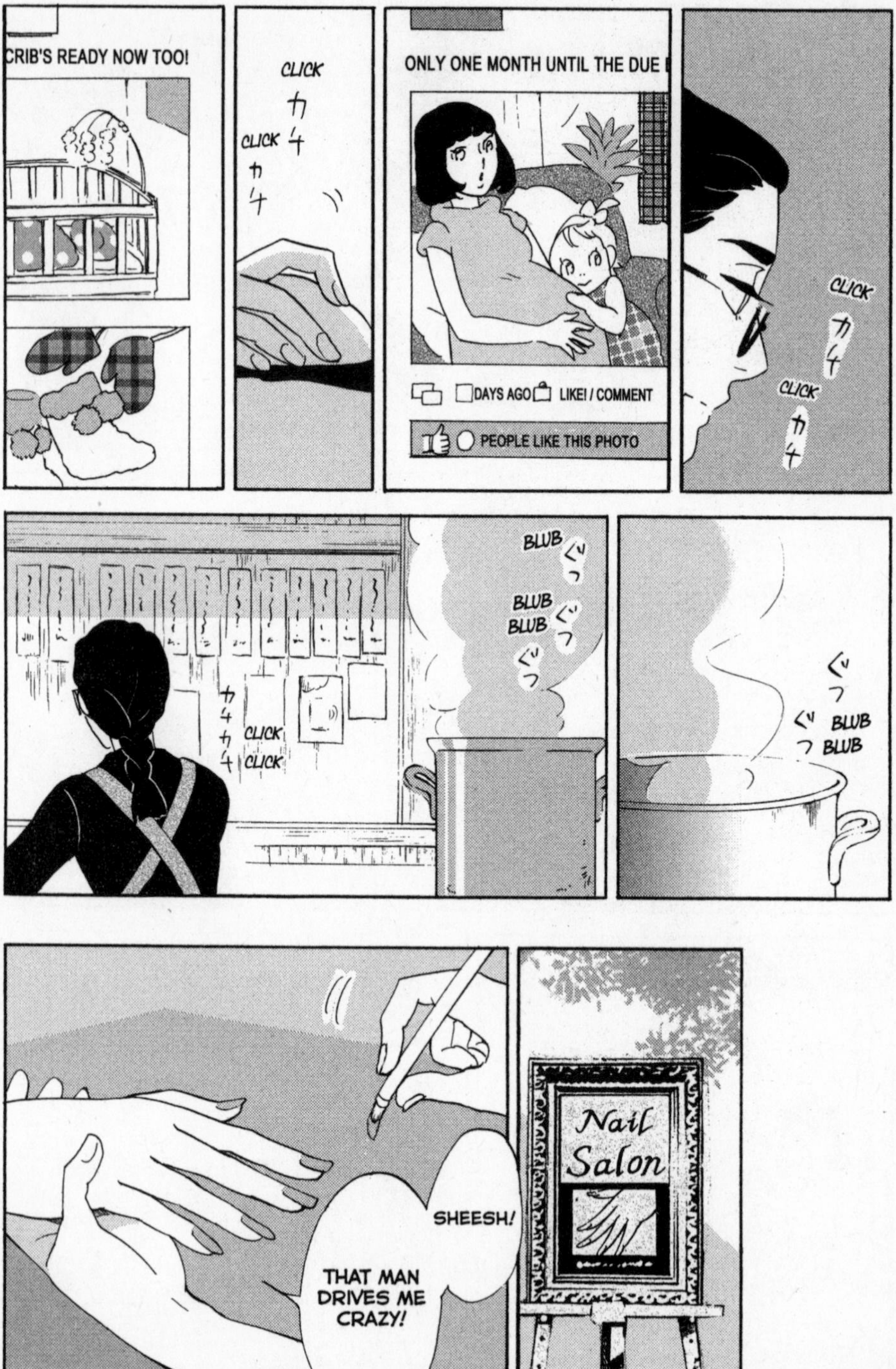
CLICK
カチ
CLICK
カチ
ONLY ONE MONTH UNTIL THE DUE
DAYS AGO
LIKE! / COMMENT
PEOPLE LIKE THIS PHOTO
CLICK
カチ
CLICK
カチ
CRIB'S READY NOW TOO!
ぐつ
ぐつ
BLUB
BLUB
BLUB
ぐつ
BLUB
BLUB
ぐつ
ぐつ
カチ
カチ
CLICK
CLICK
Nail Salon
SHEESH!
THAT MAN DRIVES ME CRAZY!

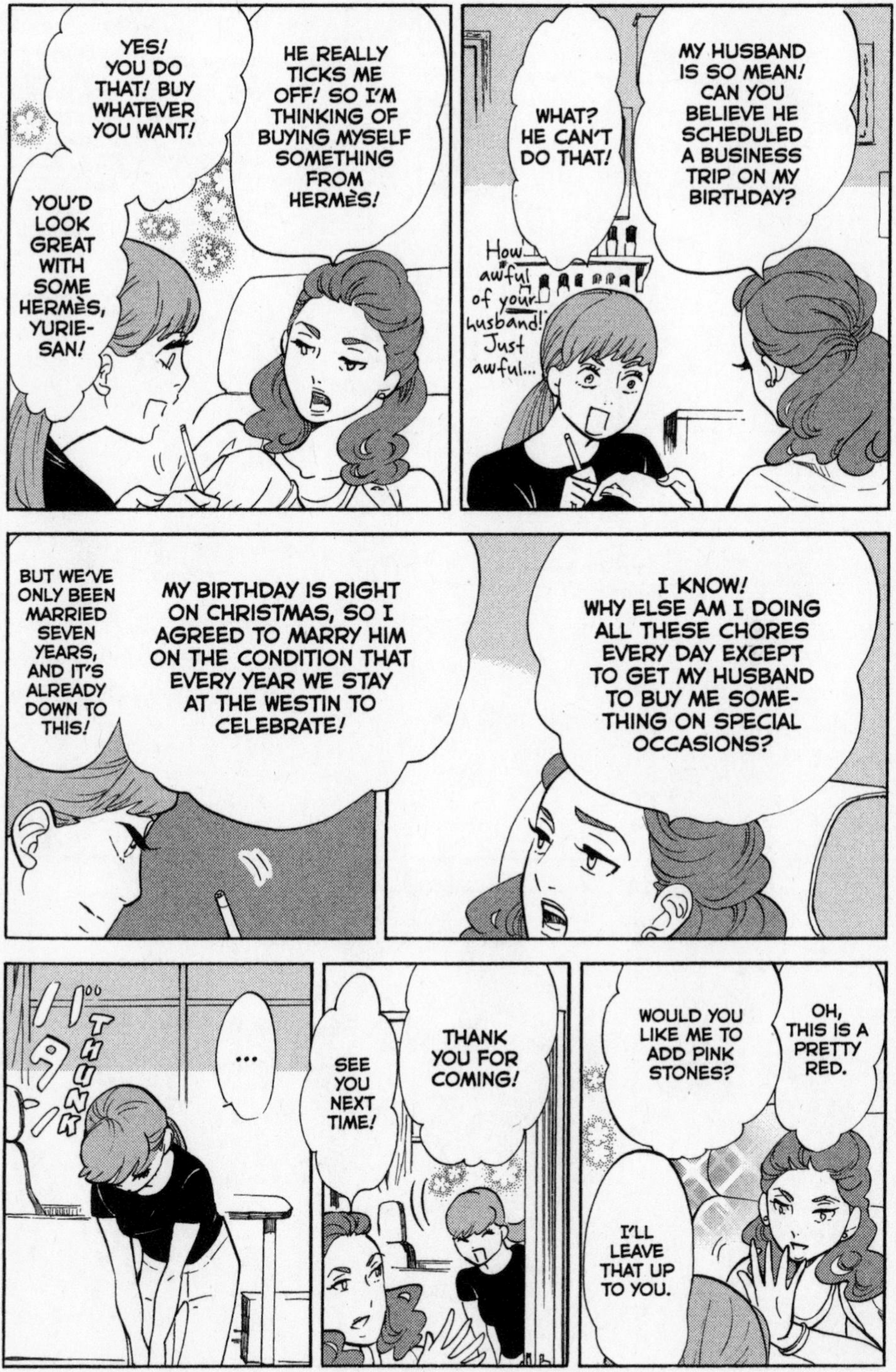
MY HUSBAND IS SO MEAN! CAN YOU BELIEVE HE SCHEDULED A BUSINESS TRIP ON MY BIRTHDAY?
WHAT? HE CAN'T DO THAT!
How awful of your husband! Just awful...
HE REALLY TICKS ME OFF! SO I'M THINKING OF BUYING MYSELF SOMETHING FROM HERMÈS!
YES! YOU DO THAT! BUY WHATEVER YOU WANT!
YOU'D LOOK GREAT WITH SOME HERMÈS, YURIE-SAN!
I KNOW! WHY ELSE AM I DOING ALL THESE CHORES EVERY DAY EXCEPT TO GET MY HUSBAND TO BUY ME SOMETHING ON SPECIAL OCCASIONS?
MY BIRTHDAY IS RIGHT ON CHRISTMAS, SO I AGREED TO MARRY HIM ON THE CONDITION THAT EVERY YEAR WE STAY AT THE WESTIN TO CELEBRATE!
BUT WE'VE ONLY BEEN MARRIED SEVEN YEARS, AND IT'S ALREADY DOWN TO THIS!
OH, THIS IS A PRETTY RED.
WOULD YOU LIKE ME TO ADD PINK STONES?
I'LL LEAVE THAT UP TO YOU.
THANK YOU FOR COMING!
SEE YOU NEXT TIME!
...
THUNK

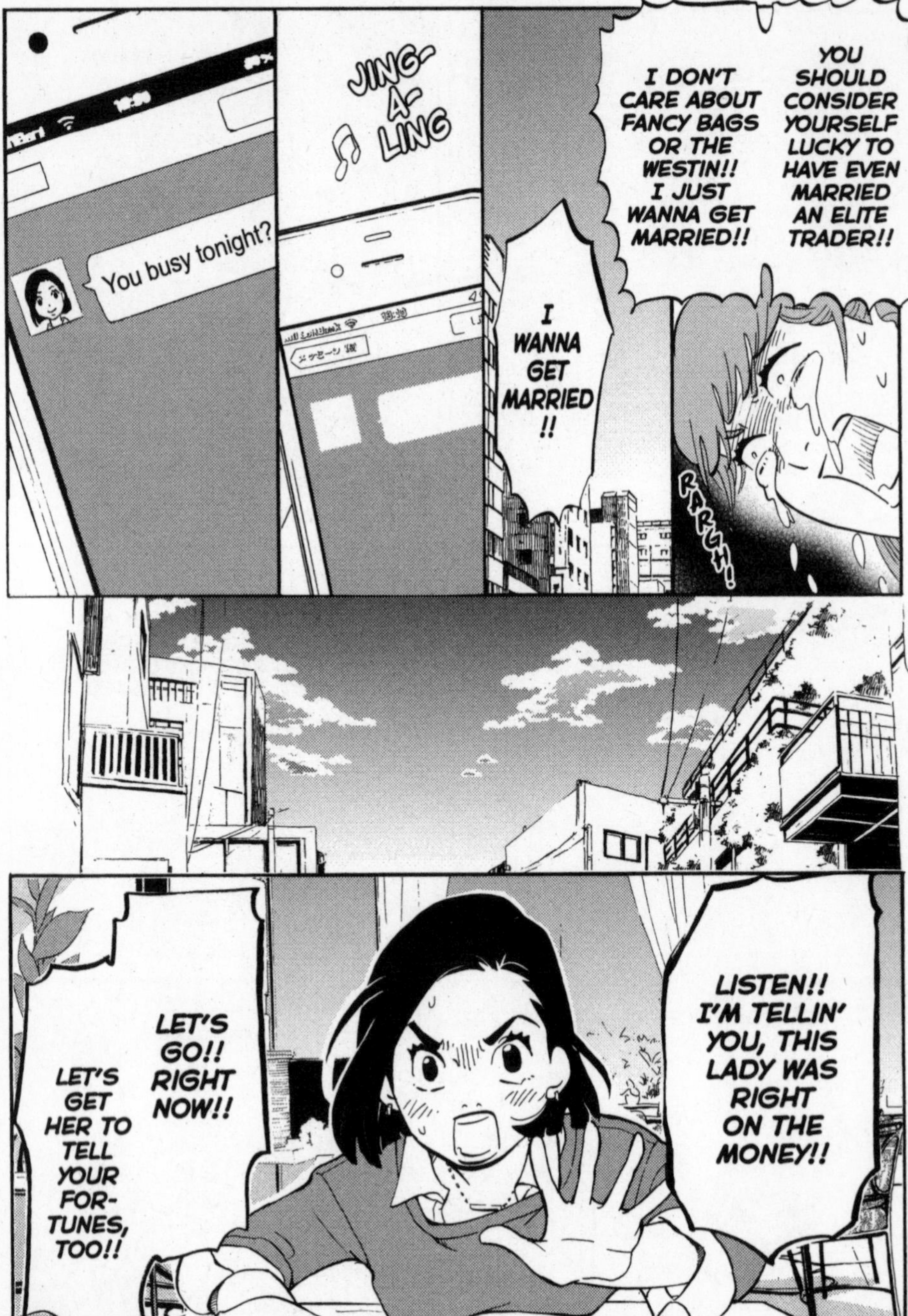
YOU SHOULD CONSIDER YOURSELF LUCKY TO HAVE EVEN MARRIED AN ELITE TRADER!!
I DON'T CARE ABOUT FANCY BAGS OR THE WESTIN!! I JUST WANNA GET MARRIED!!
I WANNA GET MARRIED!!
RARGH!
JING-A-LING
You busy tonight?
LISTEN!! I'M TELLIN' YOU, THIS LADY WAS RIGHT ON THE MONEY!!
LET'S GO!! RIGHT NOW!!
LET'S GET HER TO TELL YOUR FOR-TUNES, TOO!!

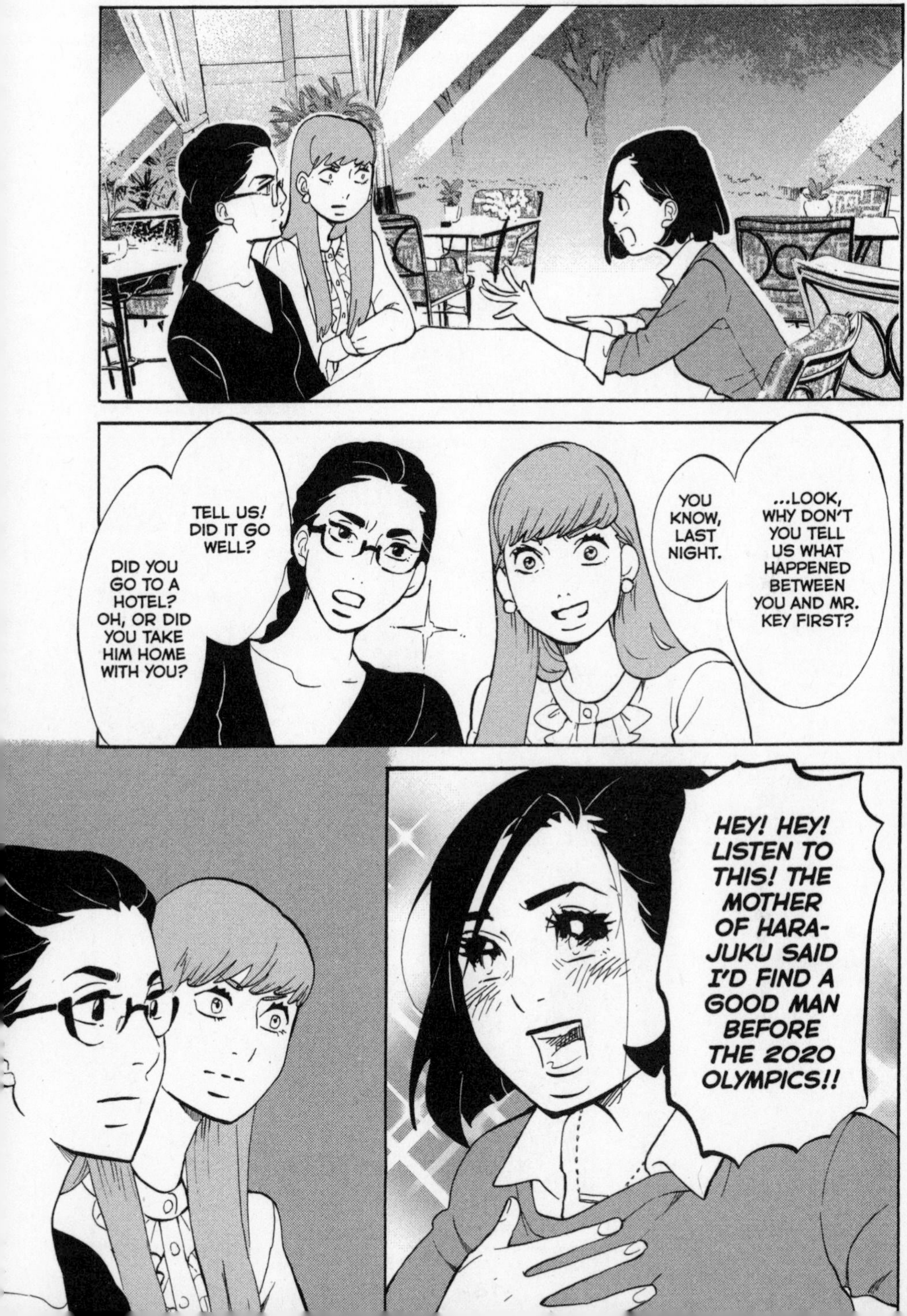
...LOOK, WHY DON'T YOU TELL US WHAT HAPPENED BETWEEN YOU AND MR. KEY FIRST?
YOU KNOW, LAST NIGHT.
TELL US! DID IT GO WELL?
DID YOU GO TO A HOTEL? OH, OR DID YOU TAKE HIM HOME WITH YOU?
HEY! HEY! LISTEN TO THIS! THE MOTHER OF HARAJUKU SAID I'D FIND A GOOD MAN BEFORE THE 2020 OLYMPICS!!

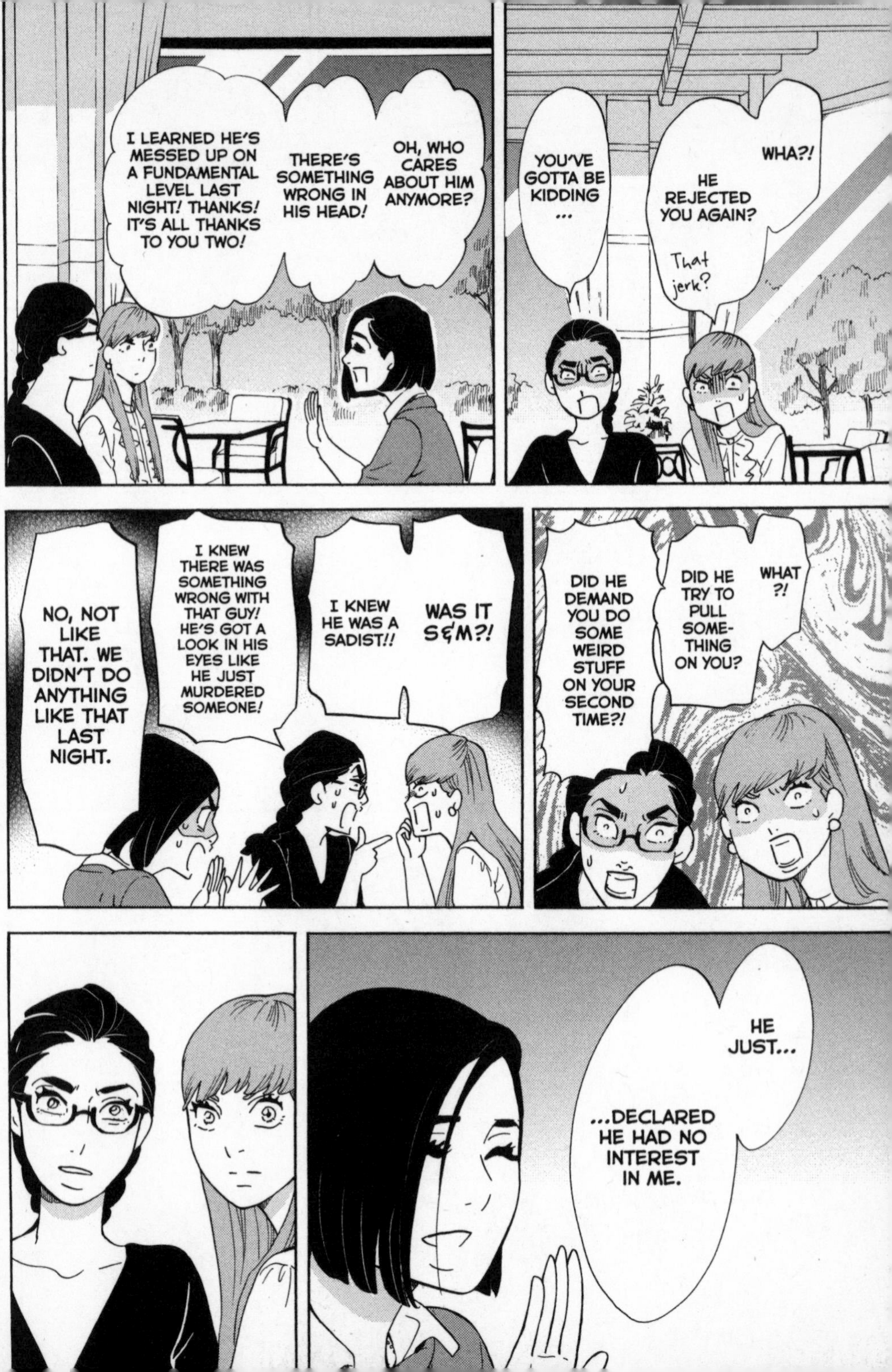
WHA?!
HE REJECTED YOU AGAIN?
That jerk?
YOU'VE GOTTA BE KIDDING ...
OH, WHO CARES ABOUT HIM ANYMORE?
THERE'S SOMETHING WRONG IN HIS HEAD!
I LEARNED HE'S MESSED UP ON A FUNDAMENTAL LEVEL LAST NIGHT! THANKS! IT'S ALL THANKS TO YOU TWO!
WHAT?!
DID HE TRY TO PULL SOME-THING ON YOU?
DID HE DEMAND YOU DO SOME WEIRD STUFF ON YOUR SECOND TIME?!
WAS IT S&M?!
I KNEW HE WAS A SADIST!!
I KNEW THERE WAS SOMETHING WRONG WITH THAT GUY! HE'S GOT A LOOK IN HIS EYES LIKE HE JUST MURDERED SOMEONE!
NO, NOT LIKE THAT. WE DIDN'T DO ANYTHING LIKE THAT LAST NIGHT.
HE JUST...
...DECLARED HE HAD NO INTEREST IN ME.

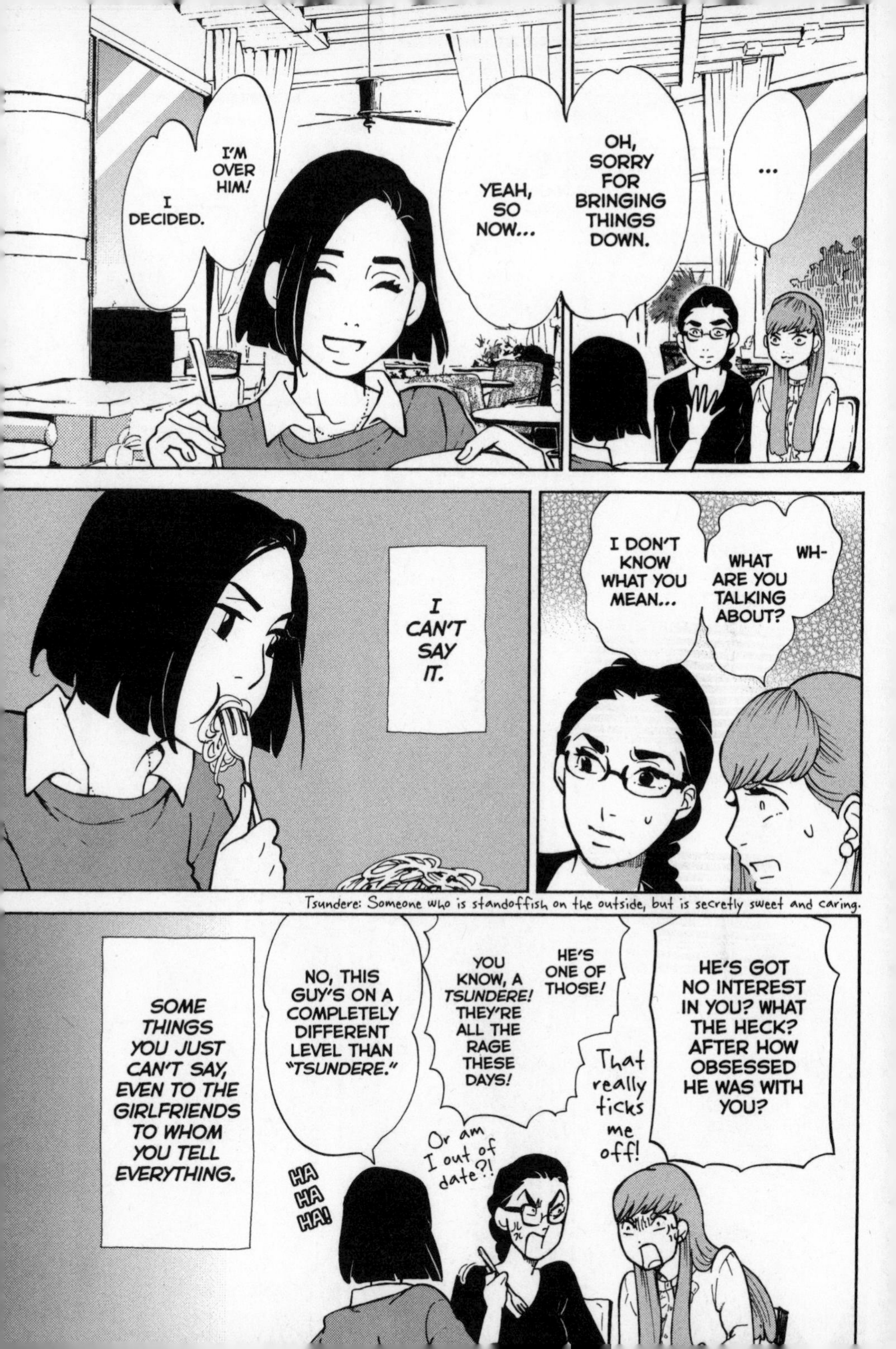
...
OH, SORRY FOR BRINGING THINGS DOWN.
YEAH, SO NOW...
I'M OVER HIM!
I DECIDED.
WH- WHAT ARE YOU TALKING ABOUT?
I DON'T KNOW WHAT YOU MEAN...
I CAN'T SAY IT.
HE'S GOT NO INTEREST IN YOU? WHAT THE HECK? AFTER HOW OBSESSED HE WAS WITH YOU?
That really ticks me off!
HE'S ONE OF THOSE!
YOU KNOW, A *TSUNDERE!* THEY'RE ALL THE RAGE THESE DAYS!
Or am I out of date?!
NO, THIS GUY'S ON A COMPLETELY DIFFERENT LEVEL THAN *"TSUNDERE."*
HA HA HA!
SOME THINGS YOU JUST CAN'T SAY, EVEN TO THE GIRLFRIENDS TO WHOM YOU TELL EVERYTHING.

Tsundere: Someone who is standoffish on the outside, but is secretly sweet and caring.

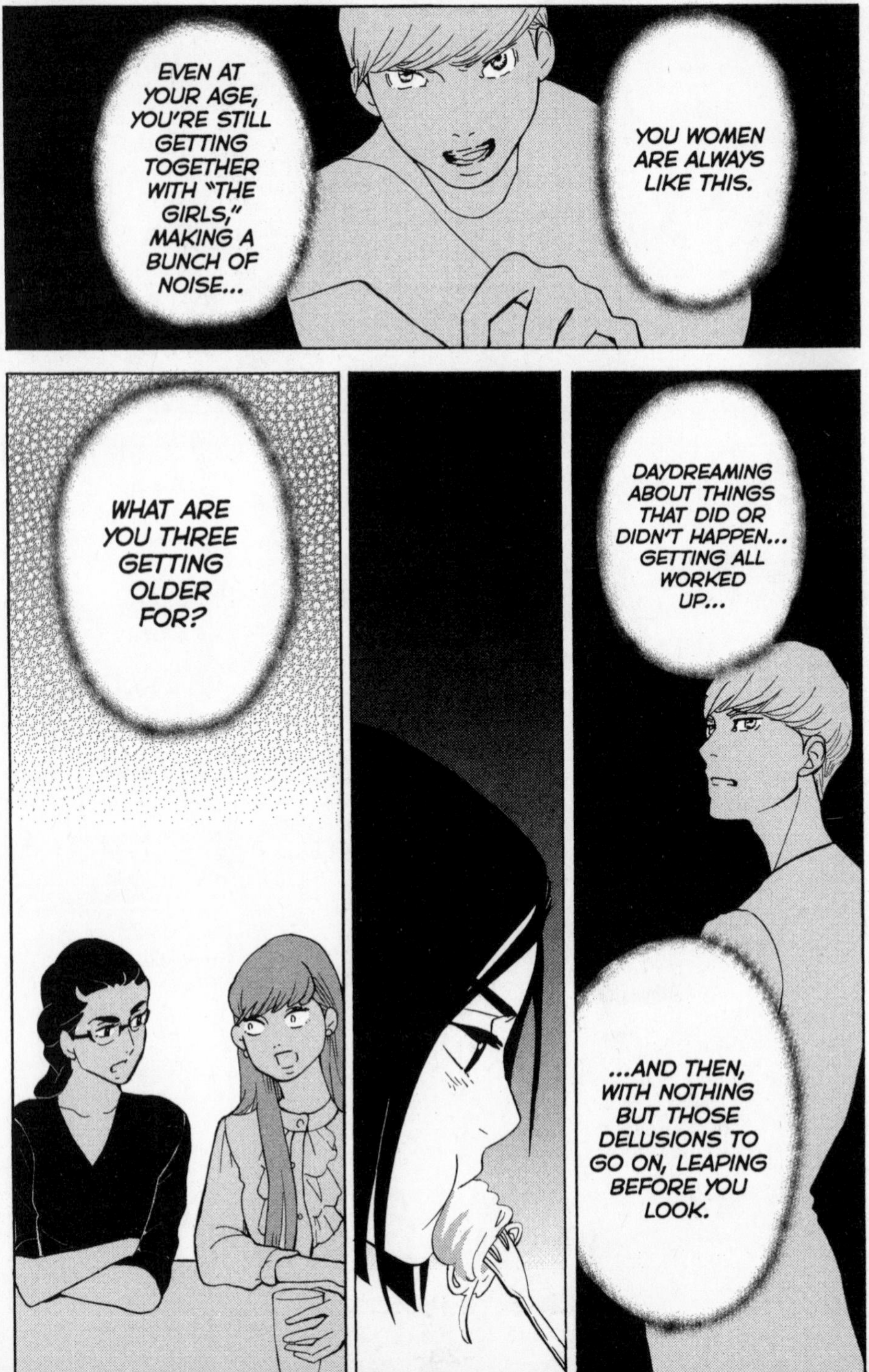
YOU WOMEN ARE ALWAYS LIKE THIS.
EVEN AT YOUR AGE, YOU'RE STILL GETTING TOGETHER WITH "THE GIRLS," MAKING A BUNCH OF NOISE...
DAYDREAMING ABOUT THINGS THAT DID OR DIDN'T HAPPEN... GETTING ALL WORKED UP...
...AND THEN, WITH NOTHING BUT THOSE DELUSIONS TO GO ON, LEAPING BEFORE YOU LOOK.
WHAT ARE YOU THREE GETTING OLDER FOR?

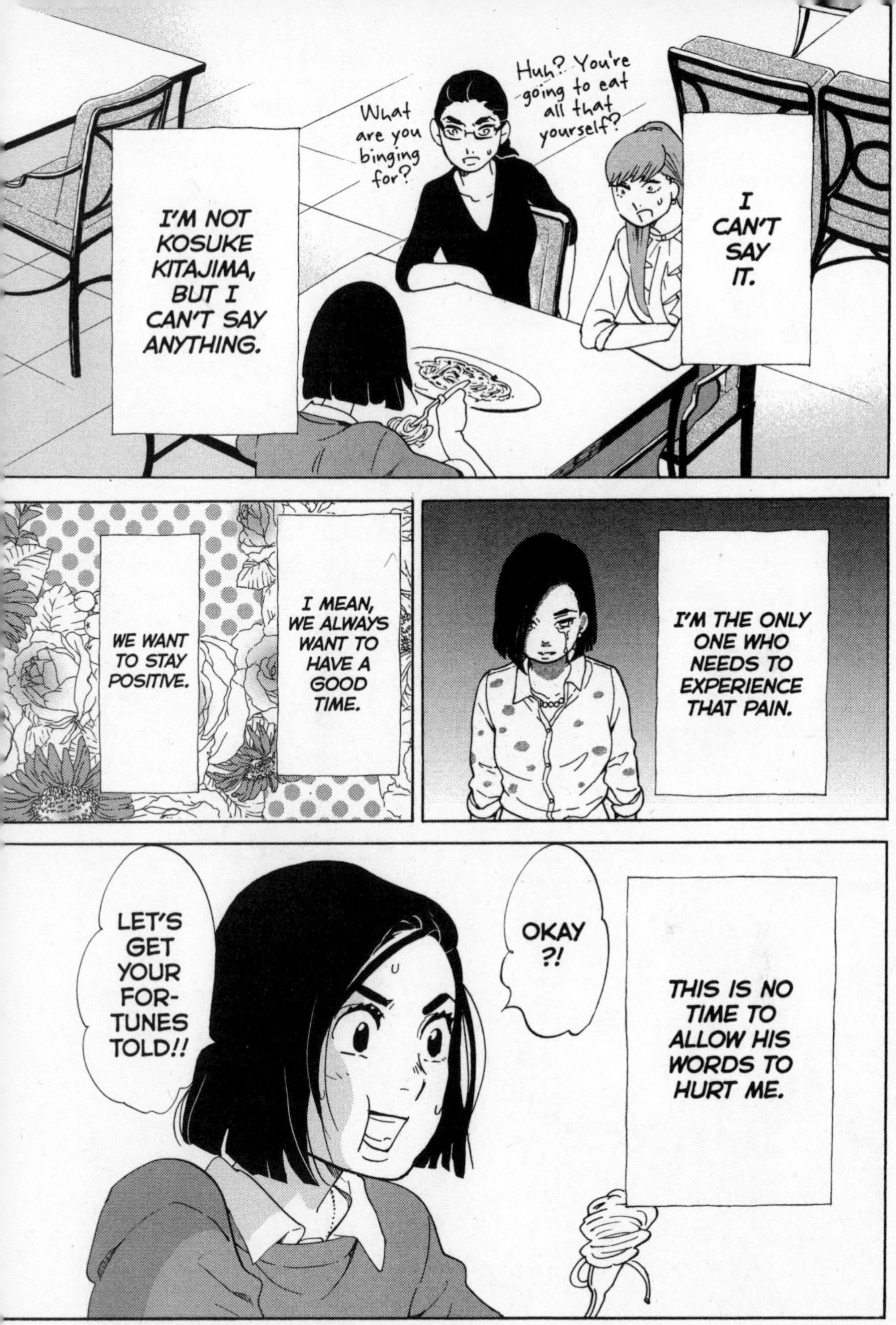

I CAN'T SAY IT.
Huh? You're going to eat all that yourself?
What are you binging for?
I'M NOT KOSUKE KITAJIMA, BUT I CAN'T SAY ANYTHING.
I'M THE ONLY ONE WHO NEEDS TO EXPERIENCE THAT PAIN.
I MEAN, WE ALWAYS WANT TO HAVE A GOOD TIME.
WE WANT TO STAY POSITIVE.
THIS IS NO TIME TO ALLOW HIS WORDS TO HURT ME.
OKAY?!
LET'S GET YOUR FOR-TUNES TOLD!!

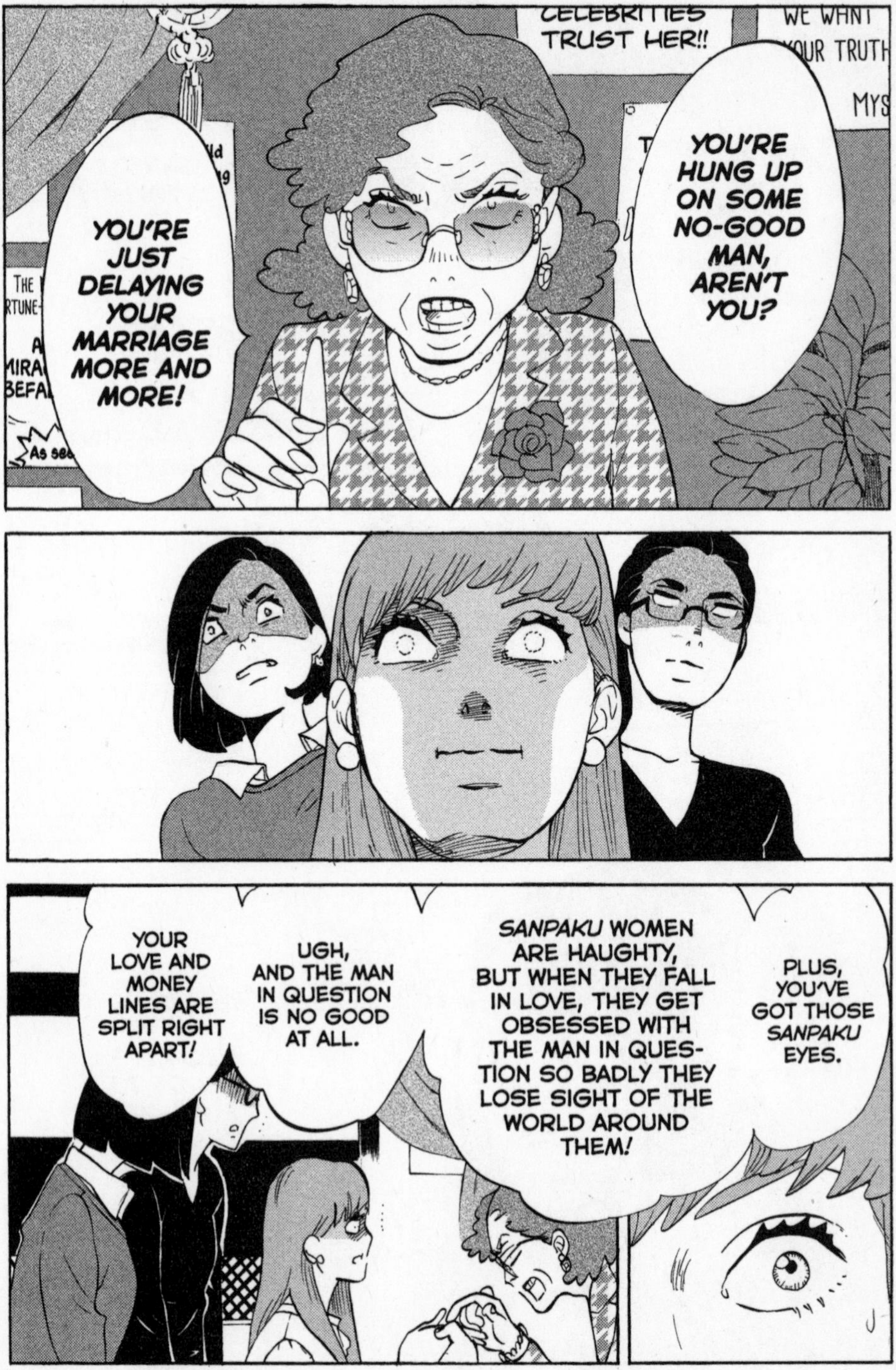
CELEBRITIES TRUST HER!!
YOU'RE HUNG UP ON SOME NO-GOOD MAN, AREN'T YOU?
YOU'RE JUST DELAYING YOUR MARRIAGE MORE AND MORE!
PLUS, YOU'VE GOT THOSE *SANPAKU* EYES.
SANPAKU WOMEN ARE HAUGHTY, BUT WHEN THEY FALL IN LOVE, THEY GET OBSESSED WITH THE MAN IN QUESTION SO BADLY THEY LOSE SIGHT OF THE WORLD AROUND THEM!
UGH, AND THE MAN IN QUESTION IS NO GOOD AT ALL.
YOUR LOVE AND MONEY LINES ARE SPLIT RIGHT APART!

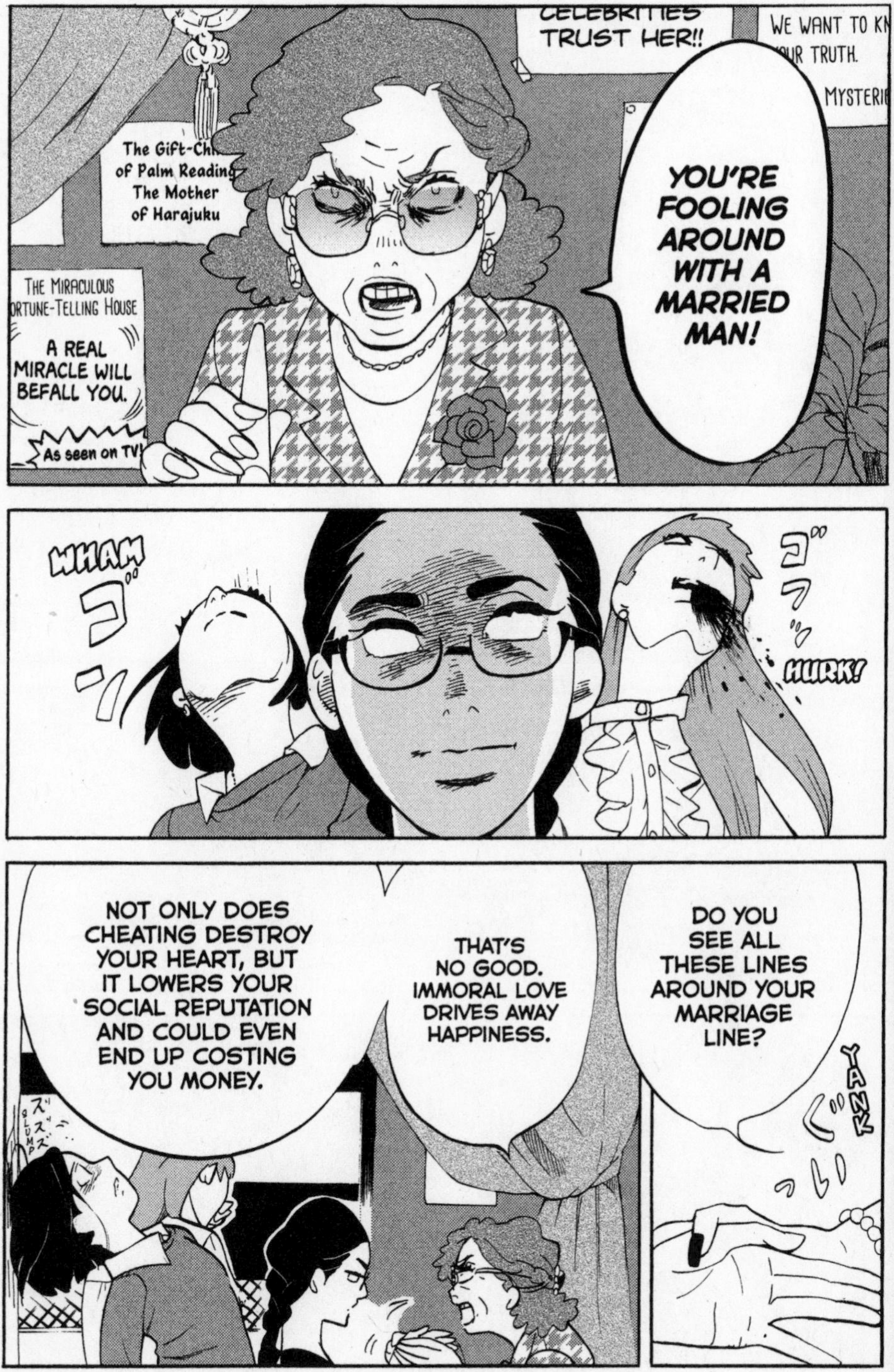

WE WANT TO KN
UR TRUTH.
MYSTERIE
CELEBRITIES
TRUST HER!!
YOU'RE FOOLING AROUND WITH A MARRIED MAN!
The Gift-Chi
of Palm Reading
The Mother
of Harajuku
THE MIRACULOUS
ORTUNE-TELLING HOUSE
A REAL MIRACLE WILL BEFALL YOU.
As seen on TV!
HURK!
WHAM
DO YOU SEE ALL THESE LINES AROUND YOUR MARRIAGE LINE?
YANK
THAT'S NO GOOD. IMMORAL LOVE DRIVES AWAY HAPPINESS.
NOT ONLY DOES CHEATING DESTROY YOUR HEART, BUT IT LOWERS YOUR SOCIAL REPUTATION AND COULD EVEN END UP COSTING YOU MONEY.
SLUMP

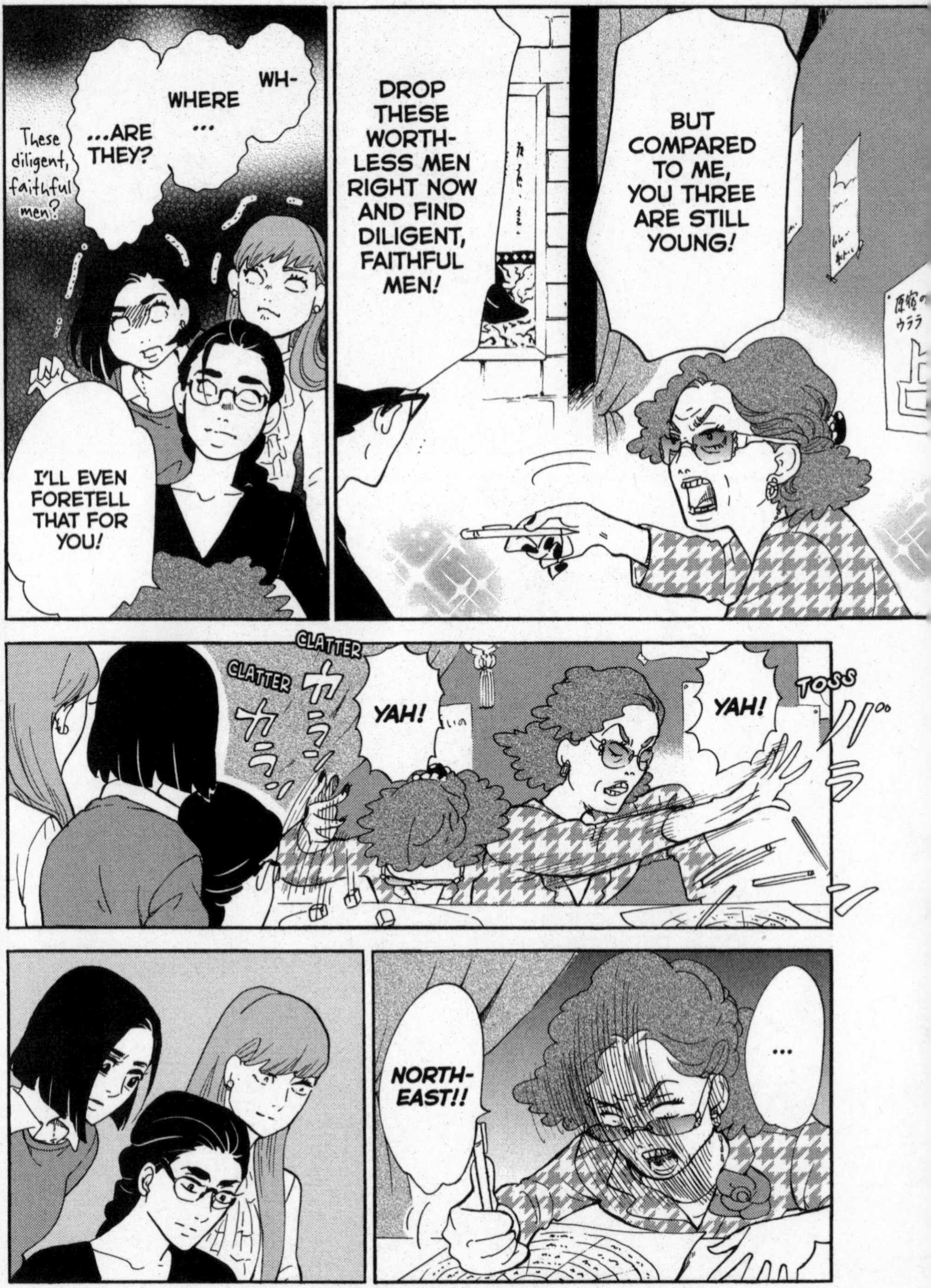
原宿の
ウララ
占
BUT COMPARED TO ME, YOU THREE ARE STILL YOUNG!
DROP THESE WORTHLESS MEN RIGHT NOW AND FIND DILIGENT, FAITHFUL MEN!
WH-
WHERE ...
...ARE THEY?
These diligent, faithful men?
I'LL EVEN FORETELL THAT FOR YOU!
TOSS
バラ
YAH!
YAH!
CLATTER
カラン
CLATTER
カラン
...
NORTH-EAST!!

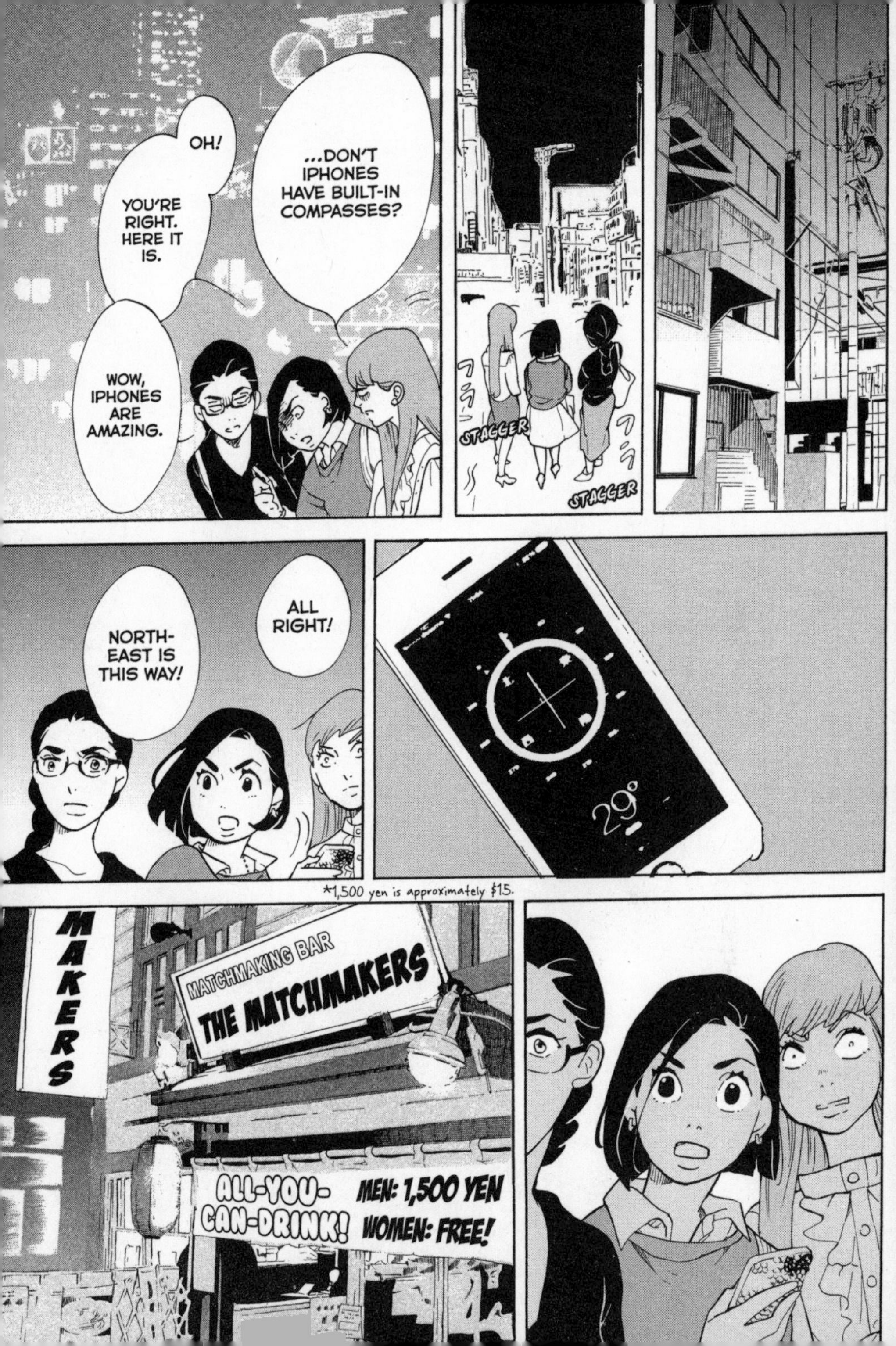
STAGGER
STAGGER
...DON'T IPHONES HAVE BUILT-IN COMPASSES?
OH!
YOU'RE RIGHT. HERE IT IS.
WOW, IPHONES ARE AMAZING.
29°
ALL RIGHT!
NORTH-EAST IS THIS WAY!
*1,500 yen is approximately $15.
MATCHMAKING BAR
THE MATCHMAKERS
MAKERS
ALL-YOU-CAN-DRINK!
MEN: 1,500 YEN
WOMEN: FREE!

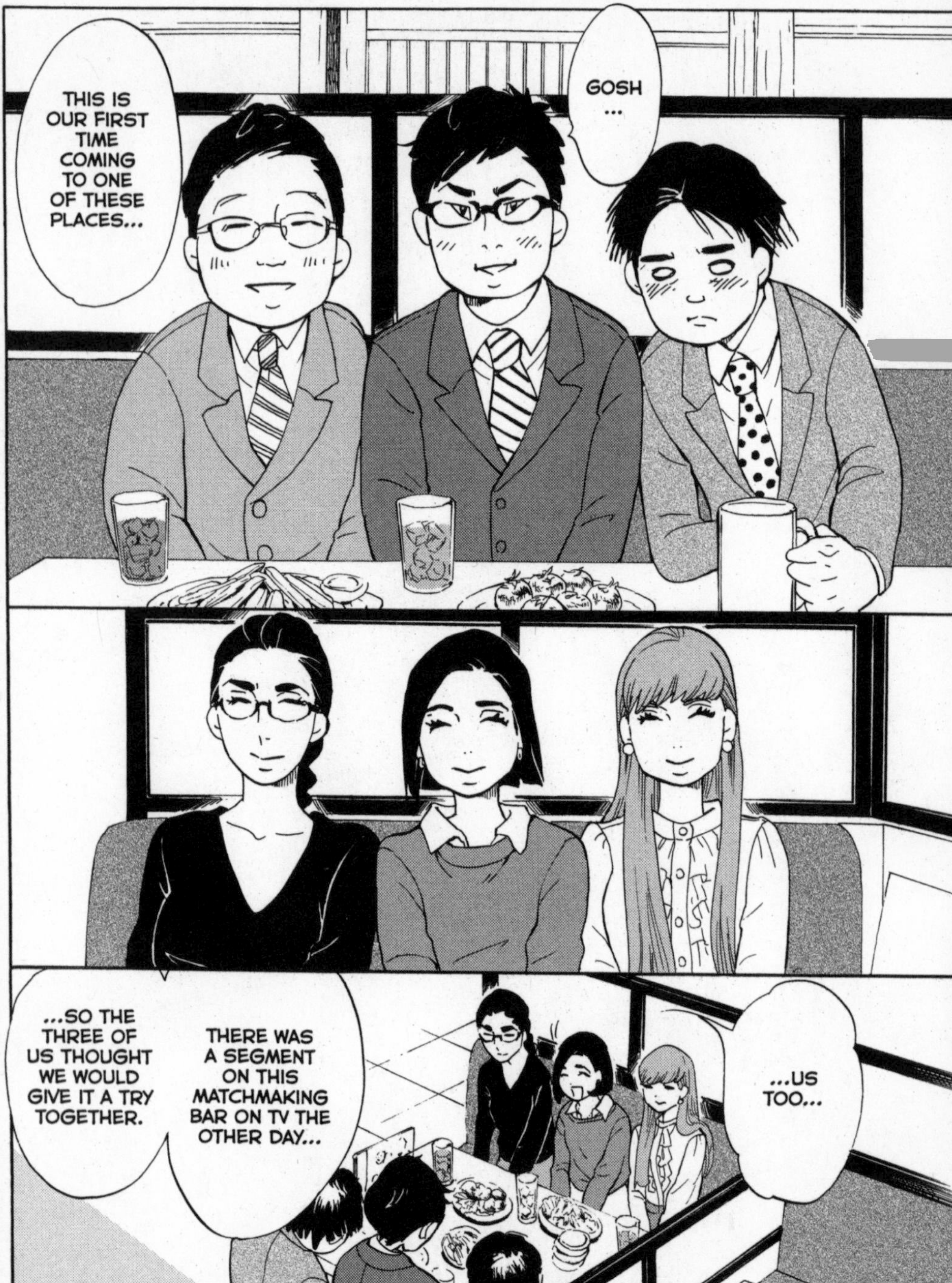
GOSH ...
THIS IS OUR FIRST TIME COMING TO ONE OF THESE PLACES...
...US TOO...
THERE WAS A SEGMENT ON THIS MATCHMAKING BAR ON TV THE OTHER DAY...
...SO THE THREE OF US THOUGHT WE WOULD GIVE IT A TRY TOGETHER.

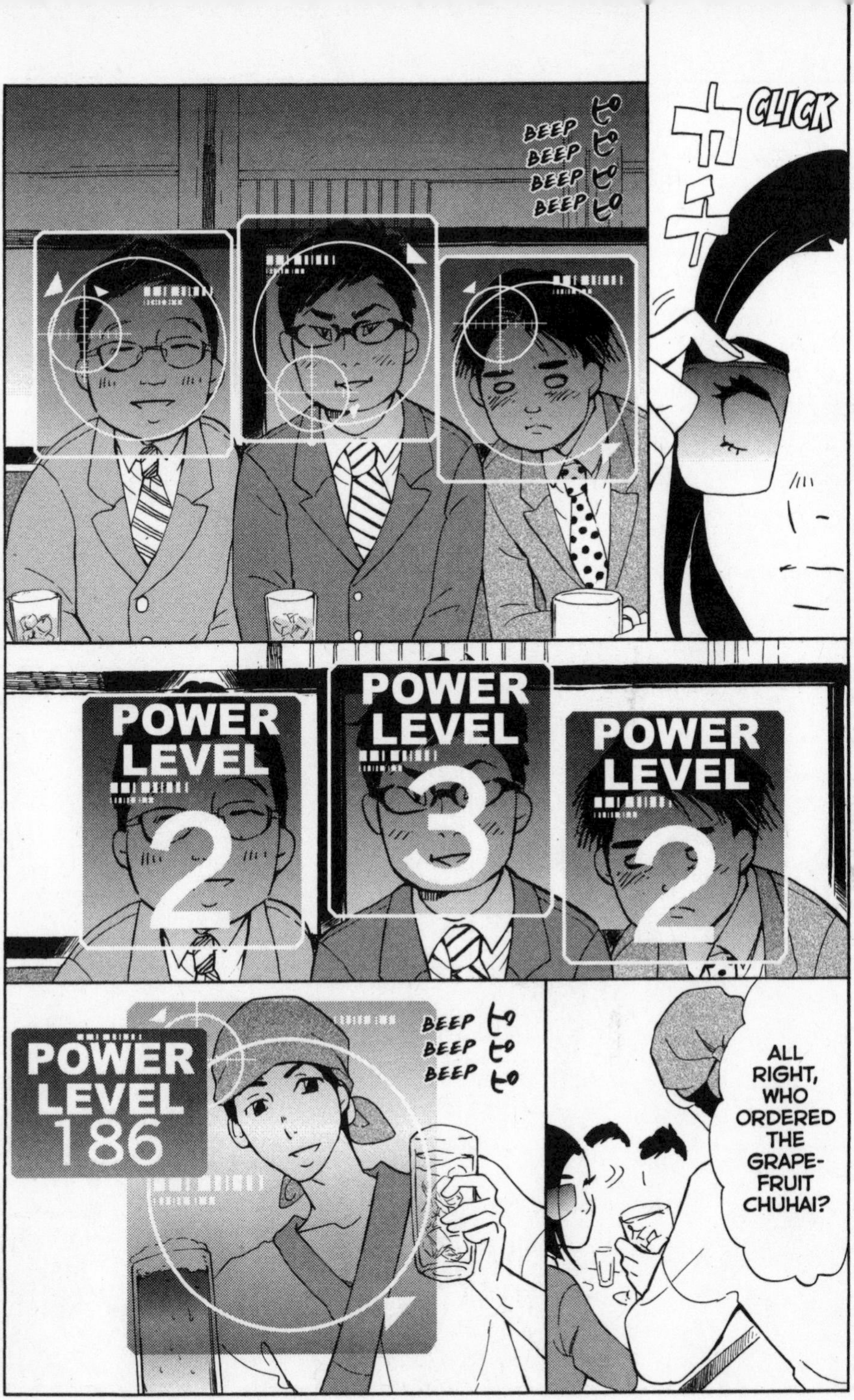
カチ
CLICK
ピピピピ
BEEP BEEP BEEP BEEP
POWER LEVEL 2
POWER LEVEL 3
POWER LEVEL 2
ALL RIGHT, WHO ORDERED THE GRAPE-FRUIT CHUHAI?
ピピピ
BEEP BEEP BEEP
POWER LEVEL 186

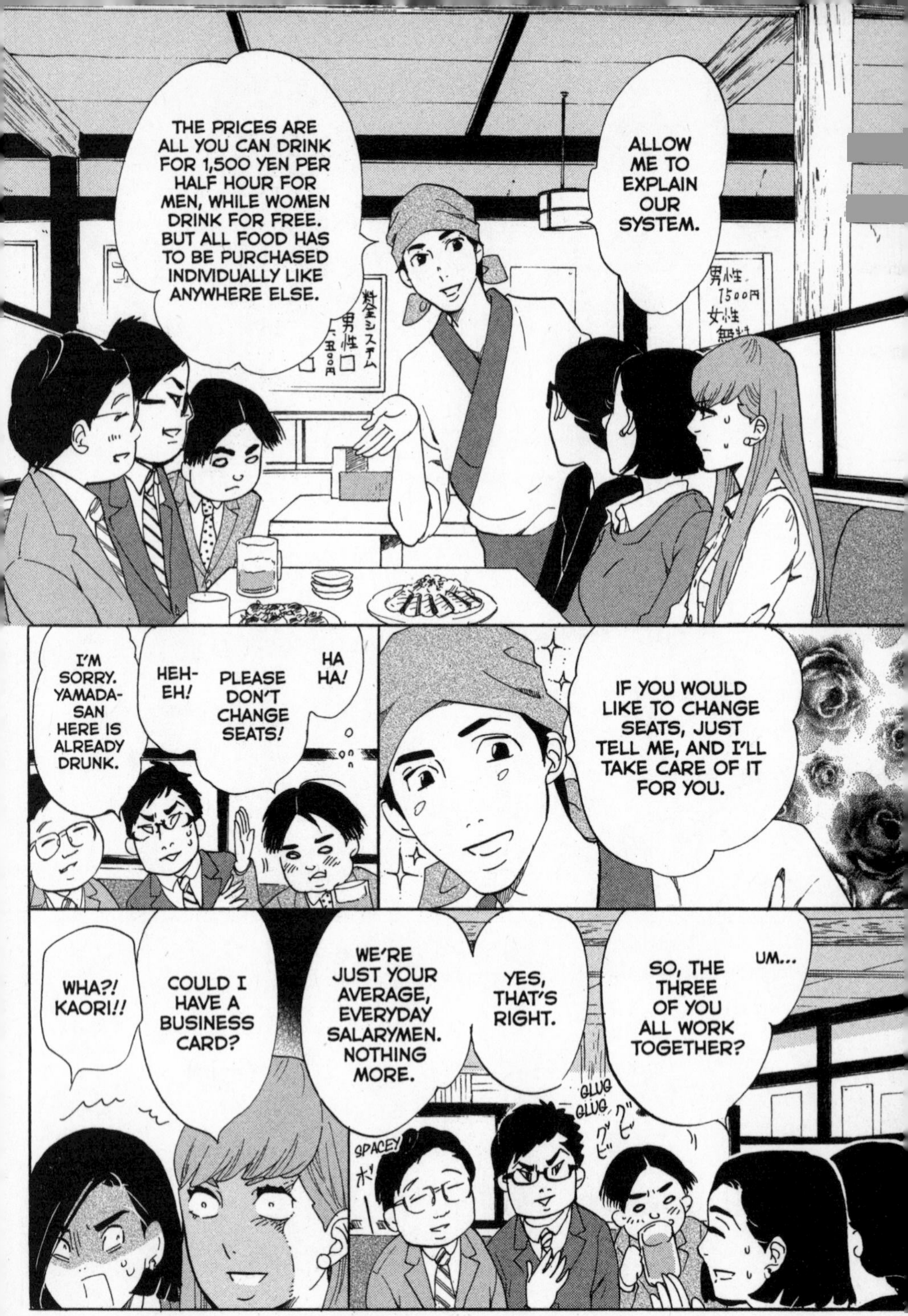
ALLOW ME TO EXPLAIN OUR SYSTEM.
THE PRICES ARE ALL YOU CAN DRINK FOR 1,500 YEN PER HALF HOUR FOR MEN, WHILE WOMEN DRINK FOR FREE. BUT ALL FOOD HAS TO BE PURCHASED INDIVIDUALLY LIKE ANYWHERE ELSE.
IF YOU WOULD LIKE TO CHANGE SEATS, JUST TELL ME, AND I'LL TAKE CARE OF IT FOR YOU.
HA HA!
PLEASE DON'T CHANGE SEATS!
HEH-EH!
I'M SORRY. YAMADA-SAN HERE IS ALREADY DRUNK.
UM...
SO, THE THREE OF YOU ALL WORK TOGETHER?
YES, THAT'S RIGHT.
GLUG GLUG
WE'RE JUST YOUR AVERAGE, EVERYDAY SALARYMEN. NOTHING MORE.
SPACEY
COULD I HAVE A BUSINESS CARD?
WHA?! KAORI!!

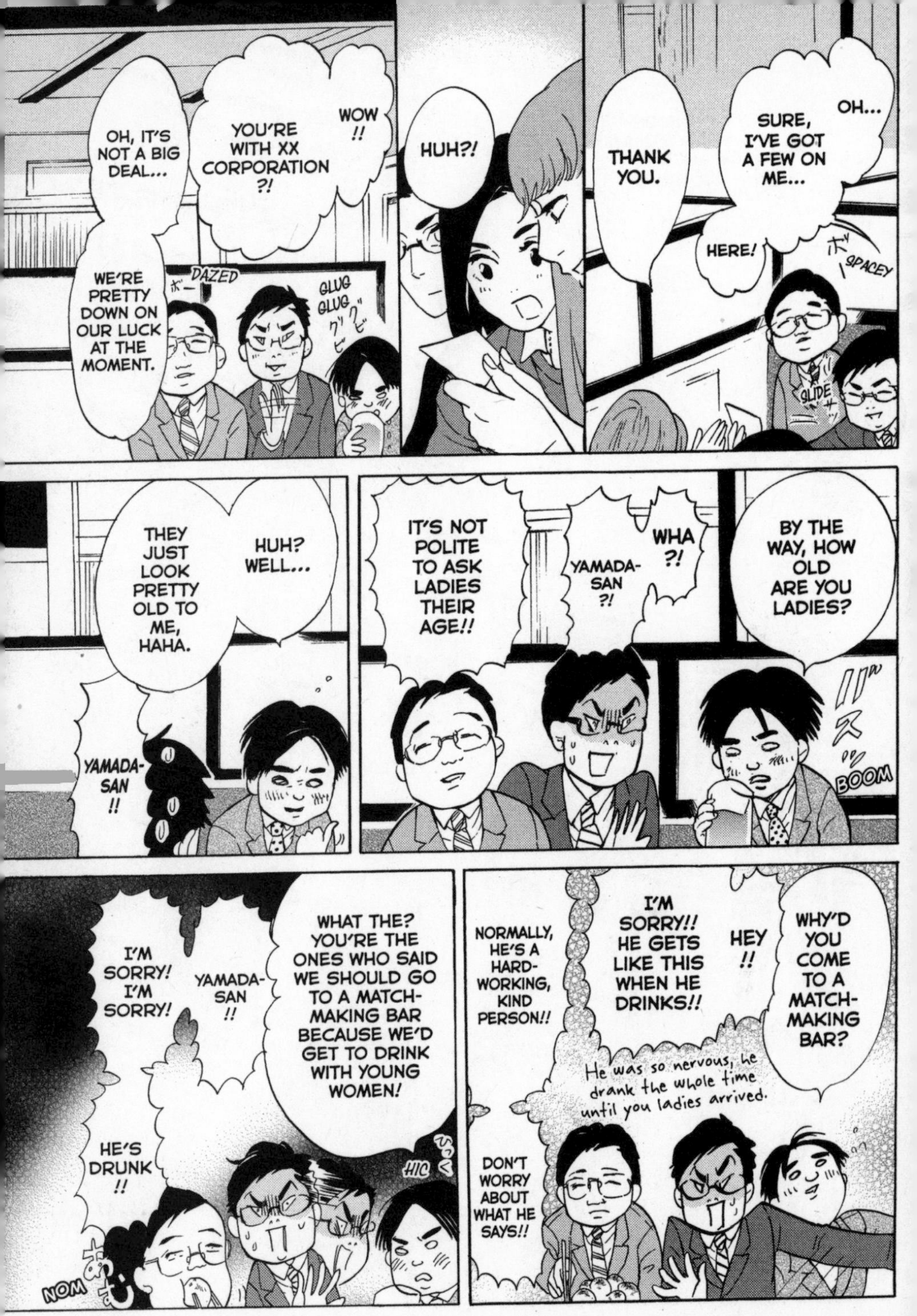
OH...
SURE, I'VE GOT A FEW ON ME...
THANK YOU.
HERE!
SPACEY
SLIDE
HUH?!
WOW!!
YOU'RE WITH XX CORPORATION?!
OH, IT'S NOT A BIG DEAL...
WE'RE PRETTY DOWN ON OUR LUCK AT THE MOMENT.
DAZED
GLUG GLUG
BY THE WAY, HOW OLD ARE YOU LADIES?
WHA?!
YAMADA-SAN?!
IT'S NOT POLITE TO ASK LADIES THEIR AGE!!
BOOM
HUH? WELL...
THEY JUST LOOK PRETTY OLD TO ME, HAHA.
YAMADA-SAN!!
WHY'D YOU COME TO A MATCH-MAKING BAR?
HEY!!
I'M SORRY!! HE GETS LIKE THIS WHEN HE DRINKS!!
NORMALLY, HE'S A HARD-WORKING, KIND PERSON!!
He was so nervous, he drank the whole time until you ladies arrived.
DON'T WORRY ABOUT WHAT HE SAYS!!
WHAT THE? YOU'RE THE ONES WHO SAID WE SHOULD GO TO A MATCH-MAKING BAR BECAUSE WE'D GET TO DRINK WITH YOUNG WOMEN!
YAMADA-SAN!!
I'M SORRY! I'M SORRY!
HIC
HE'S DRUNK!!
NOM

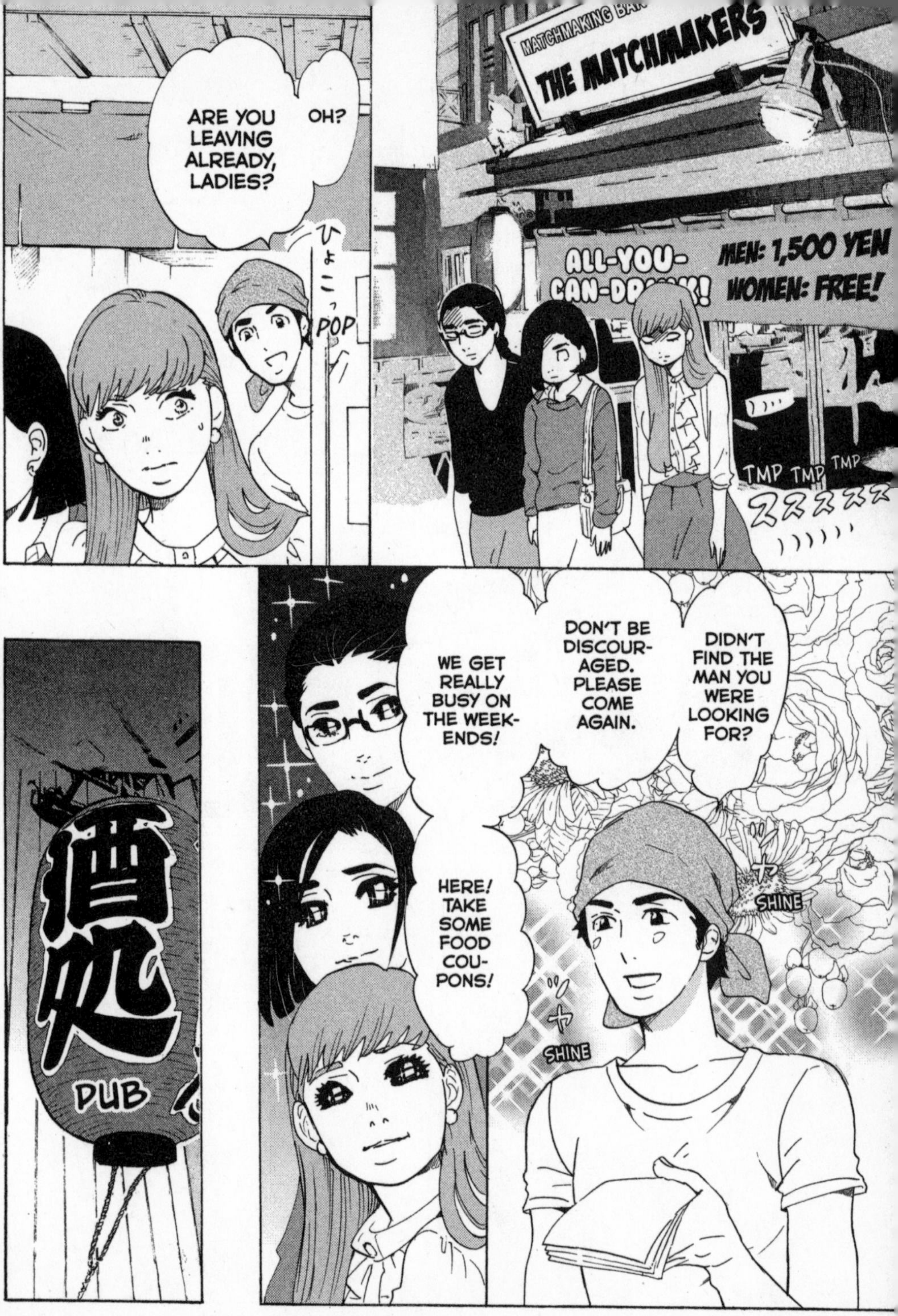
MATCHMAKING
THE MATCHMAKERS
ALL-YOU-
MEN: 1,500 YEN
WOMEN: FREE!
TMP TMP TMP
ススススス
OH?
ARE YOU LEAVING ALREADY, LADIES?
ひょこっ
POP
DIDN'T FIND THE MAN YOU WERE LOOKING FOR?
DON'T BE DISCOURAGED. PLEASE COME AGAIN.
WE GET REALLY BUSY ON THE WEEKENDS!
SHINE
HERE! TAKE SOME FOOD COUPONS!
SHINE
酒処
PUB

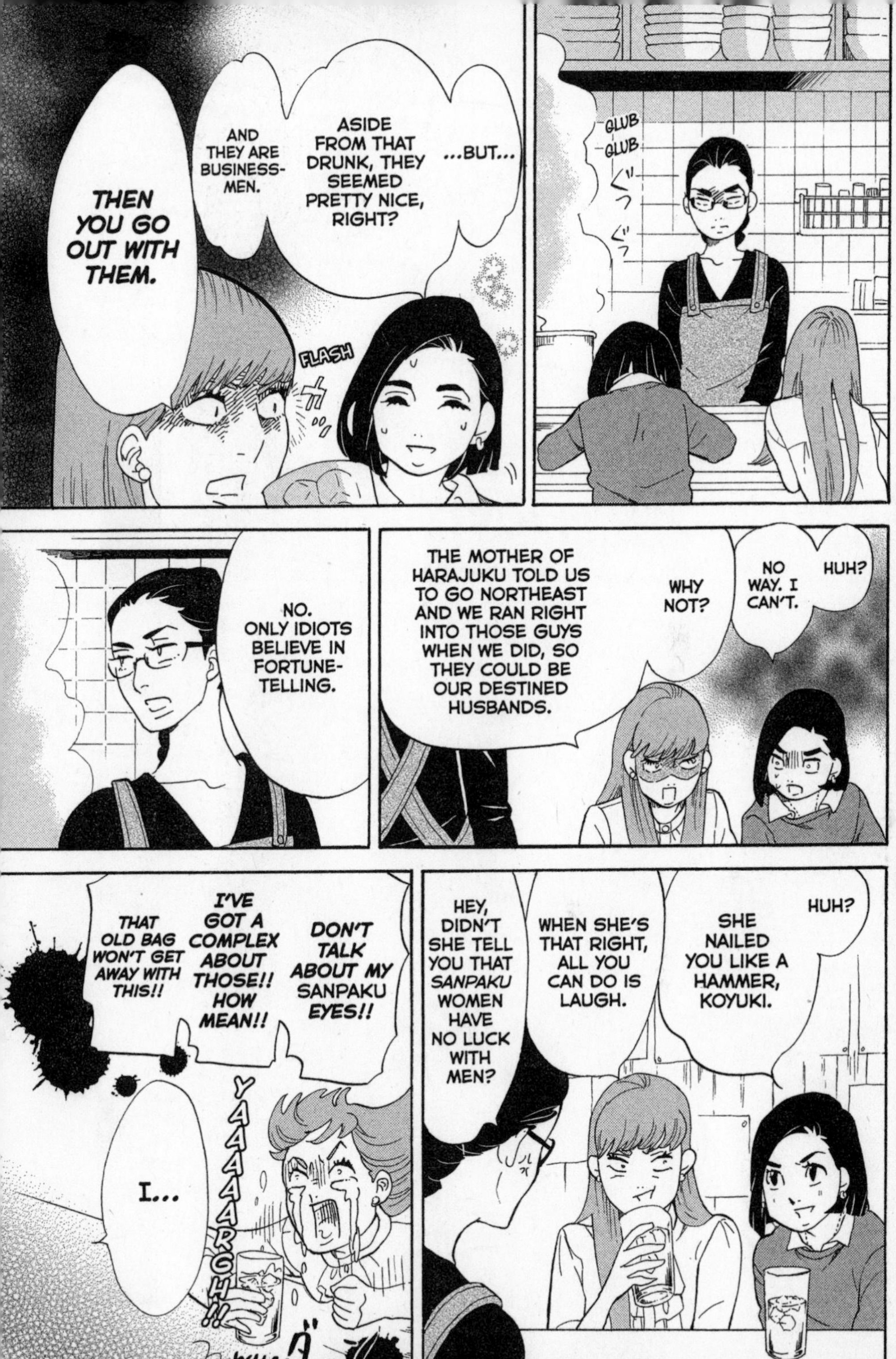
GLUB GLUB
...BUT...
ASIDE FROM THAT DRUNK, THEY SEEMED PRETTY NICE, RIGHT?
AND THEY ARE BUSINESS-MEN.
THEN YOU GO OUT WITH THEM.
FLASH
HUH?
NO WAY. I CAN'T.
WHY NOT?
THE MOTHER OF HARAJUKU TOLD US TO GO NORTHEAST AND WE RAN RIGHT INTO THOSE GUYS WHEN WE DID, SO THEY COULD BE OUR DESTINED HUSBANDS.
NO. ONLY IDIOTS BELIEVE IN FORTUNE-TELLING.
HUH?
SHE NAILED YOU LIKE A HAMMER, KOYUKI.
WHEN SHE'S THAT RIGHT, ALL YOU CAN DO IS LAUGH.
HEY, DIDN'T SHE TELL YOU THAT SANPAKU WOMEN HAVE NO LUCK WITH MEN?
DON'T TALK ABOUT MY SANPAKU EYES!!
I'VE GOT A COMPLEX ABOUT THOSE!! HOW MEAN!!
THAT OLD BAG WON'T GET AWAY WITH THIS!!
YAAAAARGH!!
I...
WHAM

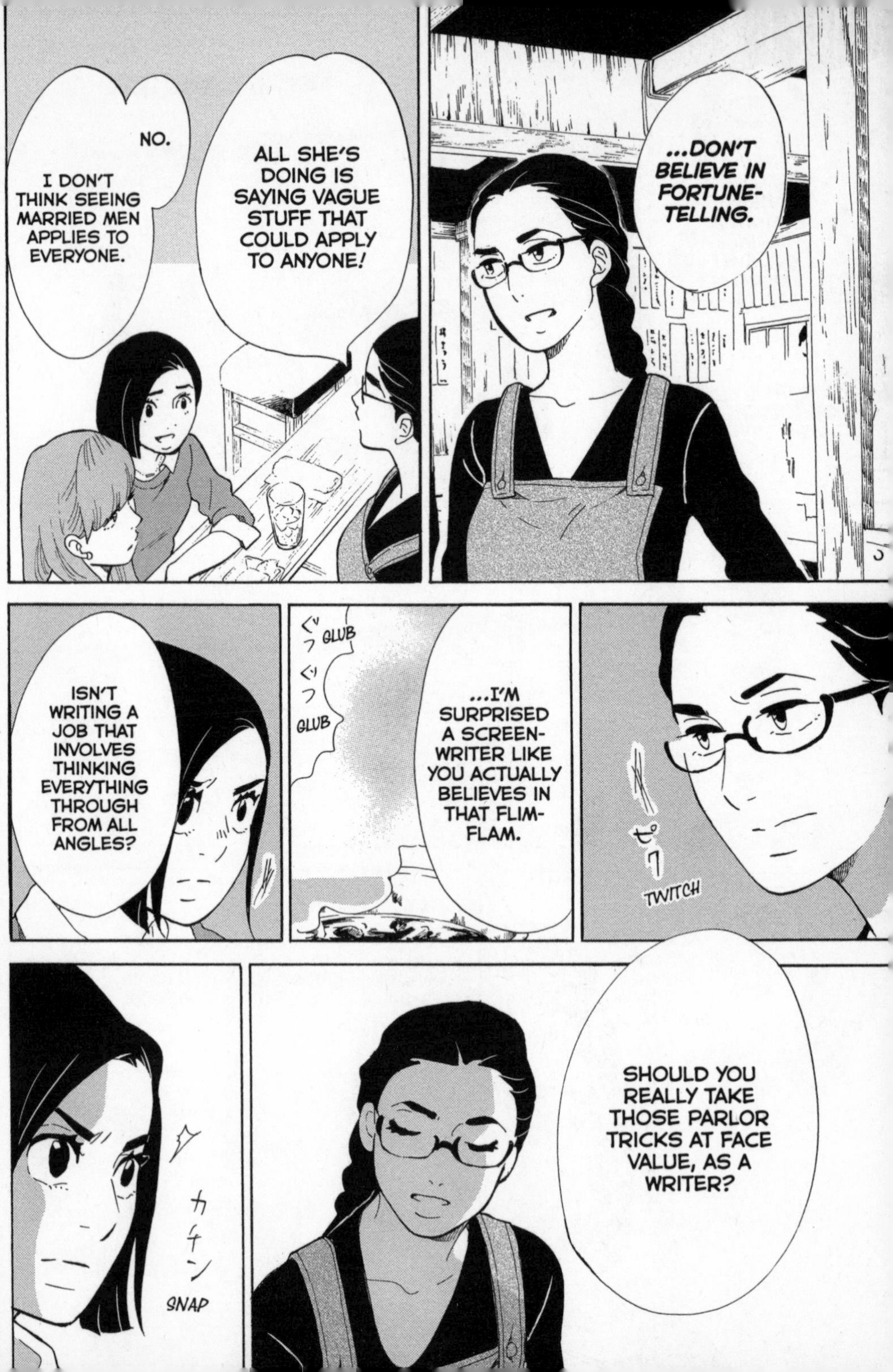
...DON'T BELIEVE IN FORTUNE-TELLING.
ALL SHE'S DOING IS SAYING VAGUE STUFF THAT COULD APPLY TO ANYONE!
NO.
I DON'T THINK SEEING MARRIED MEN APPLIES TO EVERYONE.
ピク
TWITCH
...I'M SURPRISED A SCREEN-WRITER LIKE YOU ACTUALLY BELIEVES IN THAT FLIM-FLAM.
ぐつ
GLUB
ぐつ
GLUB
ISN'T WRITING A JOB THAT INVOLVES THINKING EVERYTHING THROUGH FROM ALL ANGLES?
SHOULD YOU REALLY TAKE THOSE PARLOR TRICKS AT FACE VALUE, AS A WRITER?
カチン
SNAP

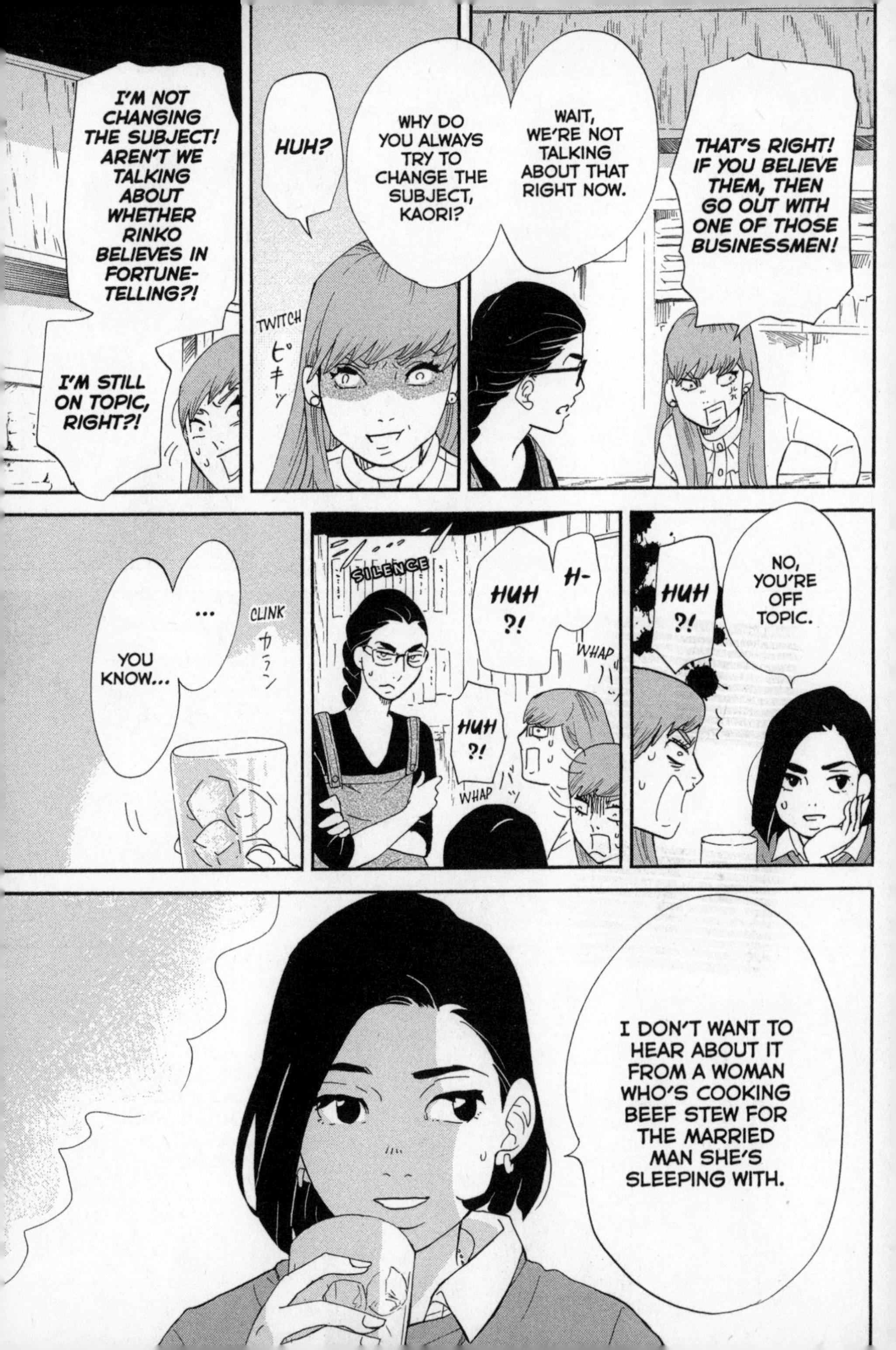
THAT'S RIGHT! IF YOU BELIEVE THEM, THEN GO OUT WITH ONE OF THOSE BUSINESSMEN!
WAIT, WE'RE NOT TALKING ABOUT THAT RIGHT NOW.
WHY DO YOU ALWAYS TRY TO CHANGE THE SUBJECT, KAORI?
HUH?
TWITCH
ピキッ
I'M NOT CHANGING THE SUBJECT! AREN'T WE TALKING ABOUT WHETHER RINKO BELIEVES IN FORTUNE-TELLING?!
I'M STILL ON TOPIC, RIGHT?!
NO, YOU'RE OFF TOPIC.
HUH ?!
H- HUH ?!
SILENCE
WHAP
バッ
HUH ?!
WHAP
バッ
CLINK
カラン
...
YOU KNOW...
I DON'T WANT TO HEAR ABOUT IT FROM A WOMAN WHO'S COOKING BEEF STEW FOR THE MARRIED MAN SHE'S SLEEPING WITH.

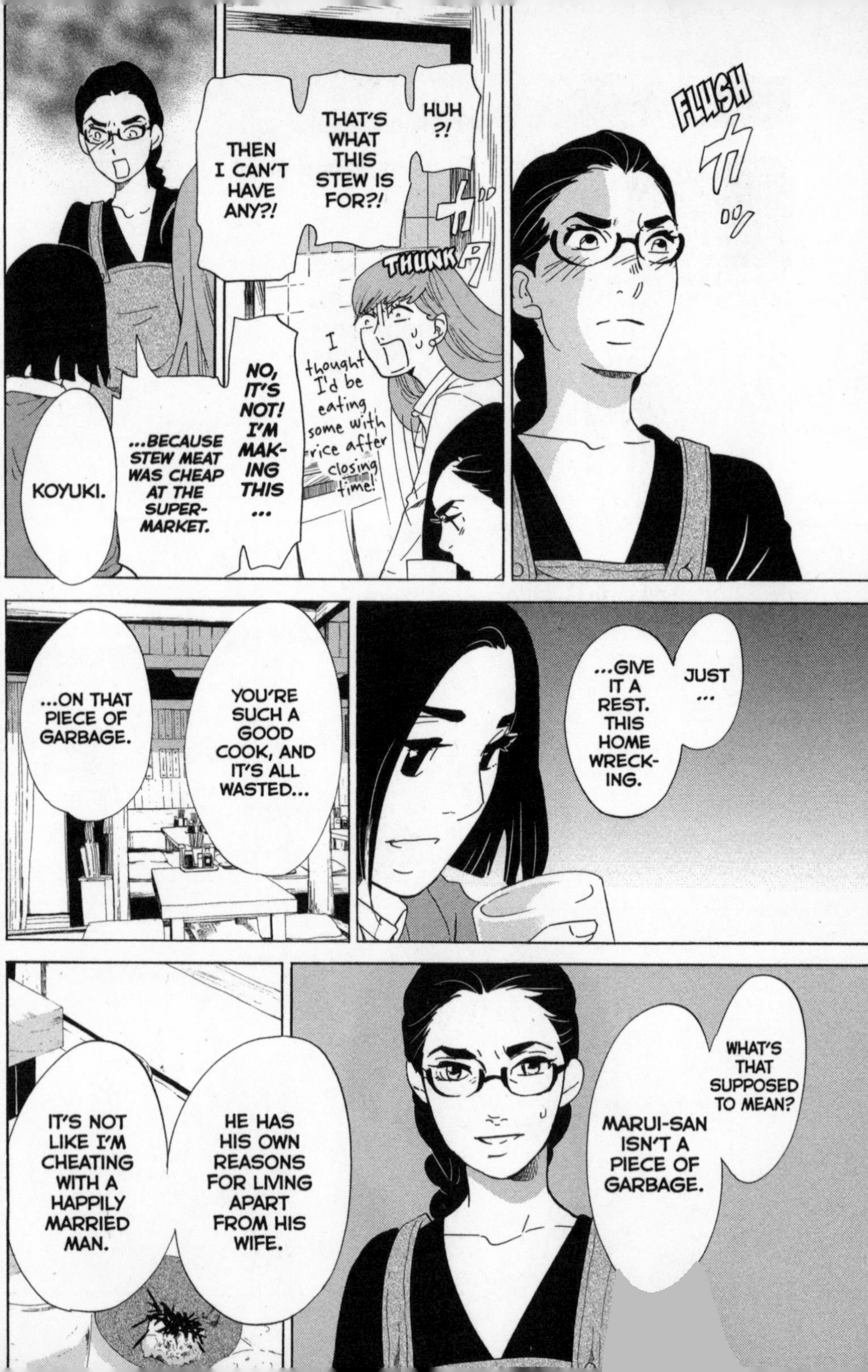
FLUSH
カッ
HUH?!
THAT'S WHAT THIS STEW IS FOR?!
THEN I CAN'T HAVE ANY?!
THUNK
I thought I'd be eating some with rice after closing time!
NO, IT'S NOT! I'M MAKING THIS...
...BECAUSE STEW MEAT WAS CHEAP AT THE SUPERMARKET.
KOYUKI.
JUST...
...GIVE IT A REST. THIS HOME WRECKING.
YOU'RE SUCH A GOOD COOK, AND IT'S ALL WASTED...
...ON THAT PIECE OF GARBAGE.
WHAT'S THAT SUPPOSED TO MEAN?
MARUI-SAN ISN'T A PIECE OF GARBAGE.
HE HAS HIS OWN REASONS FOR LIVING APART FROM HIS WIFE.
IT'S NOT LIKE I'M CHEATING WITH A HAPPILY MARRIED MAN.

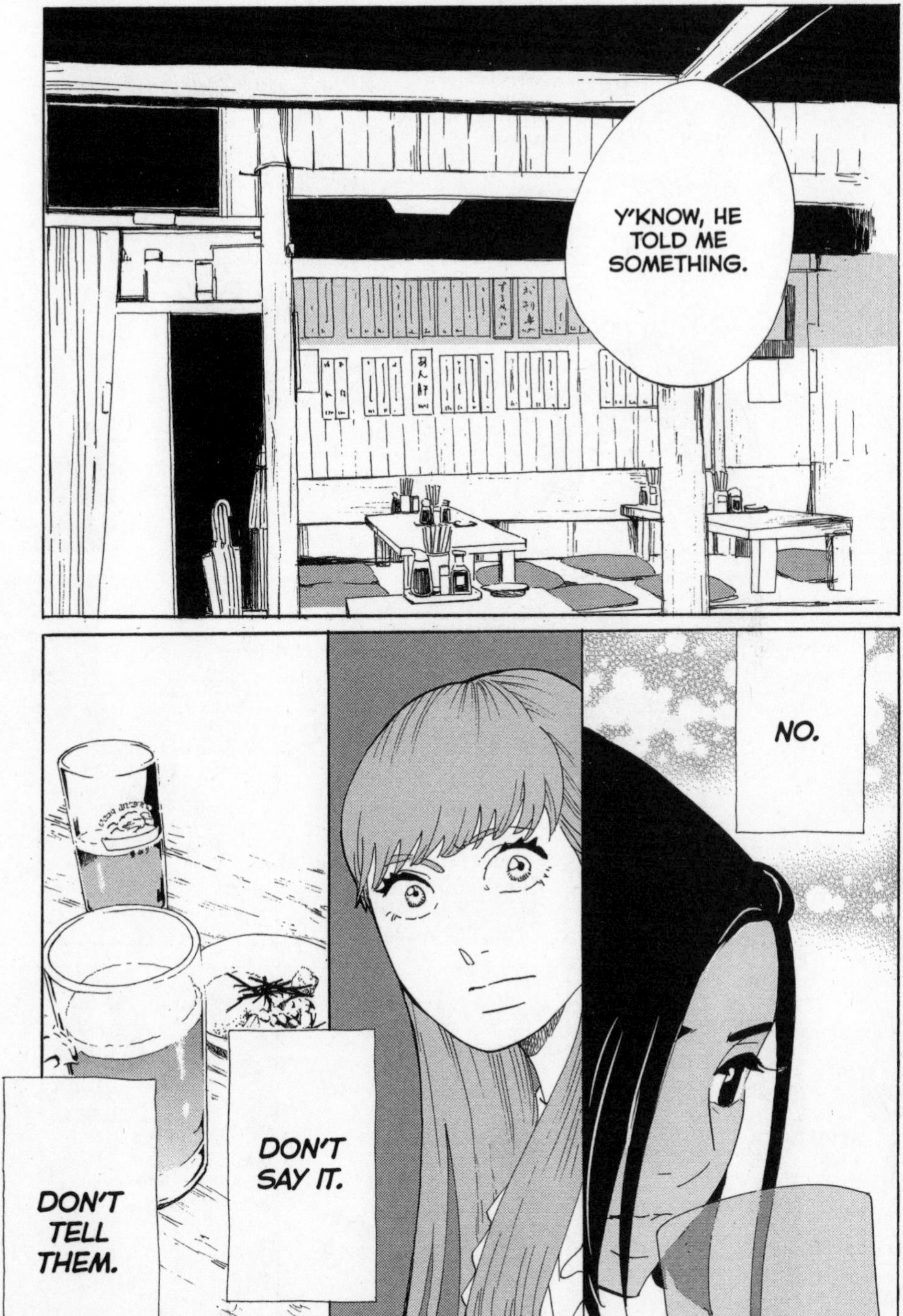
Y'KNOW, HE TOLD ME SOMETHING.
NO.
DON'T SAY IT.
DON'T TELL THEM.

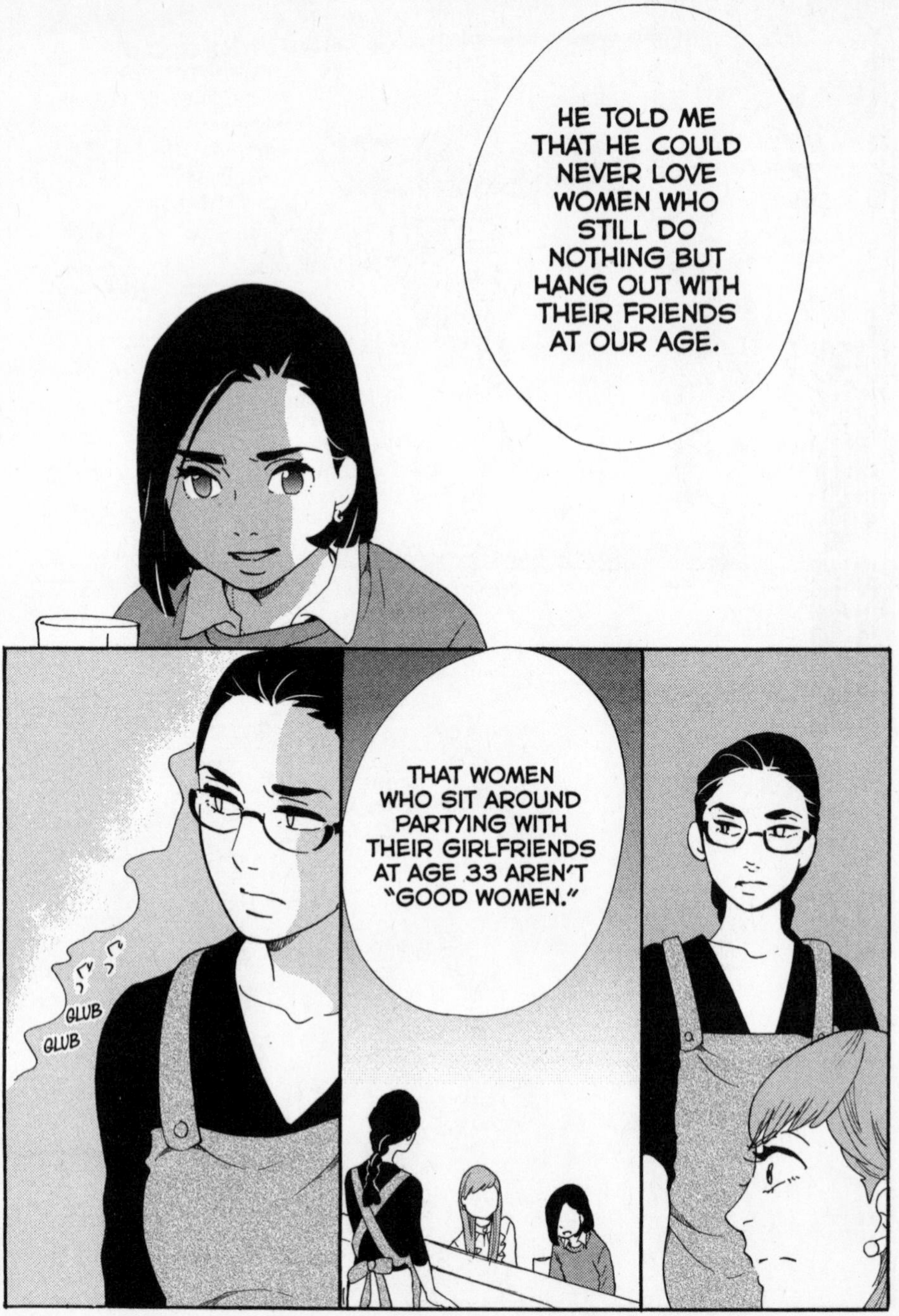
HE TOLD ME THAT HE COULD NEVER LOVE WOMEN WHO STILL DO NOTHING BUT HANG OUT WITH THEIR FRIENDS AT OUR AGE.
THAT WOMEN WHO SIT AROUND PARTYING WITH THEIR GIRLFRIENDS AT AGE 33 AREN'T "GOOD WOMEN."
GLUB GLUB

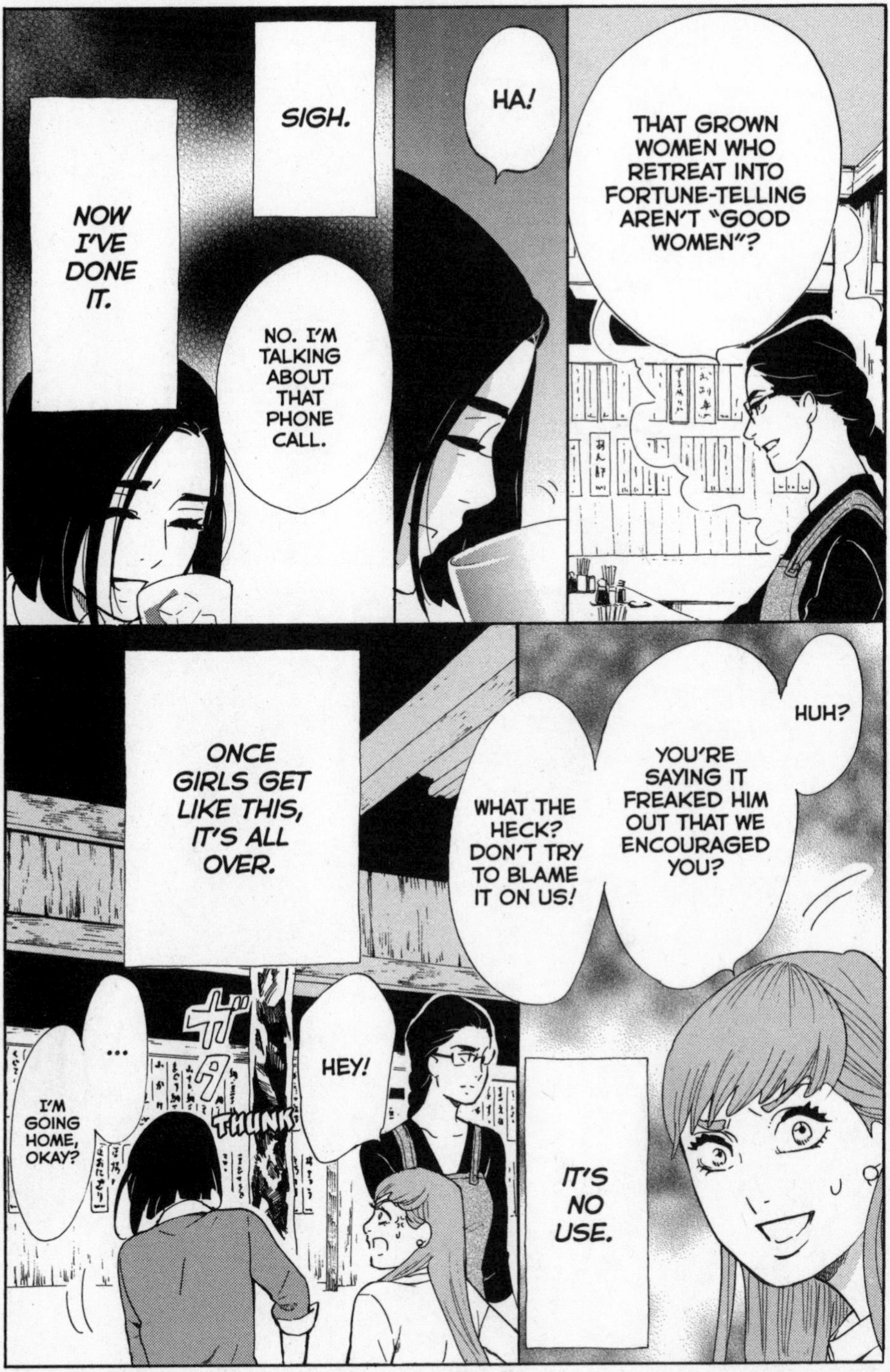
THAT GROWN WOMEN WHO RETREAT INTO FORTUNE-TELLING AREN'T "GOOD WOMEN"?
HA!
NO. I'M TALKING ABOUT THAT PHONE CALL.
SIGH.
NOW I'VE DONE IT.
HUH?
YOU'RE SAYING IT FREAKED HIM OUT THAT WE ENCOURAGED YOU?
WHAT THE HECK? DON'T TRY TO BLAME IT ON US!
IT'S NO USE.
ONCE GIRLS GET LIKE THIS, IT'S ALL OVER.
HEY!
ガタ
THUNK
...
I'M GOING HOME, OKAY?

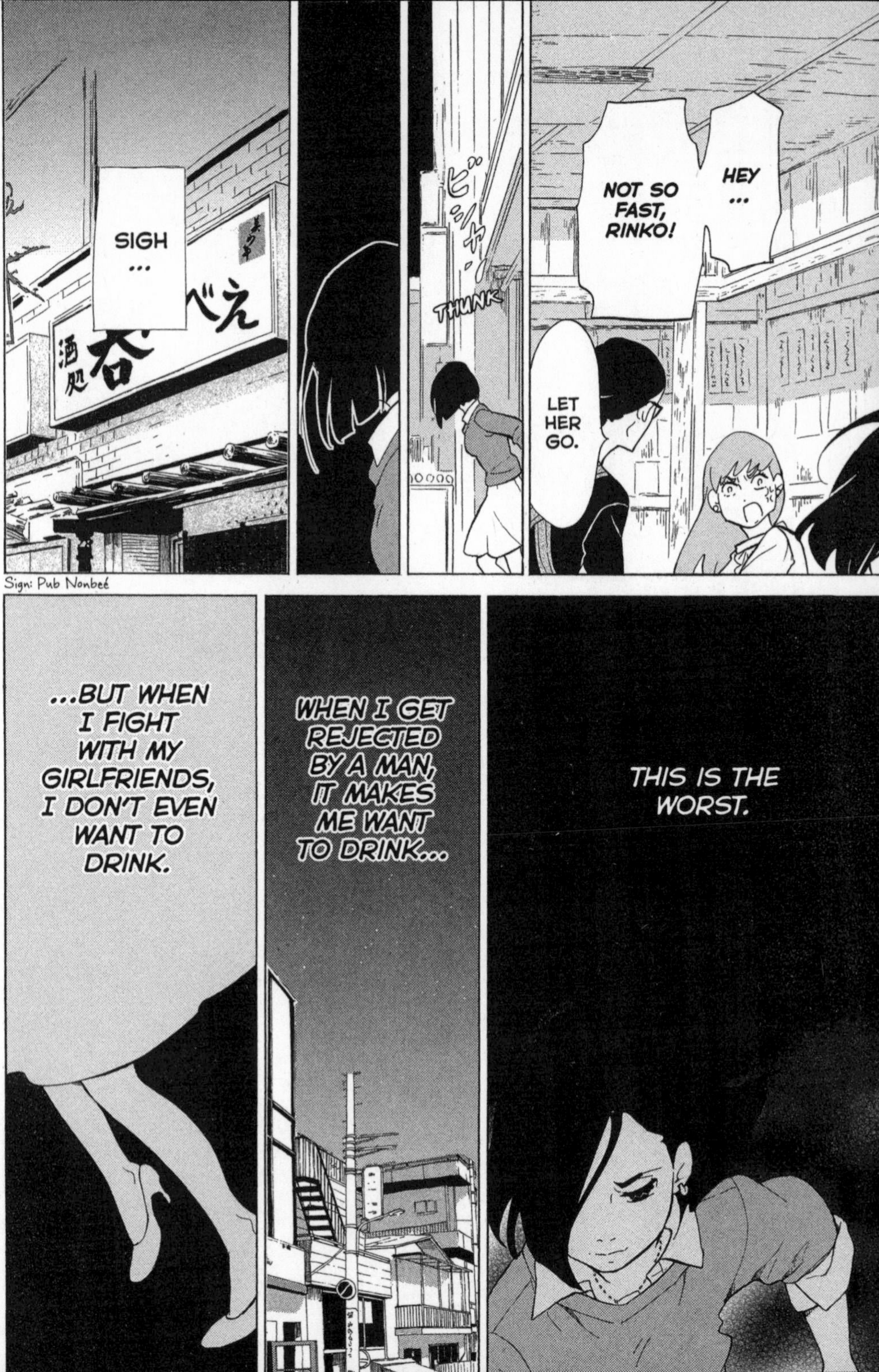
HEY ...
NOT SO FAST, RINKO!
LET HER GO.
ピシャッ
THUNK
SIGH ...
酒処
Sign: Pub Nonbeé
THIS IS THE WORST.
WHEN I GET REJECTED BY A MAN, IT MAKES ME WANT TO DRINK...
...BUT WHEN I FIGHT WITH MY GIRLFRIENDS, I DON'T EVEN WANT TO DRINK.

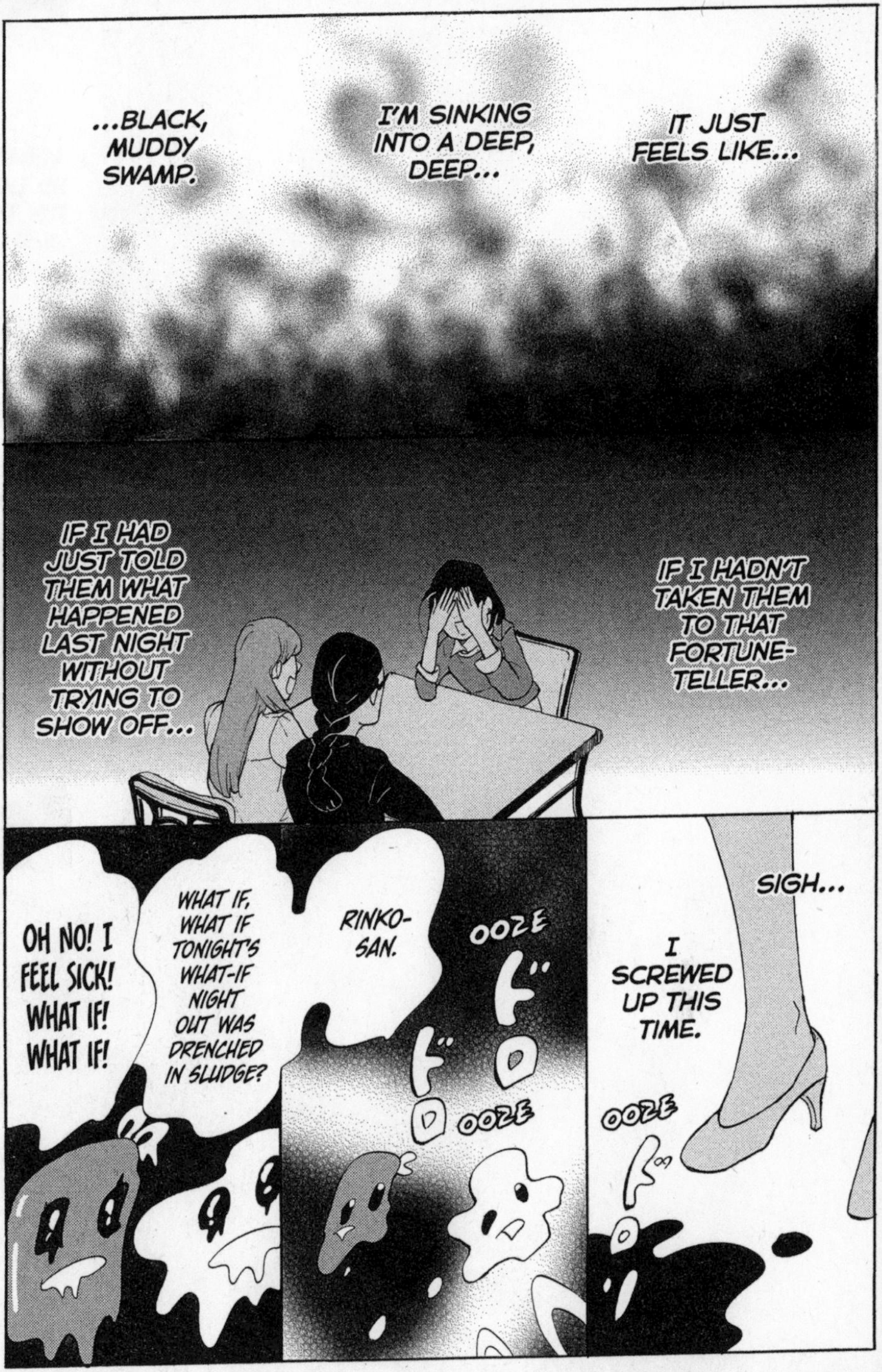
IT JUST FEELS LIKE...
I'M SINKING INTO A DEEP, DEEP...
...BLACK, MUDDY SWAMP.
IF I HADN'T TAKEN THEM TO THAT FORTUNE-TELLER...
IF I HAD JUST TOLD THEM WHAT HAPPENED LAST NIGHT WITHOUT TRYING TO SHOW OFF...
SIGH...
I SCREWED UP THIS TIME.
OOZE
ドッ
OOZE
ドロ
RINKO-SAN.
WHAT IF, WHAT IF TONIGHT'S WHAT-IF NIGHT OUT WAS DRENCHED IN SLUDGE?
OOZE
ドロ
OH NO! I FEEL SICK! WHAT IF! WHAT IF!

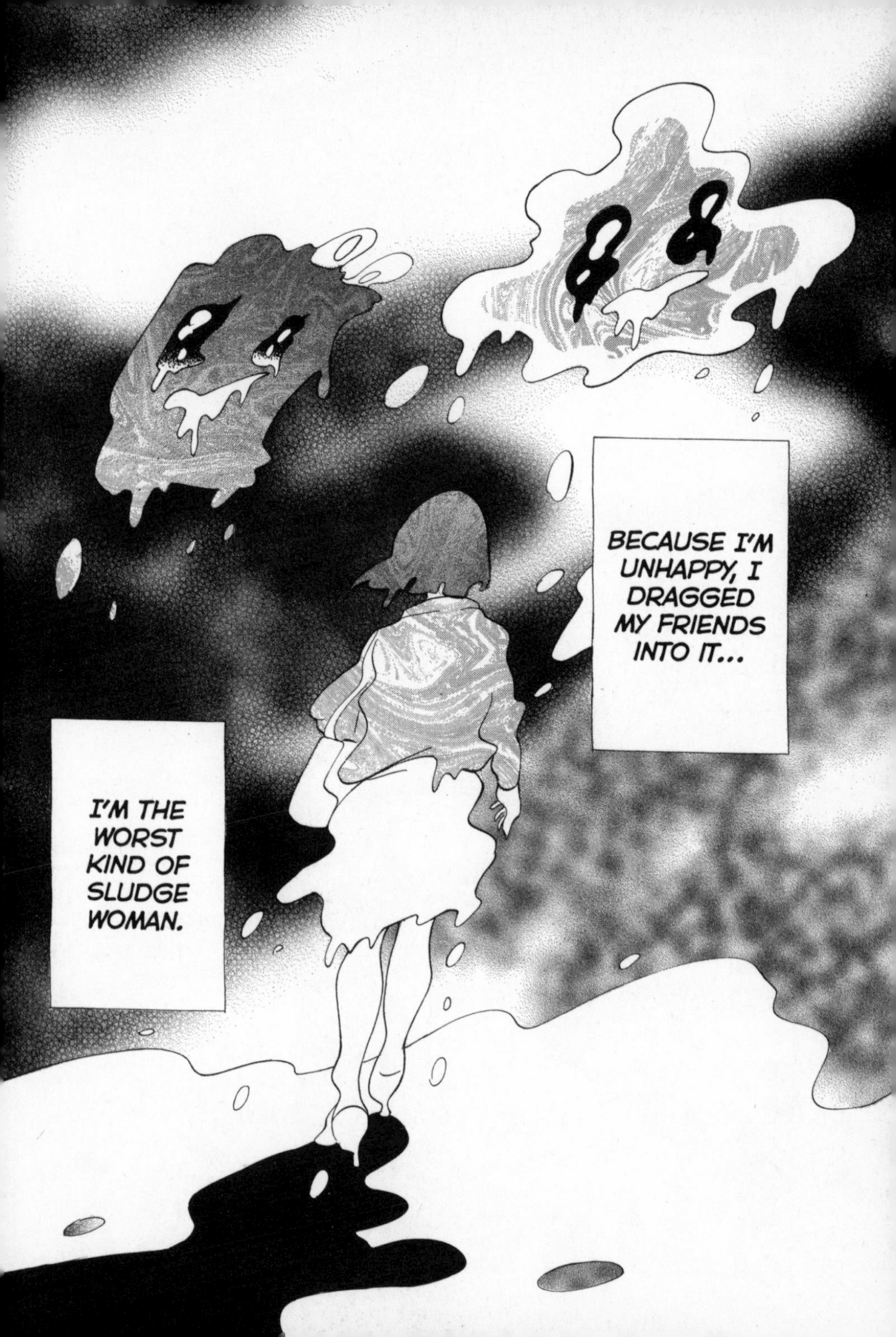
BECAUSE I'M UNHAPPY, I DRAGGED MY FRIENDS INTO IT...
I'M THE WORST KIND OF SLUDGE WOMAN.

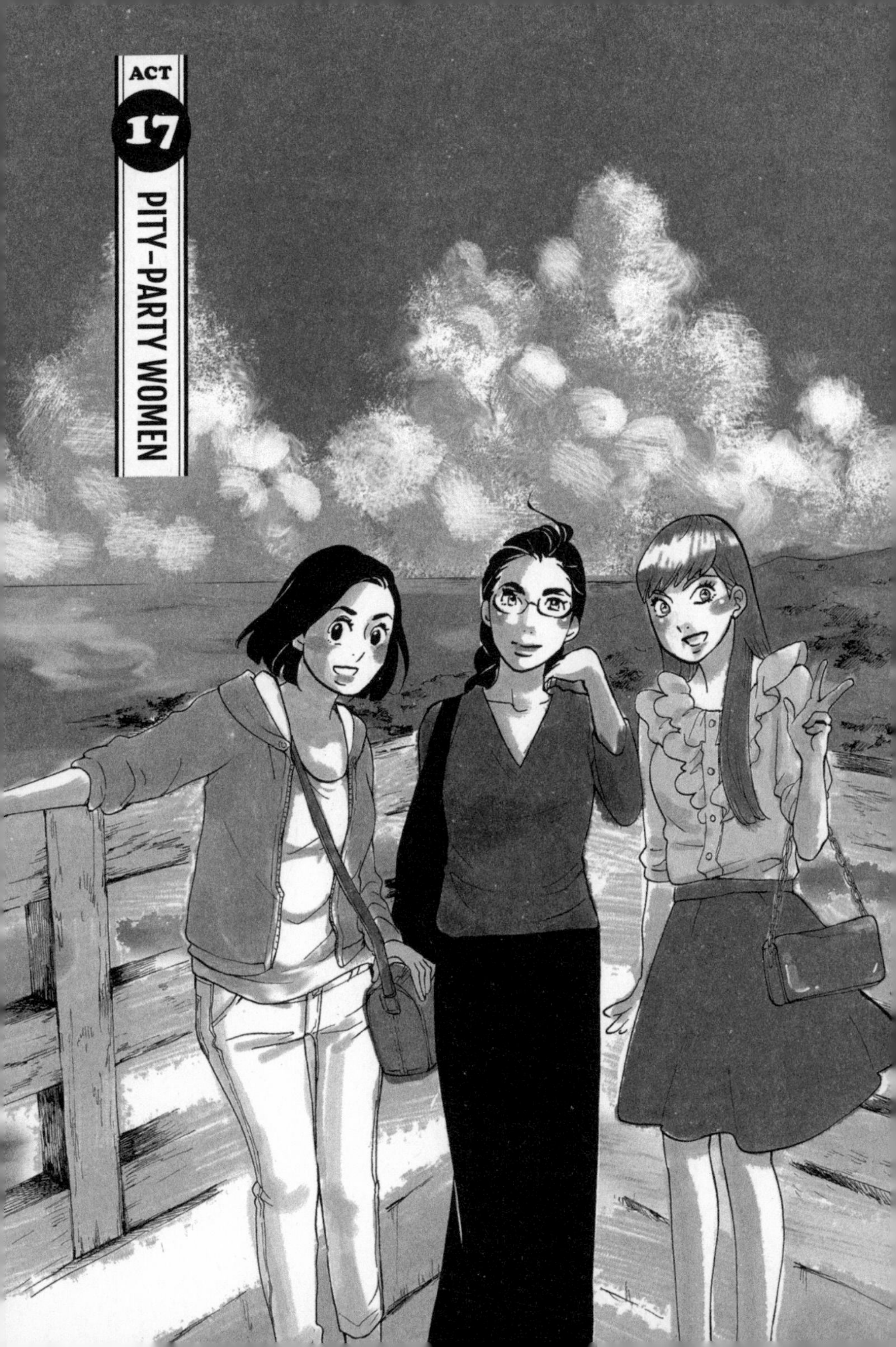
ACT
17
PITY-PARTY WOMEN

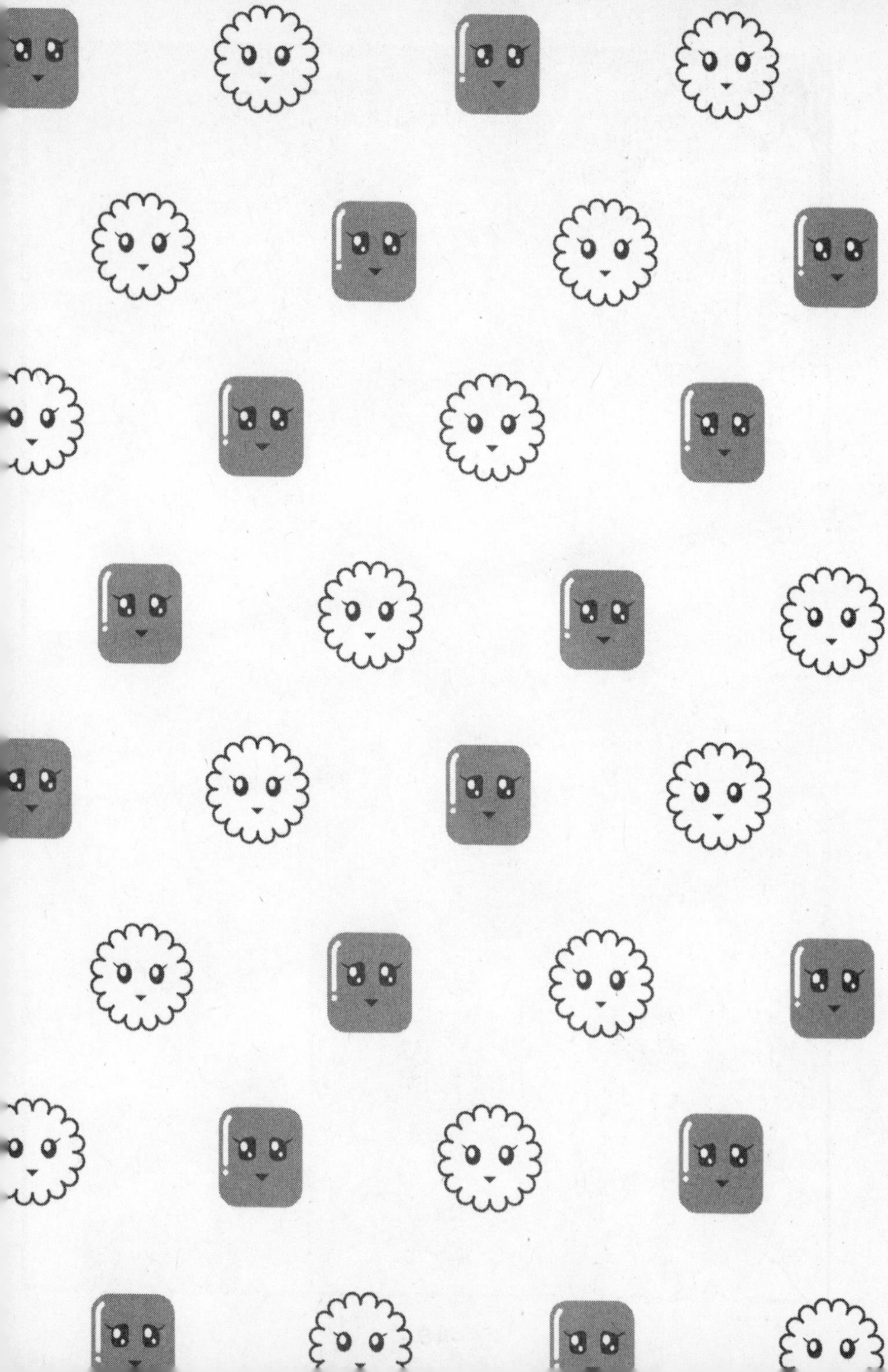

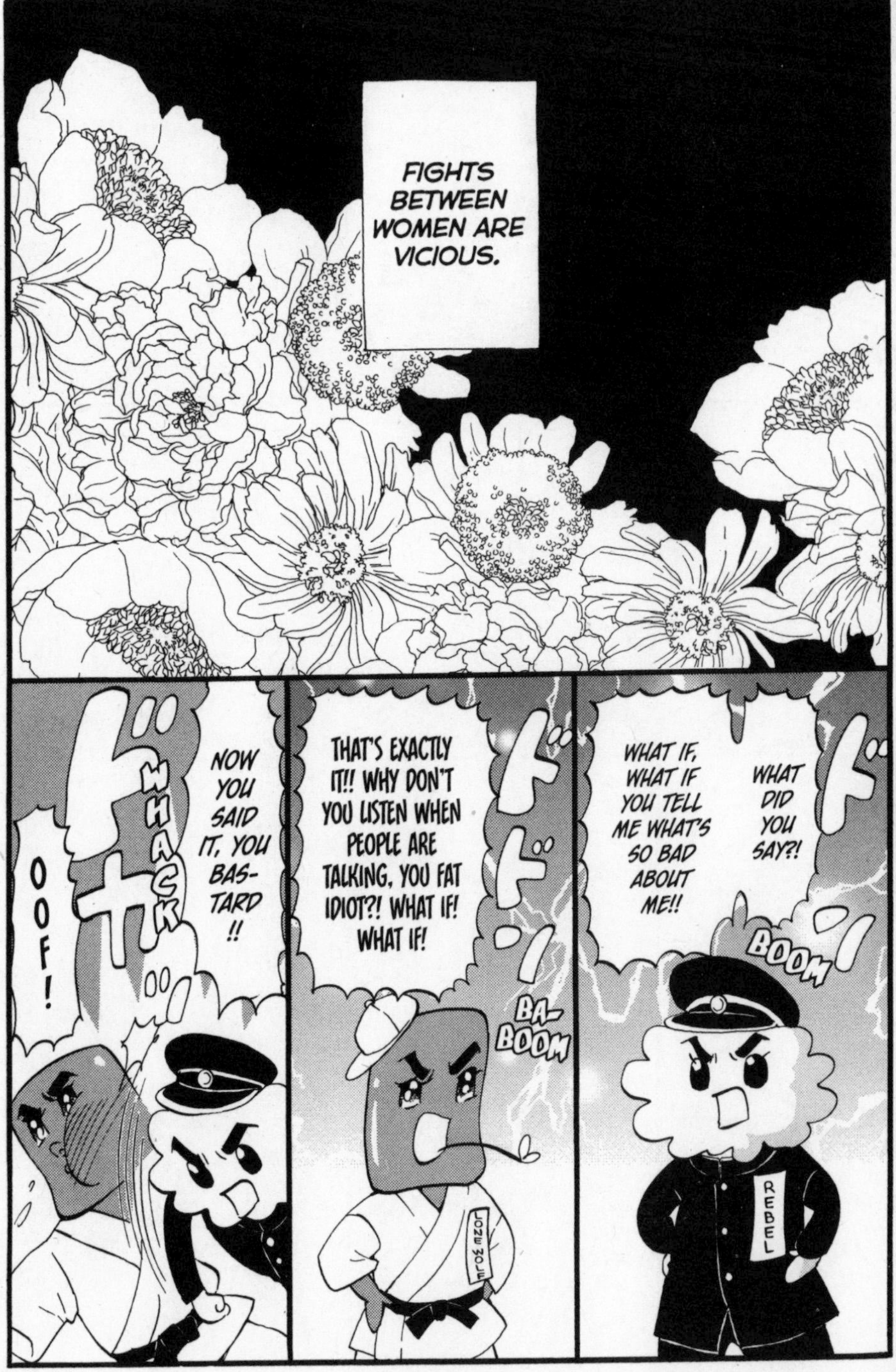
FIGHTS BETWEEN WOMEN ARE VICIOUS.
WHAT DID YOU SAY?!
WHAT IF, WHAT IF YOU TELL ME WHAT'S SO BAD ABOUT ME!!
BOOM
REBEL
THAT'S EXACTLY IT!! WHY DON'T YOU LISTEN WHEN PEOPLE ARE TALKING, YOU FAT IDIOT?! WHAT IF! WHAT IF!
BA-BOOM
LONE WOLF
NOW YOU SAID IT, YOU BAS-TARD!!
WHACK
OOF!

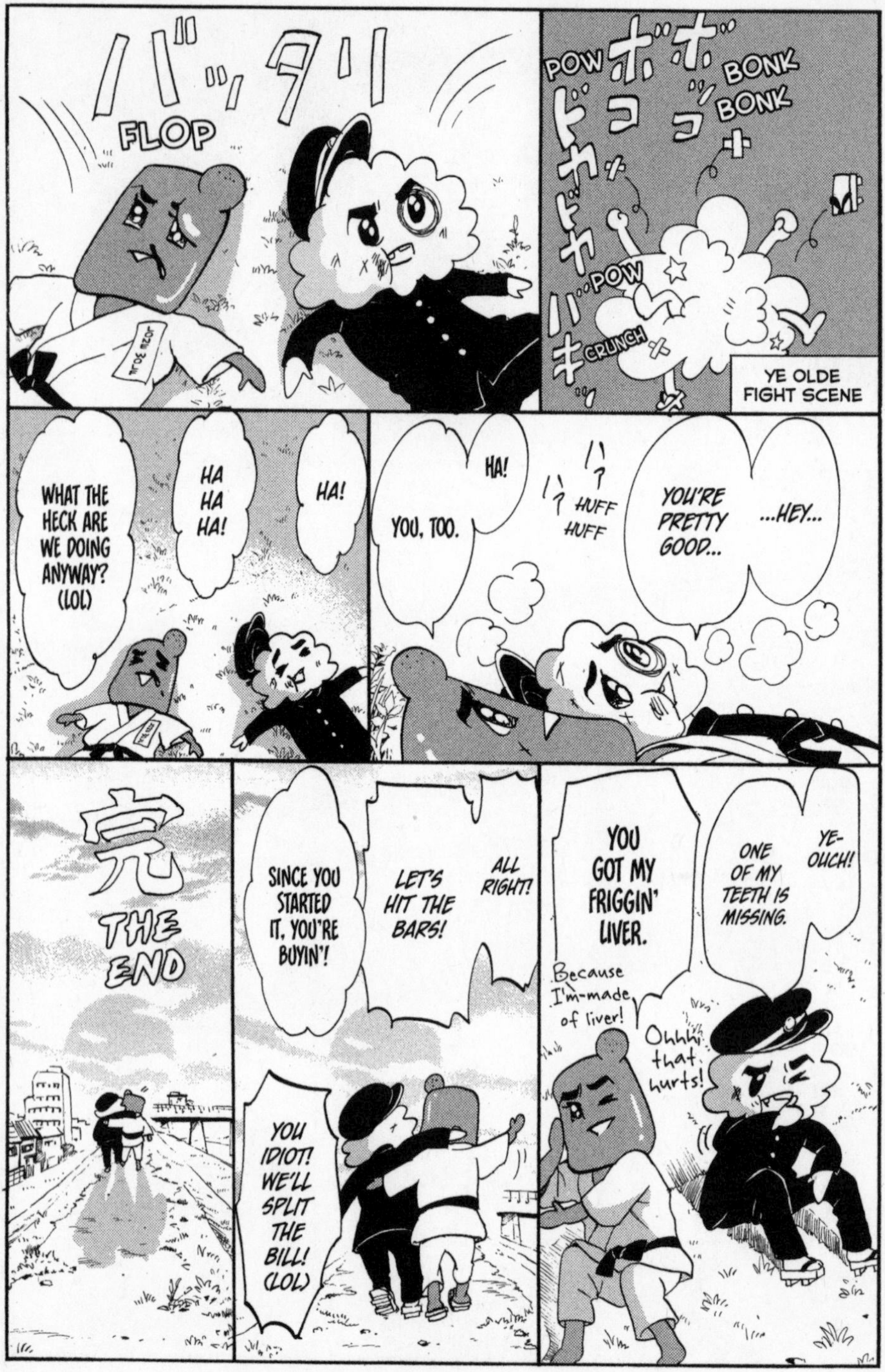
POW
BONK
BONK
POW
CRUNCH
YE OLDE FIGHT SCENE
バッタリ
FLOP
...HEY...
YOU'RE PRETTY GOOD...
HUFF HUFF
HA!
YOU, TOO.
HA!
HA HA HA!
WHAT THE HECK ARE WE DOING ANYWAY? (LOL)
YE-OUCH!
ONE OF MY TEETH IS MISSING.
YOU GOT MY FRIGGIN' LIVER.
Because I'm made of liver!
Ohhh that hurts!
ALL RIGHT!
LET'S HIT THE BARS!
SINCE YOU STARTED IT, YOU'RE BUYIN'!
YOU IDIOT! WE'LL SPLIT THE BILL! (LOL)
完
THE END

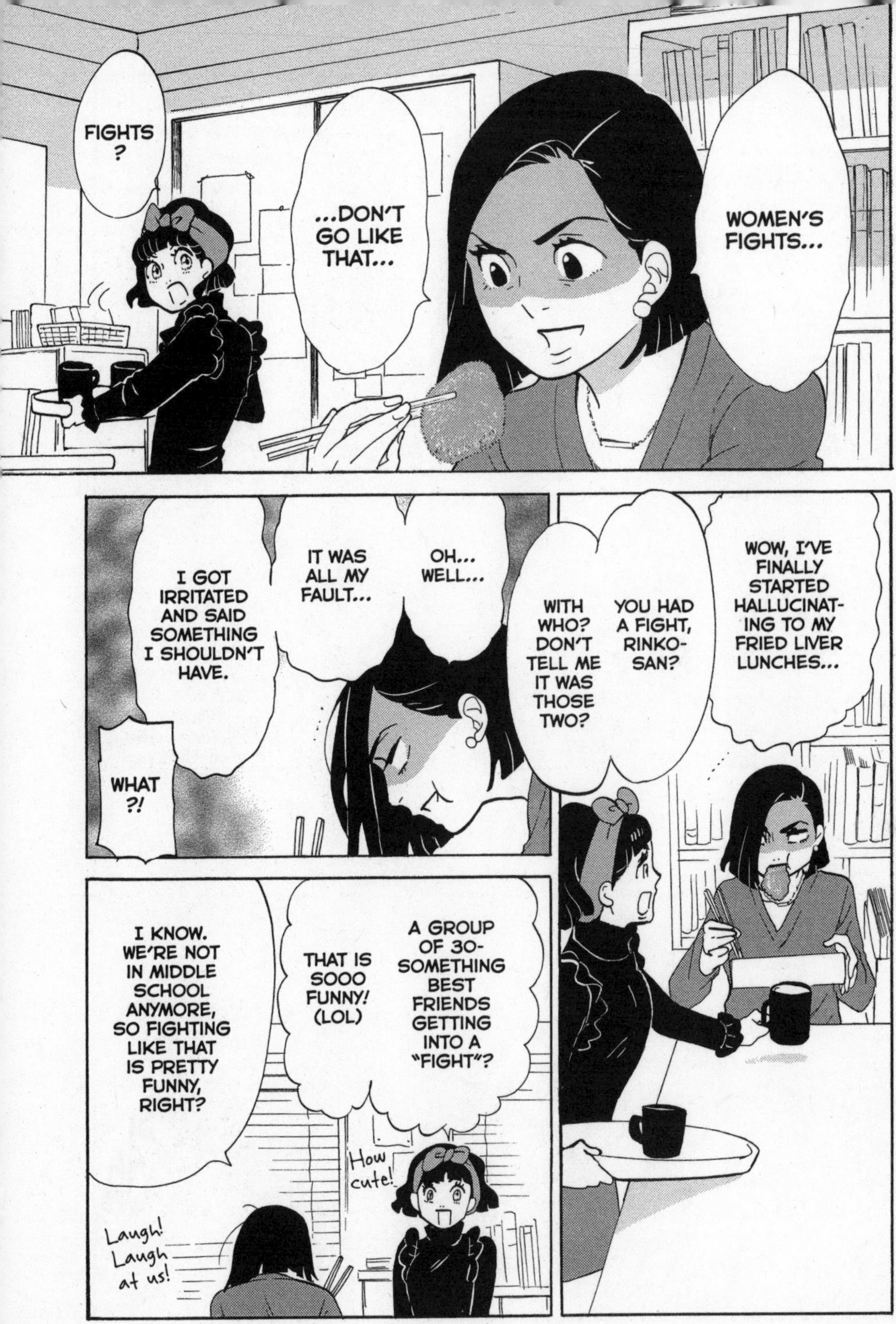

WOMEN'S FIGHTS...
...DON'T GO LIKE THAT...
FIGHTS?
WOW, I'VE FINALLY STARTED HALLUCINATING TO MY FRIED LIVER LUNCHES...
YOU HAD A FIGHT, RINKO-SAN?
WITH WHO? DON'T TELL ME IT WAS THOSE TWO?
OH... WELL...
IT WAS ALL MY FAULT...
I GOT IRRITATED AND SAID SOMETHING I SHOULDN'T HAVE.
WHAT?!
A GROUP OF 30-SOMETHING BEST FRIENDS GETTING INTO A "FIGHT"?
THAT IS SOOO FUNNY! (LOL)
How cute!
I KNOW. WE'RE NOT IN MIDDLE SCHOOL ANYMORE, SO FIGHTING LIKE THAT IS PRETTY FUNNY, RIGHT?
Laugh! Laugh at us!

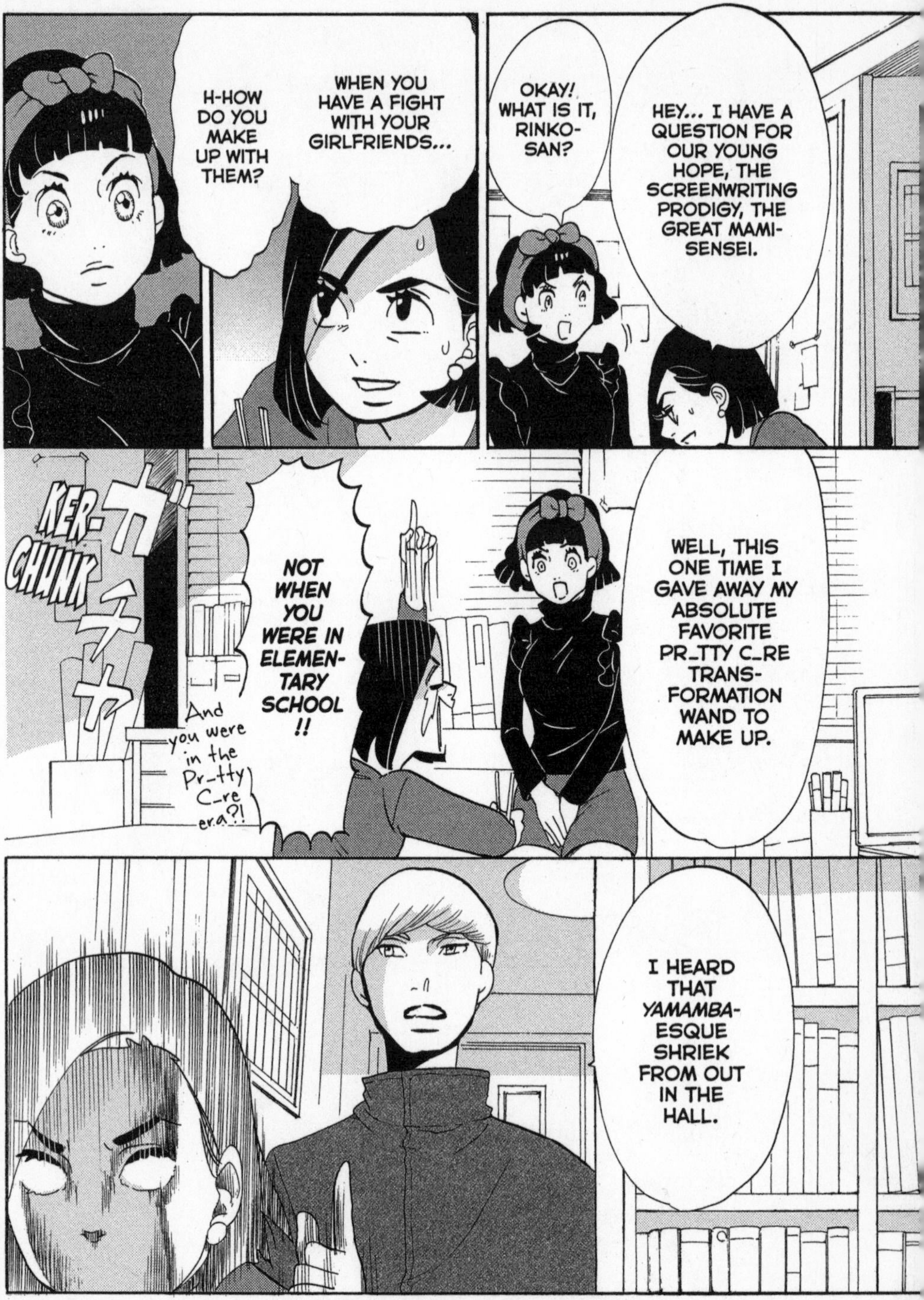
HEY... I HAVE A QUESTION FOR OUR YOUNG HOPE, THE SCREENWRITING PRODIGY, THE GREAT MAMI-SENSEI.
OKAY! WHAT IS IT, RINKO-SAN?
WHEN YOU HAVE A FIGHT WITH YOUR GIRLFRIENDS...
H-HOW DO YOU MAKE UP WITH THEM?
WELL, THIS ONE TIME I GAVE AWAY MY ABSOLUTE FAVORITE PR_TTY C_RE TRANSFORMATION WAND TO MAKE UP.
NOT WHEN YOU WERE IN ELEMENTARY SCHOOL !!
And you were in the Pr_tty C_re era?!
KER-CHUNK
I HEARD THAT YAMAMBA-ESQUE SHRIEK FROM OUT IN THE HALL.

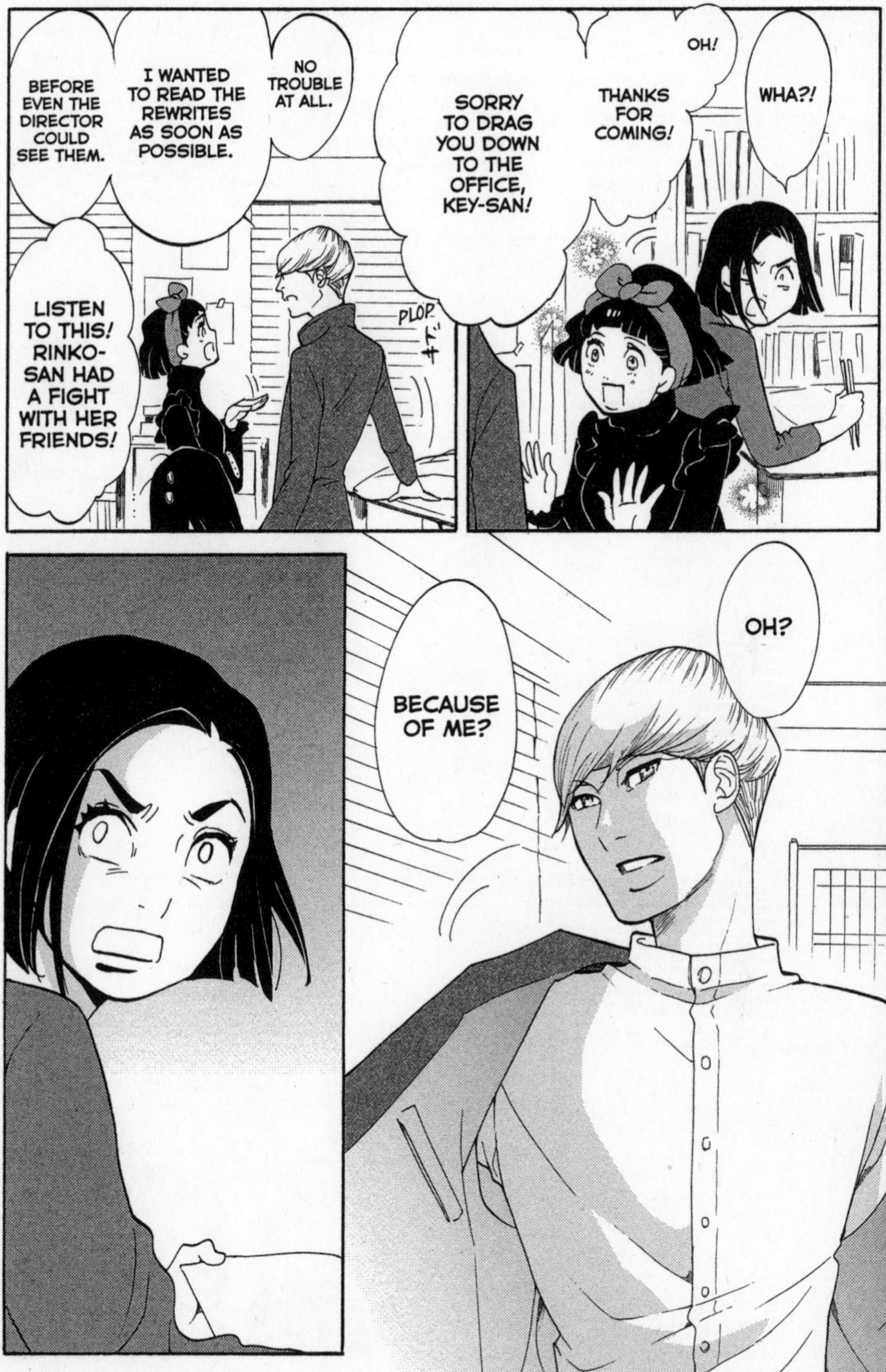
WHA?!
OH!
THANKS FOR COMING!
SORRY TO DRAG YOU DOWN TO THE OFFICE, KEY-SAN!
NO TROUBLE AT ALL.
I WANTED TO READ THE REWRITES AS SOON AS POSSIBLE.
BEFORE EVEN THE DIRECTOR COULD SEE THEM.
PLOP
LISTEN TO THIS! RINKO-SAN HAD A FIGHT WITH HER FRIENDS!
OH?
BECAUSE OF ME?

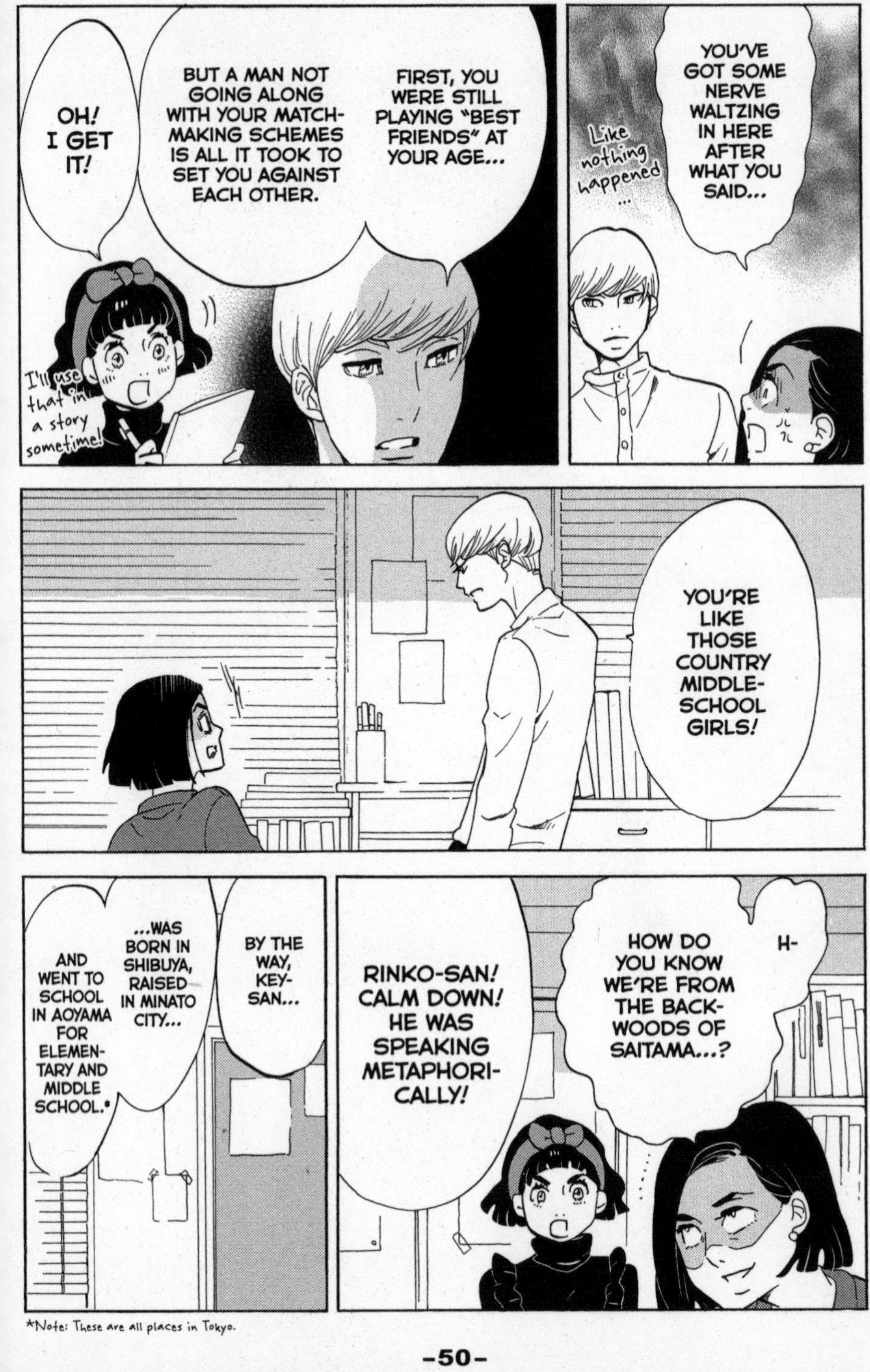
YOU'VE GOT SOME NERVE WALTZING IN HERE AFTER WHAT YOU SAID...
Like nothing happened ...
FIRST, YOU WERE STILL PLAYING "BEST FRIENDS" AT YOUR AGE...
BUT A MAN NOT GOING ALONG WITH YOUR MATCH-MAKING SCHEMES IS ALL IT TOOK TO SET YOU AGAINST EACH OTHER.
OH! I GET IT!
I'll use that in a story sometime!
YOU'RE LIKE THOSE COUNTRY MIDDLE-SCHOOL GIRLS!
H-
HOW DO YOU KNOW WE'RE FROM THE BACK-WOODS OF SAITAMA...?
RINKO-SAN! CALM DOWN! HE WAS SPEAKING METAPHORI-CALLY!
BY THE WAY, KEY-SAN...
...WAS BORN IN SHIBUYA, RAISED IN MINATO CITY...
AND WENT TO SCHOOL IN AOYAMA FOR ELEMEN-TARY AND MIDDLE SCHOOL.*

*Note: These are all places in Tokyo.

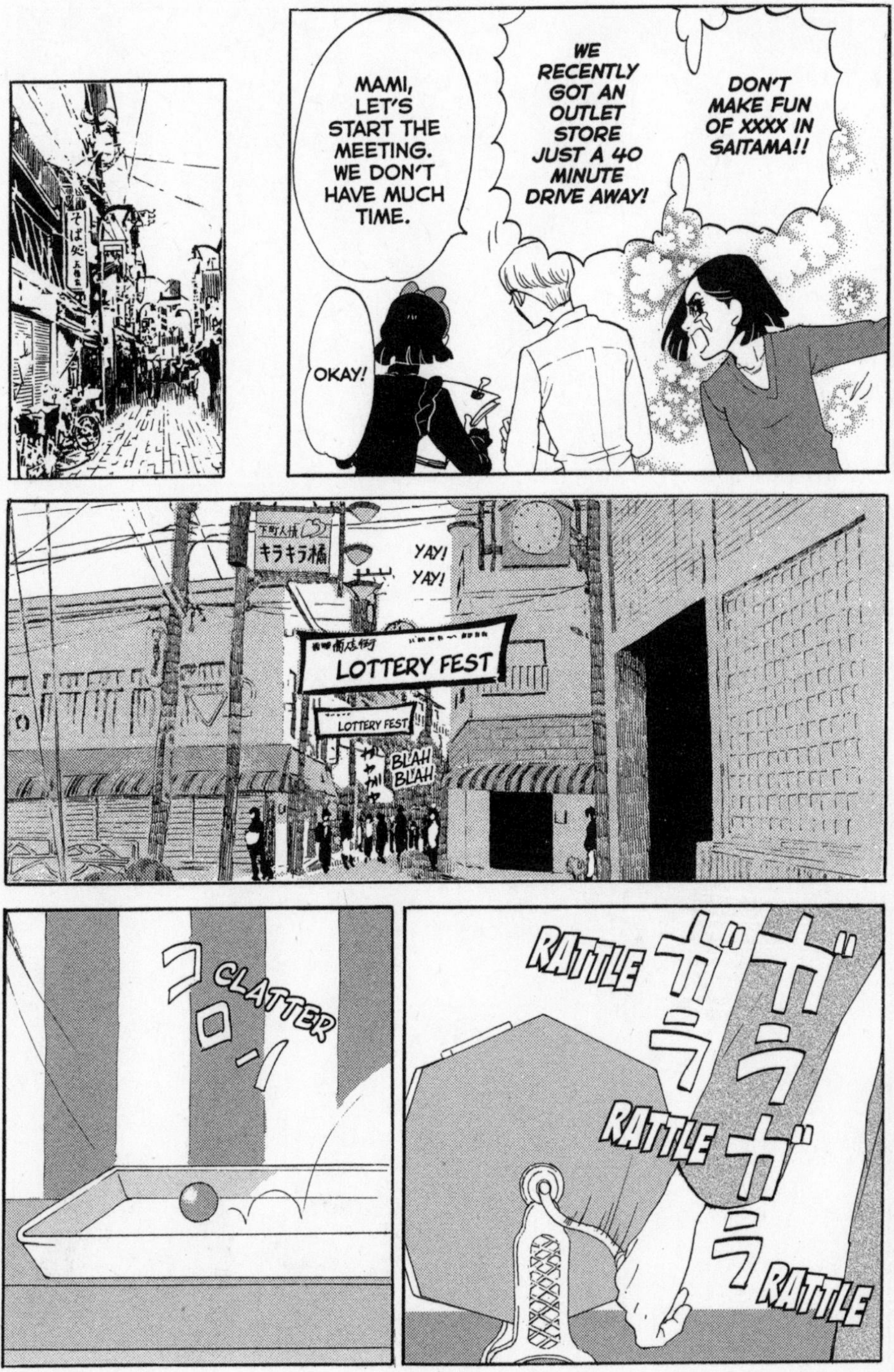
DON'T MAKE FUN OF XXXX IN SAITAMA!!
WE RECENTLY GOT AN OUTLET STORE JUST A 40 MINUTE DRIVE AWAY!
MAMI, LET'S START THE MEETING. WE DON'T HAVE MUCH TIME.
OKAY!
YAY! YAY!
キラキラ橋
LOTTERY FEST
LOTTERY FEST
BLAH BLAH
ガヤガヤ
ガラガラ
RATTLE
ガラガラ
RATTLE
RATTLE
コローン
CLATTER

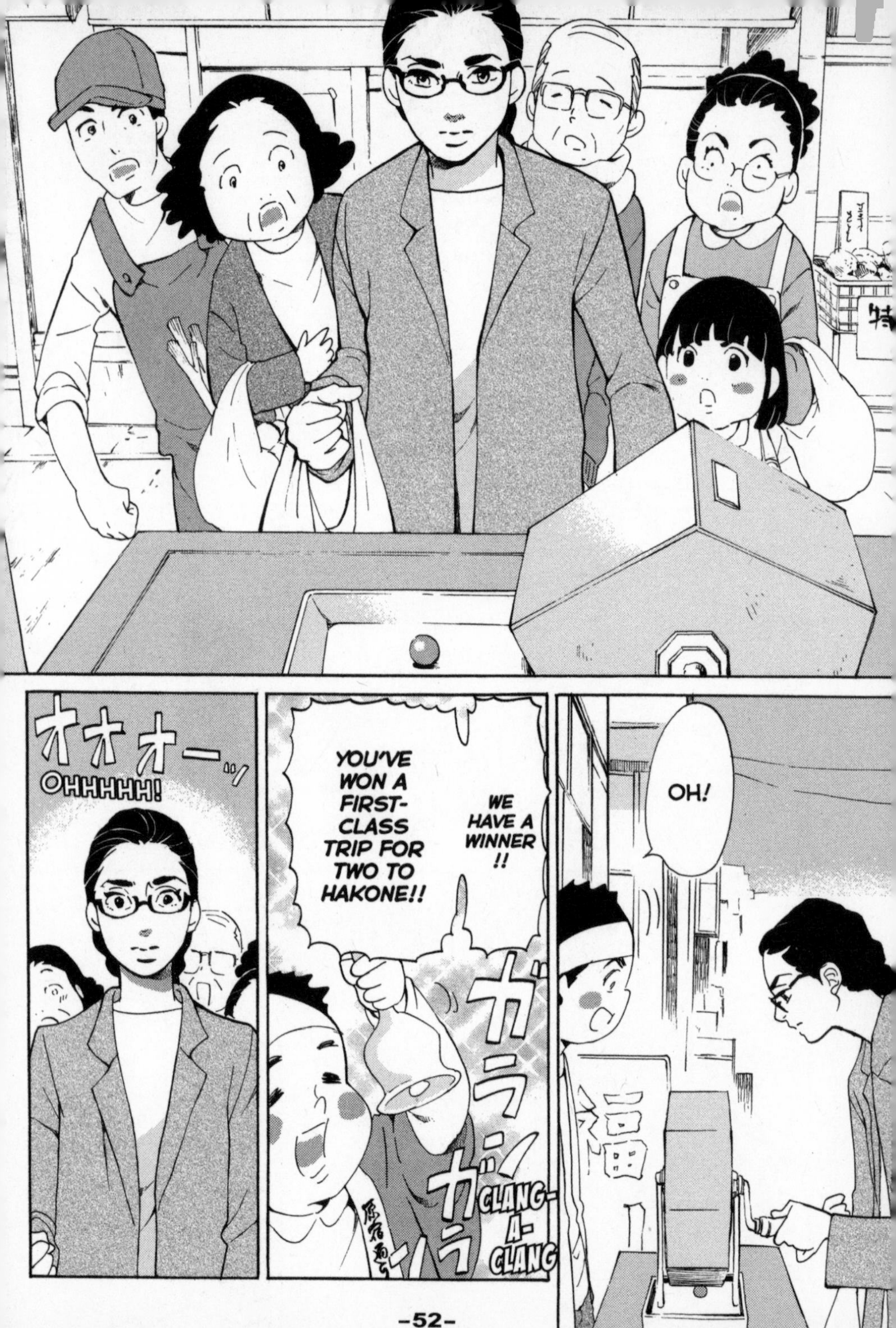
OH!
WE HAVE A WINNER!!
YOU'VE WON A FIRST-CLASS TRIP FOR TWO TO HAKONE!!
ガラン ガラン
CLANG-A-CLANG
オオオーッ
OHHHHHH!

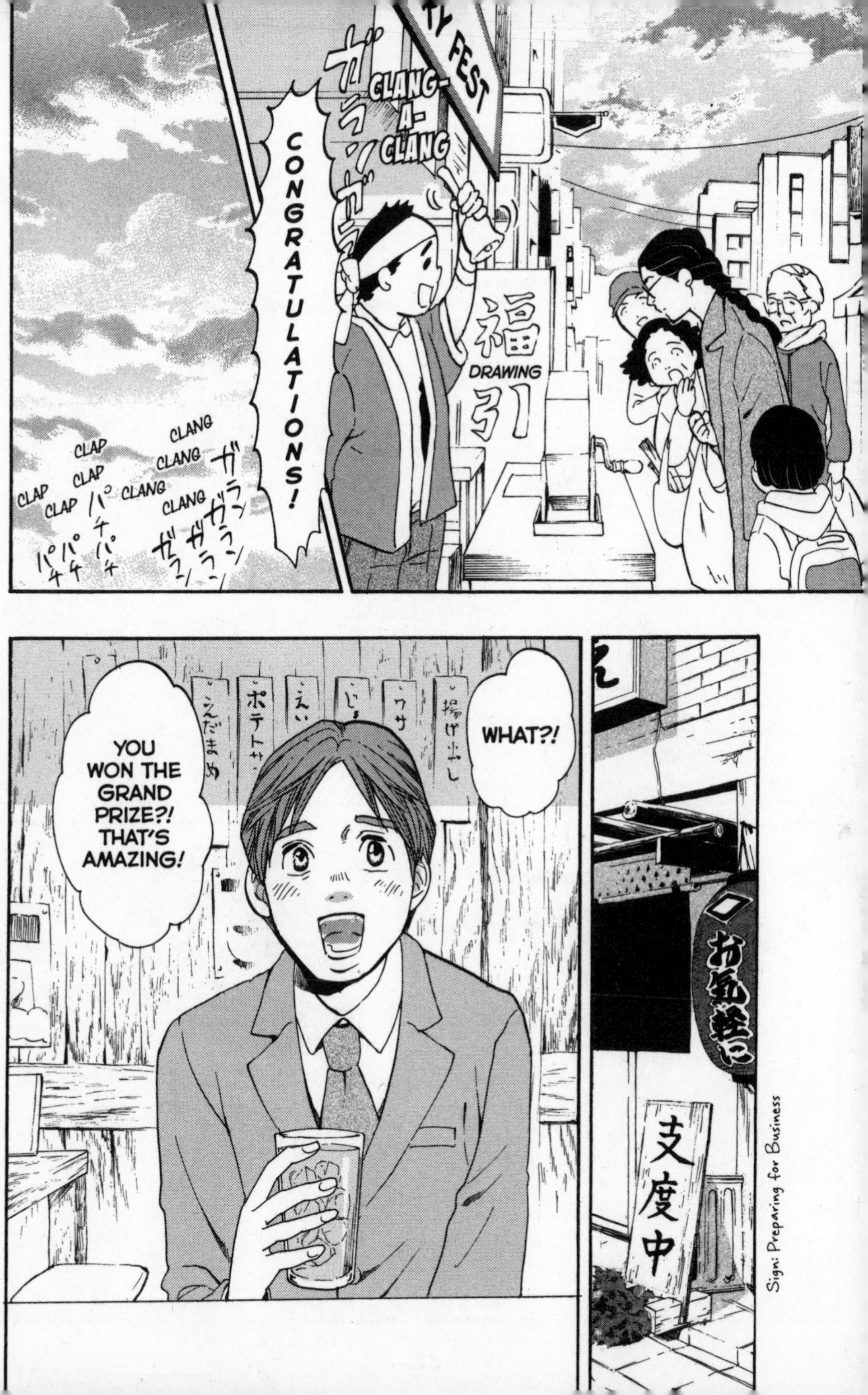
TY FEST
CLANG-A-CLANG
CONGRATULATIONS!
福
DRAWING
引
CLANG
CLANG
CLANG
CLANG
CLAP
CLAP
CLAP
CLAP
支度中
お気軽に
WHAT?!
YOU WON THE GRAND PRIZE?! THAT'S AMAZING!

Sign: Preparing for Business

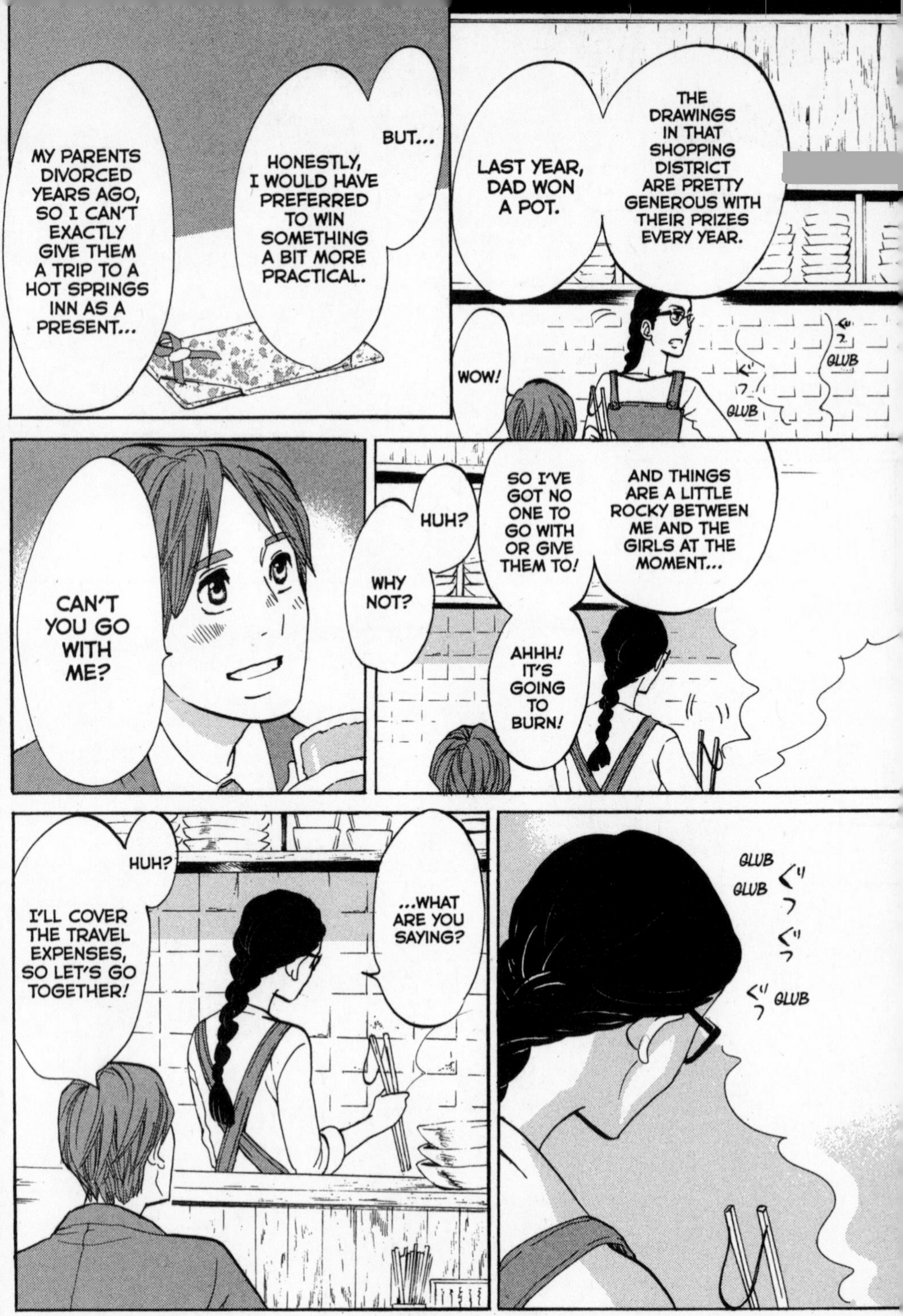
THE DRAWINGS IN THAT SHOPPING DISTRICT ARE PRETTY GENEROUS WITH THEIR PRIZES EVERY YEAR.
LAST YEAR, DAD WON A POT.
WOW!
GLUB
GLUB
BUT...
HONESTLY, I WOULD HAVE PREFERRED TO WIN SOMETHING A BIT MORE PRACTICAL.
MY PARENTS DIVORCED YEARS AGO, SO I CAN'T EXACTLY GIVE THEM A TRIP TO A HOT SPRINGS INN AS A PRESENT...
AND THINGS ARE A LITTLE ROCKY BETWEEN ME AND THE GIRLS AT THE MOMENT...
SO I'VE GOT NO ONE TO GO WITH OR GIVE THEM TO!
HUH?
WHY NOT?
AHHH! IT'S GOING TO BURN!
CAN'T YOU GO WITH ME?
GLUB
GLUB
GLUB
...WHAT ARE YOU SAYING?
HUH?
I'LL COVER THE TRAVEL EXPENSES, SO LET'S GO TOGETHER!

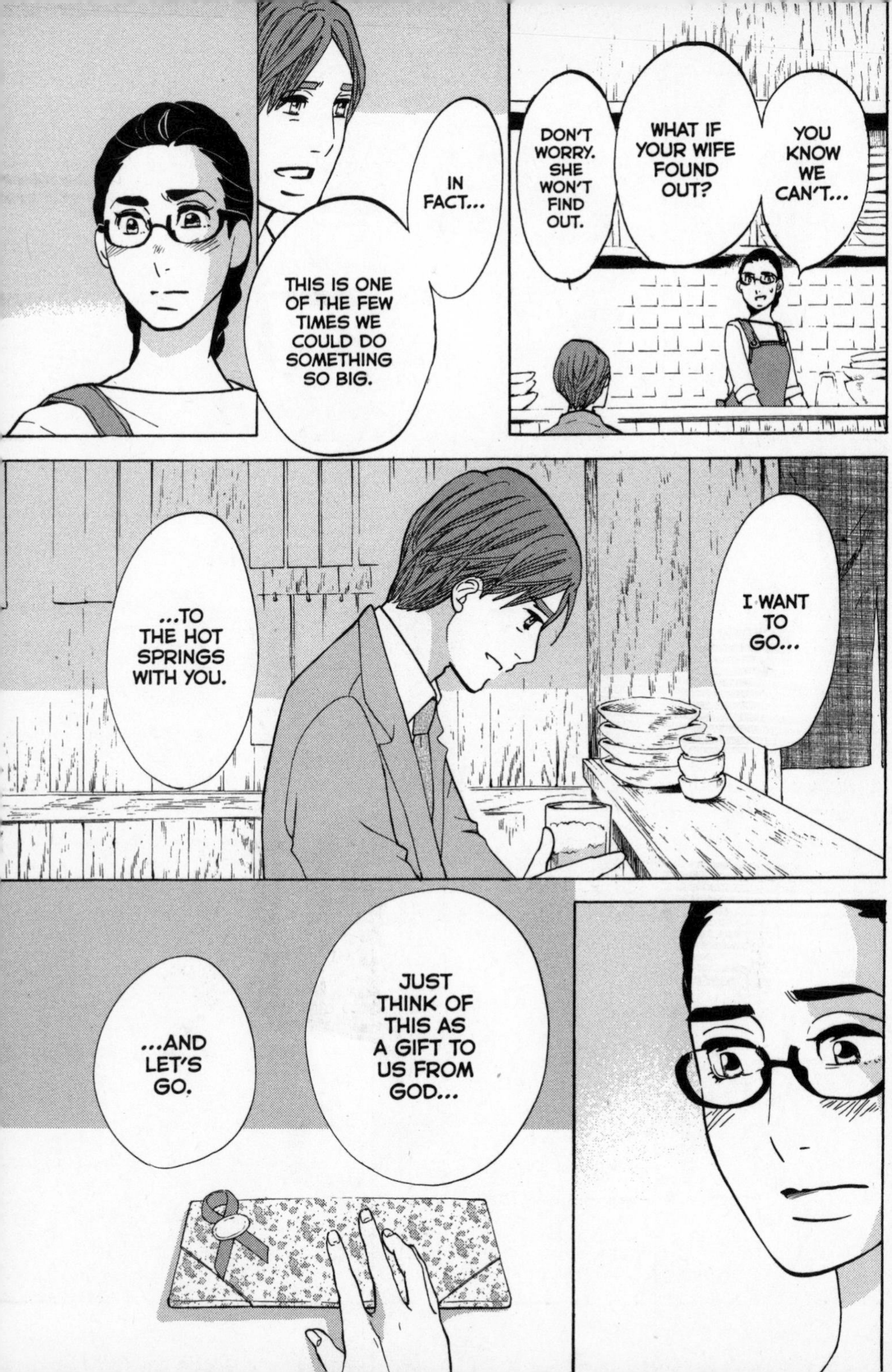
YOU KNOW WE CAN'T...
WHAT IF YOUR WIFE FOUND OUT?
DON'T WORRY. SHE WON'T FIND OUT.
IN FACT...
THIS IS ONE OF THE FEW TIMES WE COULD DO SOMETHING SO BIG.
I WANT TO GO...
...TO THE HOT SPRINGS WITH YOU.
JUST THINK OF THIS AS A GIFT TO US FROM GOD...
...AND LET'S GO.

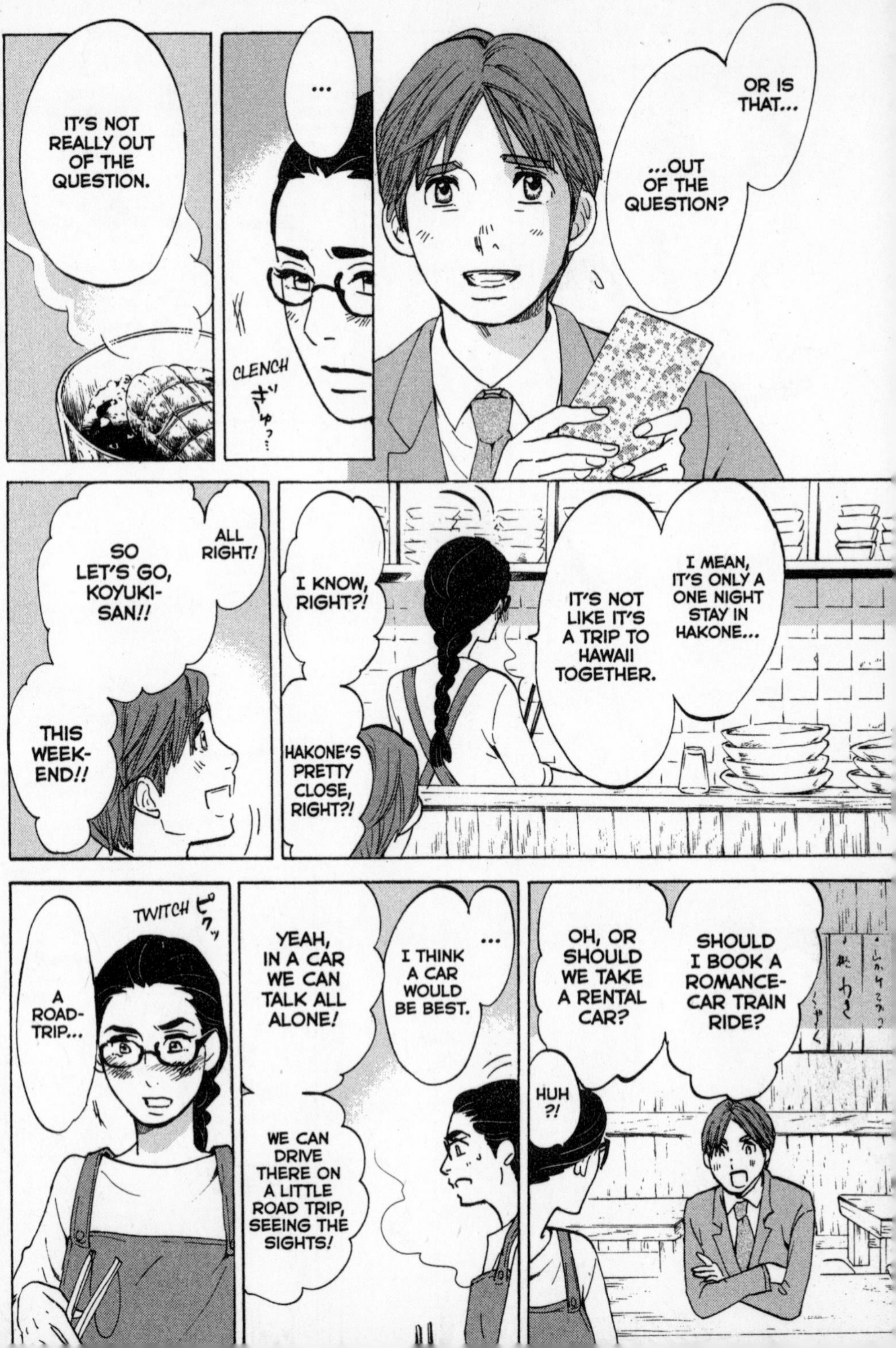
OR IS THAT...
...OUT OF THE QUESTION?
...
CLENCH
IT'S NOT REALLY OUT OF THE QUESTION.
I MEAN, IT'S ONLY A ONE NIGHT STAY IN HAKONE...
IT'S NOT LIKE IT'S A TRIP TO HAWAII TOGETHER.
I KNOW, RIGHT?!
HAKONE'S PRETTY CLOSE, RIGHT?!
ALL RIGHT!
SO LET'S GO, KOYUKI-SAN!!
THIS WEEK-END!!
SHOULD I BOOK A ROMANCE-CAR TRAIN RIDE?
OH, OR SHOULD WE TAKE A RENTAL CAR?
HUH?!
...
I THINK A CAR WOULD BE BEST.
YEAH, IN A CAR WE CAN TALK ALL ALONE!
WE CAN DRIVE THERE ON A LITTLE ROAD TRIP, SEEING THE SIGHTS!
TWITCH ピクッ
A ROAD-TRIP...

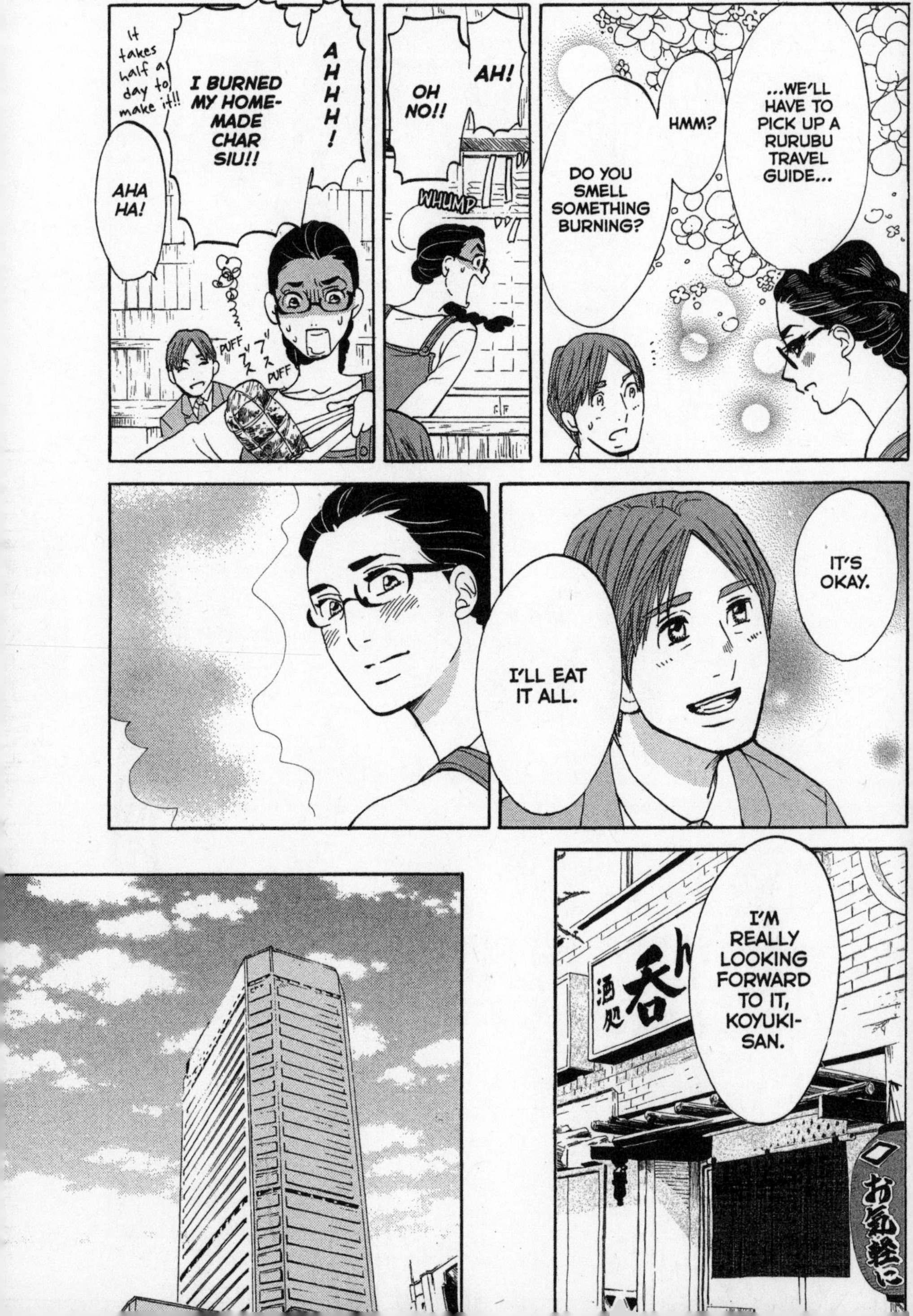
...WE'LL HAVE TO PICK UP A RURUBU TRAVEL GUIDE...
HMM?
DO YOU SMELL SOMETHING BURNING?
AH!
OH NO!!
WHUMP
AHHHH!
I BURNED MY HOME-MADE CHAR SIU!!
It takes half a day to make it!!
PUFF
PUFF
AHA HA!
IT'S OKAY.
I'LL EAT IT ALL.
I'M REALLY LOOKING FORWARD TO IT, KOYUKI-SAN.
お気軽に

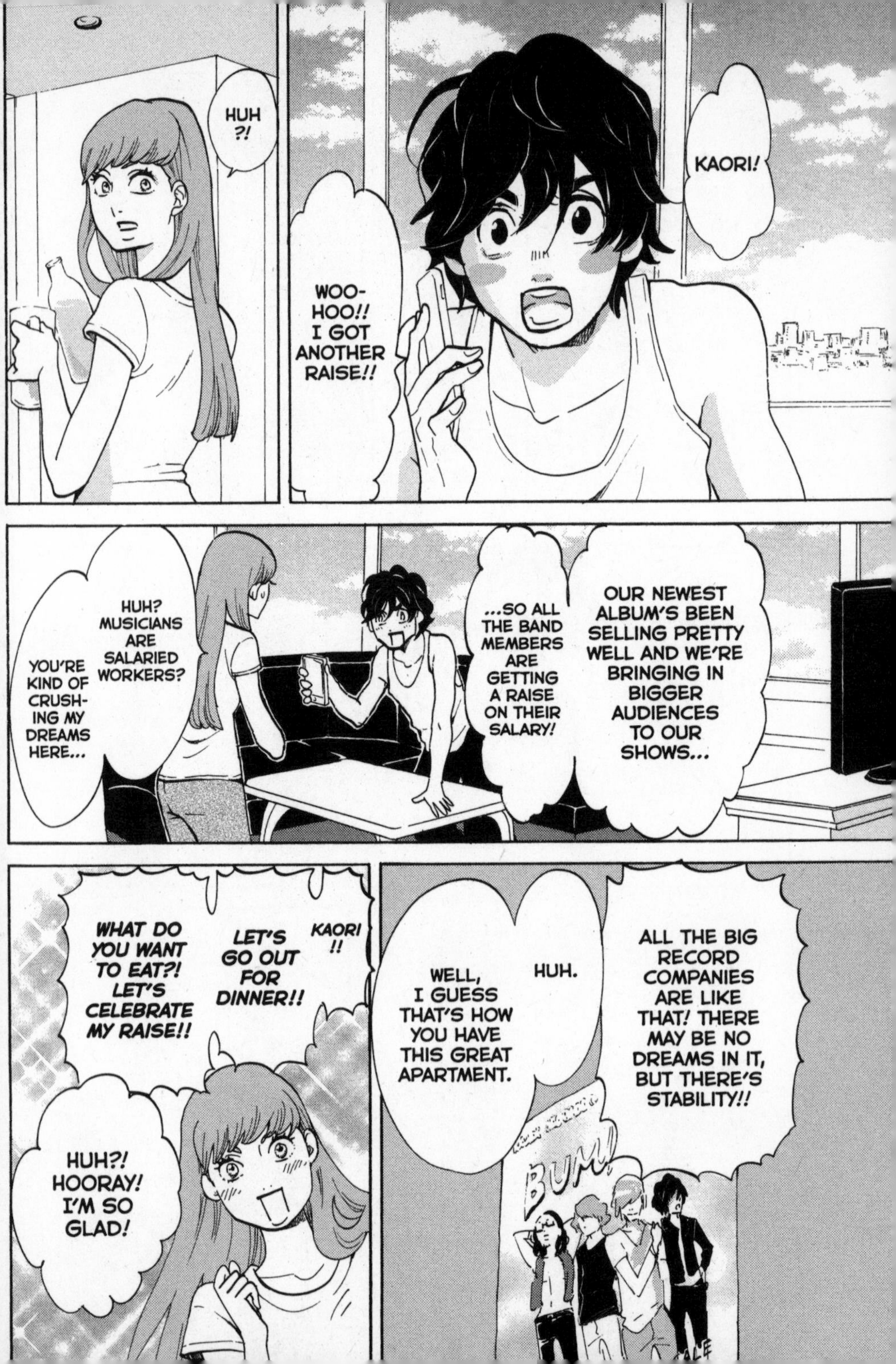
KAORI!
WOO-HOO!! I GOT ANOTHER RAISE!!
HUH ?!
OUR NEWEST ALBUM'S BEEN SELLING PRETTY WELL AND WE'RE BRINGING IN BIGGER AUDIENCES TO OUR SHOWS...
...SO ALL THE BAND MEMBERS ARE GETTING A RAISE ON THEIR SALARY!
HUH? MUSICIANS ARE SALARIED WORKERS?
YOU'RE KIND OF CRUSHING MY DREAMS HERE...
ALL THE BIG RECORD COMPANIES ARE LIKE THAT! THERE MAY BE NO DREAMS IN IT, BUT THERE'S STABILITY!!
HUH.
WELL, I GUESS THAT'S HOW YOU HAVE THIS GREAT APARTMENT.
BUM!
KAORI !!
LET'S GO OUT FOR DINNER!!
WHAT DO YOU WANT TO EAT?! LET'S CELEBRATE MY RAISE!!
HUH?! HOORAY! I'M SO GLAD!

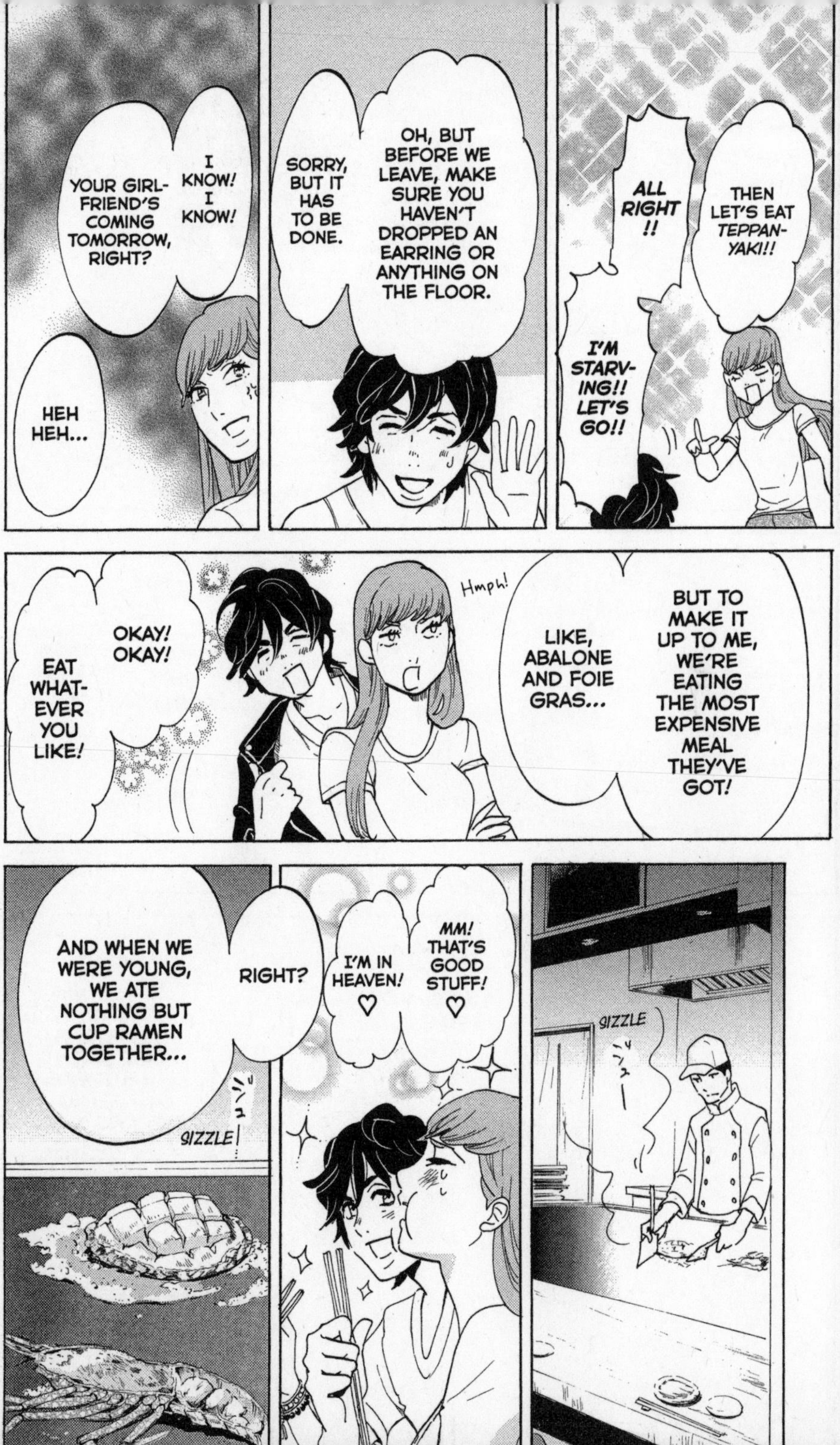
THEN LET'S EAT TEPPAN-YAKI!!
ALL RIGHT!!
I'M STARVING!! LET'S GO!!
OH, BUT BEFORE WE LEAVE, MAKE SURE YOU HAVEN'T DROPPED AN EARRING OR ANYTHING ON THE FLOOR.
SORRY, BUT IT HAS TO BE DONE.
I KNOW! I KNOW!
YOUR GIRL-FRIEND'S COMING TOMORROW, RIGHT?
HEH HEH...
BUT TO MAKE IT UP TO ME, WE'RE EATING THE MOST EXPENSIVE MEAL THEY'VE GOT!
LIKE, ABALONE AND FOIE GRAS...
Hmph!
OKAY! OKAY!
EAT WHAT-EVER YOU LIKE!
SIZZLE
MM! THAT'S GOOD STUFF! ♡
I'M IN HEAVEN! ♡
RIGHT?
AND WHEN WE WERE YOUNG, WE ATE NOTHING BUT CUP RAMEN TOGETHER...
SIZZLE

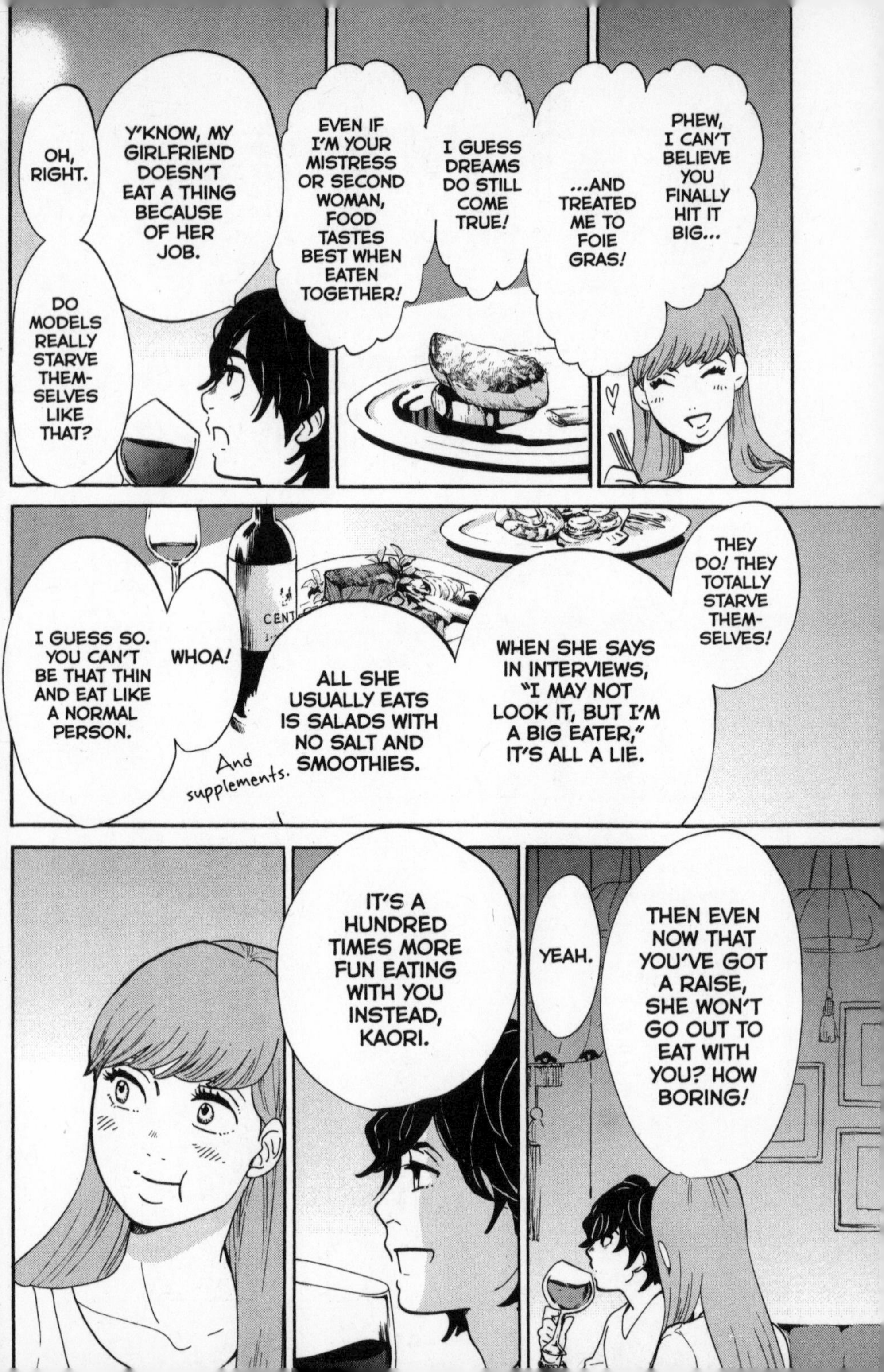
PHEW, I CAN'T BELIEVE YOU FINALLY HIT IT BIG...
...AND TREATED ME TO FOIE GRAS!
I GUESS DREAMS DO STILL COME TRUE!
EVEN IF I'M YOUR MISTRESS OR SECOND WOMAN, FOOD TASTES BEST WHEN EATEN TOGETHER!
Y'KNOW, MY GIRLFRIEND DOESN'T EAT A THING BECAUSE OF HER JOB.
OH, RIGHT.
DO MODELS REALLY STARVE THEMSELVES LIKE THAT?
THEY DO! THEY TOTALLY STARVE THEMSELVES!
WHEN SHE SAYS IN INTERVIEWS, "I MAY NOT LOOK IT, BUT I'M A BIG EATER," IT'S ALL A LIE.
ALL SHE USUALLY EATS IS SALADS WITH NO SALT AND SMOOTHIES.
And supplements.
WHOA!
I GUESS SO. YOU CAN'T BE THAT THIN AND EAT LIKE A NORMAL PERSON.
THEN EVEN NOW THAT YOU'VE GOT A RAISE, SHE WON'T GO OUT TO EAT WITH YOU? HOW BORING!
YEAH.
IT'S A HUNDRED TIMES MORE FUN EATING WITH YOU INSTEAD, KAORI.

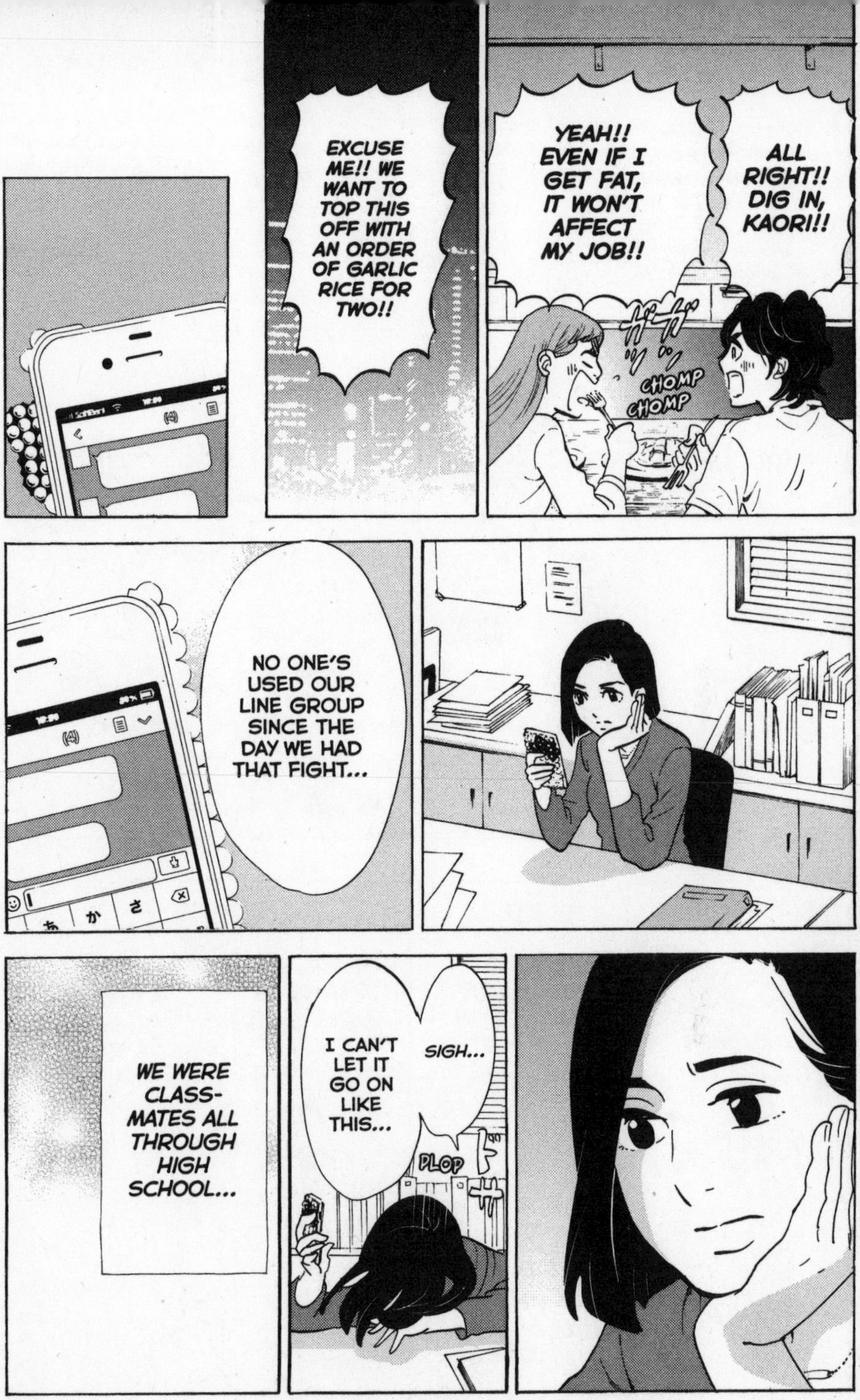
ALL RIGHT!! DIG IN, KAORI!!
YEAH!! EVEN IF I GET FAT, IT WON'T AFFECT MY JOB!!
CHOMP CHOMP
EXCUSE ME!! WE WANT TO TOP THIS OFF WITH AN ORDER OF GARLIC RICE FOR TWO!!
NO ONE'S USED OUR LINE GROUP SINCE THE DAY WE HAD THAT FIGHT...
SIGH...
I CAN'T LET IT GO ON LIKE THIS...
PLOP
WE WERE CLASSMATES ALL THROUGH HIGH SCHOOL...

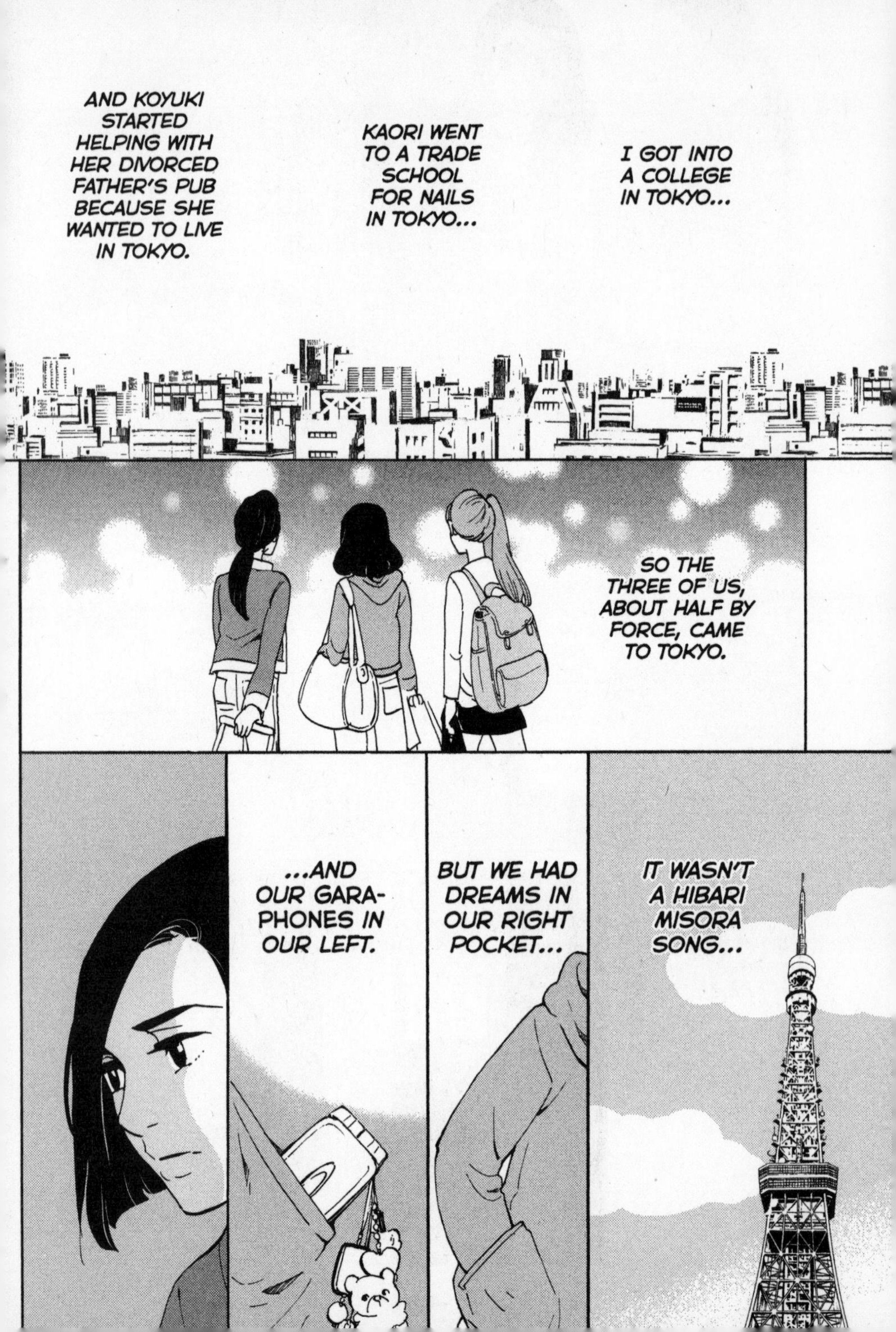
I GOT INTO A COLLEGE IN TOKYO...
KAORI WENT TO A TRADE SCHOOL FOR NAILS IN TOKYO...
AND KOYUKI STARTED HELPING WITH HER DIVORCED FATHER'S PUB BECAUSE SHE WANTED TO LIVE IN TOKYO.
SO THE THREE OF US, ABOUT HALF BY FORCE, CAME TO TOKYO.
IT WASN'T A HIBARI MISORA SONG...
BUT WE HAD DREAMS IN OUR RIGHT POCKET...
...AND OUR GARA-PHONES IN OUR LEFT.

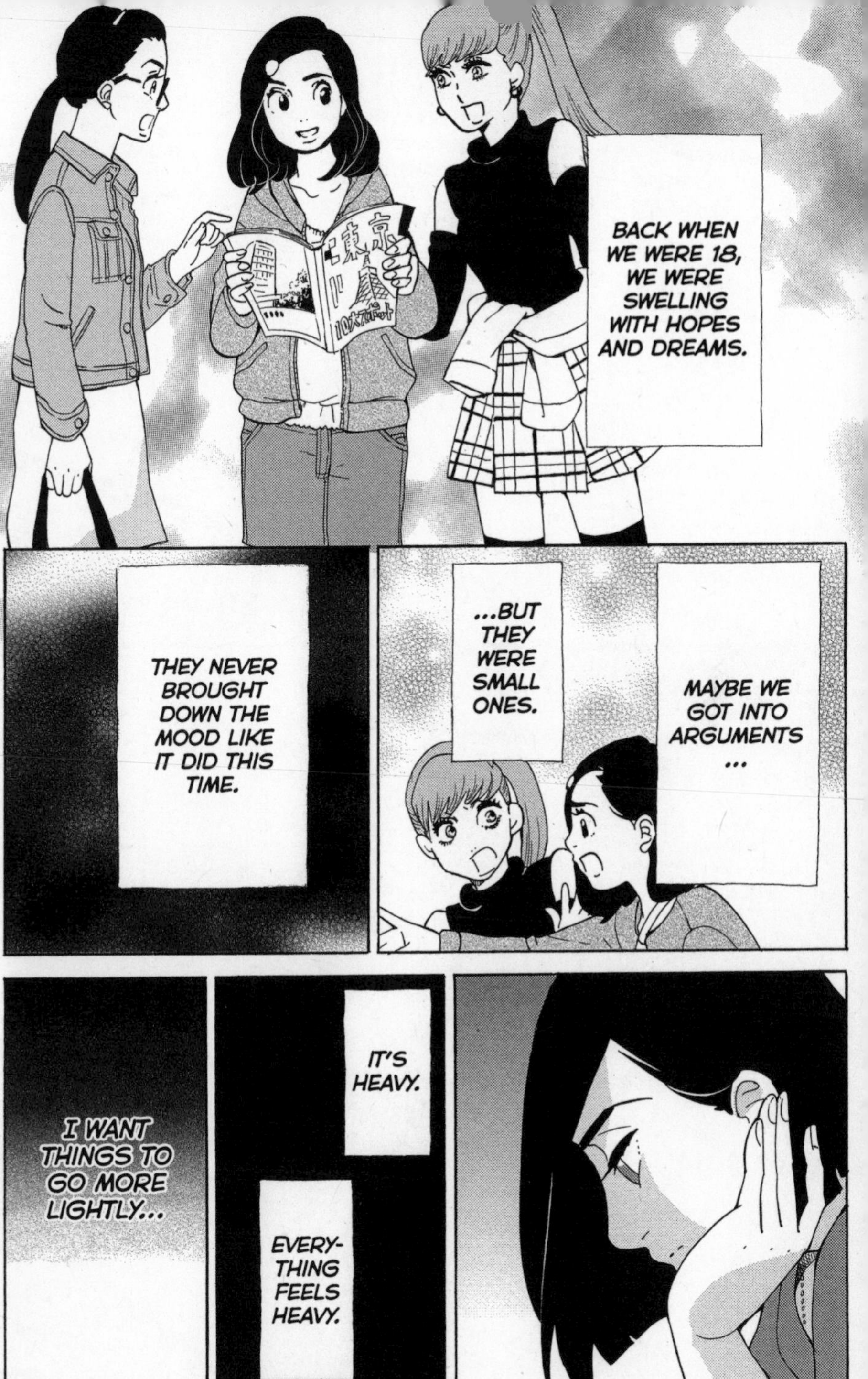
BACK WHEN WE WERE 18, WE WERE SWELLING WITH HOPES AND DREAMS.
MAYBE WE GOT INTO ARGUMENTS ...
...BUT THEY WERE SMALL ONES.
THEY NEVER BROUGHT DOWN THE MOOD LIKE IT DID THIS TIME.
IT'S HEAVY.
EVERY-THING FEELS HEAVY.
I WANT THINGS TO GO MORE LIGHTLY...

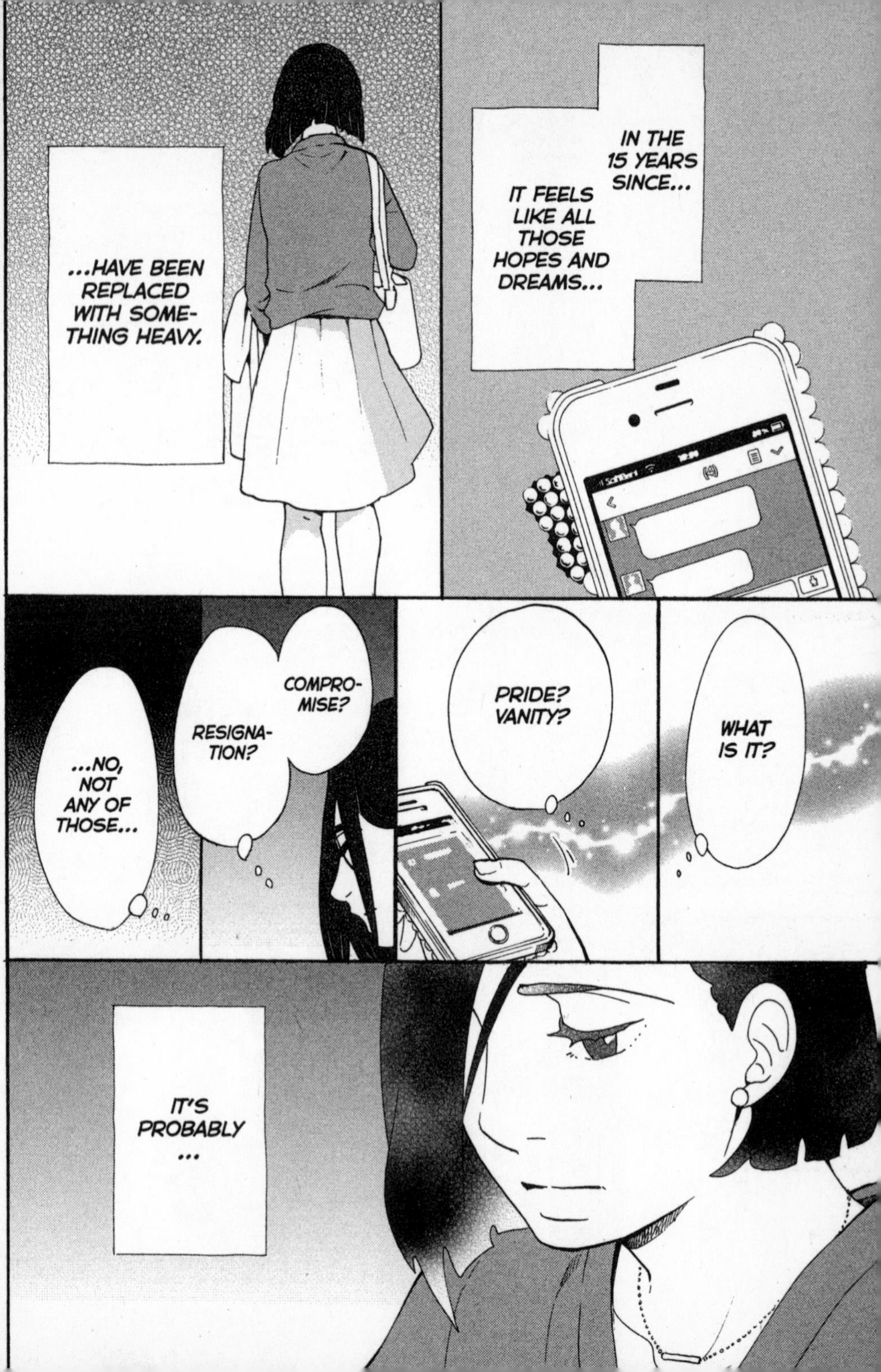
IN THE 15 YEARS SINCE...
IT FEELS LIKE ALL THOSE HOPES AND DREAMS...
...HAVE BEEN REPLACED WITH SOME-THING HEAVY.
WHAT IS IT?
PRIDE? VANITY?
COMPRO-MISE?
RESIGNA-TION?
...NO, NOT ANY OF THOSE...
IT'S PROBABLY ...

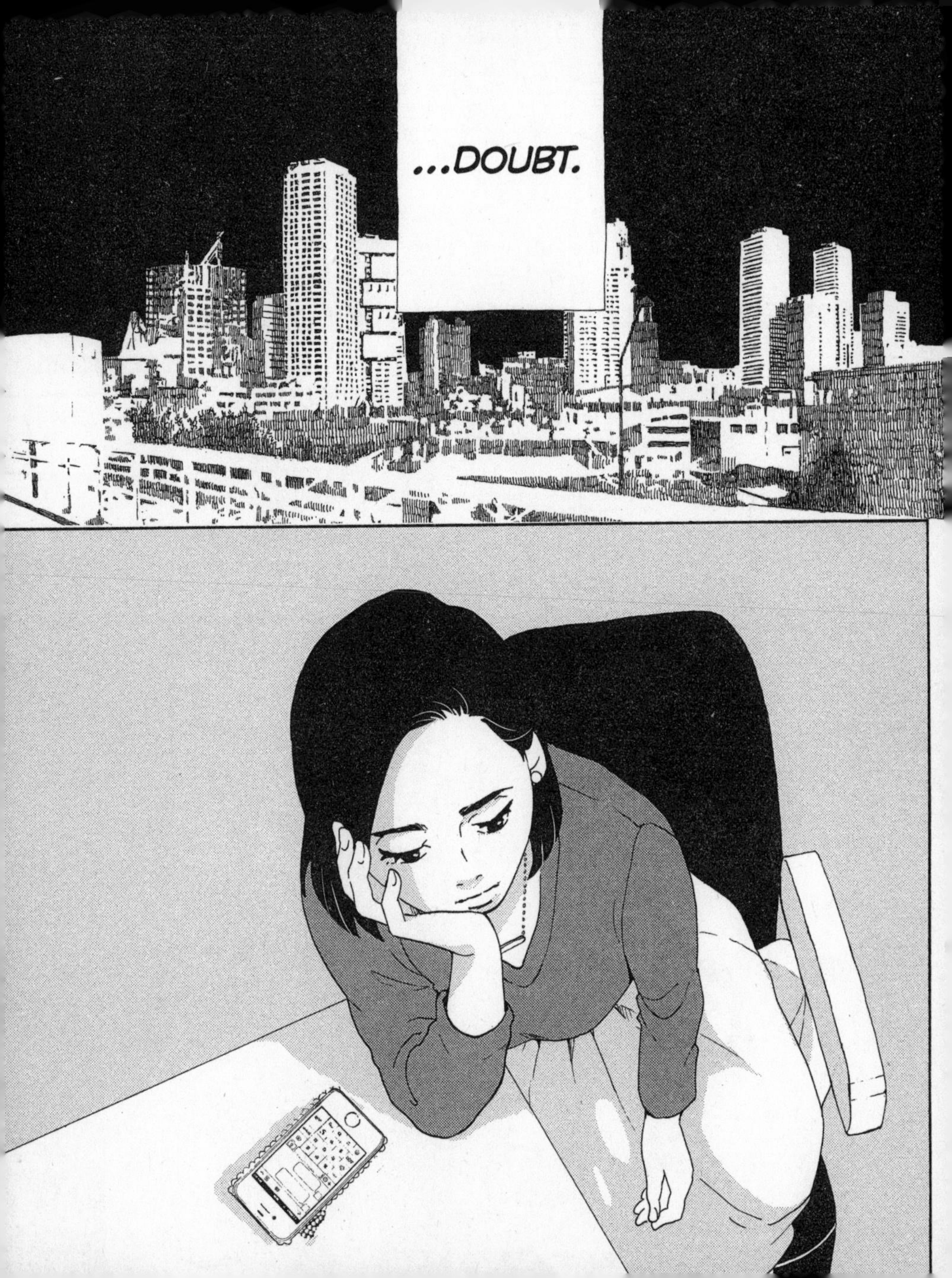
...DOUBT.

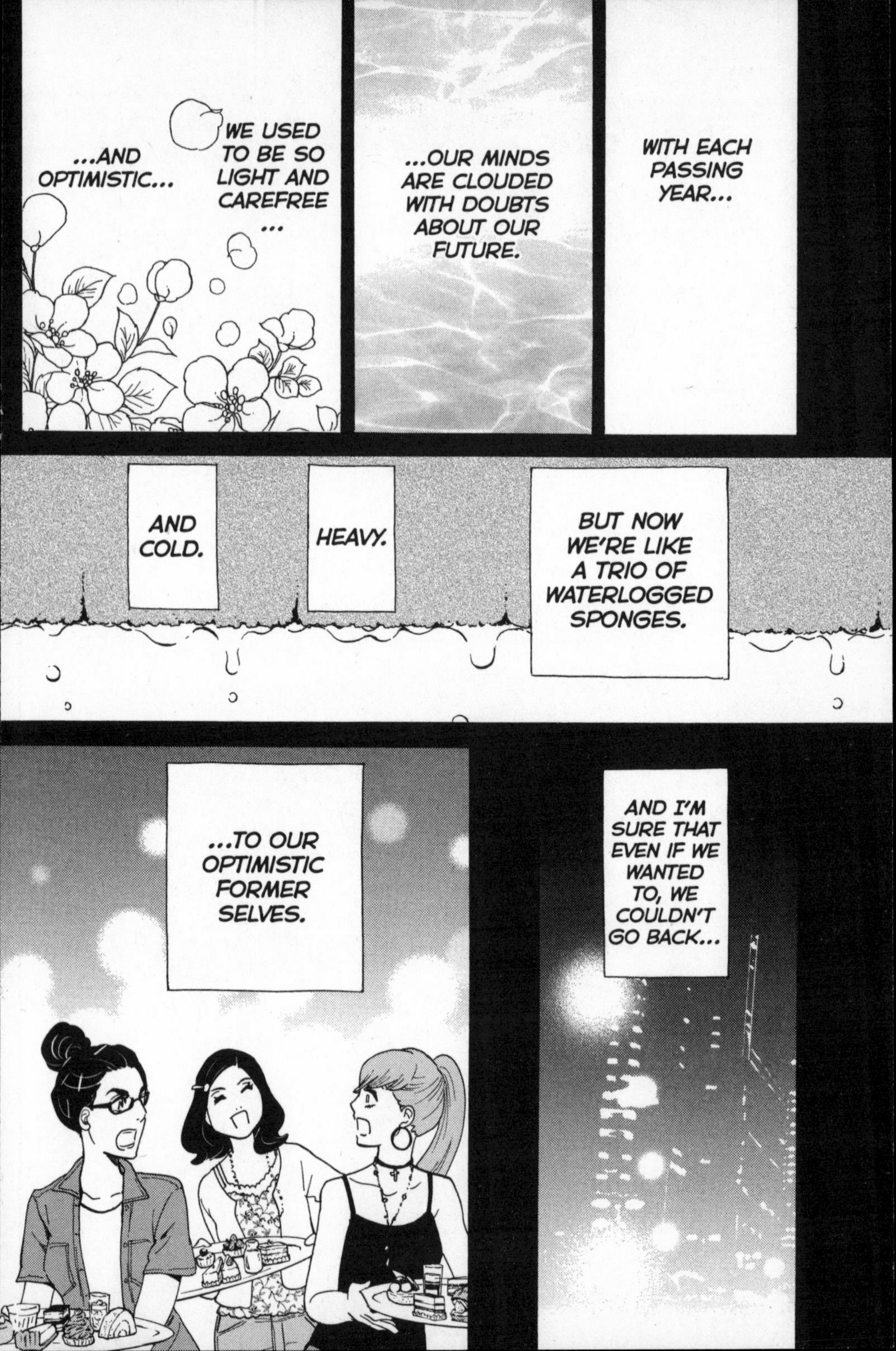
WITH EACH PASSING YEAR...
...OUR MINDS ARE CLOUDED WITH DOUBTS ABOUT OUR FUTURE.
WE USED TO BE SO LIGHT AND CAREFREE ...
...AND OPTIMISTIC...
BUT NOW WE'RE LIKE A TRIO OF WATERLOGGED SPONGES.
HEAVY.
AND COLD.
AND I'M SURE THAT EVEN IF WE WANTED TO, WE COULDN'T GO BACK...
...TO OUR OPTIMISTIC FORMER SELVES.

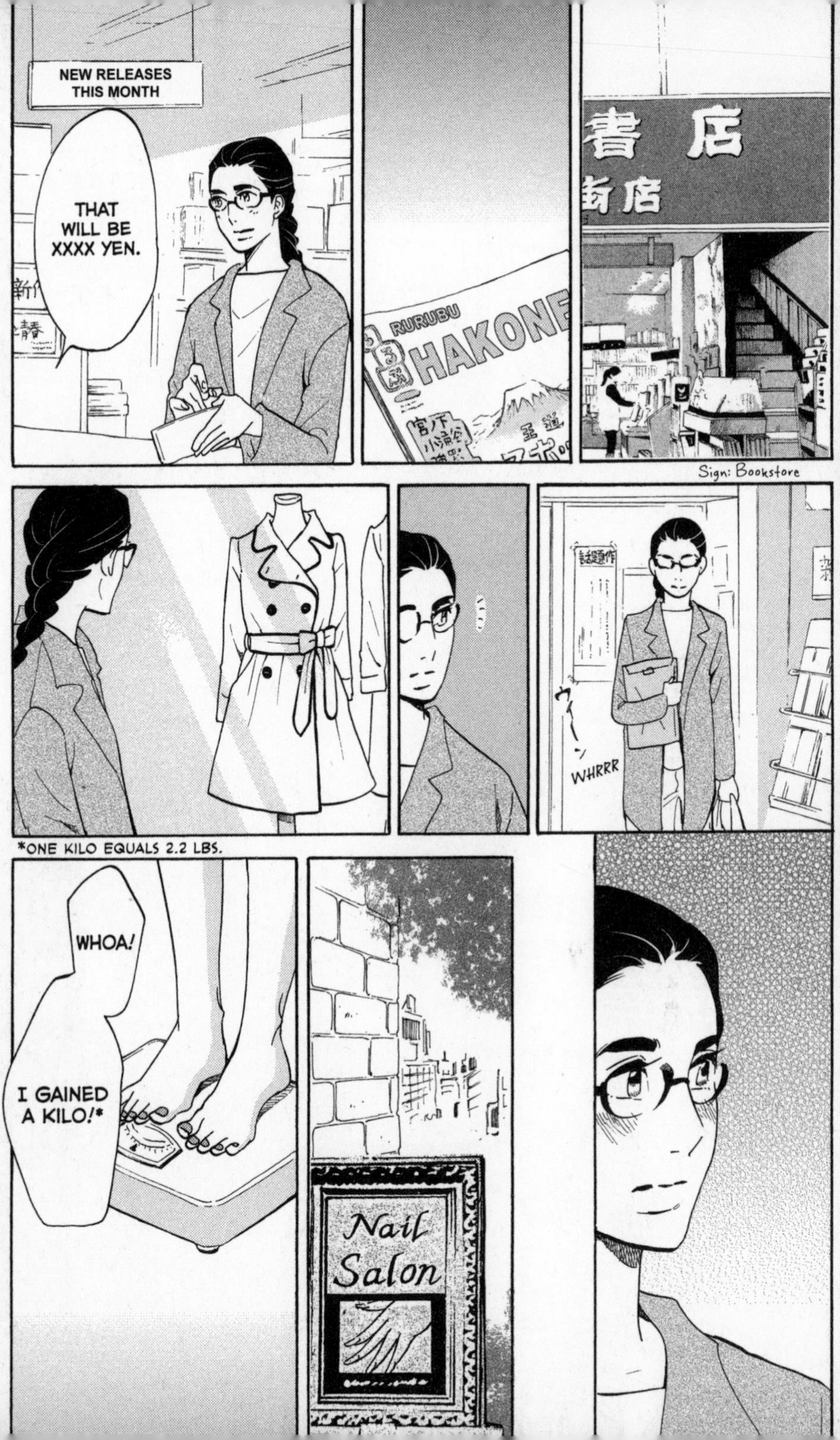
書店
Sign: Bookstore
RURUBU
HAKONE
NEW RELEASES
THIS MONTH
THAT WILL BE XXXX YEN.
話題作
ウィーン
WHRRR
Nail Salon
WHOA!
I GAINED A KILO!*
*ONE KILO EQUALS 2.2 LBS.

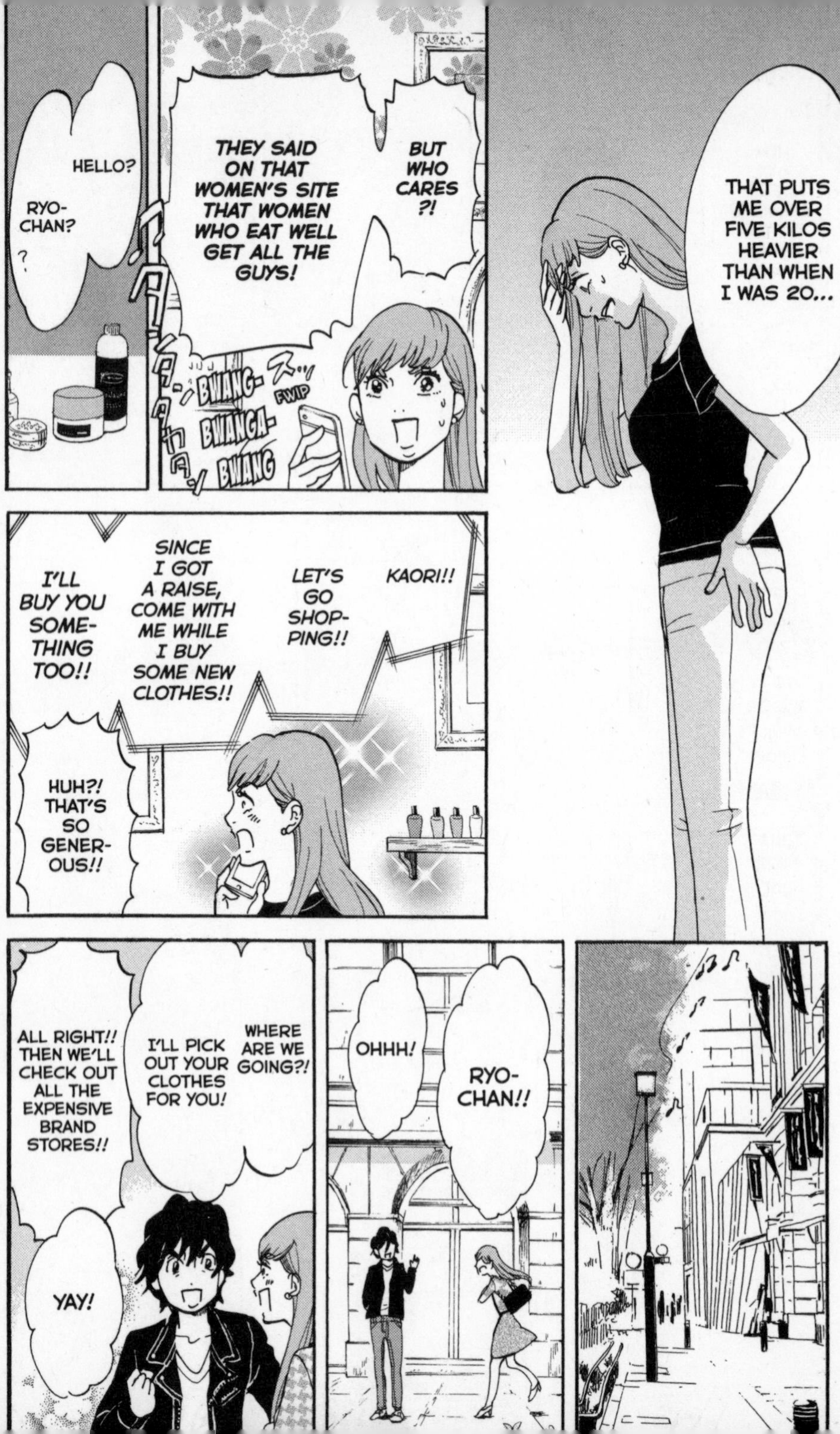
THAT PUTS ME OVER FIVE KILOS HEAVIER THAN WHEN I WAS 20...
THEY SAID ON THAT WOMEN'S SITE THAT WOMEN WHO EAT WELL GET ALL THE GUYS!
BUT WHO CARES?!
FWIP
BWANG-BWANGA-BWANG
HELLO?
RYO-CHAN?
?
KAORI!!
LET'S GO SHOP-PING!!
SINCE I GOT A RAISE, COME WITH ME WHILE I BUY SOME NEW CLOTHES!!
I'LL BUY YOU SOME-THING TOO!!
HUH?! THAT'S SO GENER-OUS!!
RYO-CHAN!!
OHHH!
WHERE ARE WE GOING?!
I'LL PICK OUT YOUR CLOTHES FOR YOU!
ALL RIGHT!! THEN WE'LL CHECK OUT ALL THE EXPENSIVE BRAND STORES!!
YAY!

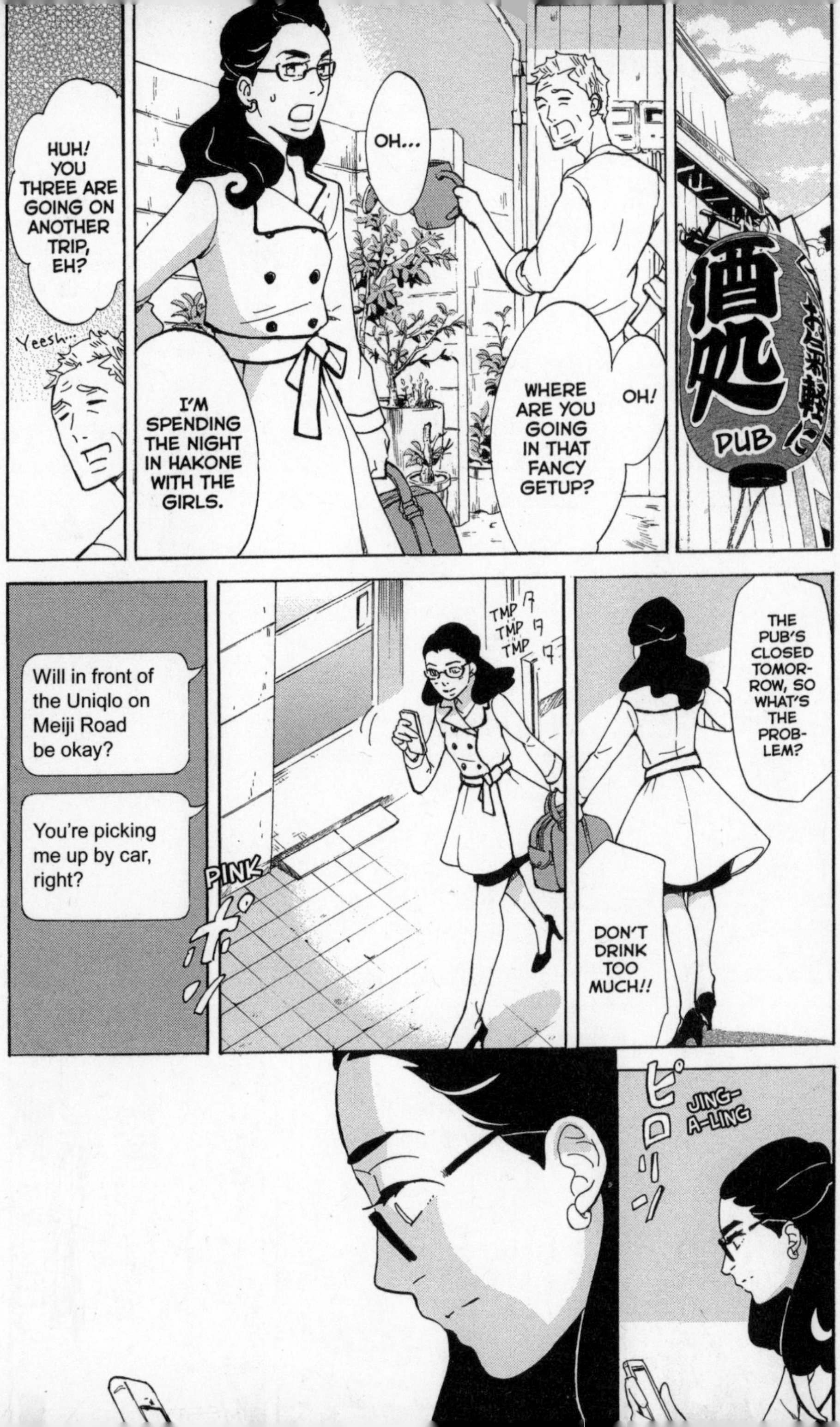
酒処
お気軽に
PUB
OH!
WHERE ARE YOU GOING IN THAT FANCY GETUP?
I'M SPENDING THE NIGHT IN HAKONE WITH THE GIRLS.
OH...
HUH! YOU THREE ARE GOING ON ANOTHER TRIP, EH?
Yeesh...
THE PUB'S CLOSED TOMOR-ROW, SO WHAT'S THE PROB-LEM?
DON'T DRINK TOO MUCH!!
TMP TMP TMP
PINK
Will in front of the Uniqlo on Meiji Road be okay?
You're picking me up by car, right?
ピロリーン
JING-A-LING

Marui

Sorry.
My wife's health took a turn for the worse, so she was emergency admitted to the hospital.

Apparently, it's that pregnancy-induced hypertension that happens with a lot of pregnancies…

JING-A-LING

But I've gotta rush down to her parents' place right now…

JING-A-LING

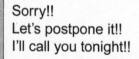

JING-A-LING

Sorry!!
Let's postpone it!!
I'll call you tonight!!

I'm really sorry, Koyuki-san!!

JING-A-LING

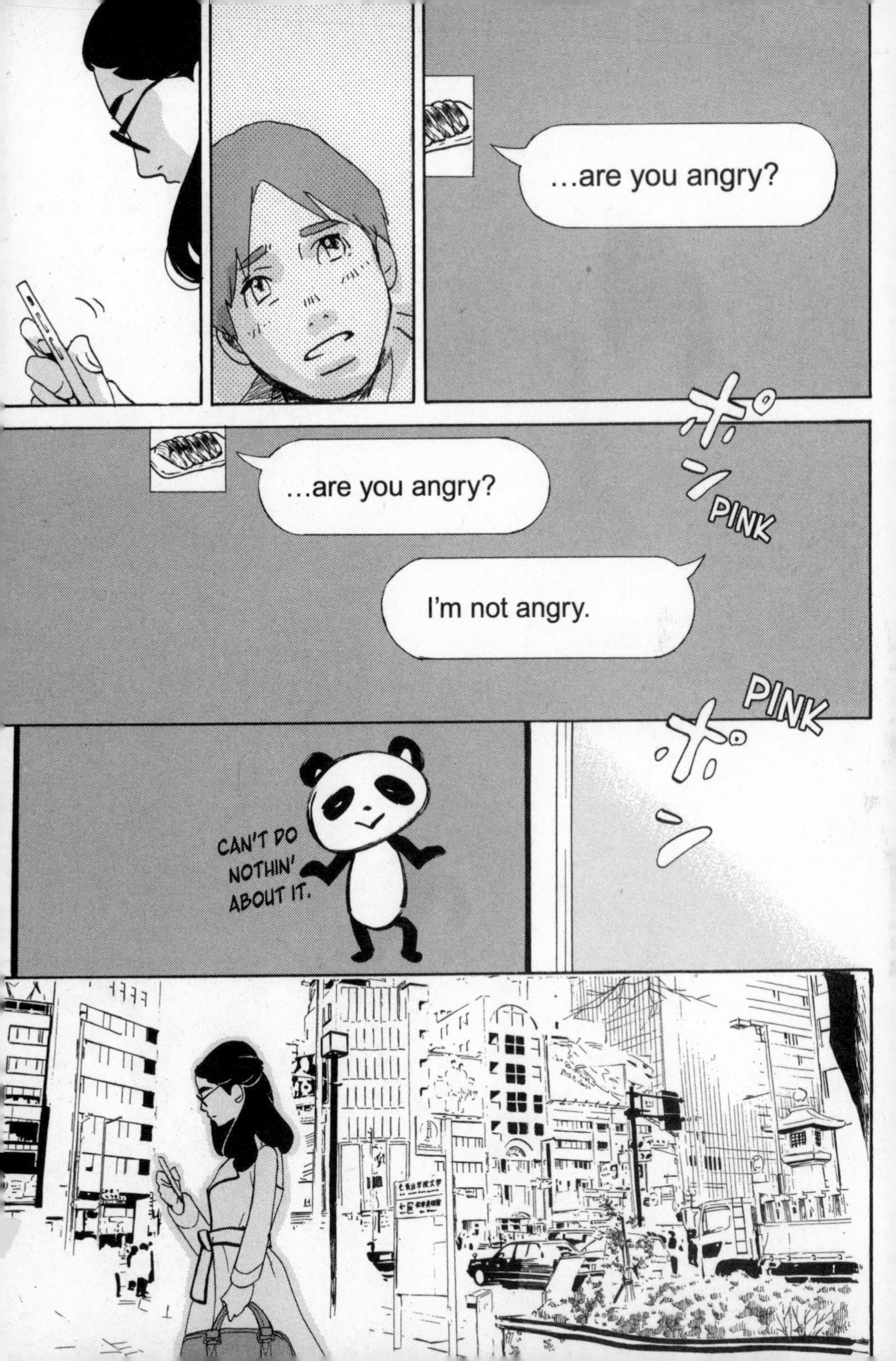
...are you angry?
...are you angry?
PINK
I'm not angry.
PINK
CAN'T DO NOTHIN' ABOUT IT.

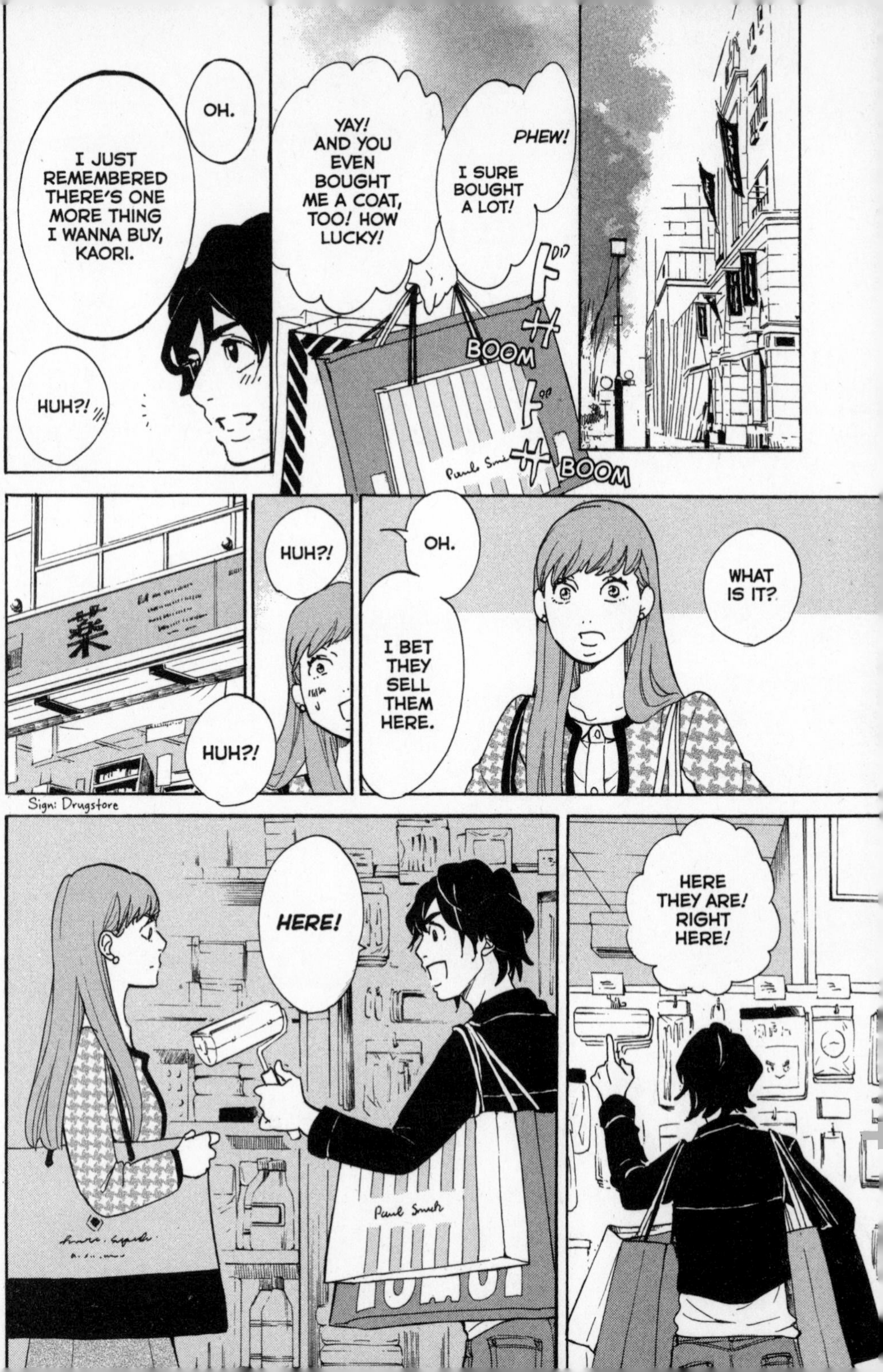
PHEW!
I SURE BOUGHT A LOT!
YAY! AND YOU EVEN BOUGHT ME A COAT, TOO! HOW LUCKY!
BOOM
BOOM
OH.
I JUST REMEMBERED THERE'S ONE MORE THING I WANNA BUY, KAORI.
HUH?!
WHAT IS IT?
OH.
I BET THEY SELL THEM HERE.
HUH?!
HUH?!
Sign: Drugstore
HERE THEY ARE! RIGHT HERE!
HERE!

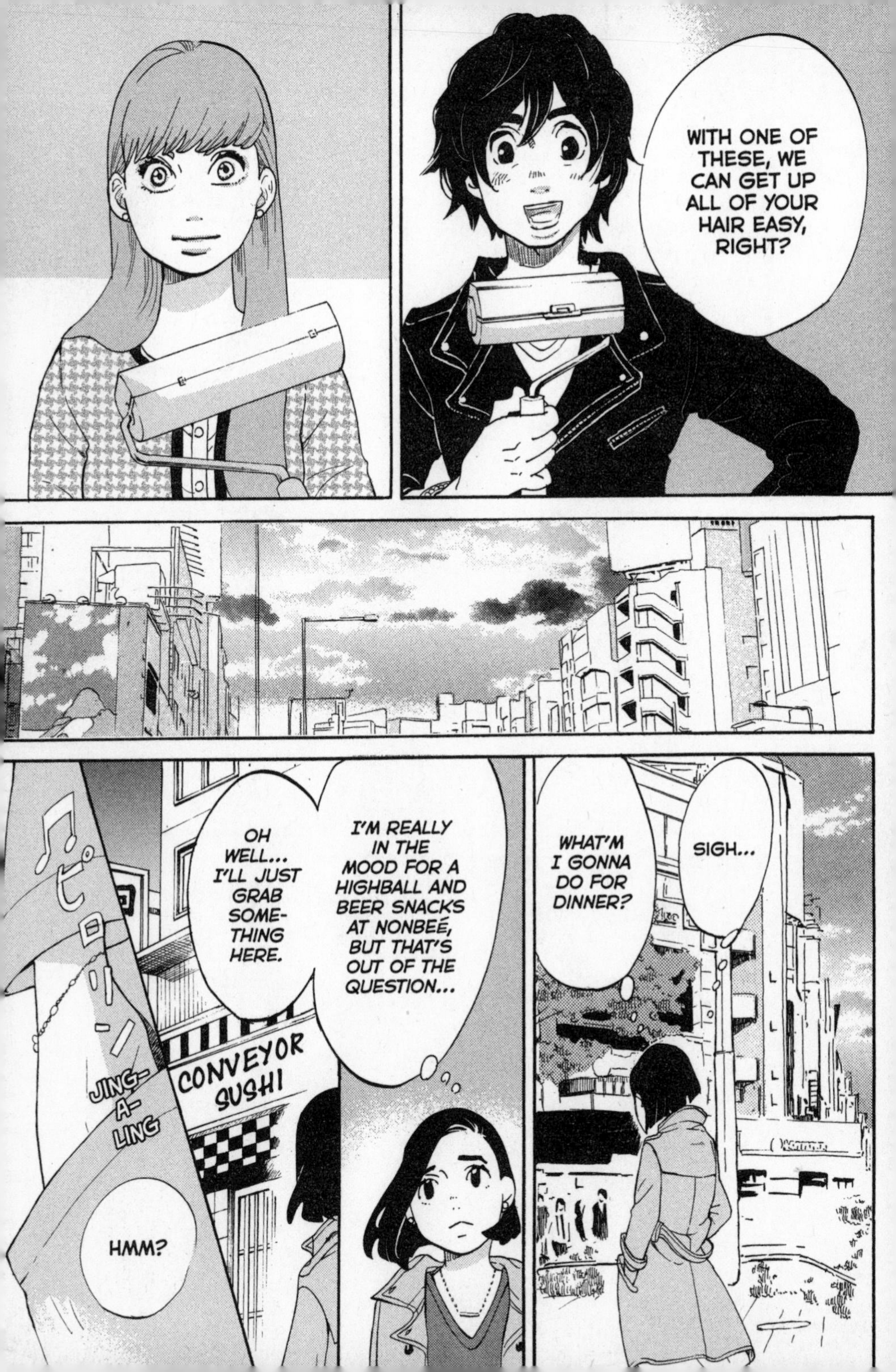
WITH ONE OF THESE, WE CAN GET UP ALL OF YOUR HAIR EASY, RIGHT?
SIGH...
WHAT'M I GONNA DO FOR DINNER?
I'M REALLY IN THE MOOD FOR A HIGHBALL AND BEER SNACKS AT NONBEÉ, BUT THAT'S OUT OF THE QUESTION...
OH WELL... I'LL JUST GRAB SOMETHING HERE.
CONVEYOR SUSHI
JING-A-LING
HMM?

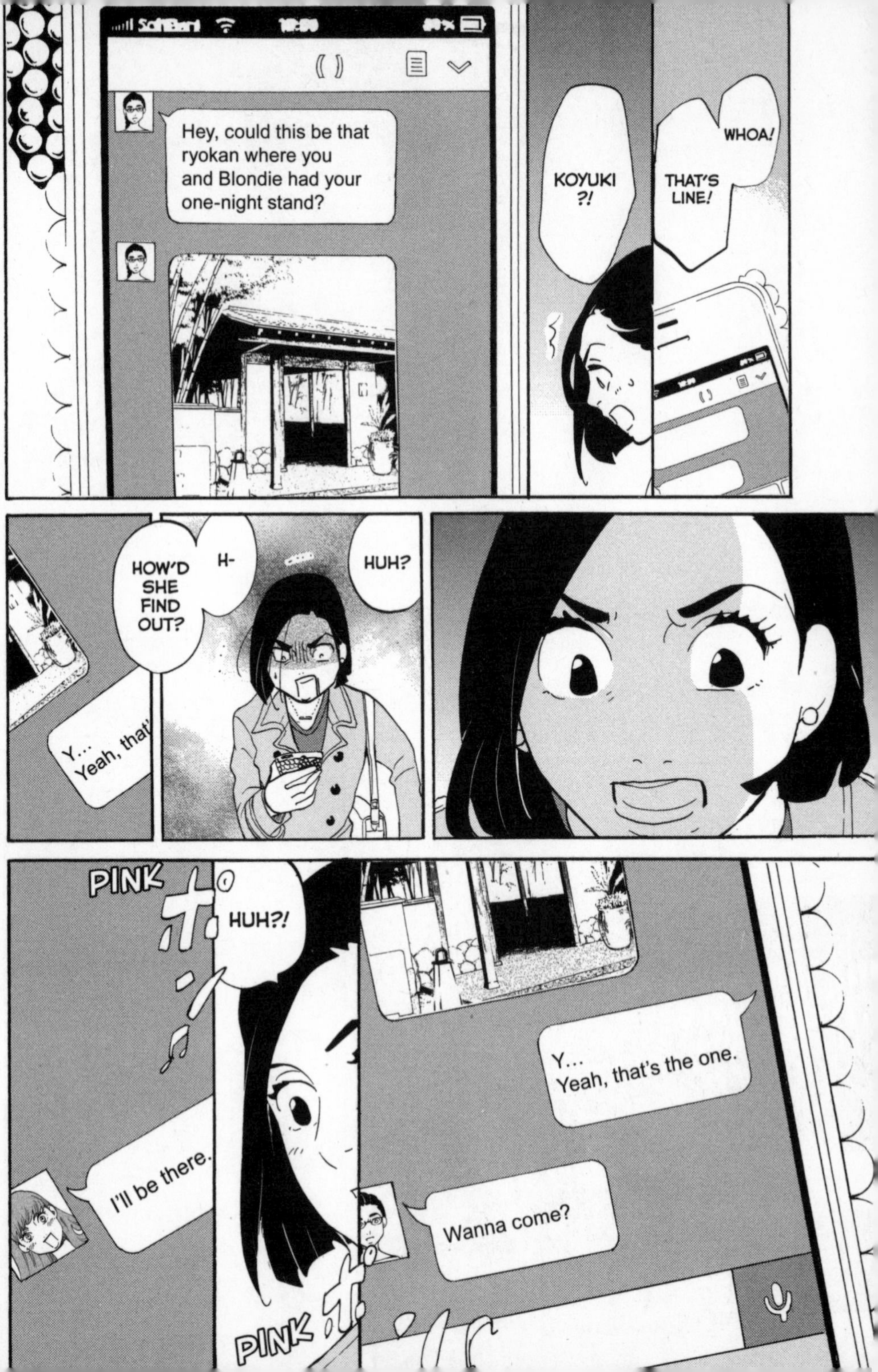
WHOA!
THAT'S LINE!
KOYUKI ?!
Hey, could this be that ryokan where you and Blondie had your one-night stand?
HUH?
H-
HOW'D SHE FIND OUT?
Y… Yeah, that'
Y… Yeah, that's the one.
Wanna come?
HUH?!
PINK
PINK
I'll be there.

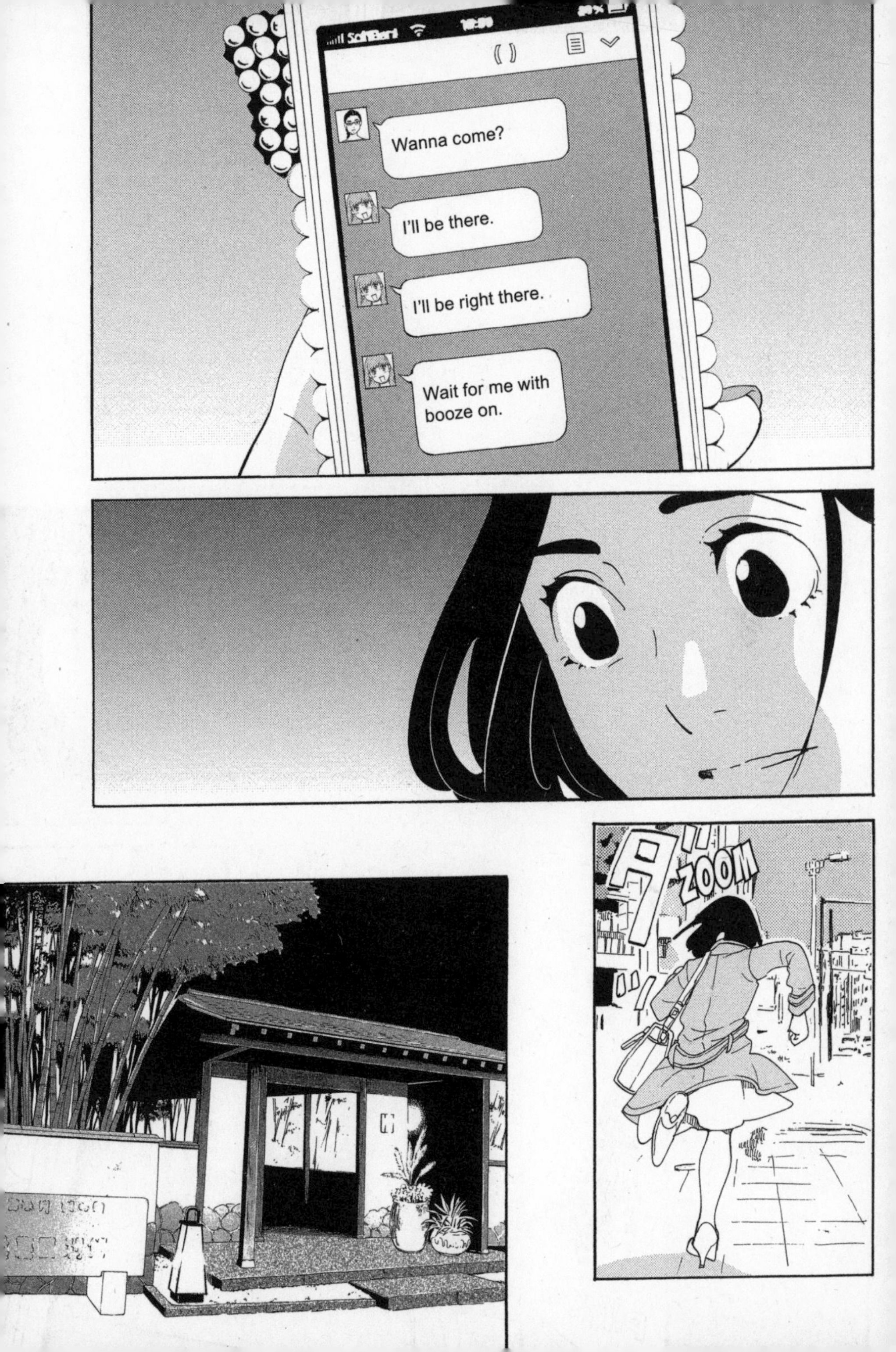
Wanna come?
I'll be there.
I'll be right there.
Wait for me with booze on.
ZOOM

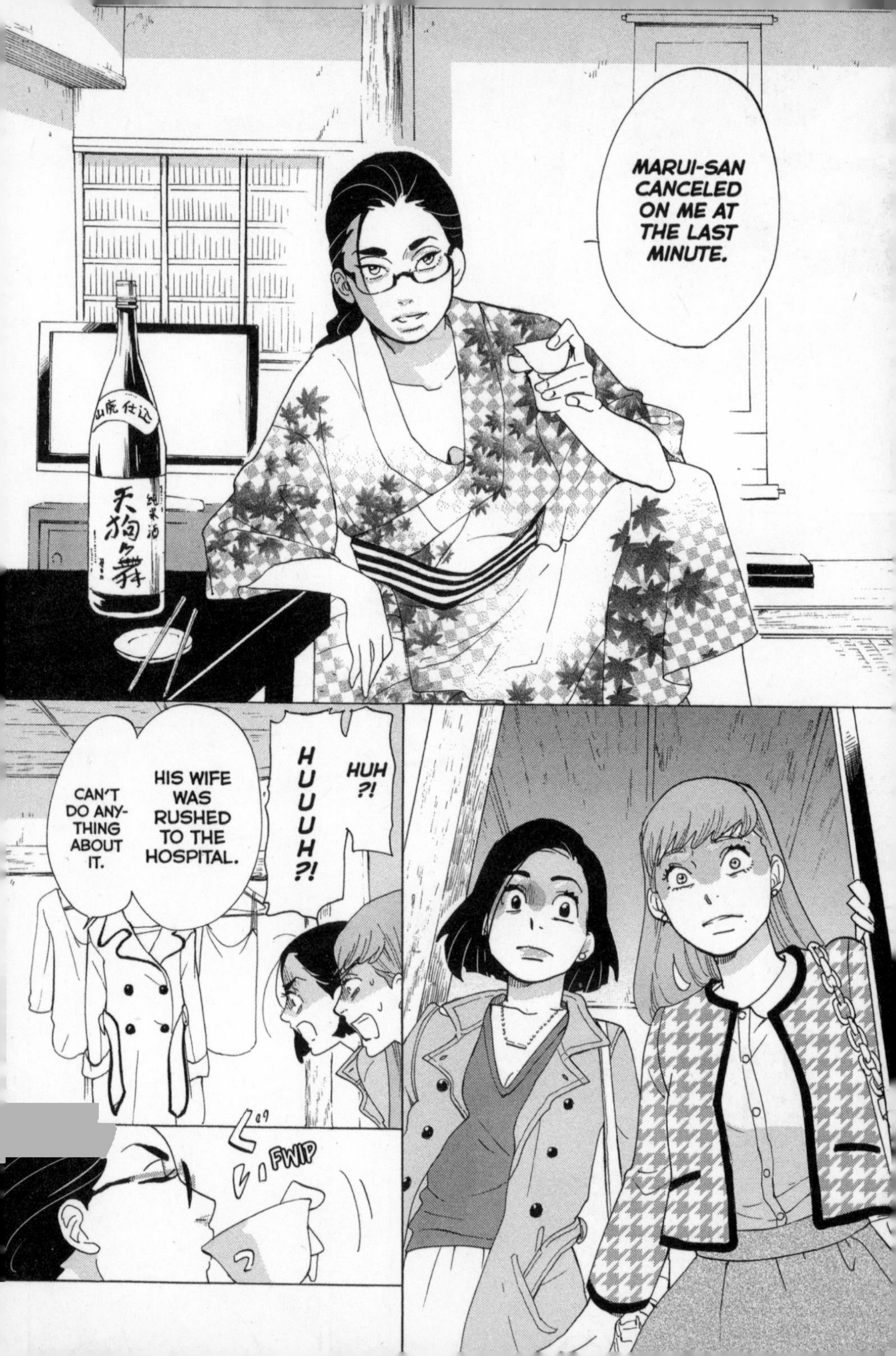
山廃仕込
純米酒
天狗舞
MARUI-SAN CANCELED ON ME AT THE LAST MINUTE.
HUH?!
HUUUUH?!
HIS WIFE WAS RUSHED TO THE HOSPITAL.
CAN'T DO ANY-THING ABOUT IT.
FWIP

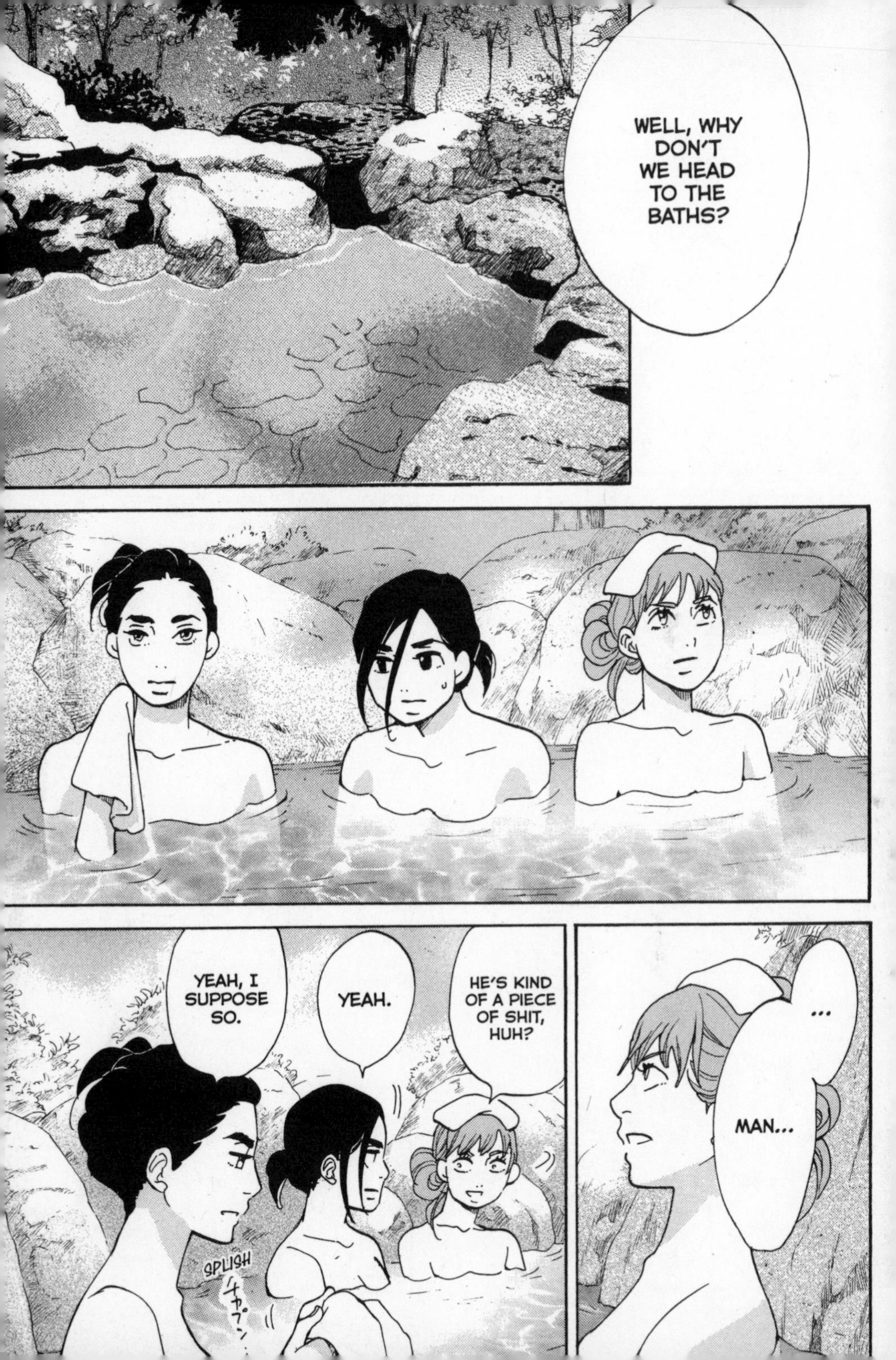
WELL, WHY DON'T WE HEAD TO THE BATHS?
...
MAN...
HE'S KIND OF A PIECE OF SHIT, HUH?
YEAH.
YEAH, I SUPPOSE SO.
SPLISH
チャプン

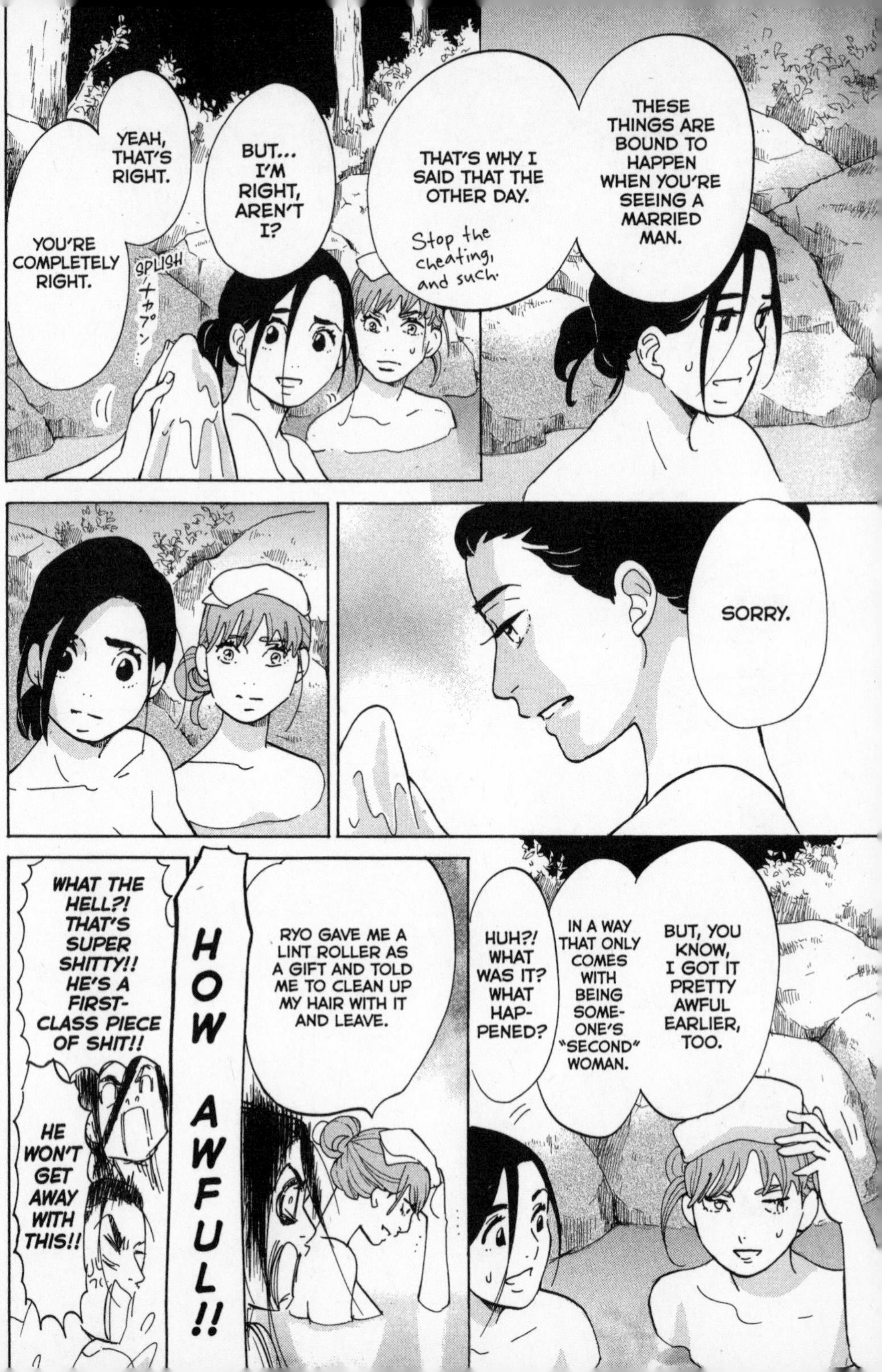
THESE THINGS ARE BOUND TO HAPPEN WHEN YOU'RE SEEING A MARRIED MAN.
THAT'S WHY I SAID THAT THE OTHER DAY.
Stop the cheating, and such.
BUT... I'M RIGHT, AREN'T I?
YEAH, THAT'S RIGHT.
YOU'RE COMPLETELY RIGHT.
SPLISH
チャプン
SORRY.
BUT, YOU KNOW, I GOT IT PRETTY AWFUL EARLIER, TOO.
IN A WAY THAT ONLY COMES WITH BEING SOME-ONE'S "SECOND" WOMAN.
HUH?! WHAT WAS IT? WHAT HAP-PENED?
RYO GAVE ME A LINT ROLLER AS A GIFT AND TOLD ME TO CLEAN UP MY HAIR WITH IT AND LEAVE.
HOW AWFUL!!
WHAT THE HELL?! THAT'S SUPER SHITTY!! HE'S A FIRST-CLASS PIECE OF SHIT!!
HE WON'T GET AWAY WITH THIS!!

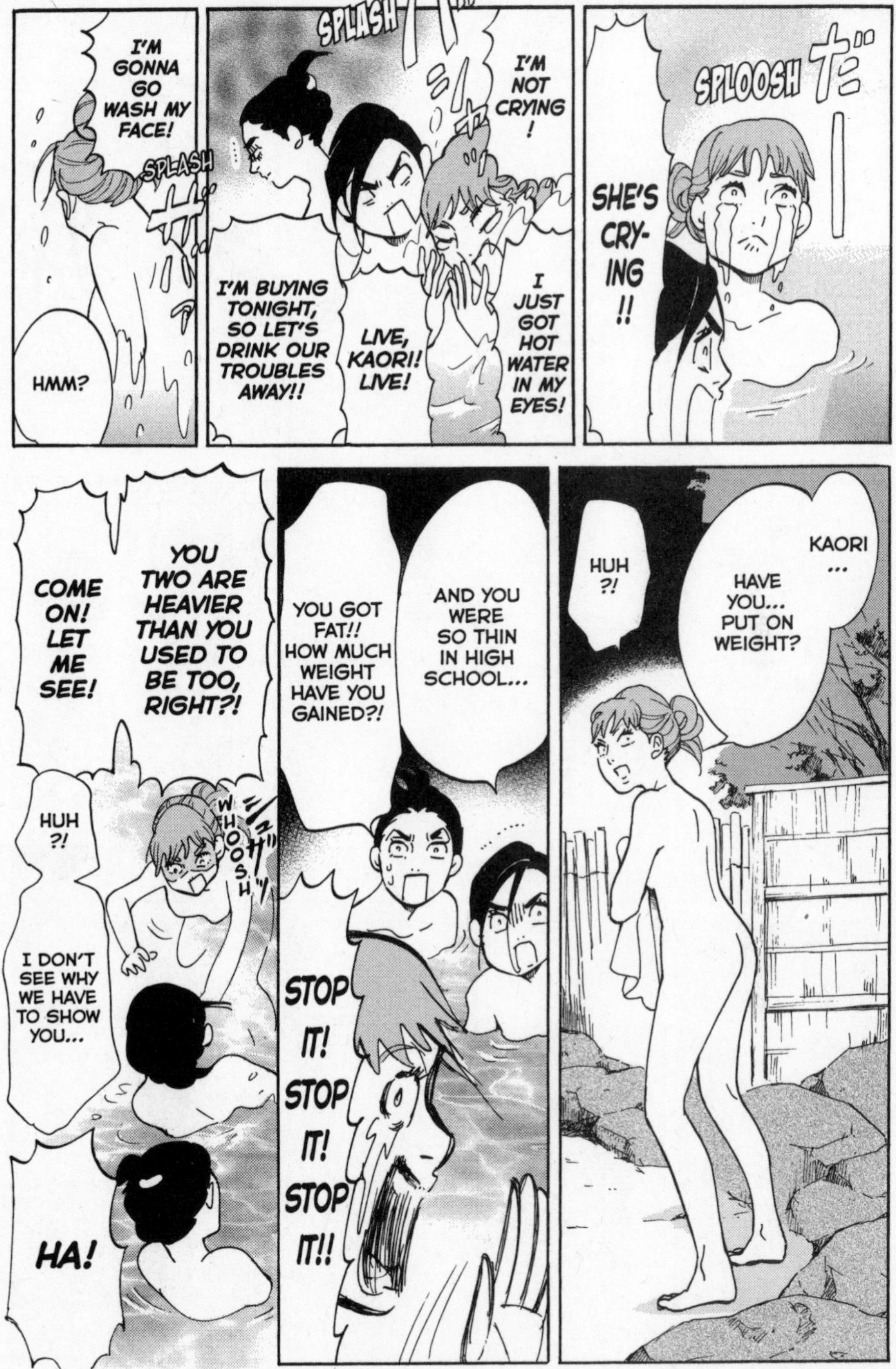
SPLOOSH
SHE'S CRY-ING!!
SPLASH
I'M NOT CRYING!
I JUST GOT HOT WATER IN MY EYES!
LIVE, KAORI! LIVE!
I'M BUYING TONIGHT, SO LET'S DRINK OUR TROUBLES AWAY!!
I'M GONNA GO WASH MY FACE!
SPLASH
HMM?
KAORI...
HAVE YOU... PUT ON WEIGHT?
HUH?!
AND YOU WERE SO THIN IN HIGH SCHOOL...
YOU GOT FAT!! HOW MUCH WEIGHT HAVE YOU GAINED?!
STOP IT! STOP IT! STOP IT!!
YOU TWO ARE HEAVIER THAN YOU USED TO BE TOO, RIGHT?!
COME ON! LET ME SEE!
WHOOSH
HUH?!
I DON'T SEE WHY WE HAVE TO SHOW YOU...
HA!

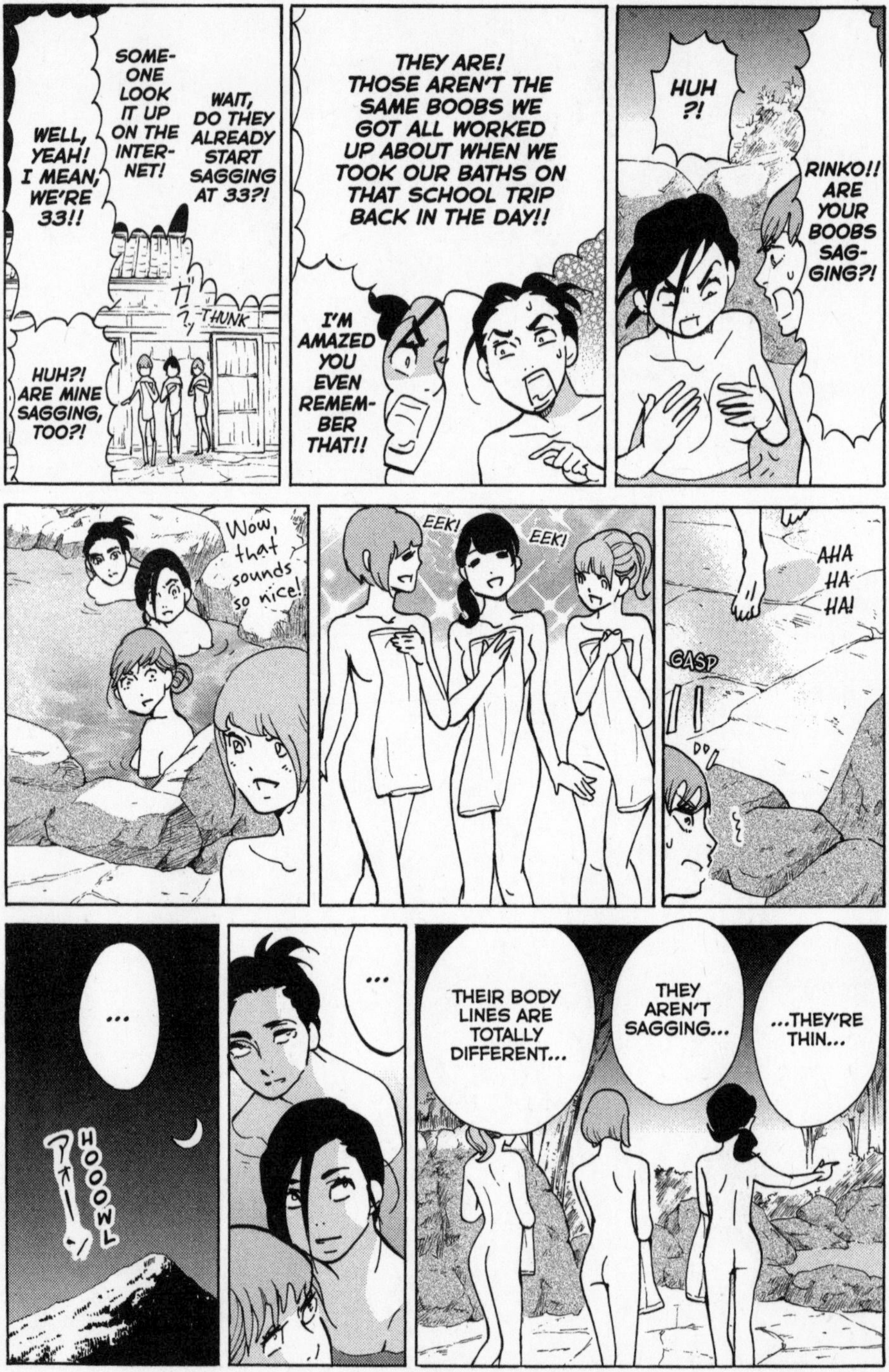
RINKO!! ARE YOUR BOOBS SAG-GING?!
HUH ?!
THEY ARE! THOSE AREN'T THE SAME BOOBS WE GOT ALL WORKED UP ABOUT WHEN WE TOOK OUR BATHS ON THAT SCHOOL TRIP BACK IN THE DAY!!
I'M AMAZED YOU EVEN REMEM-BER THAT!!
WAIT, DO THEY ALREADY START SAGGING AT 33?!
SOME-ONE LOOK IT UP ON THE INTER-NET!
WELL, YEAH! I MEAN, WE'RE 33!!
THUNK
HUH?! ARE MINE SAGGING, TOO?!
AHA HA HA!
GASP
EEK!
EEK!
Wow, that sounds so nice!
...THEY'RE THIN...
THEY AREN'T SAGGING...
THEIR BODY LINES ARE TOTALLY DIFFERENT...
...
...
HOOOWL

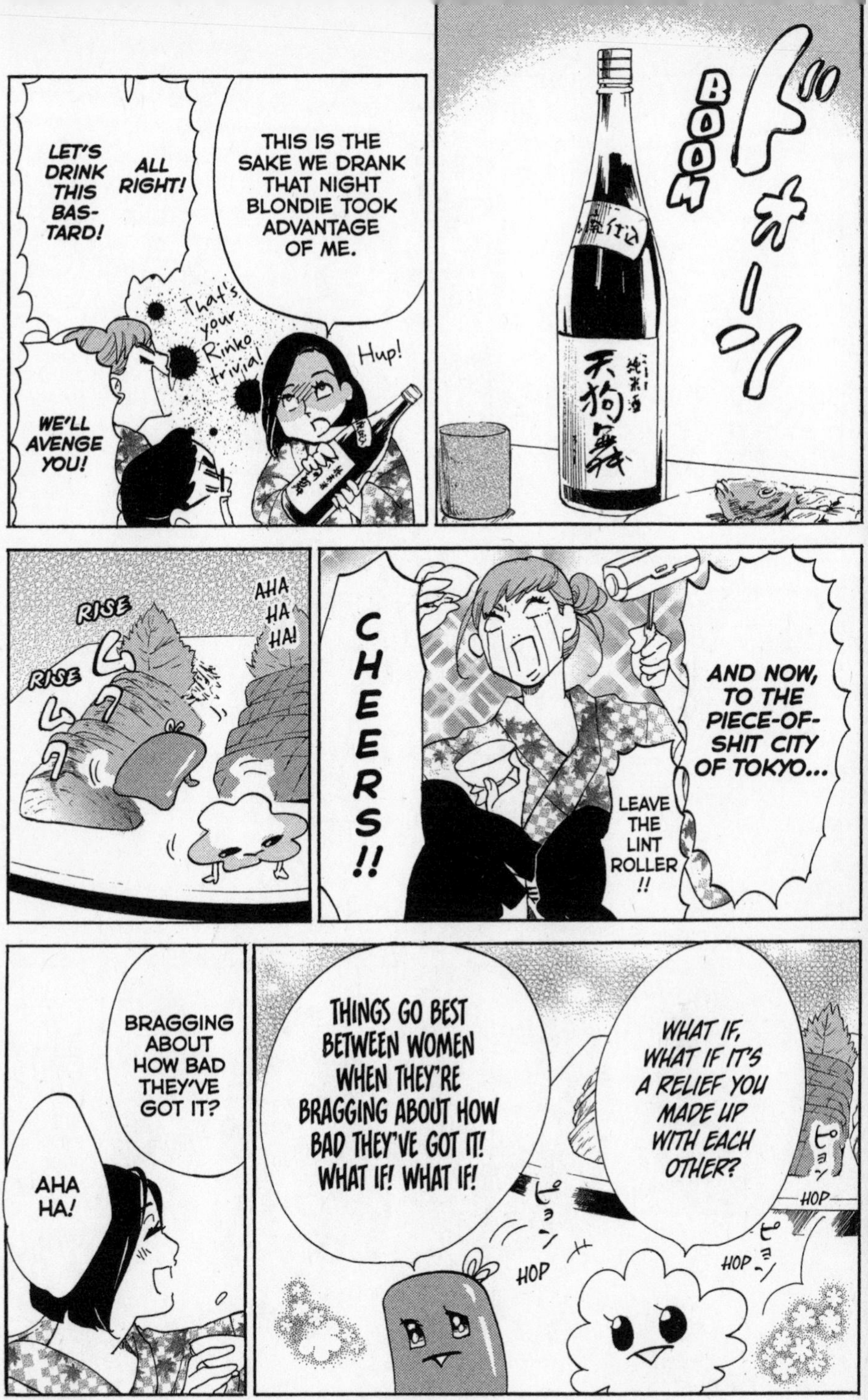

BOOM
純米酒
天狗舞
THIS IS THE SAKE WE DRANK THAT NIGHT BLONDIE TOOK ADVANTAGE OF ME.
Hup!
That's your Rinko trivia!
ALL RIGHT!
LET'S DRINK THIS BASTARD!
WE'LL AVENGE YOU!
AND NOW, TO THE PIECE-OF-SHIT CITY OF TOKYO...
CHEERS!!
LEAVE THE LINT ROLLER!!
AHA HA HA!
RISE
RISE
WHAT IF, WHAT IF IT'S A RELIEF YOU MADE UP WITH EACH OTHER?
HOP
THINGS GO BEST BETWEEN WOMEN WHEN THEY'RE BRAGGING ABOUT HOW BAD THEY'VE GOT IT! WHAT IF! WHAT IF!
HOP
HOP
BRAGGING ABOUT HOW BAD THEY'VE GOT IT?
AHA HA!

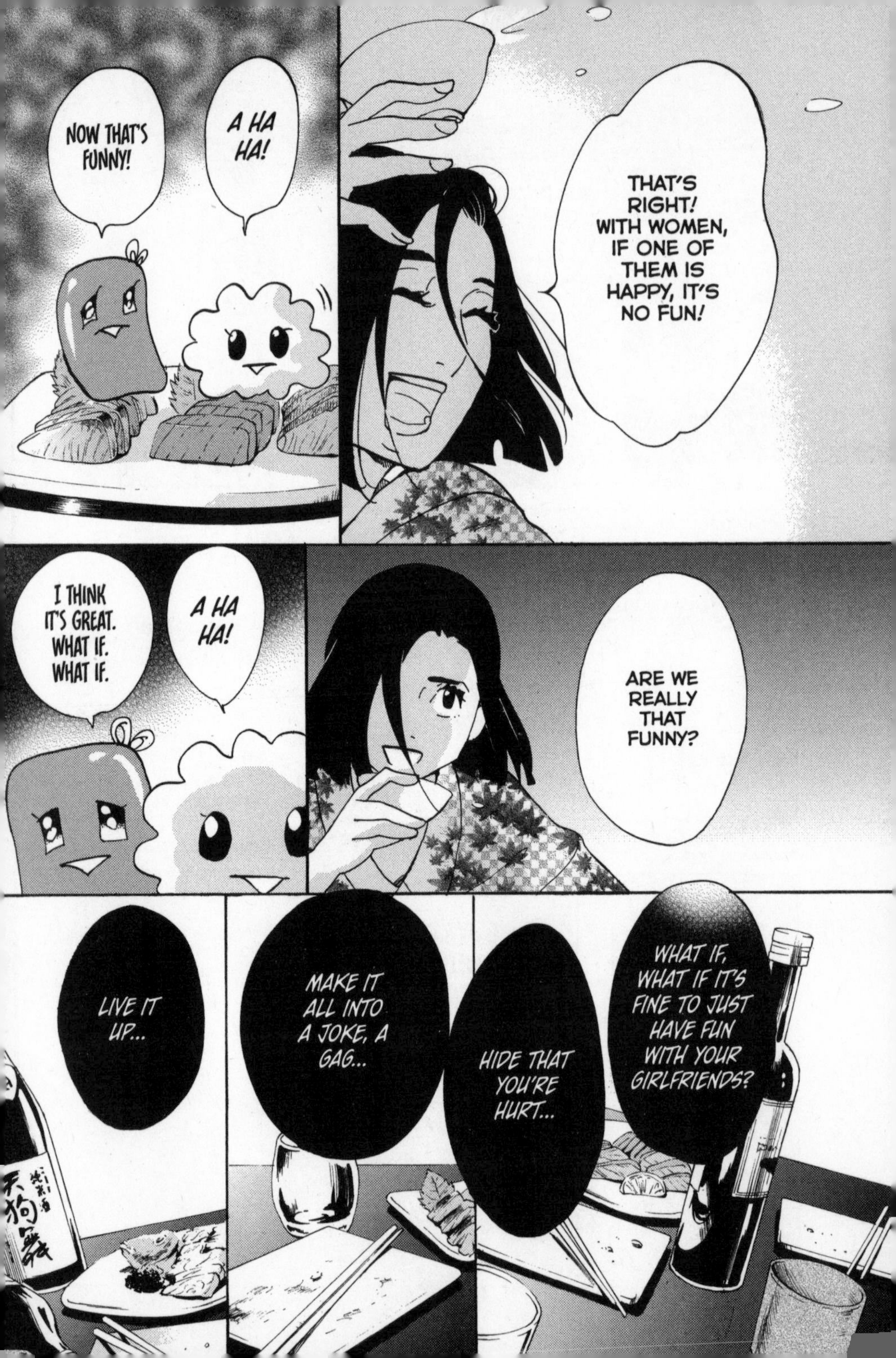
THAT'S RIGHT! WITH WOMEN, IF ONE OF THEM IS HAPPY, IT'S NO FUN!
A HA HA!
NOW THAT'S FUNNY!
ARE WE REALLY THAT FUNNY?
A HA HA!
I THINK IT'S GREAT. WHAT IF. WHAT IF.
WHAT IF, WHAT IF IT'S FINE TO JUST HAVE FUN WITH YOUR GIRLFRIENDS?
HIDE THAT YOU'RE HURT...
MAKE IT ALL INTO A JOKE, A GAG...
LIVE IT UP...

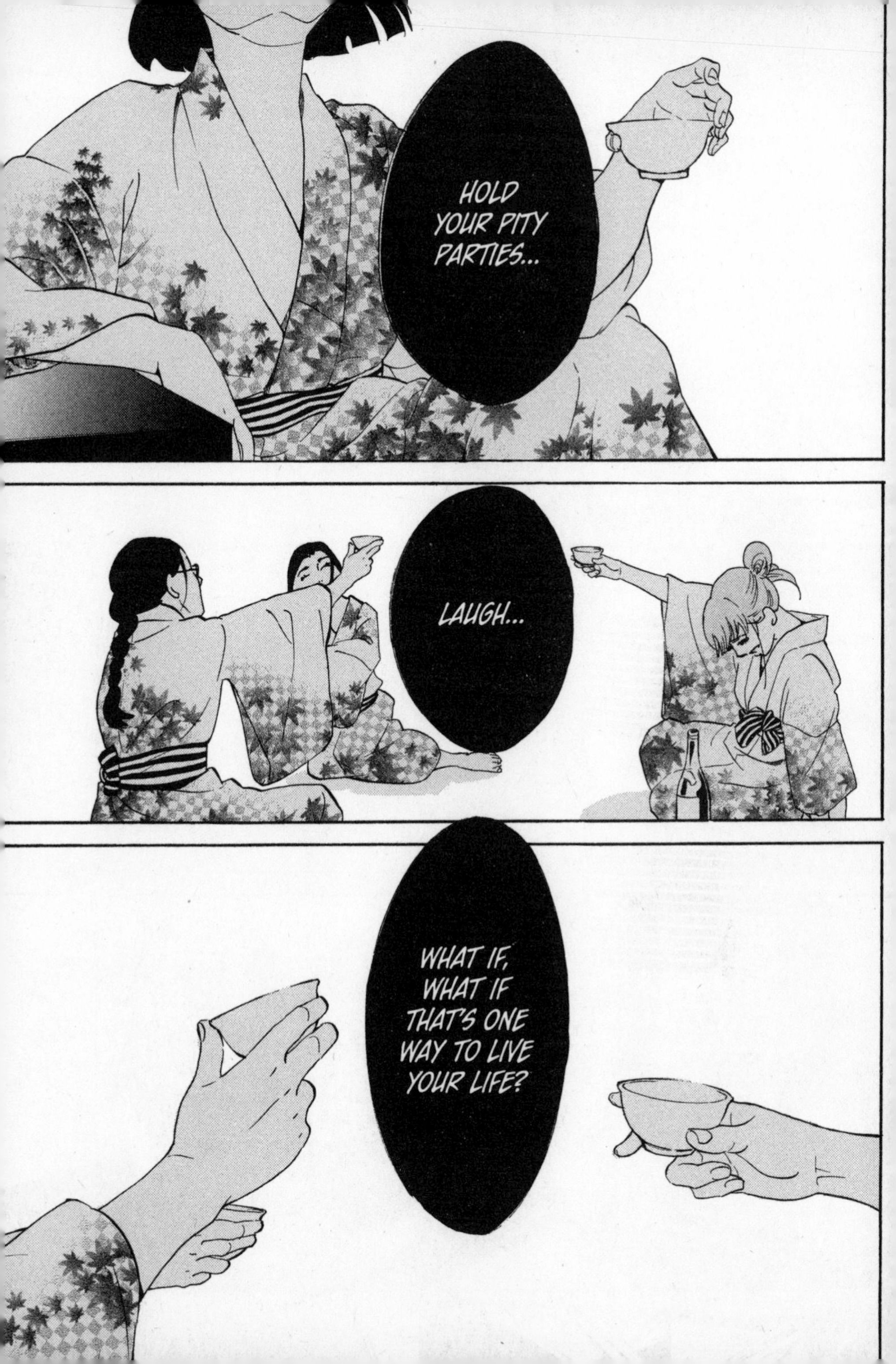
HOLD YOUR PITY PARTIES...
LAUGH...
WHAT IF, WHAT IF THAT'S ONE WAY TO LIVE YOUR LIFE?

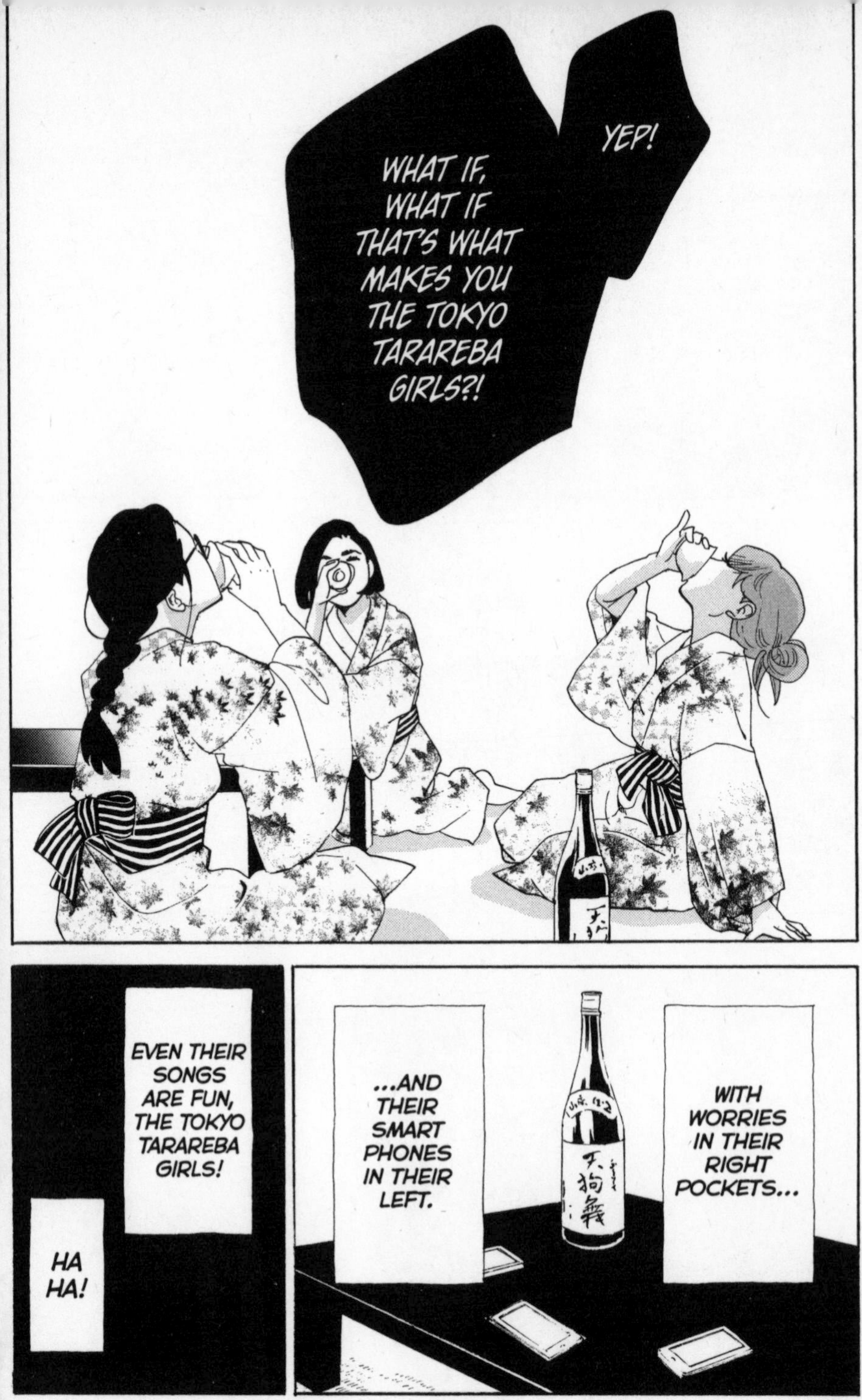
YEP!
WHAT IF, WHAT IF THAT'S WHAT MAKES YOU THE TOKYO TARAREBA GIRLS?!
WITH WORRIES IN THEIR RIGHT POCKETS...
...AND THEIR SMART PHONES IN THEIR LEFT.
EVEN THEIR SONGS ARE FUN, THE TOKYO TARAREBA GIRLS!
HA HA!

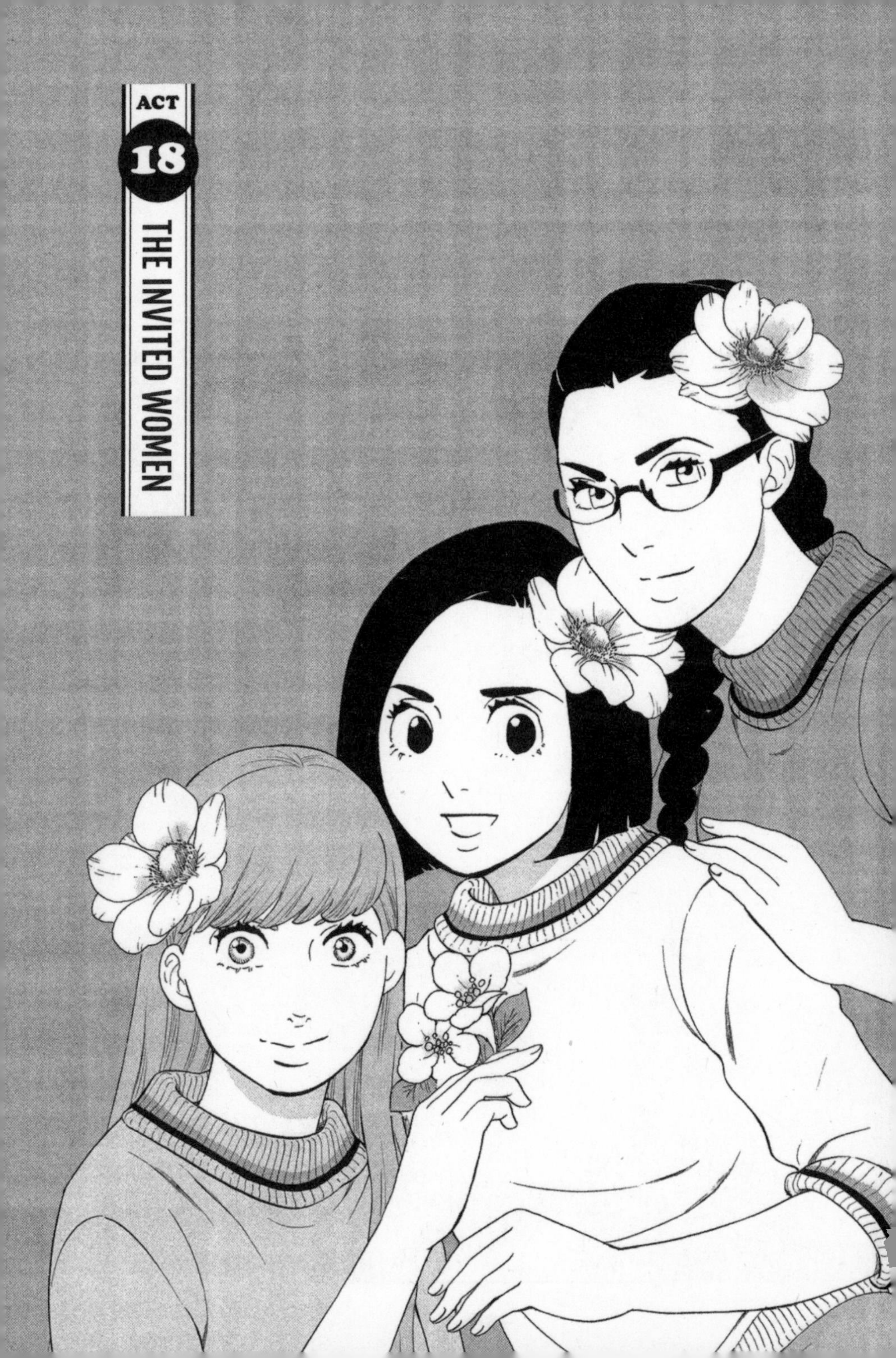
ACT
18
THE INVITED WOMEN

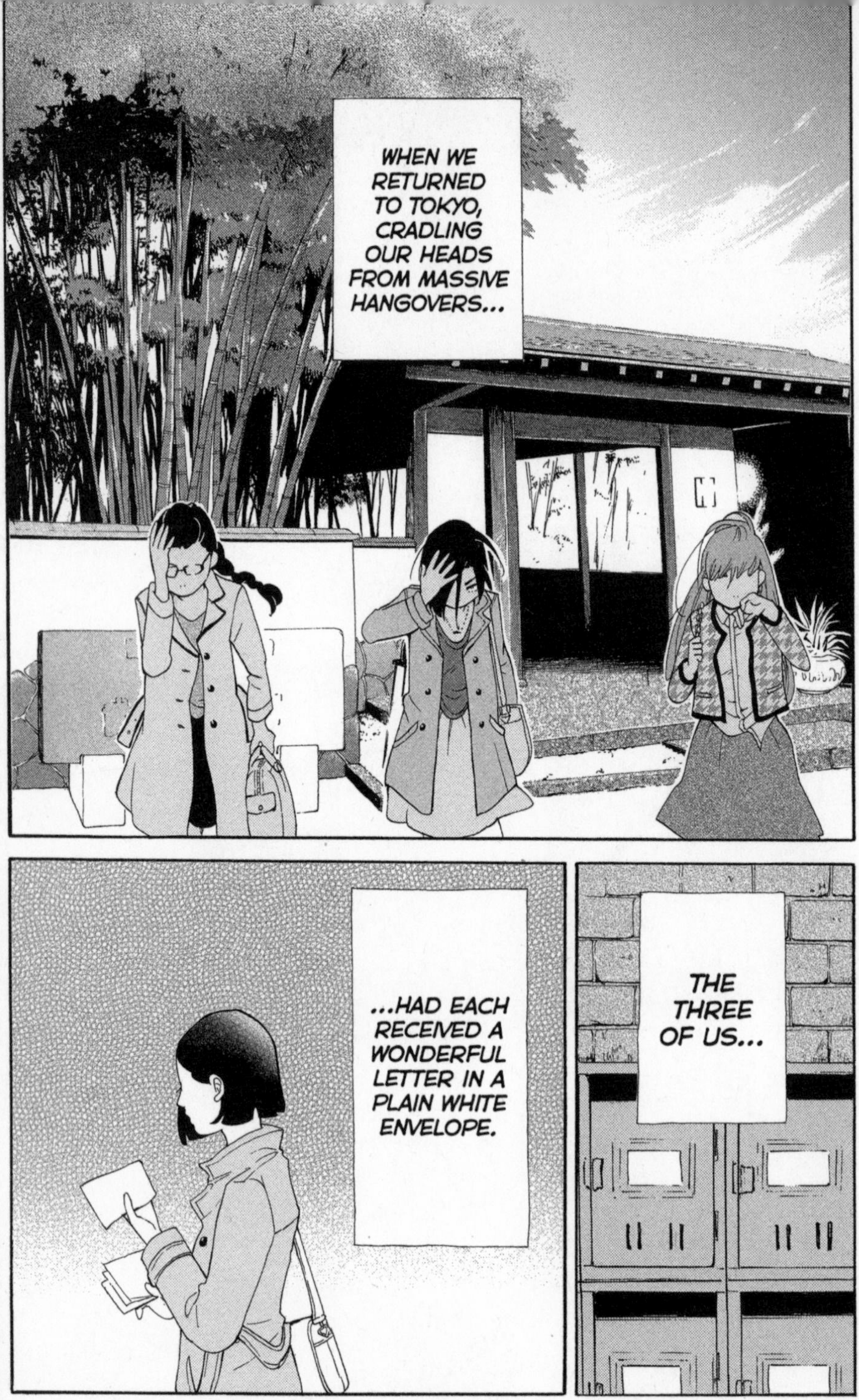
WHEN WE RETURNED TO TOKYO, CRADLING OUR HEADS FROM MASSIVE HANGOVERS...
THE THREE OF US...
...HAD EACH RECEIVED A WONDERFUL LETTER IN A PLAIN WHITE ENVELOPE.

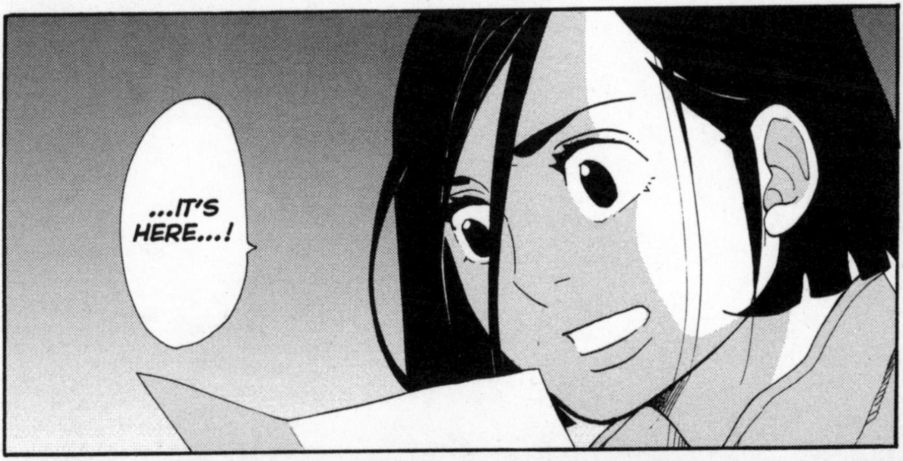
...IT'S HERE...!

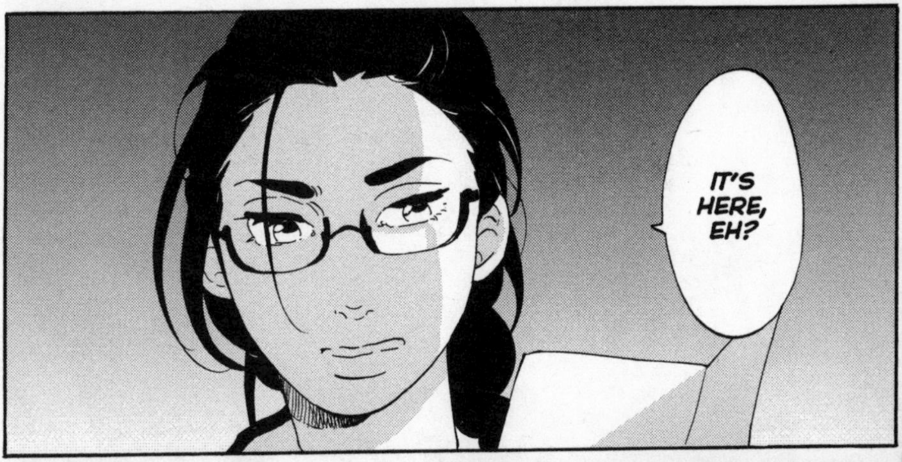
IT'S HERE, EH?

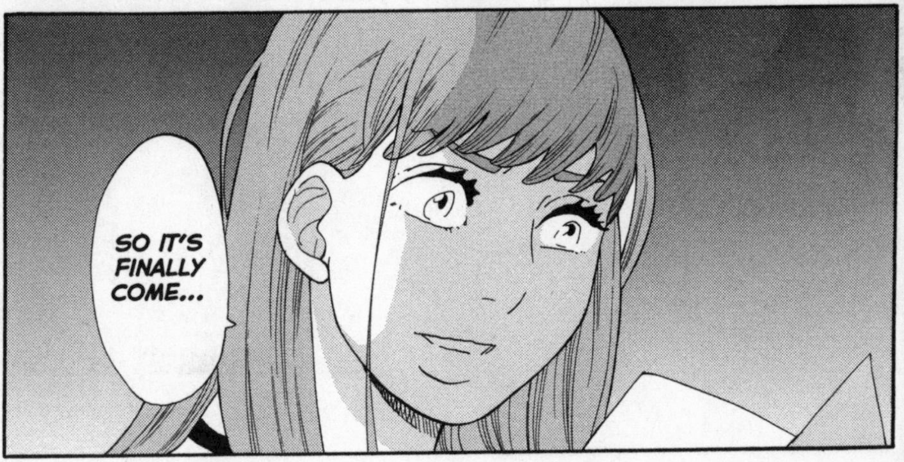
SO IT'S FINALLY COME...

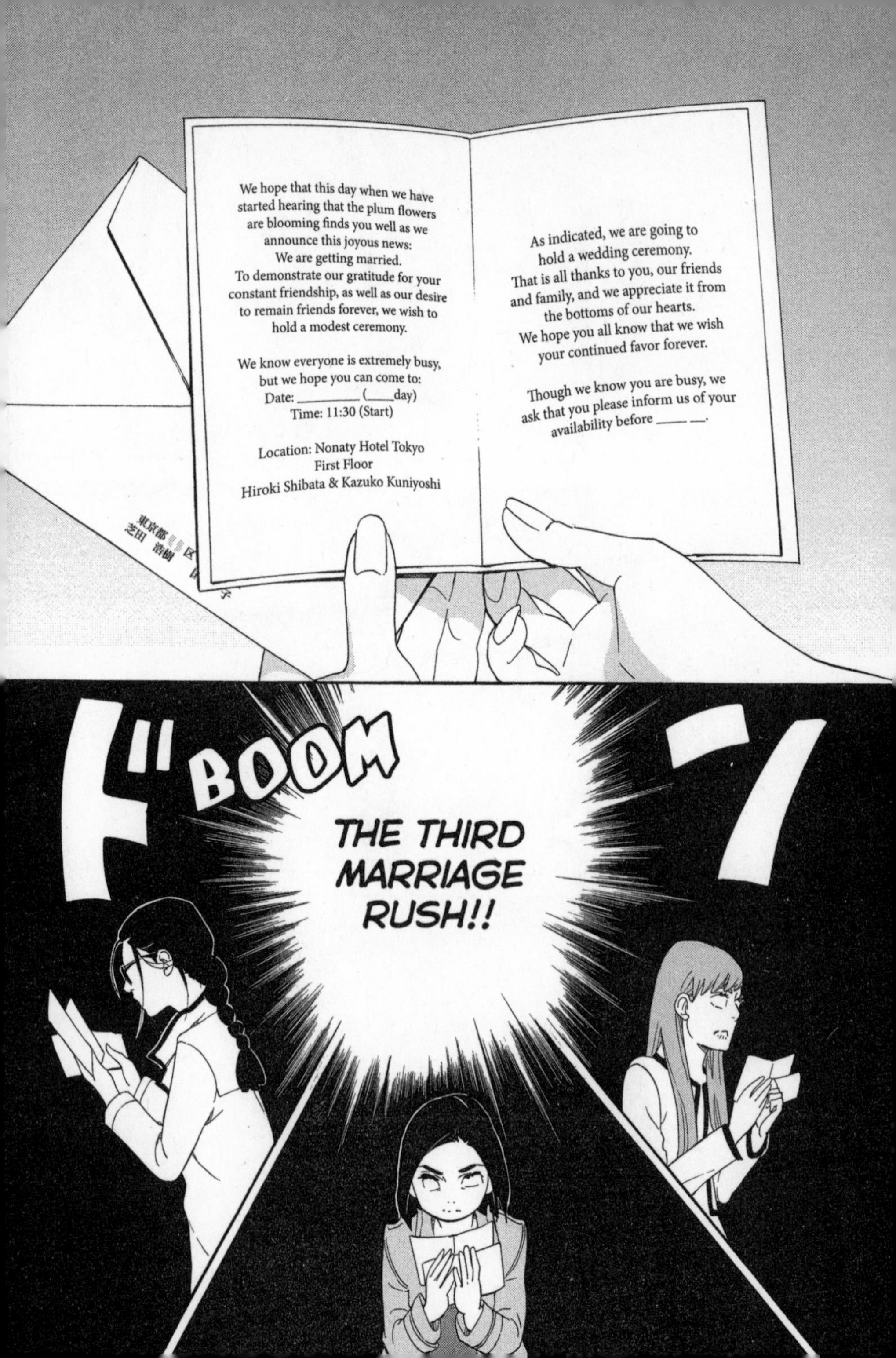
We hope that this day when we have started hearing that the plum flowers are blooming finds you well as we announce this joyous news:
We are getting married.
To demonstrate our gratitude for your constant friendship, as well as our desire to remain friends forever, we wish to hold a modest ceremony.
We know everyone is extremely busy, but we hope you can come to:
Date: ________ (____day)
Time: 11:30 (Start)
Location: Nonaty Hotel Tokyo
First Floor
Hiroki Shibata & Kazuko Kuniyoshi
As indicated, we are going to hold a wedding ceremony.
That is all thanks to you, our friends and family, and we appreciate it from the bottoms of our hearts.
We hope you all know that we wish your continued favor forever.
Though we know you are busy, we ask that you please inform us of your availability before ____ __.
東京都
芝田 浩樹
BOOM
THE THIRD MARRIAGE RUSH!!

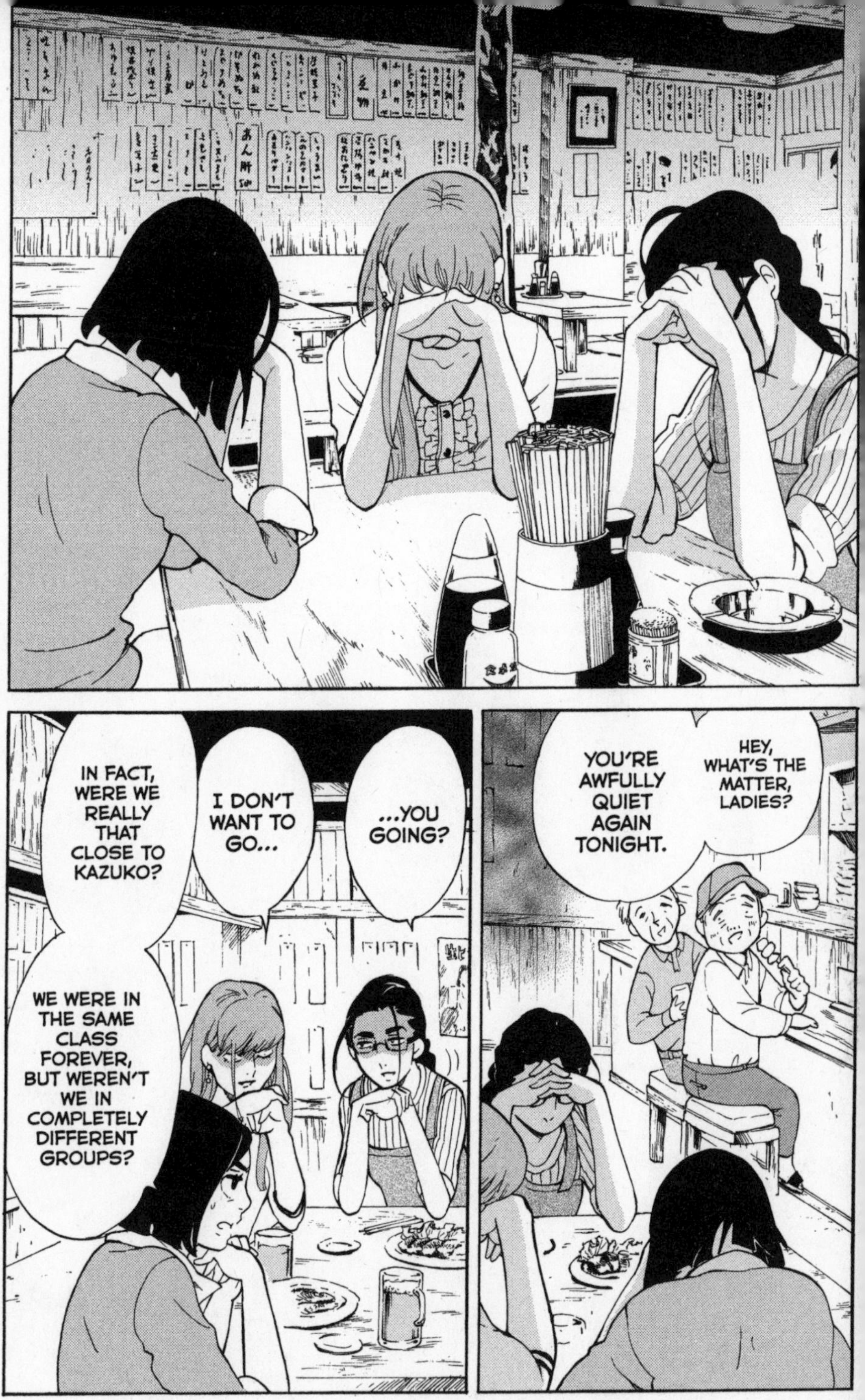
HEY, WHAT'S THE MATTER, LADIES?
YOU'RE AWFULLY QUIET AGAIN TONIGHT.
...YOU GOING?
I DON'T WANT TO GO...
IN FACT, WERE WE REALLY THAT CLOSE TO KAZUKO?
WE WERE IN THE SAME CLASS FOREVER, BUT WEREN'T WE IN COMPLETELY DIFFERENT GROUPS?

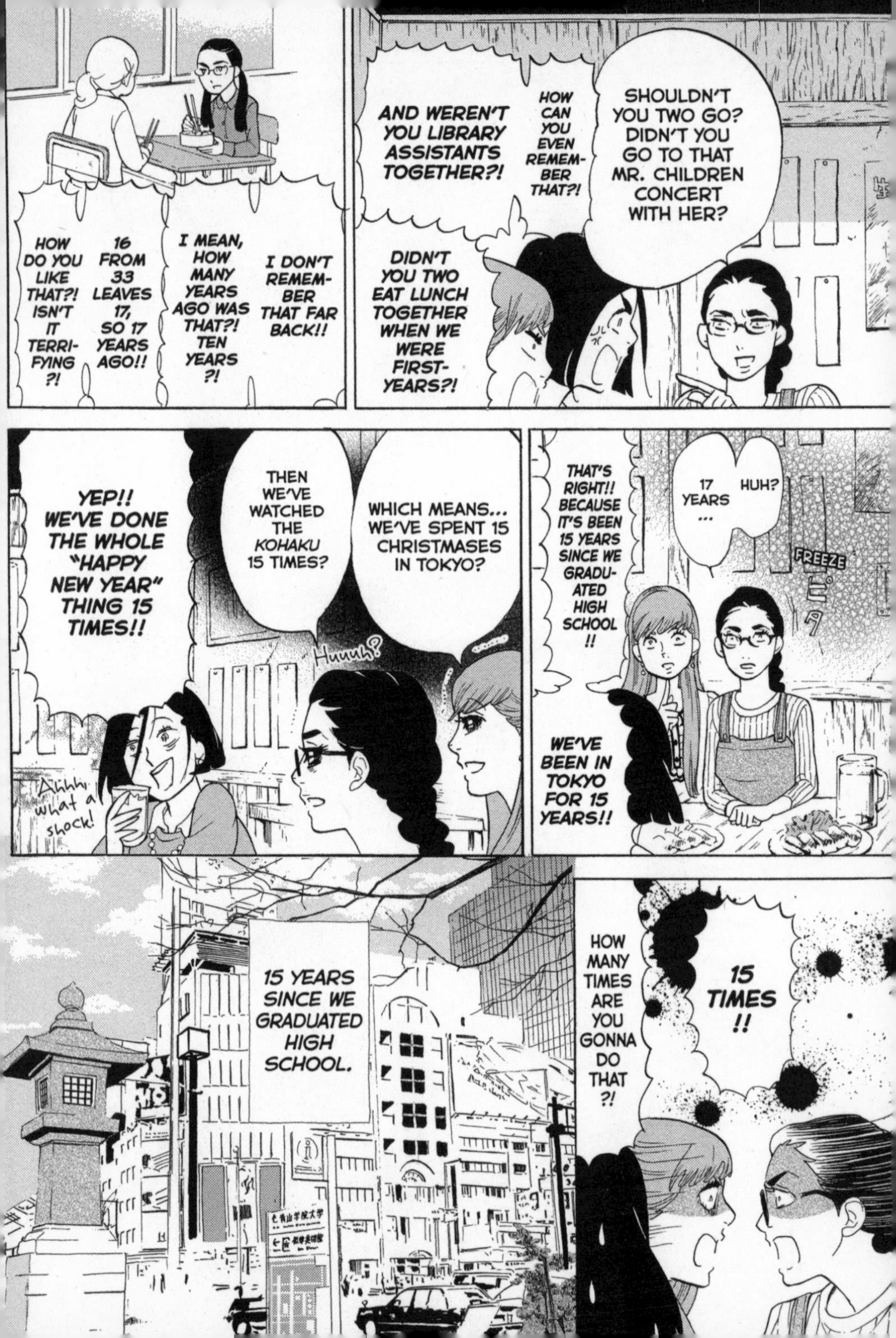
SHOULDN'T YOU TWO GO? DIDN'T YOU GO TO THAT MR. CHILDREN CONCERT WITH HER?
HOW CAN YOU EVEN REMEMBER THAT?!
AND WEREN'T YOU LIBRARY ASSISTANTS TOGETHER?!
DIDN'T YOU TWO EAT LUNCH TOGETHER WHEN WE WERE FIRST-YEARS?!
I DON'T REMEMBER THAT FAR BACK!!
I MEAN, HOW MANY YEARS AGO WAS THAT?! TEN YEARS?!
16 FROM 33 LEAVES 17, SO 17 YEARS AGO!!
HOW DO YOU LIKE THAT?! ISN'T IT TERRIFYING?!
HUH?
17 YEARS...
FREEZE
THAT'S RIGHT!! BECAUSE IT'S BEEN 15 YEARS SINCE WE GRADUATED HIGH SCHOOL!!
WE'VE BEEN IN TOKYO FOR 15 YEARS!!
WHICH MEANS... WE'VE SPENT 15 CHRISTMASES IN TOKYO?
THEN WE'VE WATCHED THE *KOHAKU* 15 TIMES?
Huuuh?
YEP!! WE'VE DONE THE WHOLE "HAPPY NEW YEAR" THING 15 TIMES!!
Ahhh what a shock!
15 TIMES!!
HOW MANY TIMES ARE YOU GONNA DO THAT?!
15 YEARS SINCE WE GRADUATED HIGH SCHOOL.

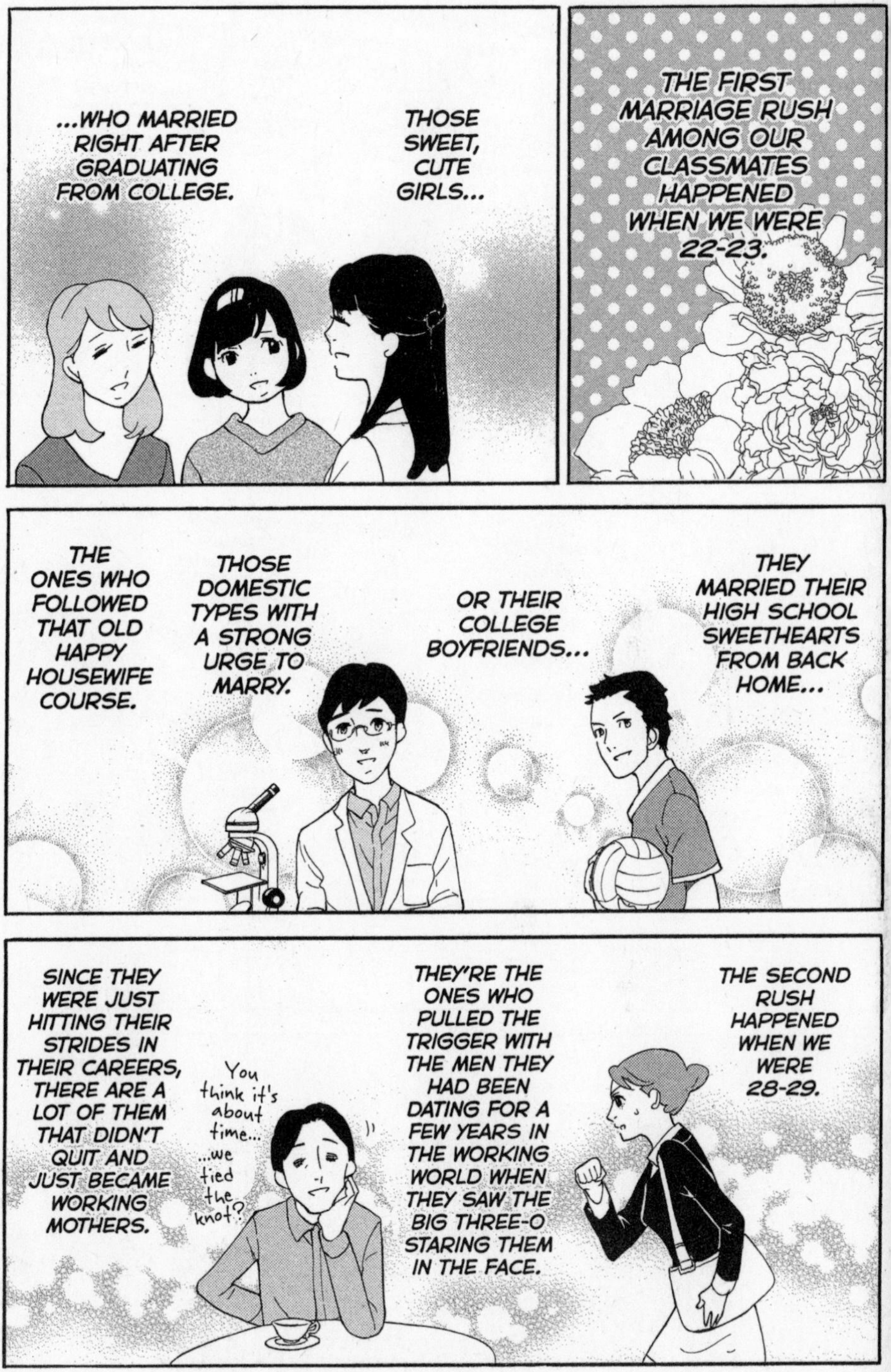
THE FIRST MARRIAGE RUSH AMONG OUR CLASSMATES HAPPENED WHEN WE WERE 22-23.
THOSE SWEET, CUTE GIRLS...
...WHO MARRIED RIGHT AFTER GRADUATING FROM COLLEGE.
THEY MARRIED THEIR HIGH SCHOOL SWEETHEARTS FROM BACK HOME...
OR THEIR COLLEGE BOYFRIENDS...
THOSE DOMESTIC TYPES WITH A STRONG URGE TO MARRY.
THE ONES WHO FOLLOWED THAT OLD HAPPY HOUSEWIFE COURSE.
THE SECOND RUSH HAPPENED WHEN WE WERE 28-29.
THEY'RE THE ONES WHO PULLED THE TRIGGER WITH THE MEN THEY HAD BEEN DATING FOR A FEW YEARS IN THE WORKING WORLD WHEN THEY SAW THE BIG THREE-O STARING THEM IN THE FACE.
You think it's about time... ...we tied the knot?
SINCE THEY WERE JUST HITTING THEIR STRIDES IN THEIR CAREERS, THERE ARE A LOT OF THEM THAT DIDN'T QUIT AND JUST BECAME WORKING MOTHERS.

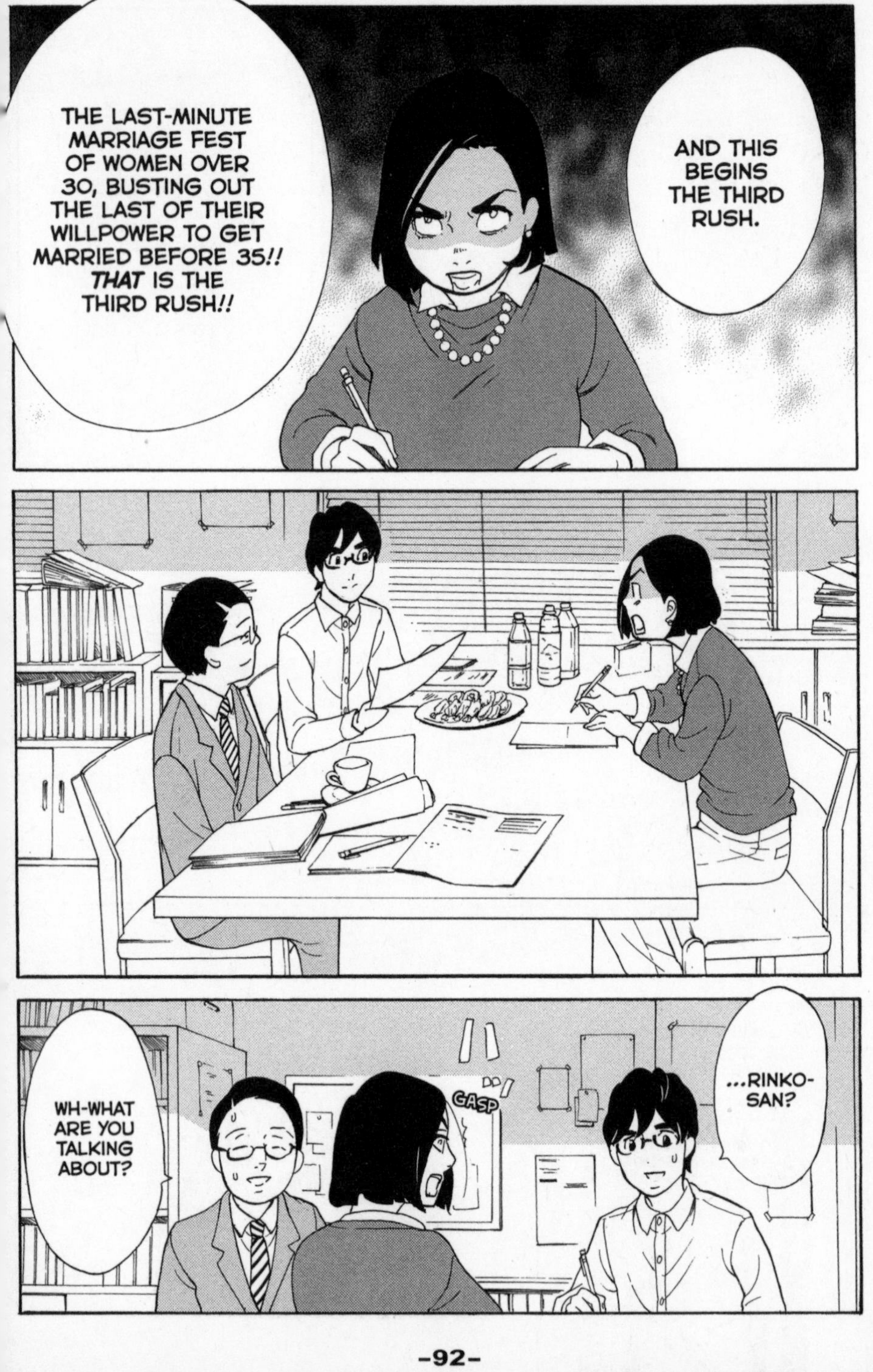
AND THIS BEGINS THE THIRD RUSH.
THE LAST-MINUTE MARRIAGE FEST OF WOMEN OVER 30, BUSTING OUT THE LAST OF THEIR WILLPOWER TO GET MARRIED BEFORE 35!! *THAT* IS THE THIRD RUSH!!
...RINKO-SAN?
GASP
WH-WHAT ARE YOU TALKING ABOUT?

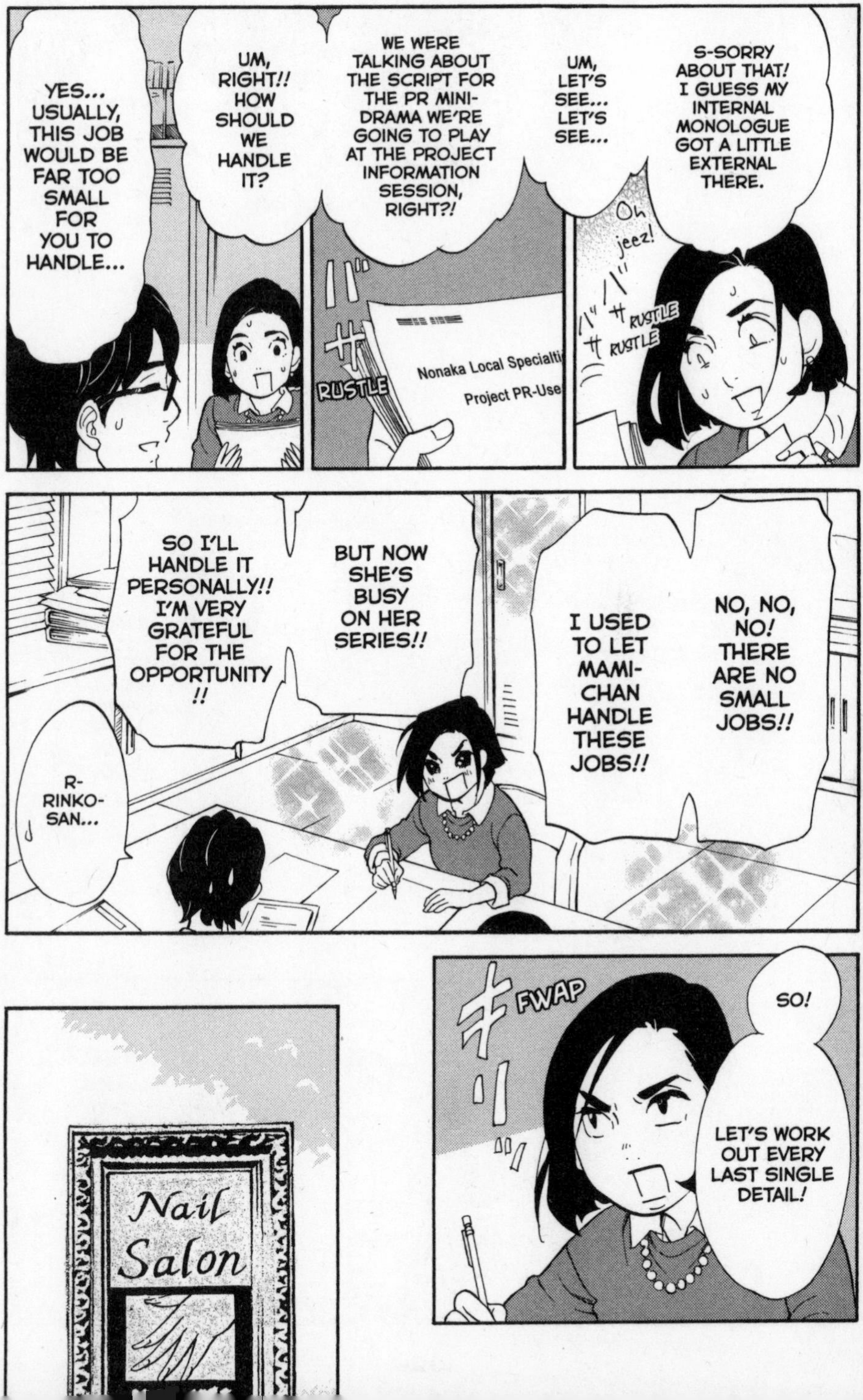

S-SORRY ABOUT THAT! I GUESS MY INTERNAL MONOLOGUE GOT A LITTLE EXTERNAL THERE.
UM, LET'S SEE... LET'S SEE...
Oh jeez!
RUSTLE RUSTLE
WE WERE TALKING ABOUT THE SCRIPT FOR THE PR MINI-DRAMA WE'RE GOING TO PLAY AT THE PROJECT INFORMATION SESSION, RIGHT?!
Nonaka Local Specialti
Project PR-Use
RUSTLE
UM, RIGHT!! HOW SHOULD WE HANDLE IT?
YES... USUALLY, THIS JOB WOULD BE FAR TOO SMALL FOR YOU TO HANDLE...
NO, NO, NO! THERE ARE NO SMALL JOBS!!
I USED TO LET MAMI-CHAN HANDLE THESE JOBS!!
BUT NOW SHE'S BUSY ON HER SERIES!!
SO I'LL HANDLE IT PERSONALLY!! I'M VERY GRATEFUL FOR THE OPPORTUNITY!!
R-RINKO-SAN...
FWAP
SO!
LET'S WORK OUT EVERY LAST SINGLE DETAIL!
Nail Salon

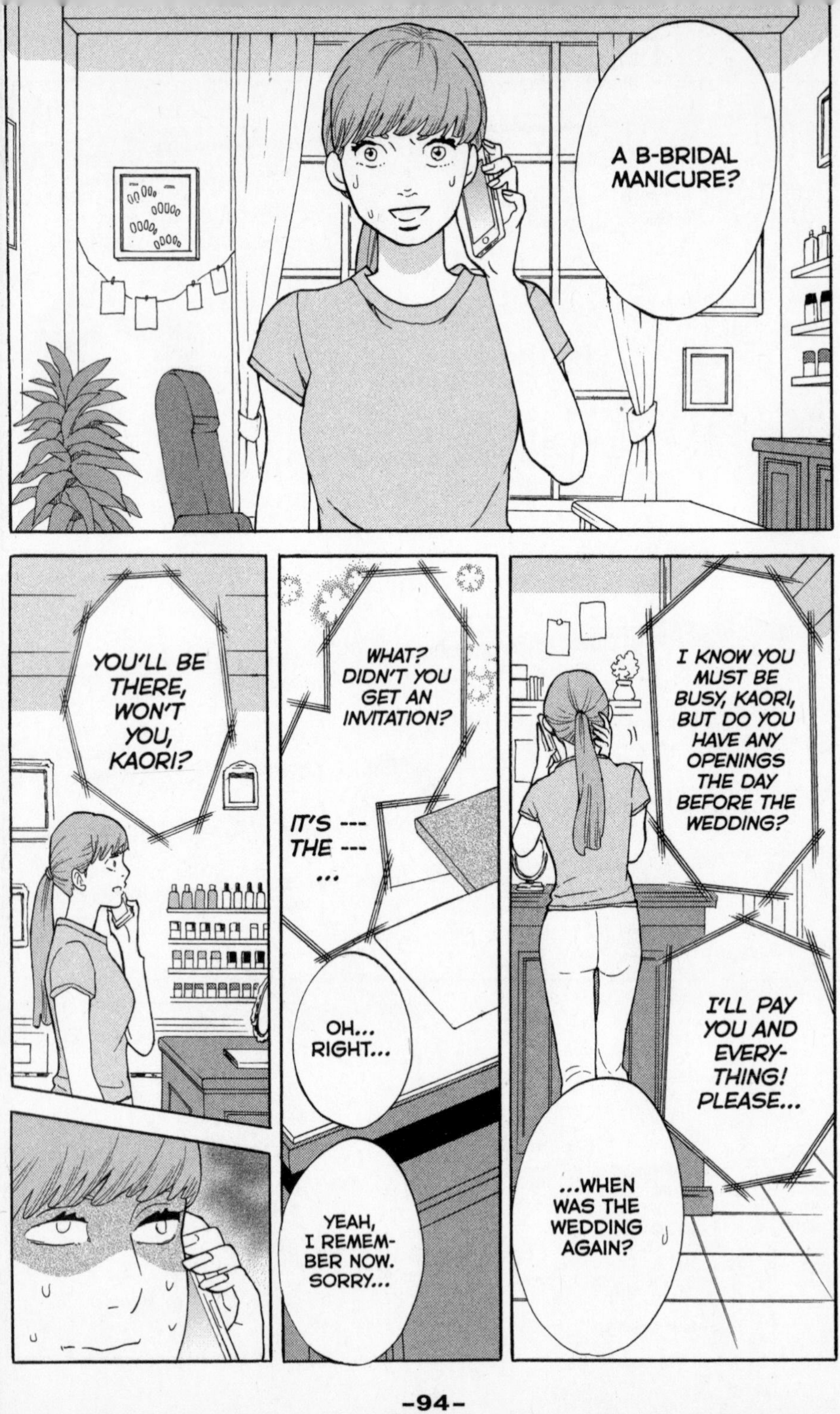
A B-BRIDAL MANICURE?
I KNOW YOU MUST BE BUSY, KAORI, BUT DO YOU HAVE ANY OPENINGS THE DAY BEFORE THE WEDDING?
I'LL PAY YOU AND EVERYTHING! PLEASE...
...WHEN WAS THE WEDDING AGAIN?
WHAT? DIDN'T YOU GET AN INVITATION?
IT'S --- THE --- ...
OH... RIGHT...
YEAH, I REMEMBER NOW. SORRY...
YOU'LL BE THERE, WON'T YOU, KAORI?

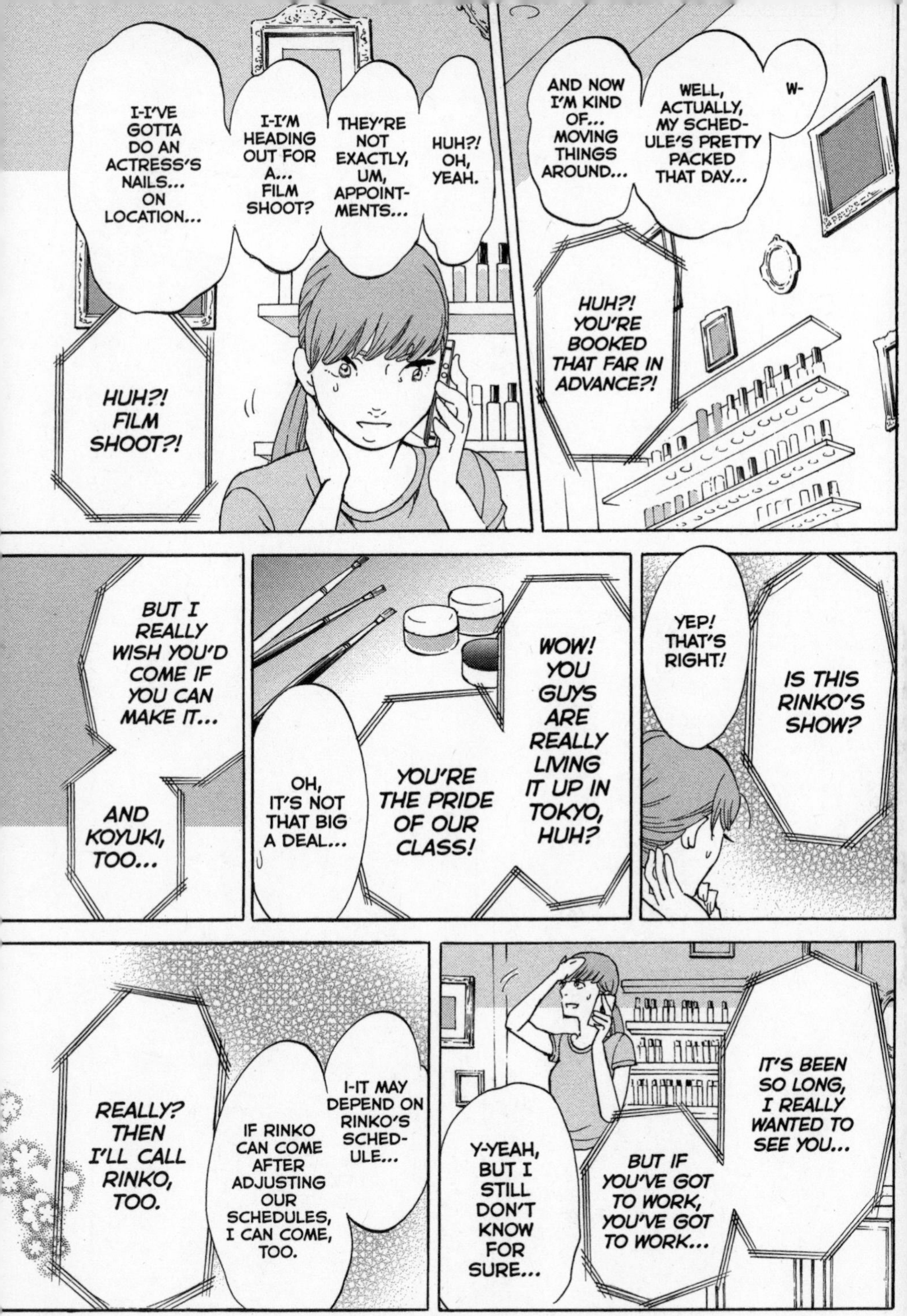
W-
WELL, ACTUALLY, MY SCHEDULE'S PRETTY PACKED THAT DAY...
AND NOW I'M KIND OF... MOVING THINGS AROUND...
HUH?! YOU'RE BOOKED THAT FAR IN ADVANCE?!
HUH?! OH, YEAH.
THEY'RE NOT EXACTLY, UM, APPOINTMENTS...
I-I'M HEADING OUT FOR A... FILM SHOOT?
I-I'VE GOTTA DO AN ACTRESS'S NAILS... ON LOCATION...
HUH?! FILM SHOOT?!
IS THIS RINKO'S SHOW?
YEP! THAT'S RIGHT!
WOW! YOU GUYS ARE REALLY LIVING IT UP IN TOKYO, HUH?
YOU'RE THE PRIDE OF OUR CLASS!
OH, IT'S NOT THAT BIG A DEAL...
BUT I REALLY WISH YOU'D COME IF YOU CAN MAKE IT...
AND KOYUKI, TOO...
IT'S BEEN SO LONG, I REALLY WANTED TO SEE YOU...
BUT IF YOU'VE GOT TO WORK, YOU'VE GOT TO WORK...
Y-YEAH, BUT I STILL DON'T KNOW FOR SURE...
I-IT MAY DEPEND ON RINKO'S SCHEDULE...
IF RINKO CAN COME AFTER ADJUSTING OUR SCHEDULES, I CAN COME, TOO.
REALLY? THEN I'LL CALL RINKO, TOO.

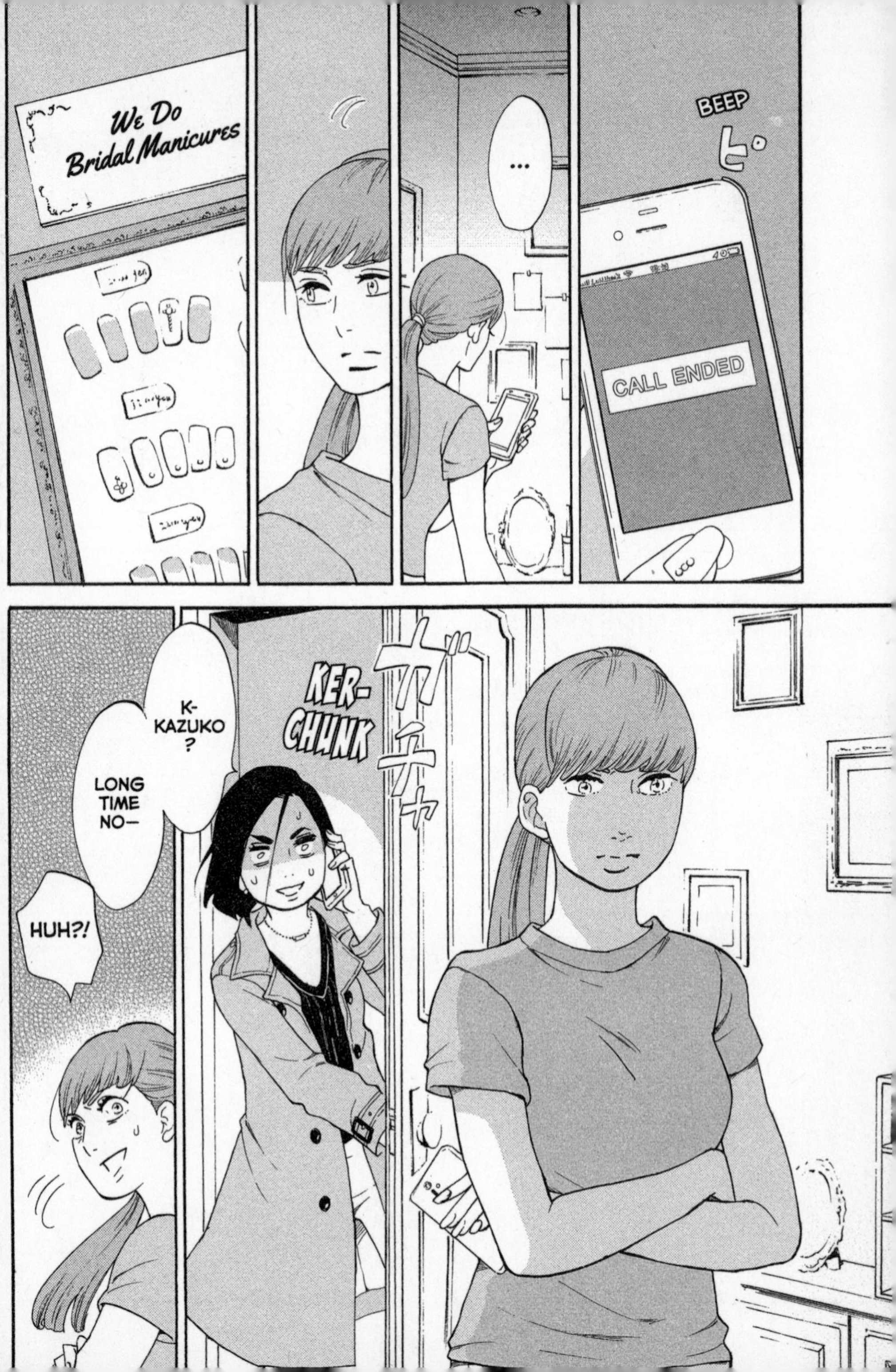
BEEP
ピ
CALL ENDED
...
We Do Bridal Manicures
KER-CHUNK
ガチャ
K-KAZUKO? LONG TIME NO—
HUH?!

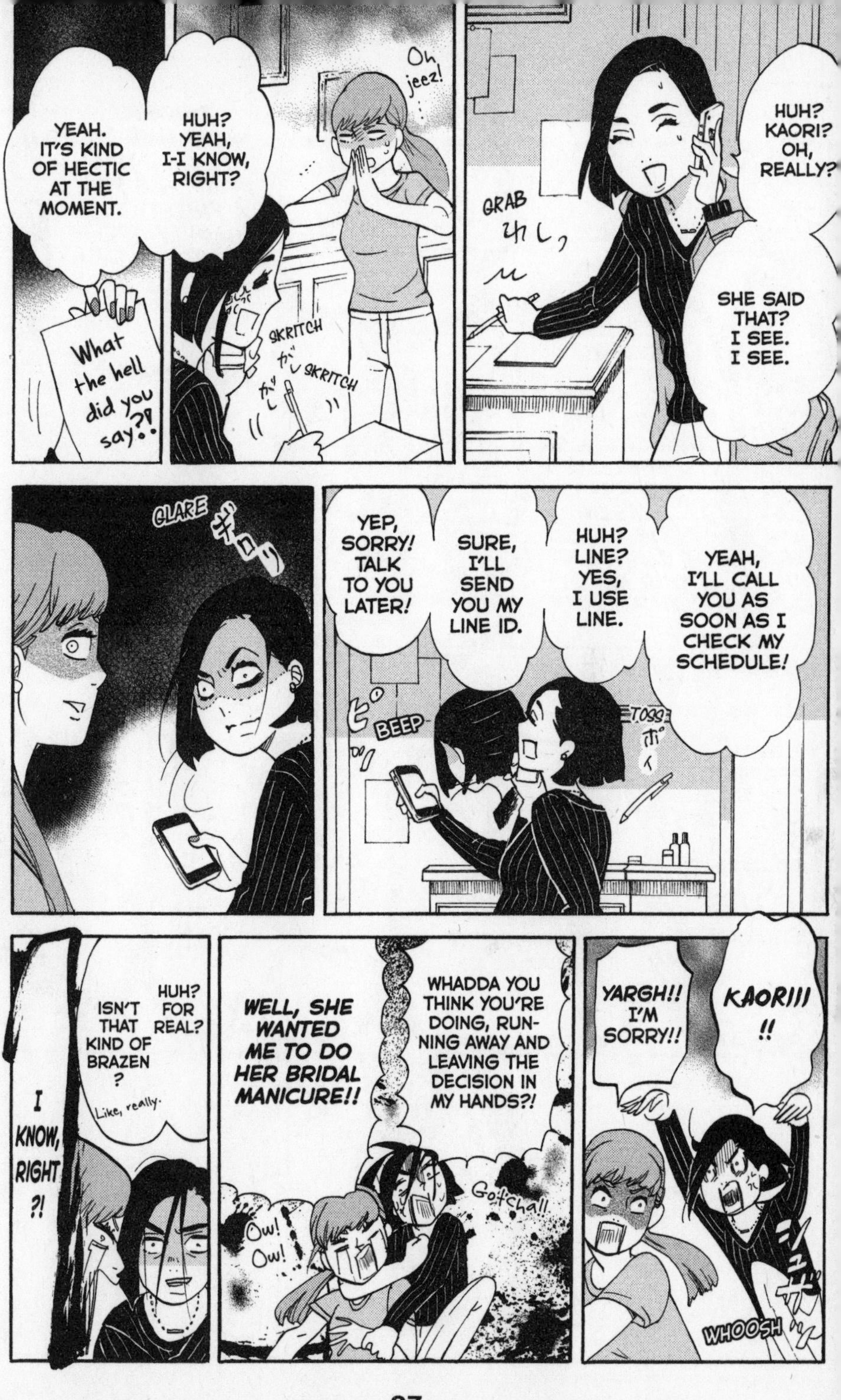
HUH? KAORI? OH, REALLY?
SHE SAID THAT? I SEE. I SEE.
GRAB
Oh jeez!
HUH? YEAH, I-I KNOW, RIGHT?
SKRITCH
SKRITCH
YEAH. IT'S KIND OF HECTIC AT THE MOMENT.
What the hell did you say?!
YEAH, I'LL CALL YOU AS SOON AS I CHECK MY SCHEDULE!
HUH? LINE? YES, I USE LINE.
SURE, I'LL SEND YOU MY LINE ID.
YEP, SORRY! TALK TO YOU LATER!
TOSS
BEEP
GLARE
KAORI!!!!
YARGH!! I'M SORRY!!
WHOOSH
WHADDA YOU THINK YOU'RE DOING, RUNNING AWAY AND LEAVING THE DECISION IN MY HANDS?!
Gotcha!!
WELL, SHE WANTED ME TO DO HER BRIDAL MANICURE!!
Ow! Ow!
HUH? FOR REAL?
ISN'T THAT KIND OF BRAZEN?
Like, really.
I KNOW, RIGHT?!

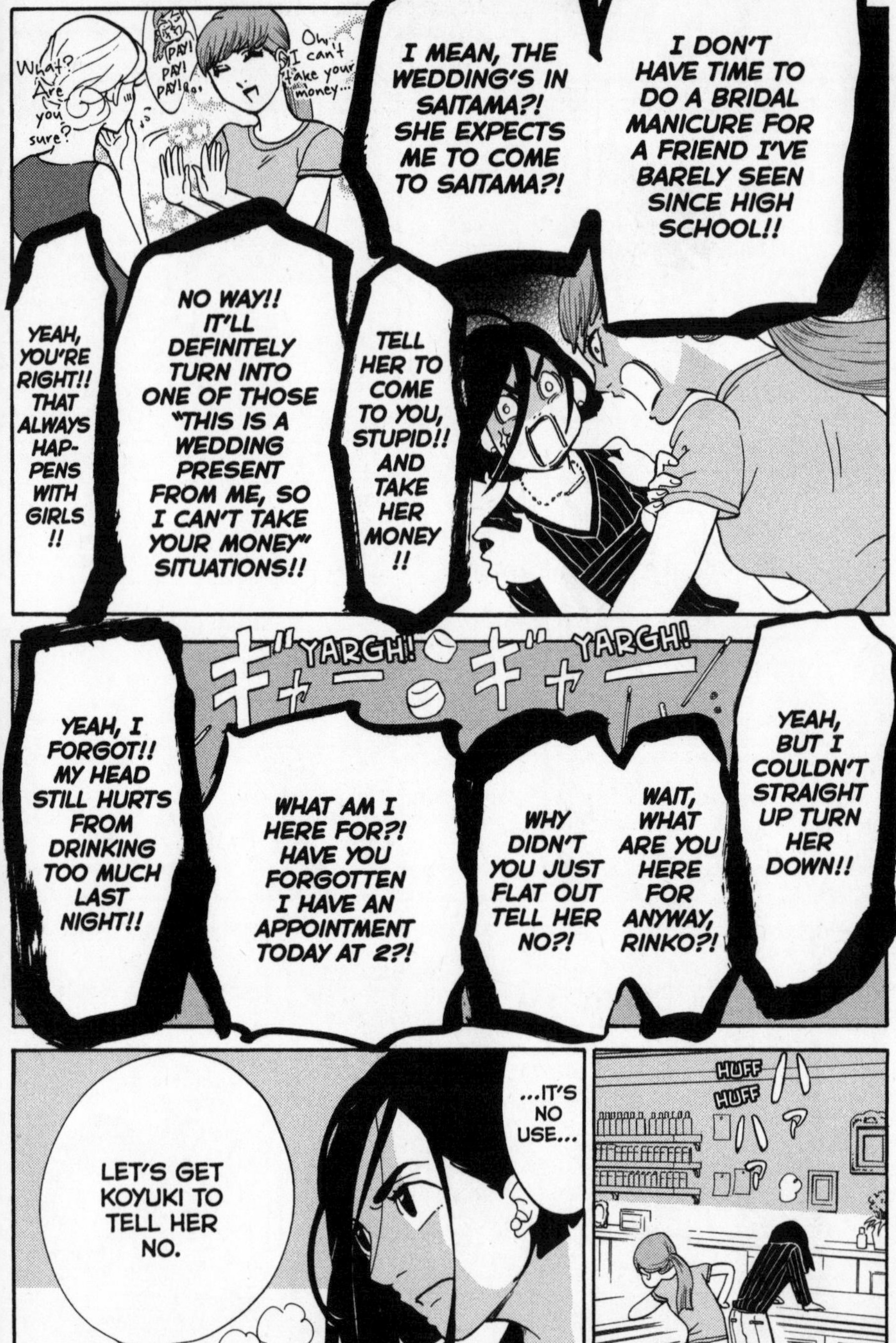
I DON'T HAVE TIME TO DO A BRIDAL MANICURE FOR A FRIEND I'VE BARELY SEEN SINCE HIGH SCHOOL!!
I MEAN, THE WEDDING'S IN SAITAMA?! SHE EXPECTS ME TO COME TO SAITAMA?!
Oh, I can't take your money...
PAY! PAY! PAY!
What? Are you sure?
TELL HER TO COME TO YOU, STUPID!! AND TAKE HER MONEY!!
NO WAY!! IT'LL DEFINITELY TURN INTO ONE OF THOSE "THIS IS A WEDDING PRESENT FROM ME, SO I CAN'T TAKE YOUR MONEY" SITUATIONS!!
YEAH, YOU'RE RIGHT!! THAT ALWAYS HAPPENS WITH GIRLS!!
YARGH!
YARGH!
YEAH, BUT I COULDN'T STRAIGHT UP TURN HER DOWN!!
WAIT, WHAT ARE YOU HERE FOR ANYWAY, RINKO?!
WHY DIDN'T YOU JUST FLAT OUT TELL HER NO?!
WHAT AM I HERE FOR?! HAVE YOU FORGOTTEN I HAVE AN APPOINTMENT TODAY AT 2?!
YEAH, I FORGOT!! MY HEAD STILL HURTS FROM DRINKING TOO MUCH LAST NIGHT!!
HUFF
HUFF
...IT'S NO USE...
LET'S GET KOYUKI TO TELL HER NO.

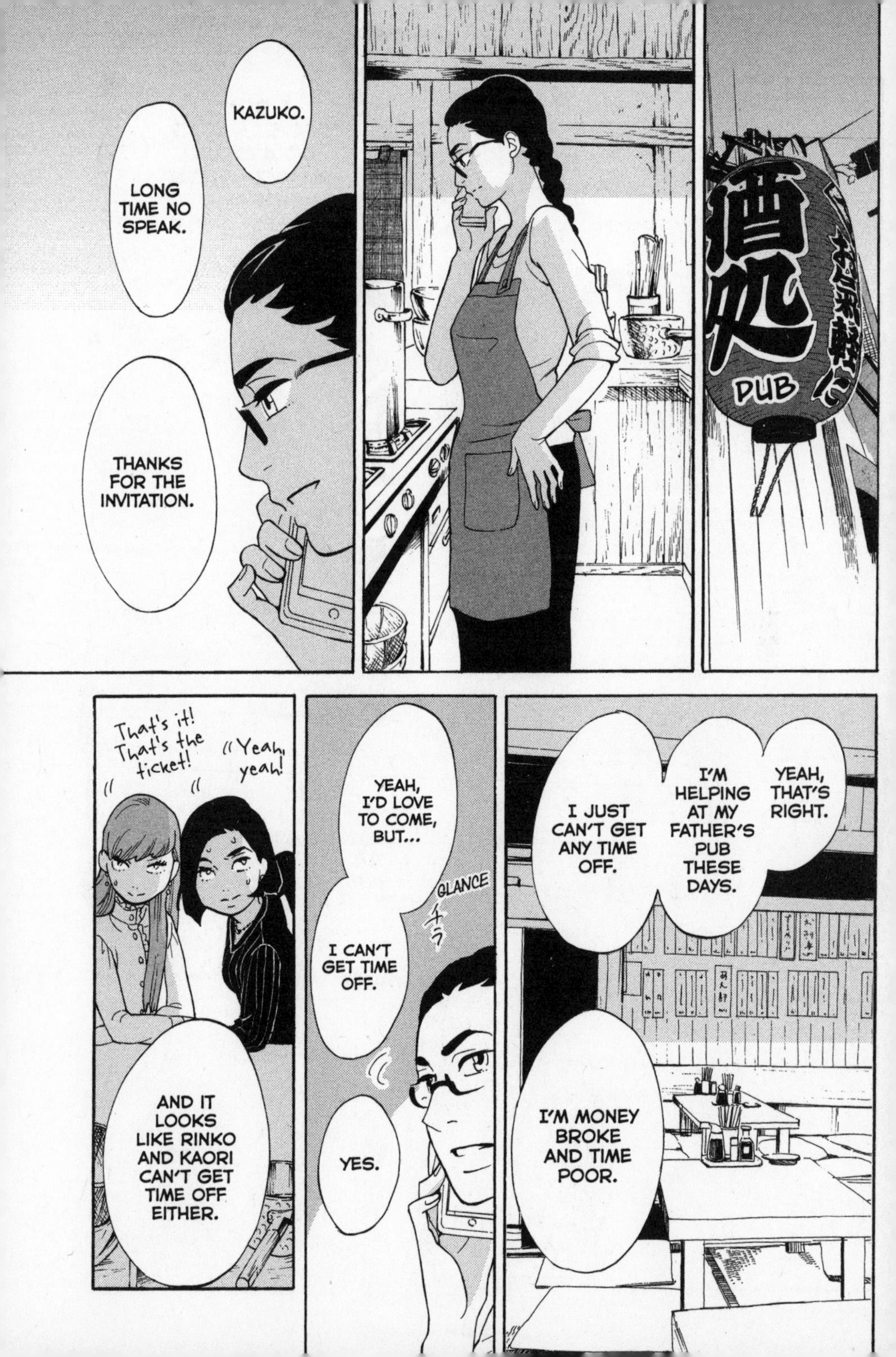
酒処
PUB
KAZUKO.
LONG TIME NO SPEAK.
THANKS FOR THE INVITATION.
YEAH, THAT'S RIGHT.
I'M HELPING AT MY FATHER'S PUB THESE DAYS.
I JUST CAN'T GET ANY TIME OFF.
I'M MONEY BROKE AND TIME POOR.
YEAH, I'D LOVE TO COME, BUT...
GLANCE
チラ
I CAN'T GET TIME OFF.
YES.
That's it! That's the ticket!
Yeah, yeah!
AND IT LOOKS LIKE RINKO AND KAORI CAN'T GET TIME OFF EITHER.

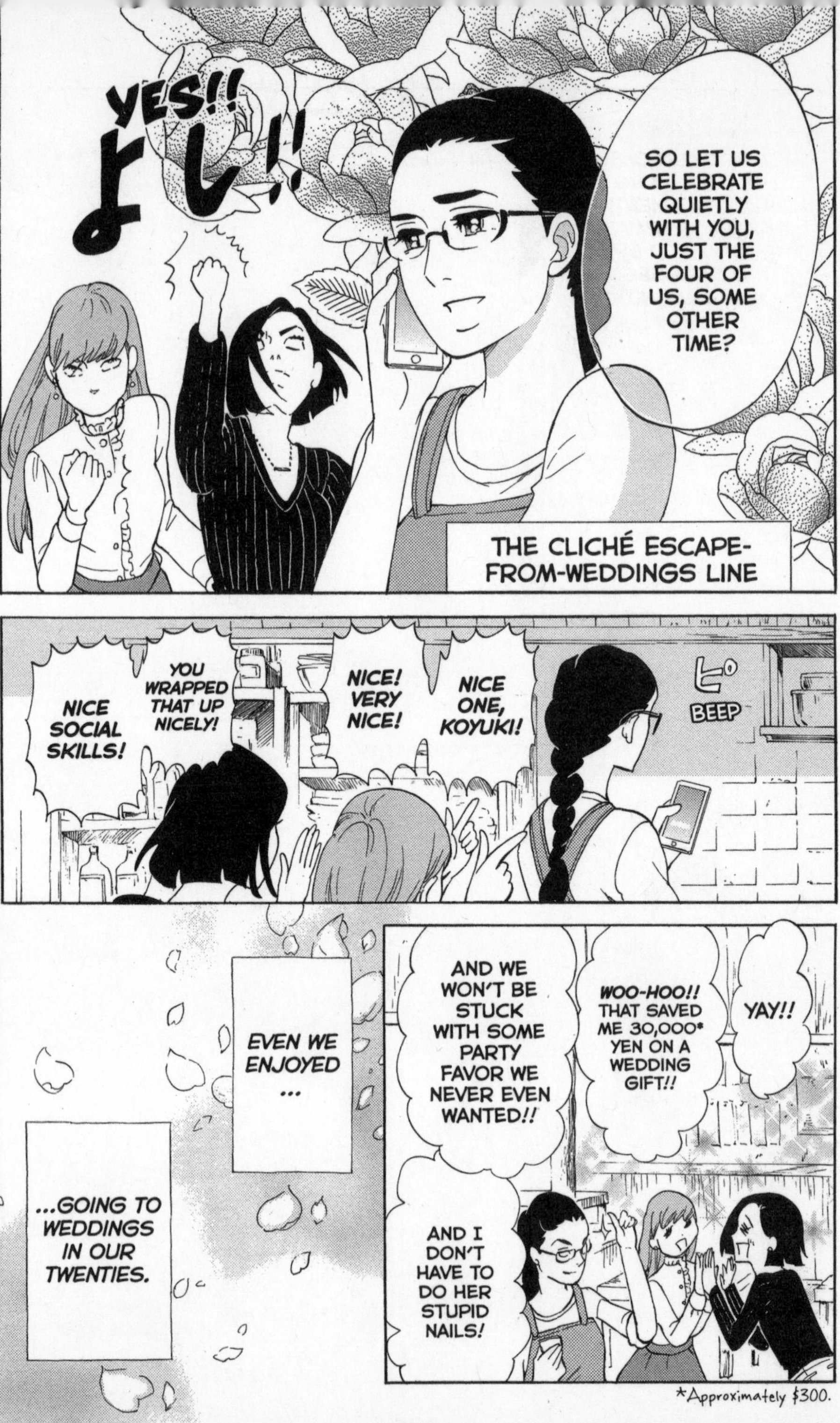
SO LET US CELEBRATE QUIETLY WITH YOU, JUST THE FOUR OF US, SOME OTHER TIME?
THE CLICHÉ ESCAPE-FROM-WEDDINGS LINE
YES!!
よし!!
ピ
BEEP
NICE ONE, KOYUKI!
NICE! VERY NICE!
YOU WRAPPED THAT UP NICELY!
NICE SOCIAL SKILLS!
YAY!!
WOO-HOO!! THAT SAVED ME 30,000* YEN ON A WEDDING GIFT!!
AND WE WON'T BE STUCK WITH SOME PARTY FAVOR WE NEVER EVEN WANTED!!
AND I DON'T HAVE TO DO HER STUPID NAILS!
EVEN WE ENJOYED ...
...GOING TO WEDDINGS IN OUR TWENTIES.

*Approximately $300.

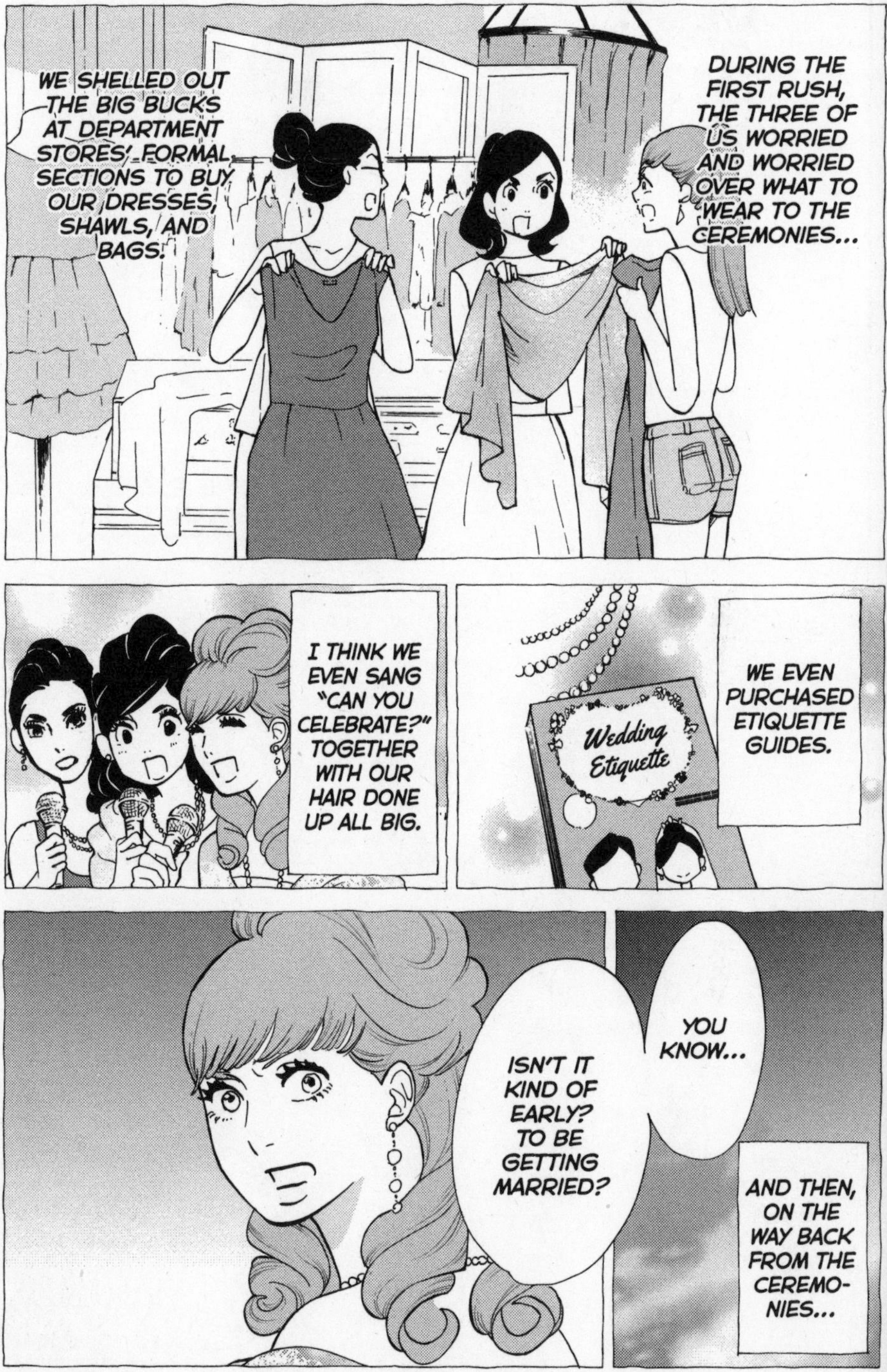
DURING THE FIRST RUSH, THE THREE OF US WORRIED AND WORRIED OVER WHAT TO WEAR TO THE CEREMONIES...
WE SHELLED OUT THE BIG BUCKS AT DEPARTMENT STORES' FORMAL SECTIONS TO BUY OUR DRESSES, SHAWLS, AND BAGS.
WE EVEN PURCHASED ETIQUETTE GUIDES.
Wedding Etiquette
I THINK WE EVEN SANG "CAN YOU CELEBRATE?" TOGETHER WITH OUR HAIR DONE UP ALL BIG.
AND THEN, ON THE WAY BACK FROM THE CEREMO-NIES...
YOU KNOW...
ISN'T IT KIND OF EARLY? TO BE GETTING MARRIED?

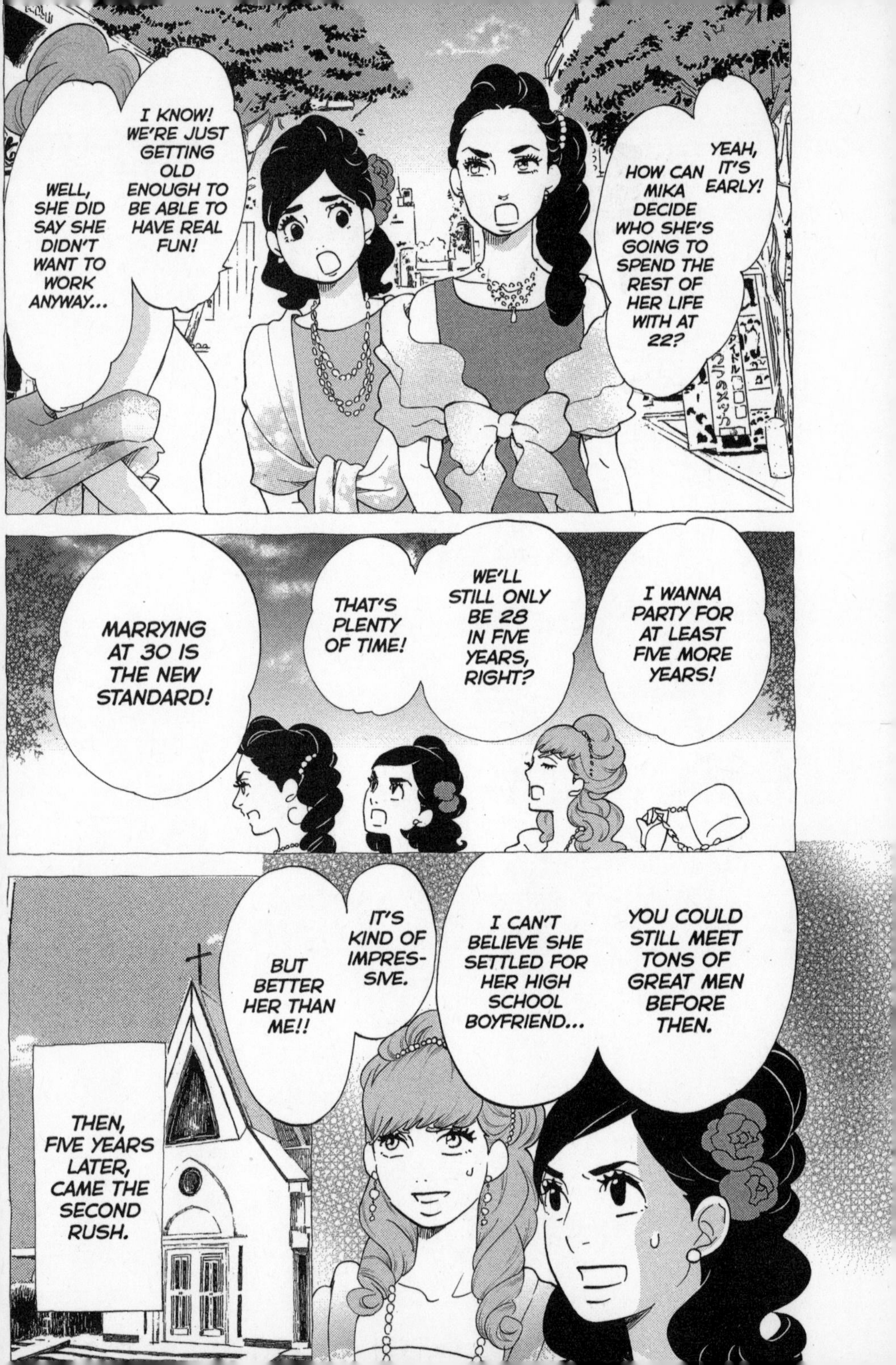
YEAH, IT'S EARLY!
HOW CAN MIKA DECIDE WHO SHE'S GOING TO SPEND THE REST OF HER LIFE WITH AT 22?
I KNOW! WE'RE JUST GETTING OLD ENOUGH TO BE ABLE TO HAVE REAL FUN!
WELL, SHE DID SAY SHE DIDN'T WANT TO WORK ANYWAY...
I WANNA PARTY FOR AT LEAST FIVE MORE YEARS!
WE'LL STILL ONLY BE 28 IN FIVE YEARS, RIGHT?
THAT'S PLENTY OF TIME!
MARRYING AT 30 IS THE NEW STANDARD!
YOU COULD STILL MEET TONS OF GREAT MEN BEFORE THEN.
I CAN'T BELIEVE SHE SETTLED FOR HER HIGH SCHOOL BOYFRIEND...
IT'S KIND OF IMPRES-SIVE.
BUT BETTER HER THAN ME!!
THEN, FIVE YEARS LATER, CAME THE SECOND RUSH.

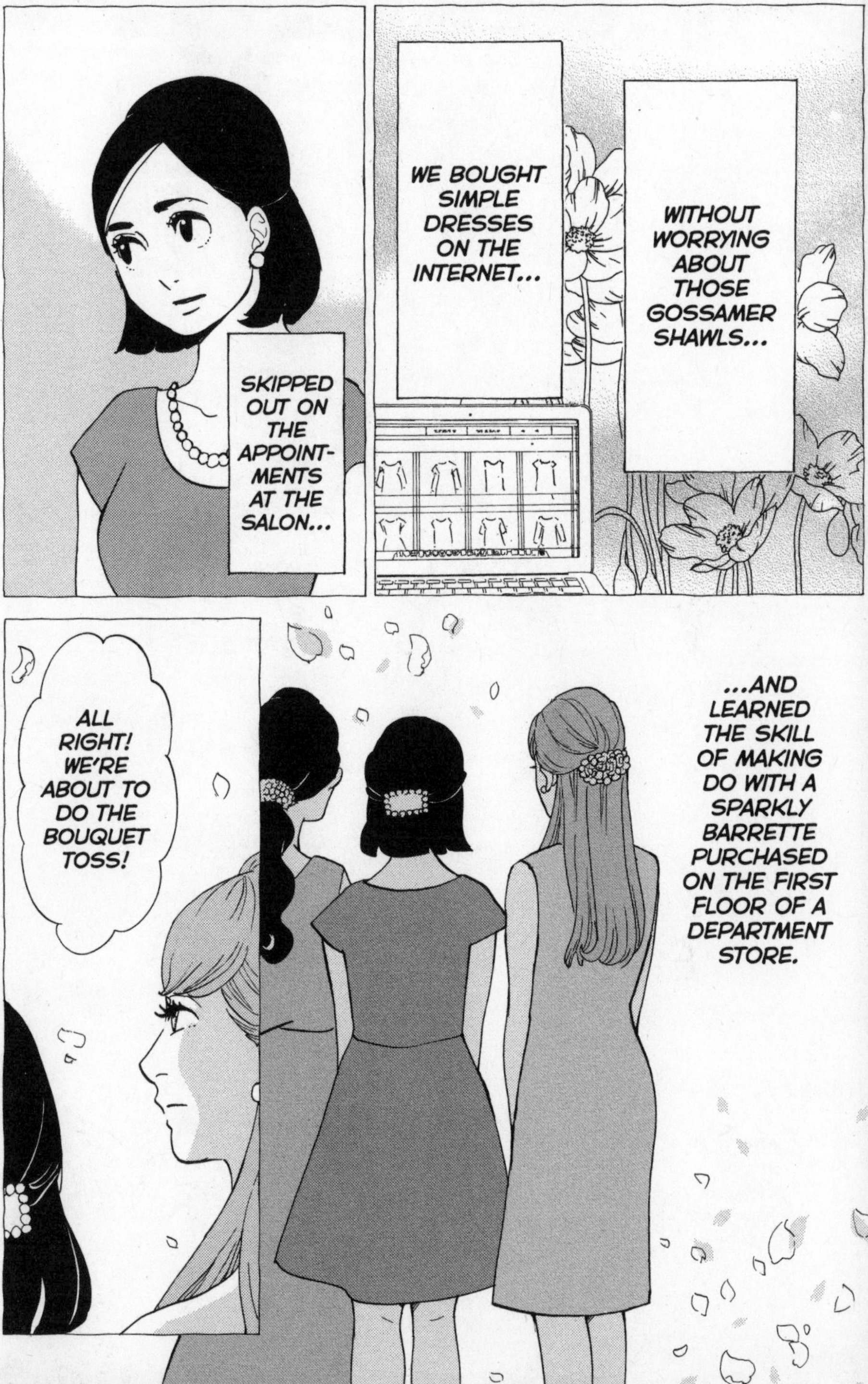
WITHOUT WORRYING ABOUT THOSE GOSSAMER SHAWLS...
WE BOUGHT SIMPLE DRESSES ON THE INTERNET...
SKIPPED OUT ON THE APPOINTMENTS AT THE SALON...
...AND LEARNED THE SKILL OF MAKING DO WITH A SPARKLY BARRETTE PURCHASED ON THE FIRST FLOOR OF A DEPARTMENT STORE.
ALL RIGHT! WE'RE ABOUT TO DO THE BOUQUET TOSS!

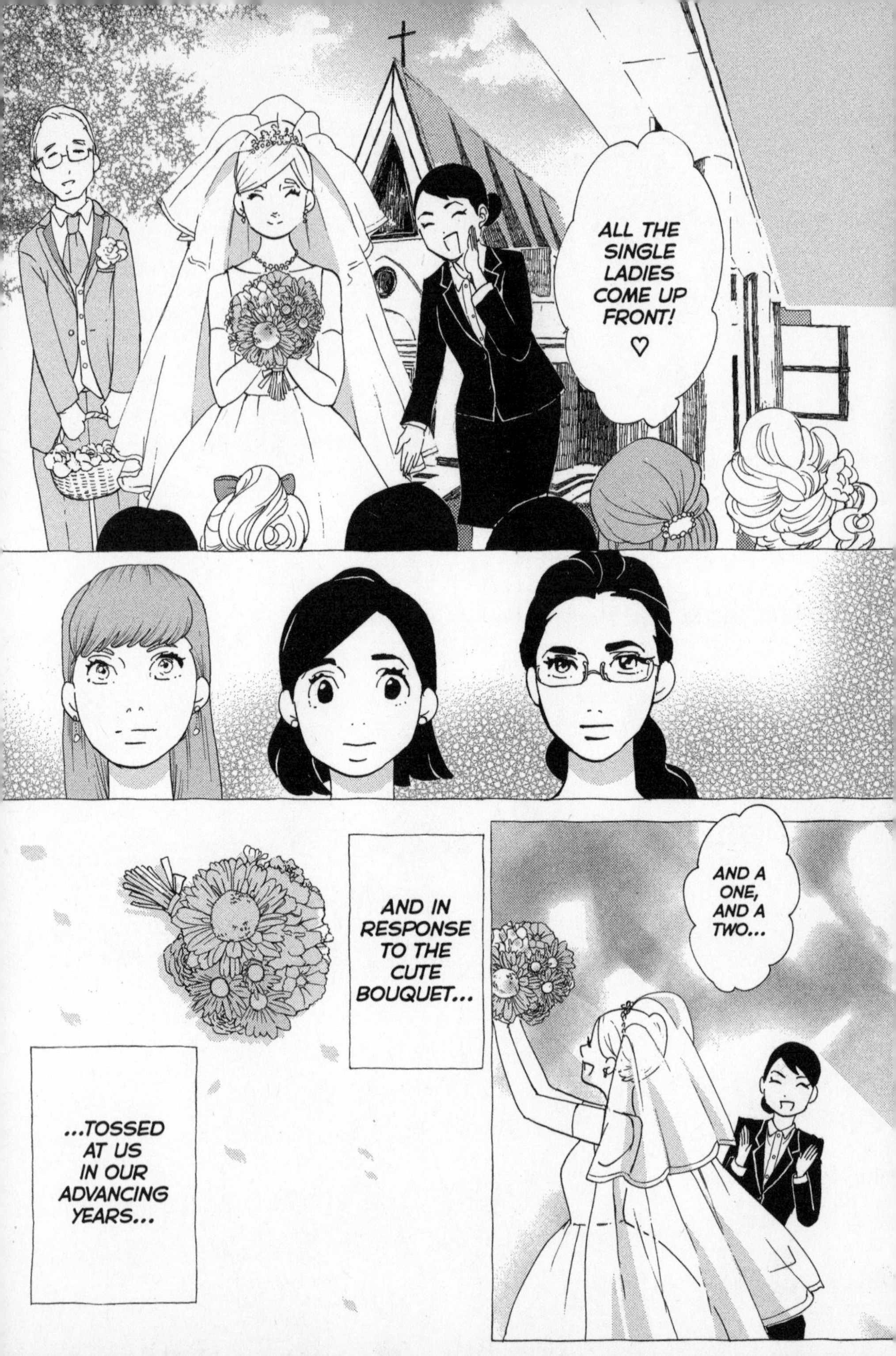
ALL THE SINGLE LADIES COME UP FRONT! ♡
AND A ONE, AND A TWO...
AND IN RESPONSE TO THE CUTE BOUQUET...
...TOSSED AT US IN OUR ADVANCING YEARS...

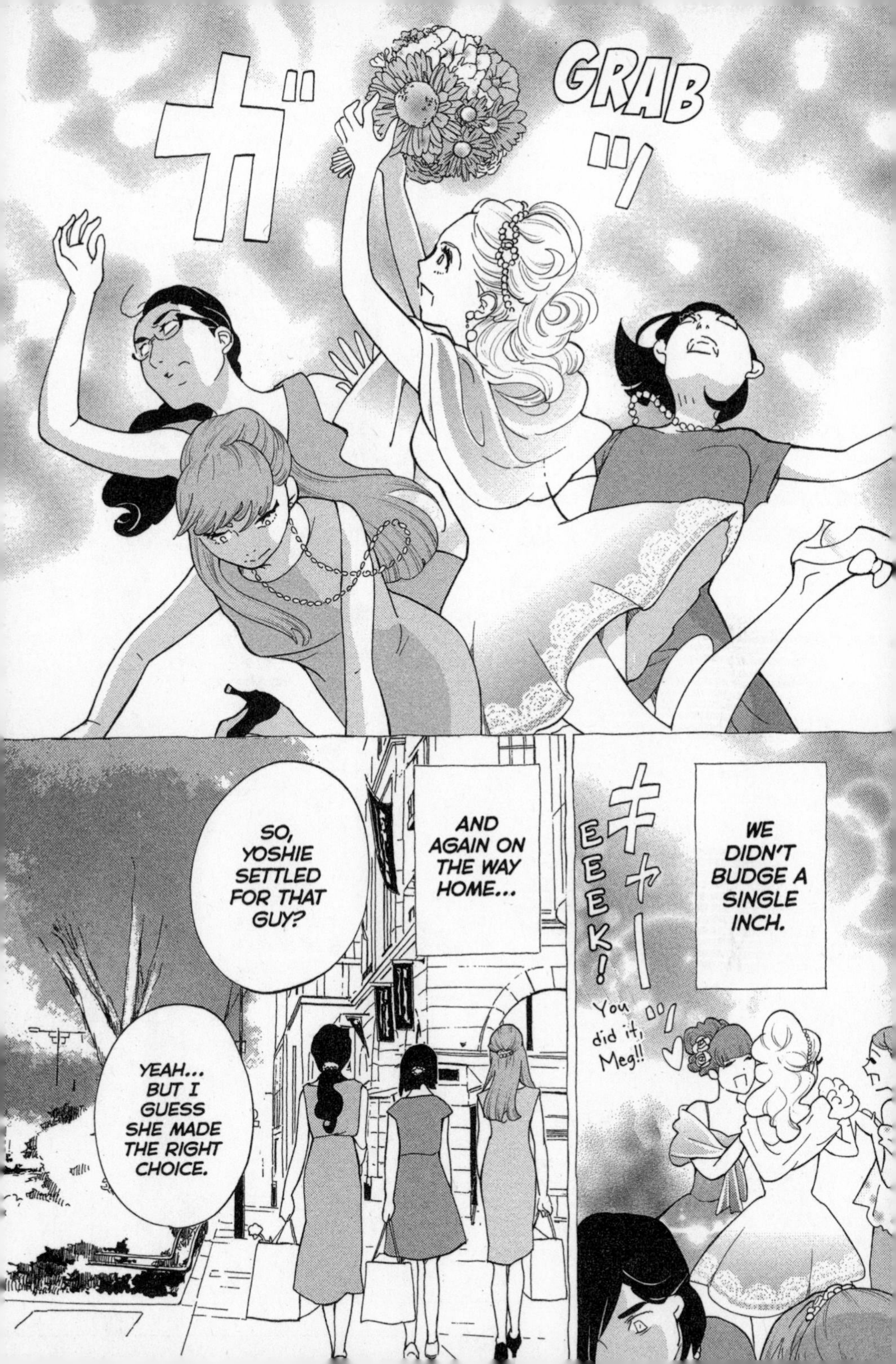
GRAB
ガッ
WE DIDN'T BUDGE A SINGLE INCH.
EEEK!
キャー
You did it, Meg!!
AND AGAIN ON THE WAY HOME...
SO, YOSHIE SETTLED FOR THAT GUY?
YEAH... BUT I GUESS SHE MADE THE RIGHT CHOICE.

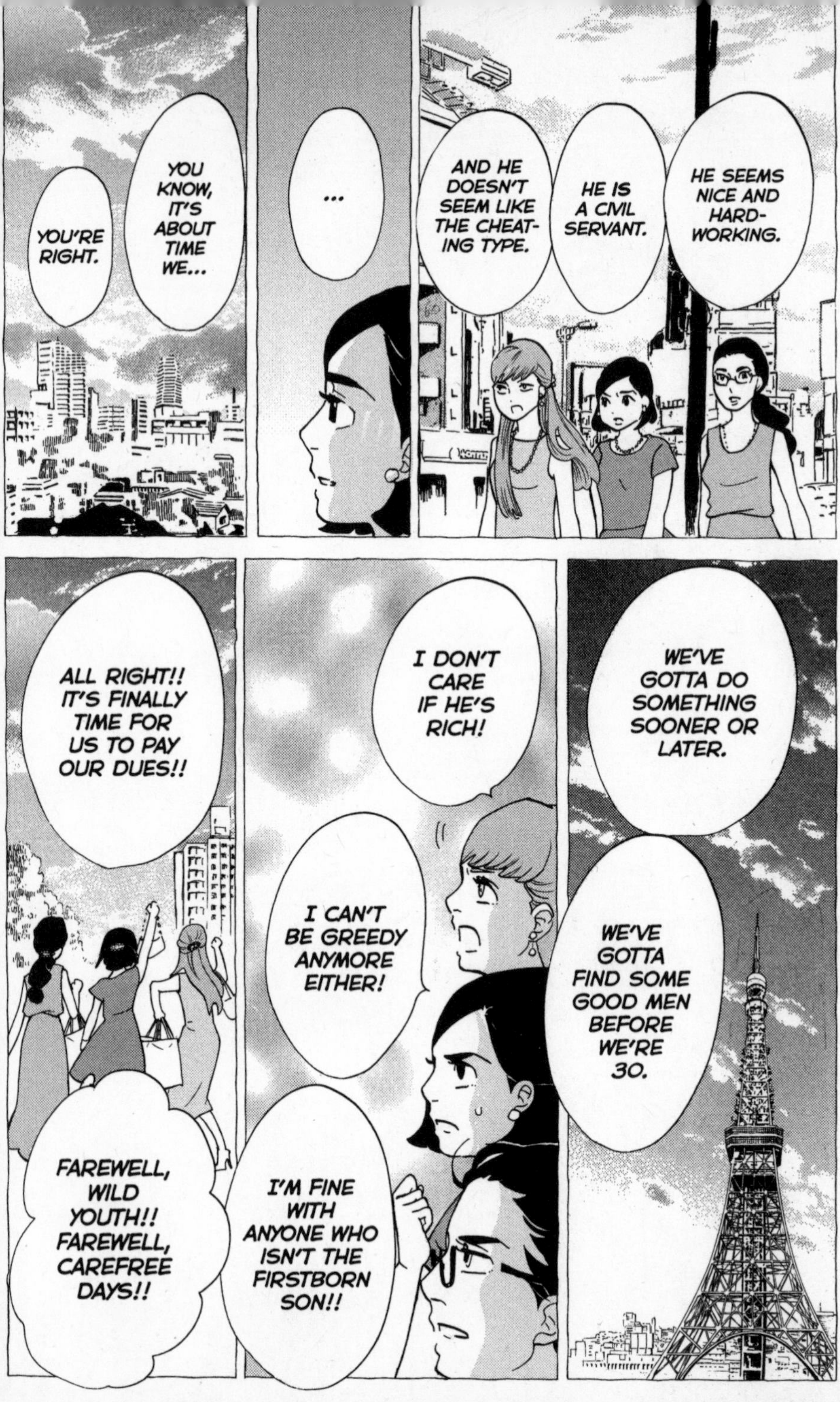
HE SEEMS NICE AND HARD-WORKING.
HE IS A CIVIL SERVANT.
AND HE DOESN'T SEEM LIKE THE CHEATING TYPE.
...
YOU KNOW, IT'S ABOUT TIME WE...
YOU'RE RIGHT.
WE'VE GOTTA DO SOMETHING SOONER OR LATER.
WE'VE GOTTA FIND SOME GOOD MEN BEFORE WE'RE 30.
I DON'T CARE IF HE'S RICH!
I CAN'T BE GREEDY ANYMORE EITHER!
I'M FINE WITH ANYONE WHO ISN'T THE FIRSTBORN SON!!
ALL RIGHT!! IT'S FINALLY TIME FOR US TO PAY OUR DUES!!
FAREWELL, WILD YOUTH!! FAREWELL, CAREFREE DAYS!!

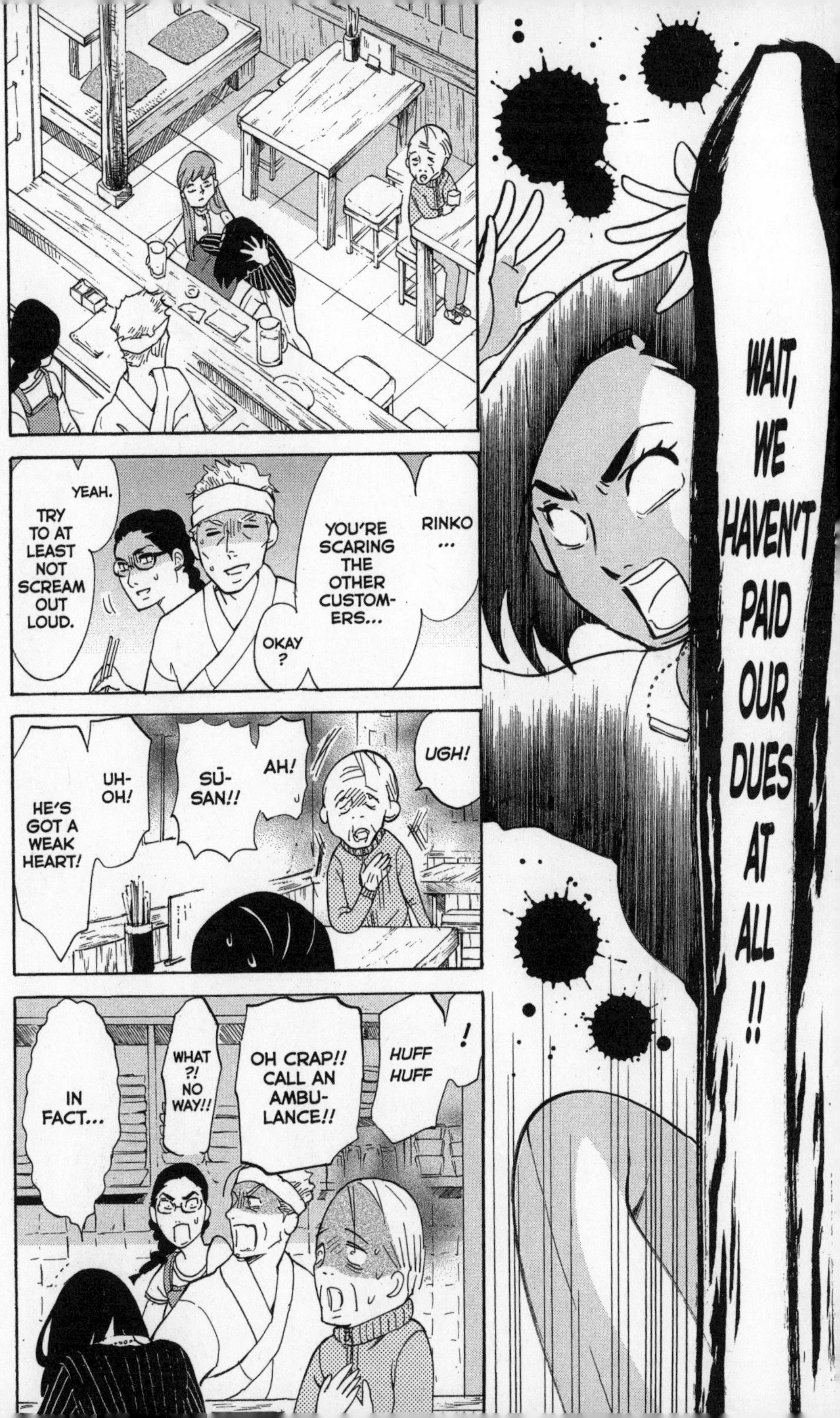
WAIT, WE HAVEN'T PAID OUR DUES AT ALL!!
RINKO ...
YOU'RE SCARING THE OTHER CUSTOM-ERS...
OKAY ?
YEAH.
TRY TO AT LEAST NOT SCREAM OUT LOUD.
UGH!
AH!
SŪ-SAN!!
UH-OH!
HE'S GOT A WEAK HEART!
!
HUFF HUFF
OH CRAP!! CALL AN AMBU-LANCE!!
WHAT ?! NO WAY!!
IN FACT...

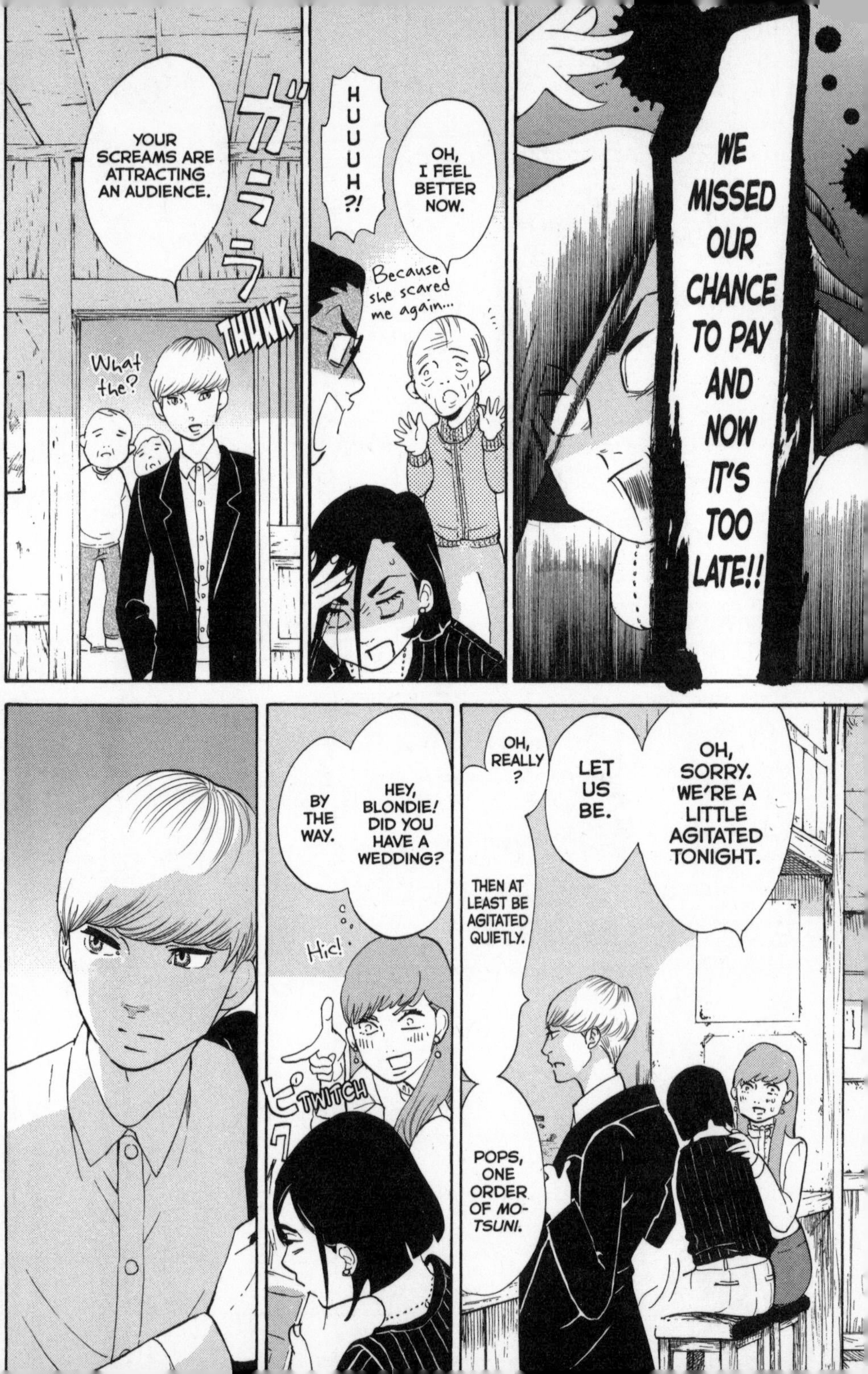
WE MISSED OUR CHANCE TO PAY AND NOW IT'S TOO LATE!!
OH, I FEEL BETTER NOW.
Because she scared me again...
HUUUUH?!
ガララ
THUNK
YOUR SCREAMS ARE ATTRACTING AN AUDIENCE.
What the?
OH, SORRY. WE'RE A LITTLE AGITATED TONIGHT.
LET US BE.
OH, REALLY?
THEN AT LEAST BE AGITATED QUIETLY.
POPS, ONE ORDER OF MO-TSUNI.
HEY, BLONDIE! DID YOU HAVE A WEDDING?
BY THE WAY.
Hic!
ピク
TWITCH

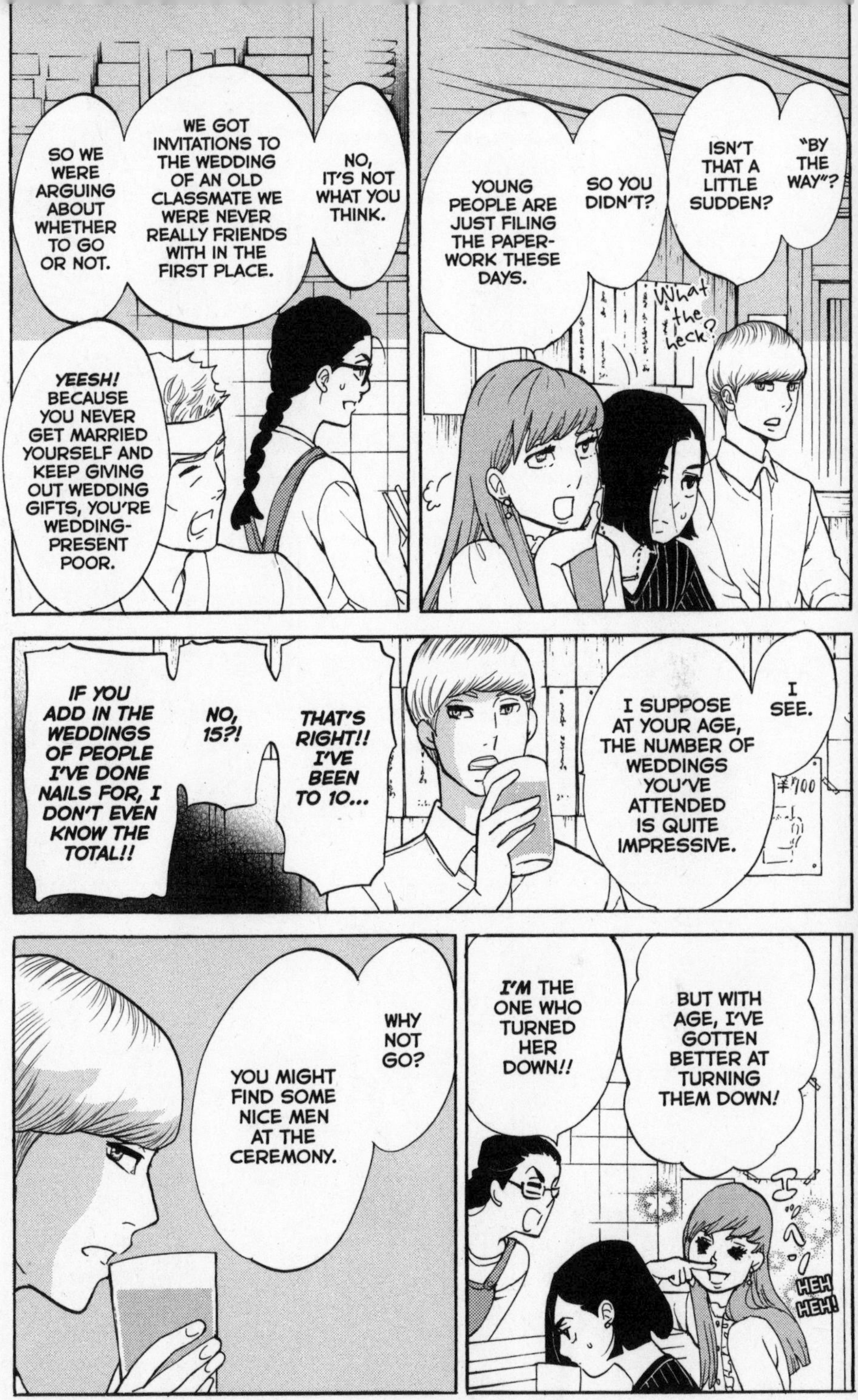
"BY THE WAY"?
ISN'T THAT A LITTLE SUDDEN?
SO YOU DIDN'T?
YOUNG PEOPLE ARE JUST FILING THE PAPERWORK THESE DAYS.
What the heck?
NO, IT'S NOT WHAT YOU THINK.
WE GOT INVITATIONS TO THE WEDDING OF AN OLD CLASSMATE WE WERE NEVER REALLY FRIENDS WITH IN THE FIRST PLACE.
SO WE WERE ARGUING ABOUT WHETHER TO GO OR NOT.
YEESH! BECAUSE YOU NEVER GET MARRIED YOURSELF AND KEEP GIVING OUT WEDDING GIFTS, YOU'RE WEDDING-PRESENT POOR.
I SEE.
I SUPPOSE AT YOUR AGE, THE NUMBER OF WEDDINGS YOU'VE ATTENDED IS QUITE IMPRESSIVE.
THAT'S RIGHT!! I'VE BEEN TO 10...
NO, 15?!
IF YOU ADD IN THE WEDDINGS OF PEOPLE I'VE DONE NAILS FOR, I DON'T EVEN KNOW THE TOTAL!!
BUT WITH AGE, I'VE GOTTEN BETTER AT TURNING THEM DOWN!
I'M THE ONE WHO TURNED HER DOWN!!
HEH HEH!
WHY NOT GO?
YOU MIGHT FIND SOME NICE MEN AT THE CEREMONY.

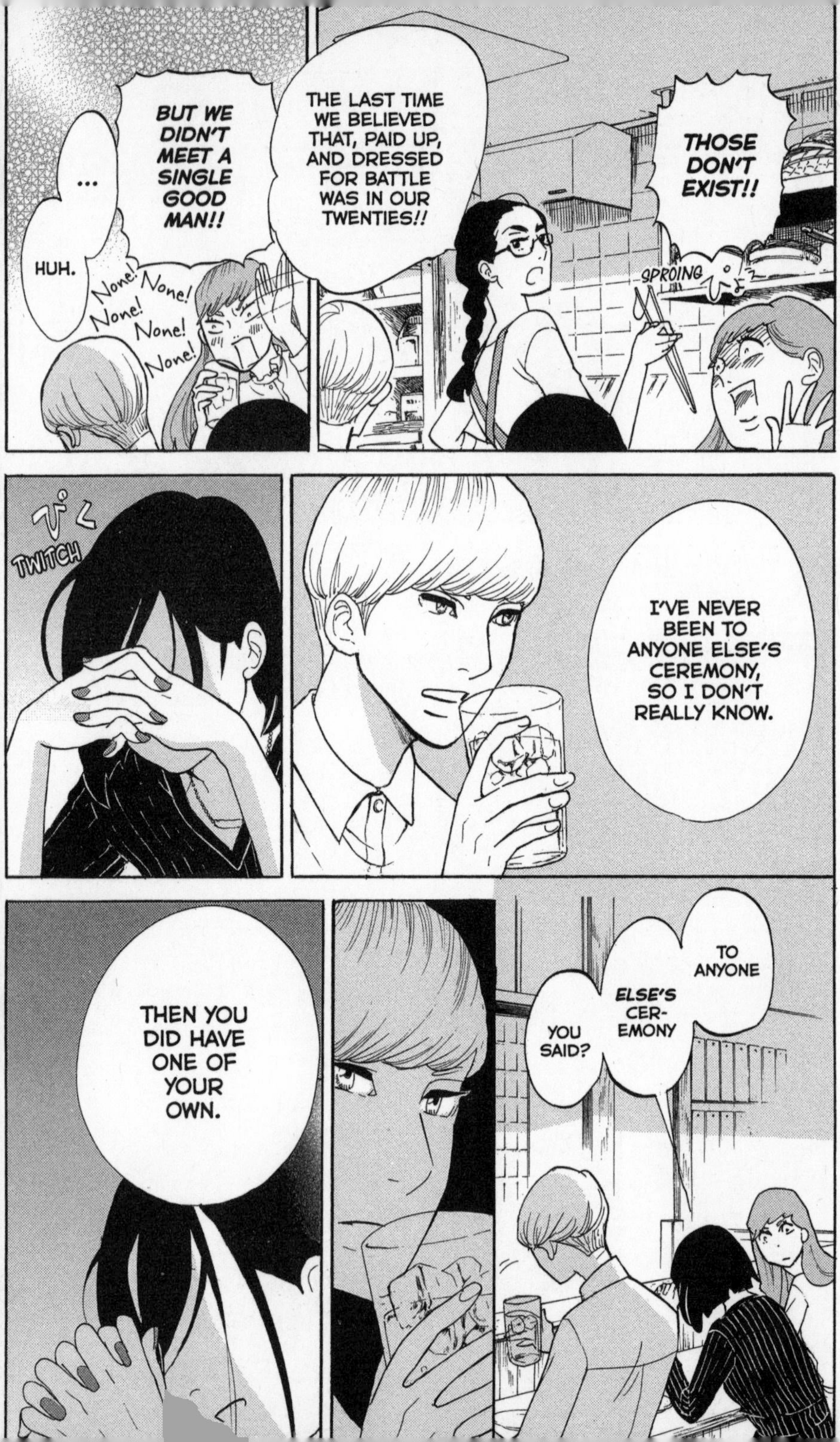
THOSE DON'T EXIST!!
THE LAST TIME WE BELIEVED THAT, PAID UP, AND DRESSED FOR BATTLE WAS IN OUR TWENTIES!!
SPROING
BUT WE DIDN'T MEET A SINGLE GOOD MAN!!
None! None! None! None! None!
...
HUH.
I'VE NEVER BEEN TO ANYONE ELSE'S CEREMONY, SO I DON'T REALLY KNOW.
ぴく
TWITCH
TO ANYONE ELSE'S CEREMONY YOU SAID?
THEN YOU DID HAVE ONE OF YOUR OWN.

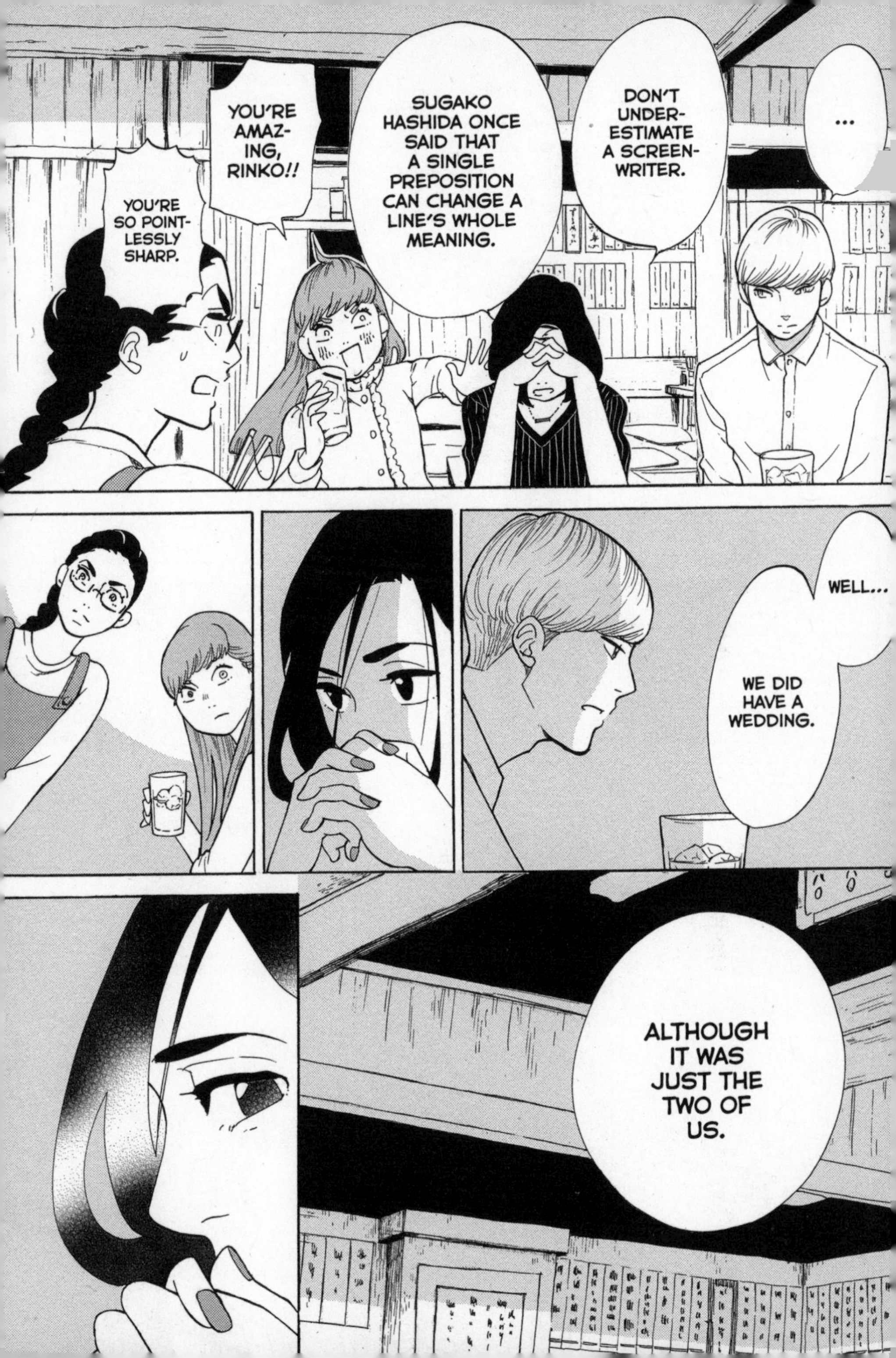
...
DON'T UNDER-ESTIMATE A SCREEN-WRITER.
SUGAKO HASHIDA ONCE SAID THAT A SINGLE PREPOSITION CAN CHANGE A LINE'S WHOLE MEANING.
YOU'RE AMAZ-ING, RINKO!!
YOU'RE SO POINT-LESSLY SHARP.
WELL...
WE DID HAVE A WEDDING.
ALTHOUGH IT WAS JUST THE TWO OF US.

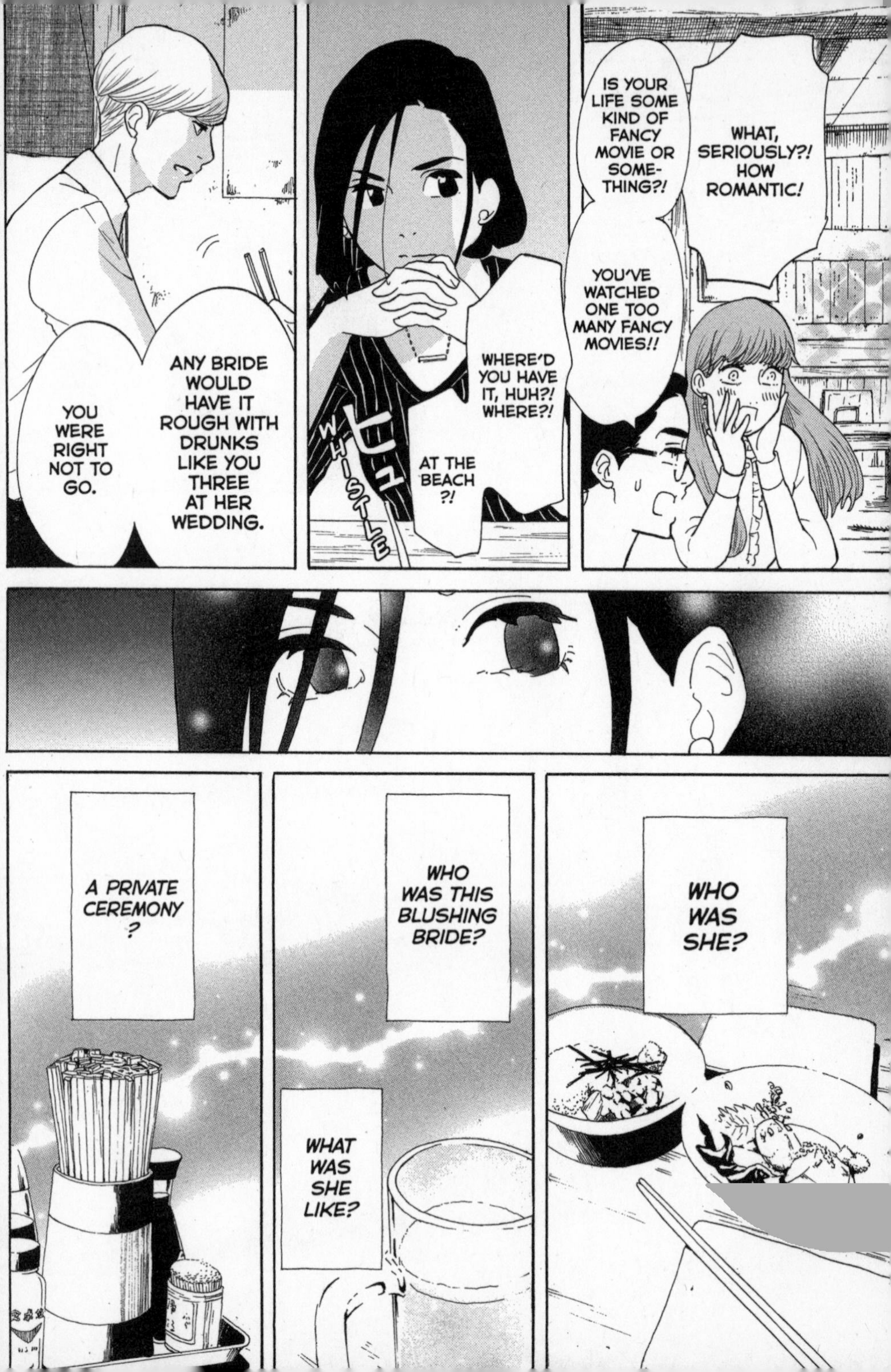
WHAT, SERIOUSLY?! HOW ROMANTIC!
IS YOUR LIFE SOME KIND OF FANCY MOVIE OR SOME-THING?!
YOU'VE WATCHED ONE TOO MANY FANCY MOVIES!!
WHERE'D YOU HAVE IT, HUH?! WHERE?!
AT THE BEACH ?!
ヒュ
WHISTLE
ANY BRIDE WOULD HAVE IT ROUGH WITH DRUNKS LIKE YOU THREE AT HER WEDDING.
YOU WERE RIGHT NOT TO GO.
WHO WAS SHE?
WHO WAS THIS BLUSHING BRIDE?
WHAT WAS SHE LIKE?
A PRIVATE CEREMONY ?

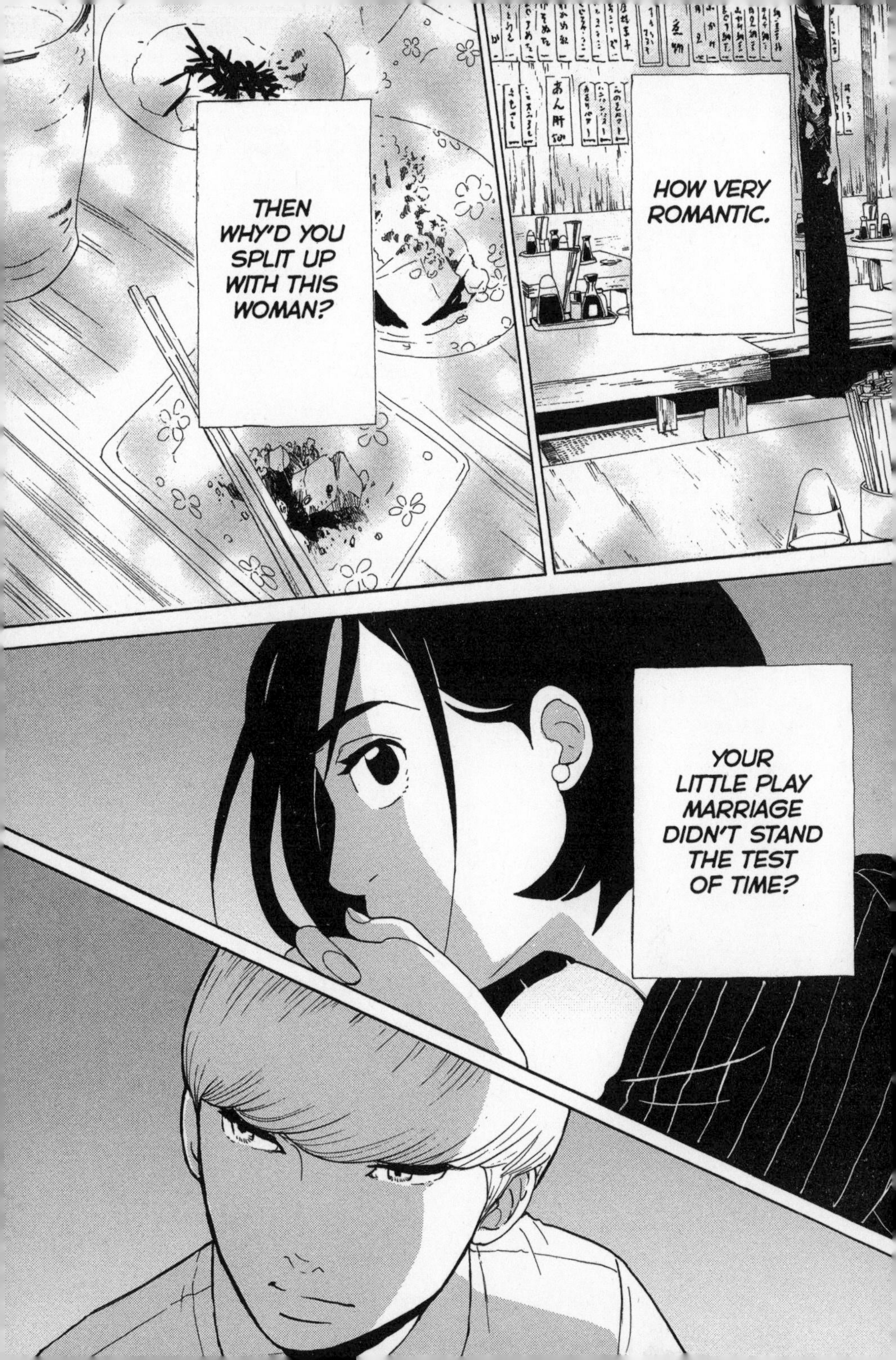
HOW VERY ROMANTIC.
THEN WHY'D YOU SPLIT UP WITH THIS WOMAN?
YOUR LITTLE PLAY MARRIAGE DIDN'T STAND THE TEST OF TIME?

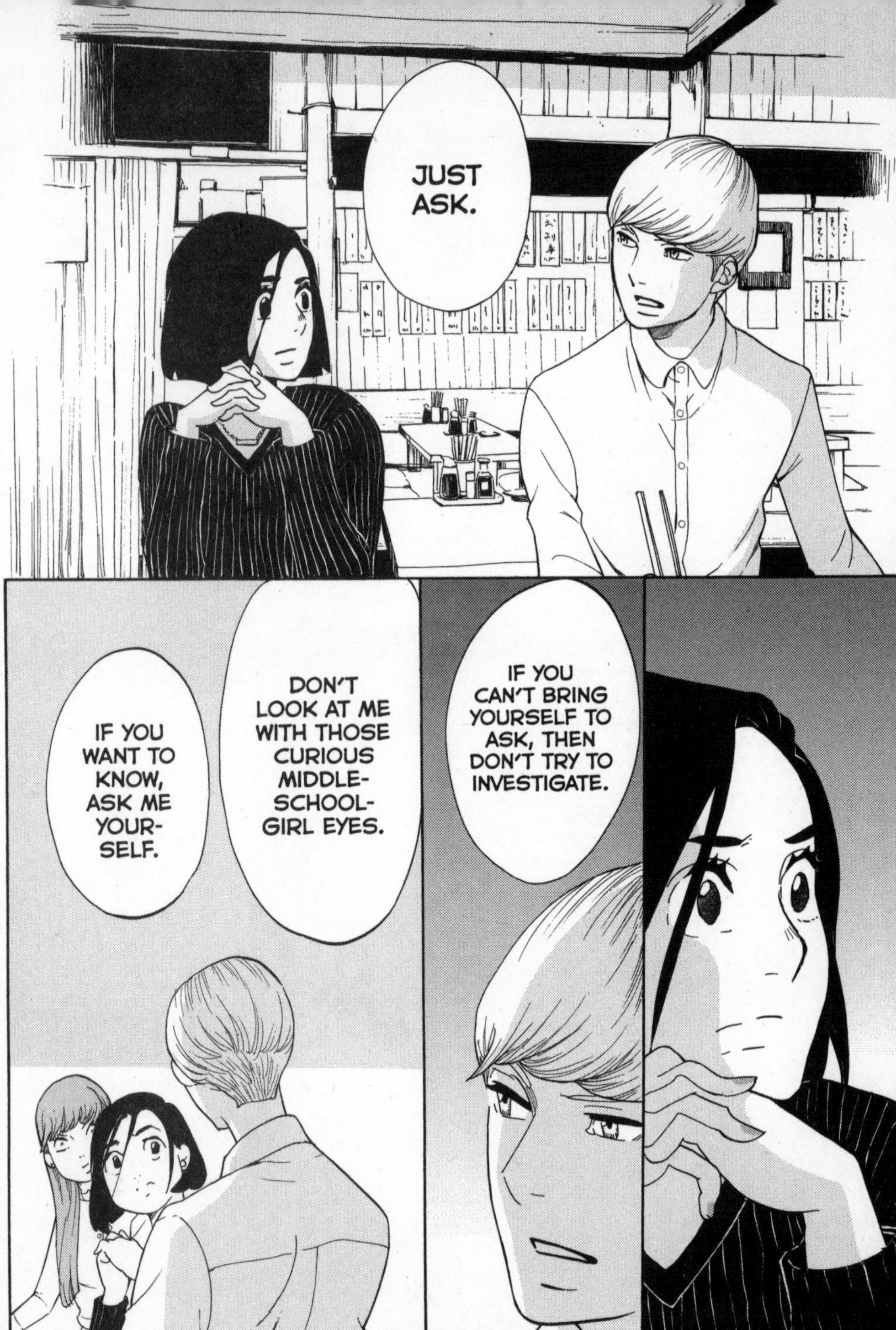
JUST ASK.
IF YOU CAN'T BRING YOURSELF TO ASK, THEN DON'T TRY TO INVESTIGATE.
DON'T LOOK AT ME WITH THOSE CURIOUS MIDDLE-SCHOOL-GIRL EYES.
IF YOU WANT TO KNOW, ASK ME YOUR-SELF.

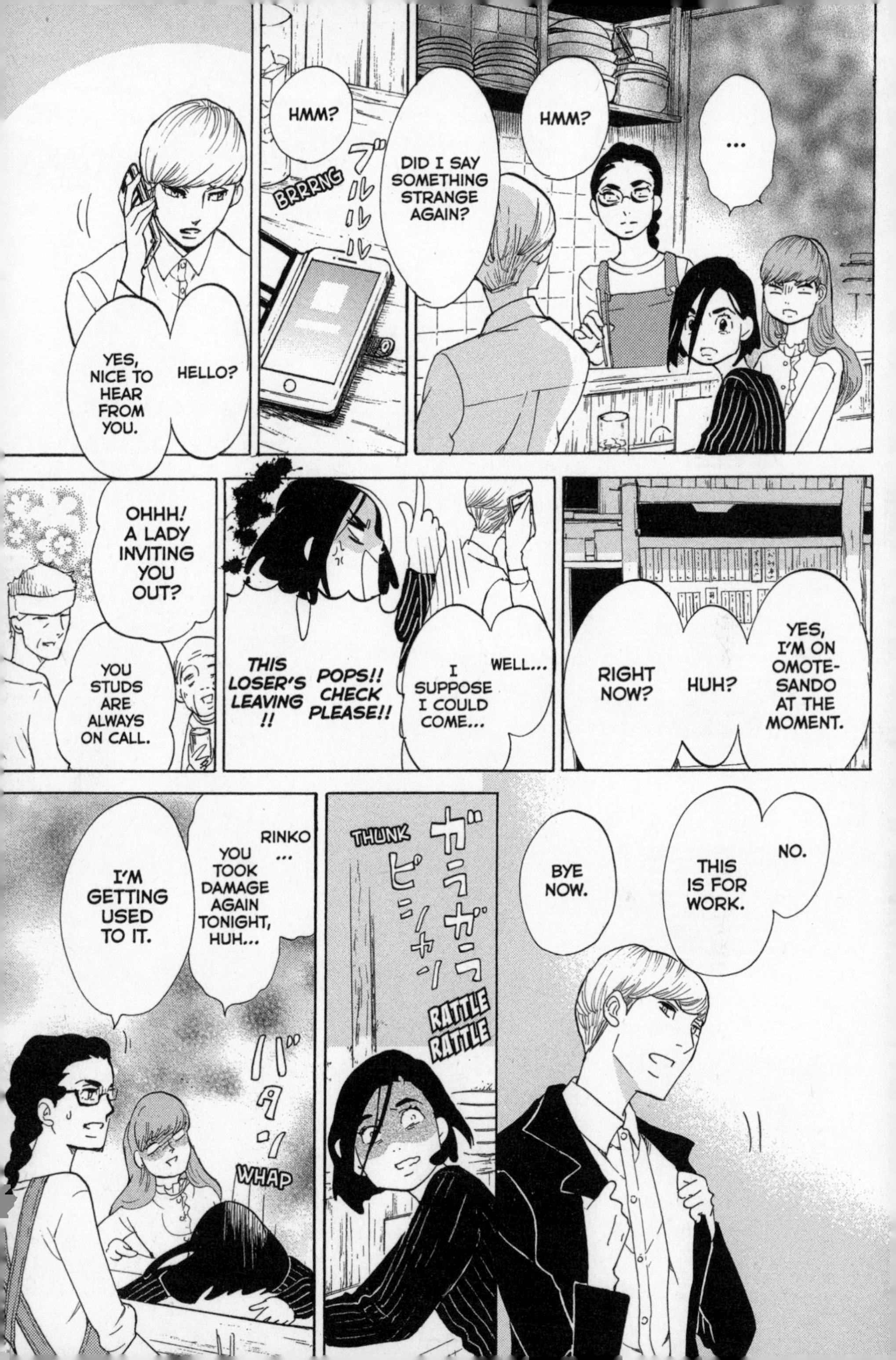
...
HMM?
DID I SAY SOMETHING STRANGE AGAIN?
HMM?
BRRRNG
HELLO?
YES, NICE TO HEAR FROM YOU.
YES, I'M ON OMOTE-SANDO AT THE MOMENT.
HUH?
RIGHT NOW?
WELL...
I SUPPOSE I COULD COME...
POPS!! CHECK PLEASE!!
THIS LOSER'S LEAVING!!
OHHH! A LADY INVITING YOU OUT?
YOU STUDS ARE ALWAYS ON CALL.
NO.
THIS IS FOR WORK.
BYE NOW.
THUNK
RATTLE RATTLE
RINKO...
YOU TOOK DAMAGE AGAIN TONIGHT, HUH...
I'M GETTING USED TO IT.
WHAP

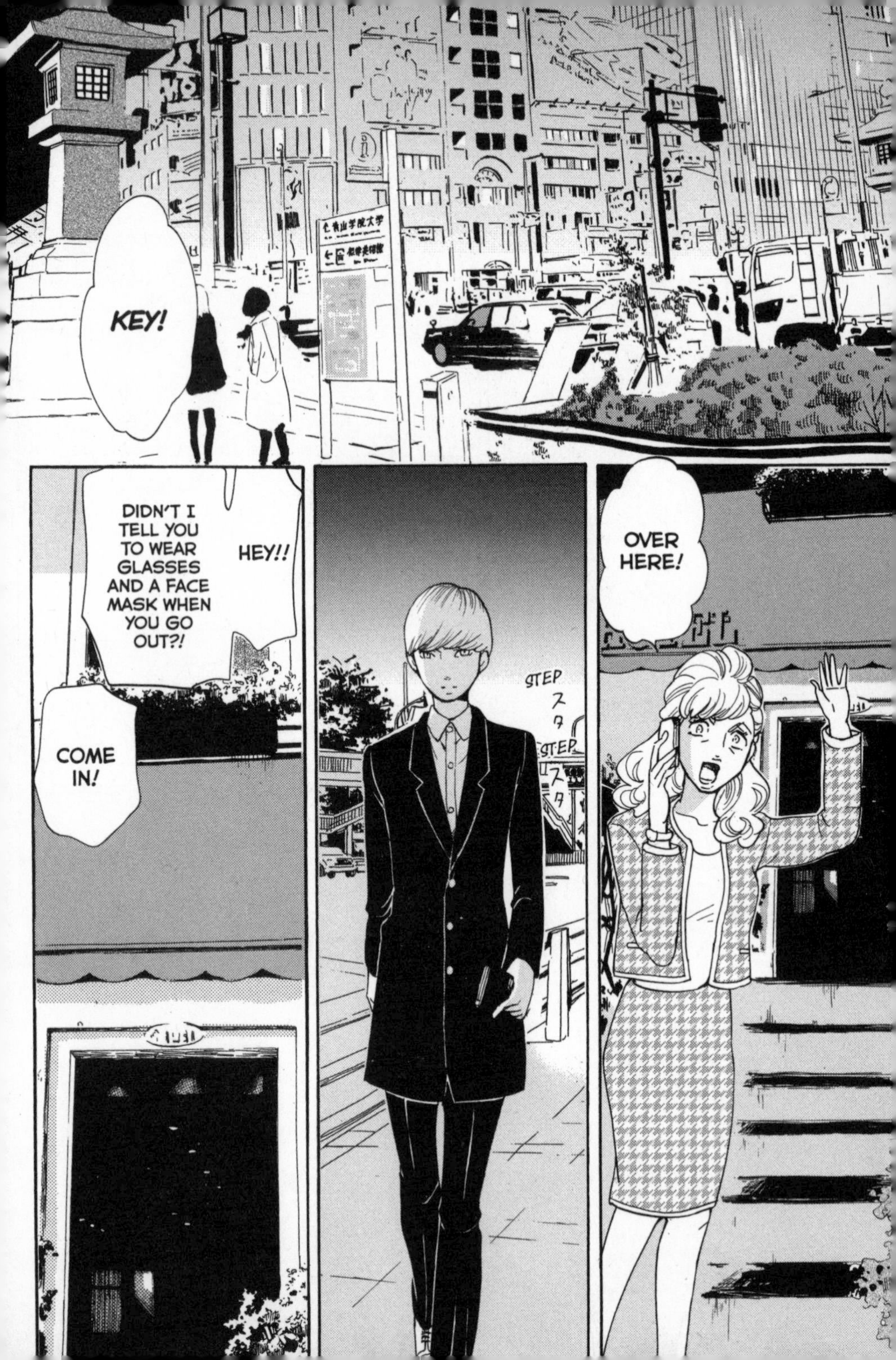
KEY!
OVER HERE!
STEP
スタ
STEP
スタ
HEY!!
DIDN'T I TELL YOU TO WEAR GLASSES AND A FACE MASK WHEN YOU GO OUT?!
COME IN!

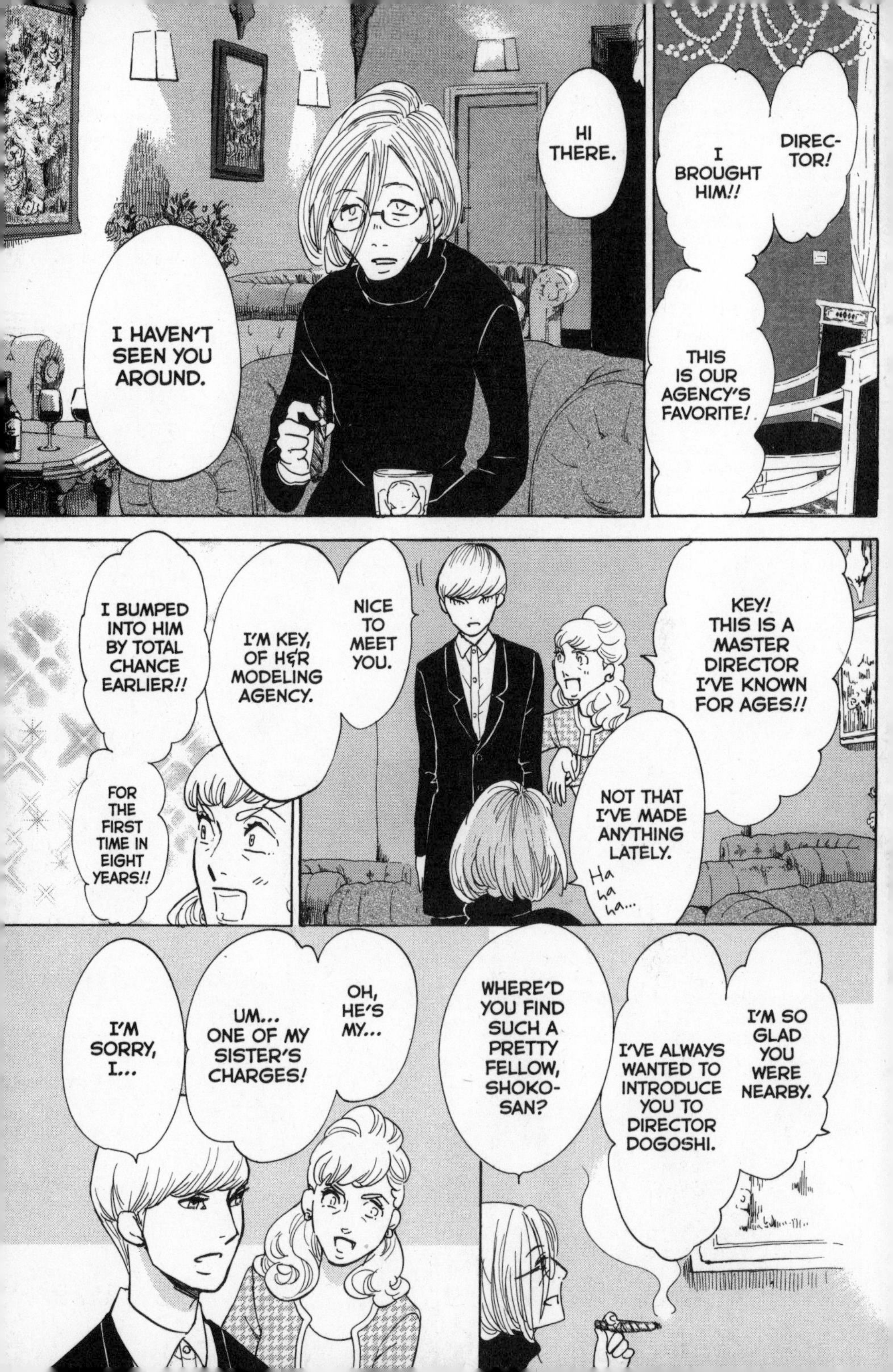
DIRECTOR!
I BROUGHT HIM!!
THIS IS OUR AGENCY'S FAVORITE!
HI THERE.
I HAVEN'T SEEN YOU AROUND.
KEY! THIS IS A MASTER DIRECTOR I'VE KNOWN FOR AGES!!
NOT THAT I'VE MADE ANYTHING LATELY.
Ha ha ha...
NICE TO MEET YOU.
I'M KEY, OF H&R MODELING AGENCY.
I BUMPED INTO HIM BY TOTAL CHANCE EARLIER!!
FOR THE FIRST TIME IN EIGHT YEARS!!
I'M SO GLAD YOU WERE NEARBY.
I'VE ALWAYS WANTED TO INTRODUCE YOU TO DIRECTOR DOGOSHI.
WHERE'D YOU FIND SUCH A PRETTY FELLOW, SHOKO-SAN?
OH, HE'S MY...
UM... ONE OF MY SISTER'S CHARGES!
I'M SORRY, I...

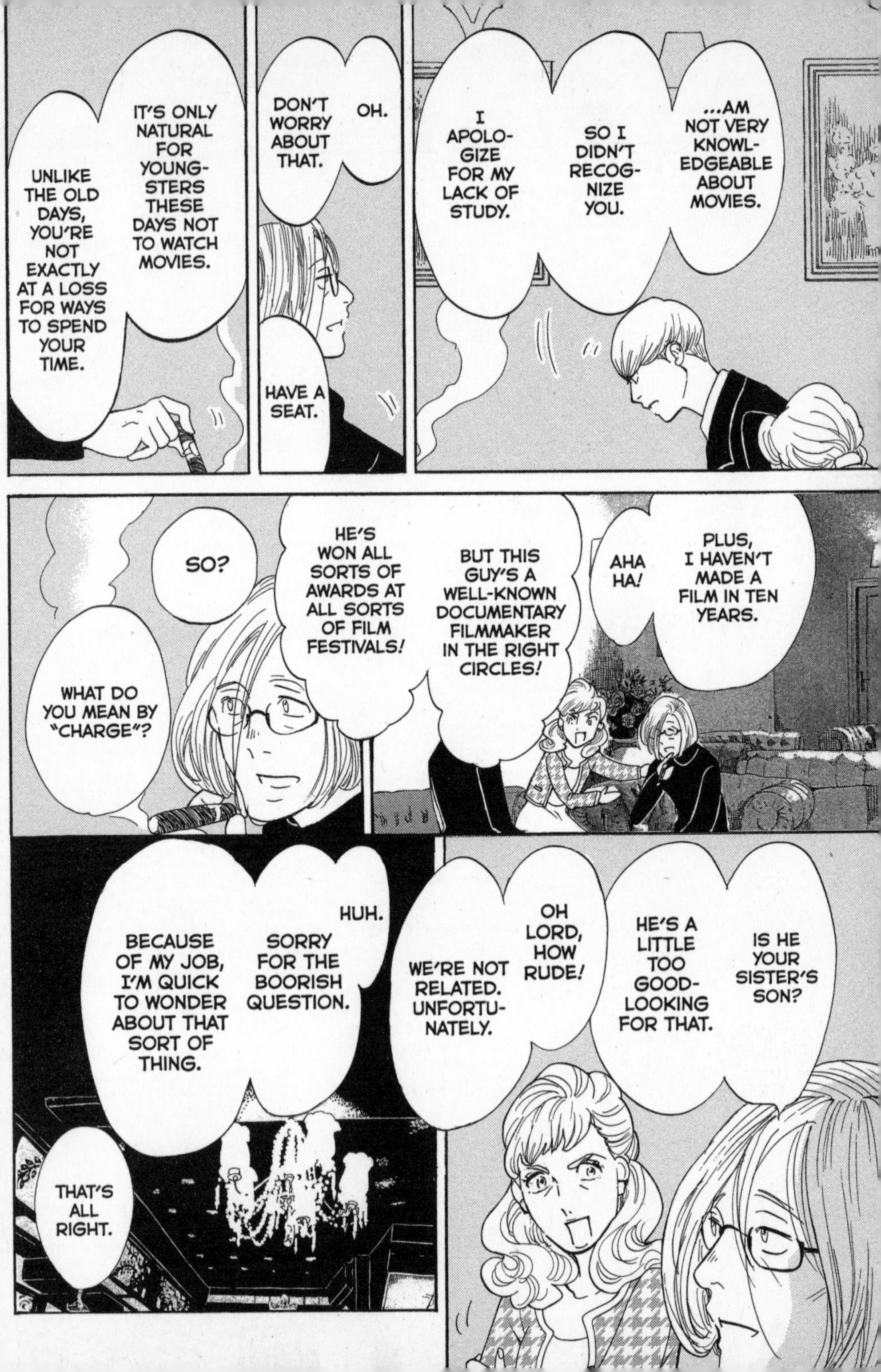
...AM NOT VERY KNOWLEDGEABLE ABOUT MOVIES.
SO I DIDN'T RECOGNIZE YOU.
I APOLOGIZE FOR MY LACK OF STUDY.
OH.
DON'T WORRY ABOUT THAT.
HAVE A SEAT.
IT'S ONLY NATURAL FOR YOUNGSTERS THESE DAYS NOT TO WATCH MOVIES.
UNLIKE THE OLD DAYS, YOU'RE NOT EXACTLY AT A LOSS FOR WAYS TO SPEND YOUR TIME.
PLUS, I HAVEN'T MADE A FILM IN TEN YEARS.
AHA HA!
BUT THIS GUY'S A WELL-KNOWN DOCUMENTARY FILMMAKER IN THE RIGHT CIRCLES!
HE'S WON ALL SORTS OF AWARDS AT ALL SORTS OF FILM FESTIVALS!
SO?
WHAT DO YOU MEAN BY "CHARGE"?
IS HE YOUR SISTER'S SON?
HE'S A LITTLE TOO GOOD-LOOKING FOR THAT.
OH LORD, HOW RUDE!
WE'RE NOT RELATED. UNFORTUNATELY.
HUH.
SORRY FOR THE BOORISH QUESTION.
BECAUSE OF MY JOB, I'M QUICK TO WONDER ABOUT THAT SORT OF THING.
THAT'S ALL RIGHT.

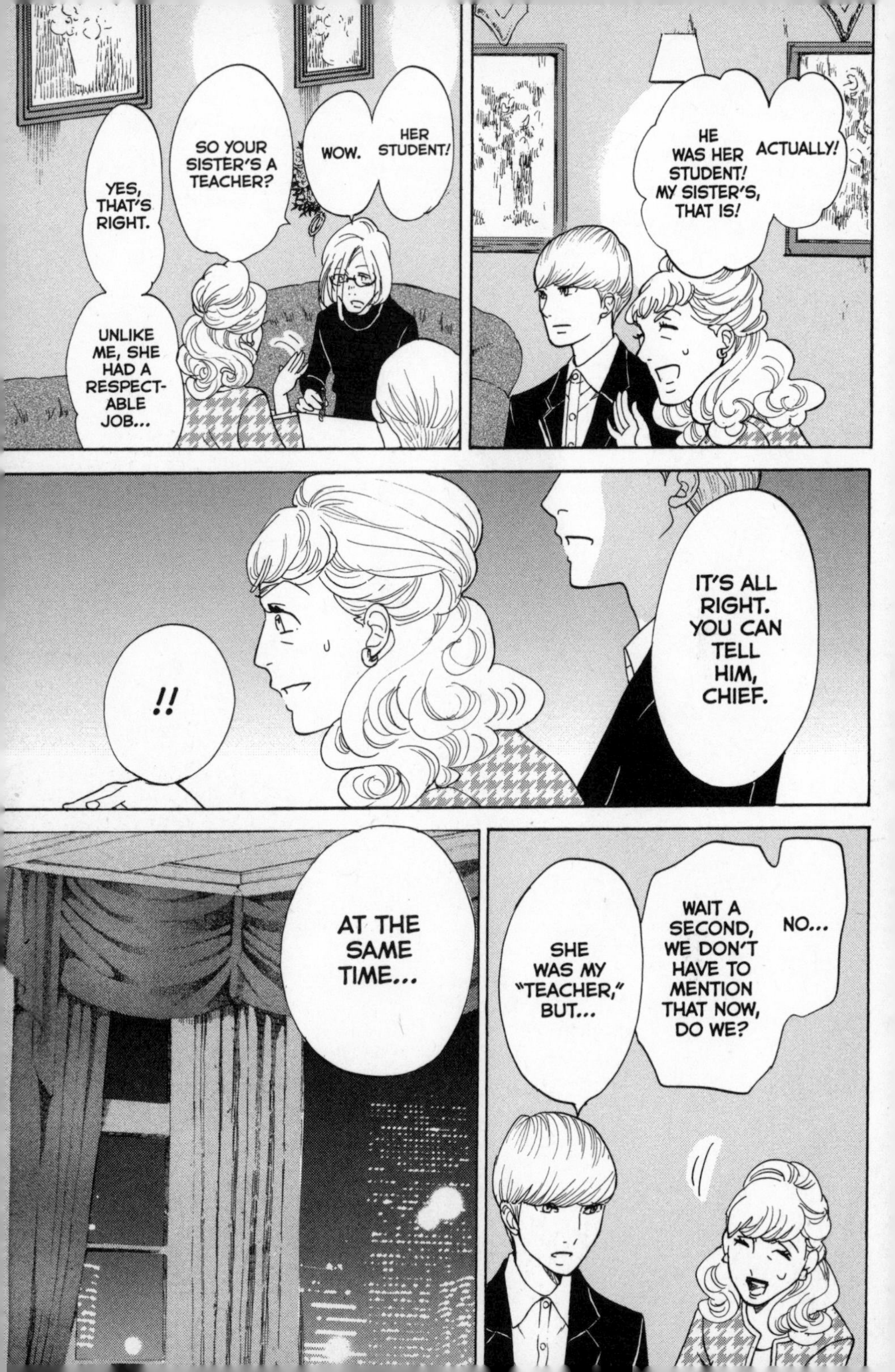
ACTUALLY! HE WAS HER STUDENT! MY SISTER'S, THAT IS!
WOW. HER STUDENT!
SO YOUR SISTER'S A TEACHER?
YES, THAT'S RIGHT.
UNLIKE ME, SHE HAD A RESPECTABLE JOB...
IT'S ALL RIGHT. YOU CAN TELL HIM, CHIEF.
!!
NO... WAIT A SECOND, WE DON'T HAVE TO MENTION THAT NOW, DO WE?
SHE WAS MY "TEACHER," BUT...
AT THE SAME TIME...

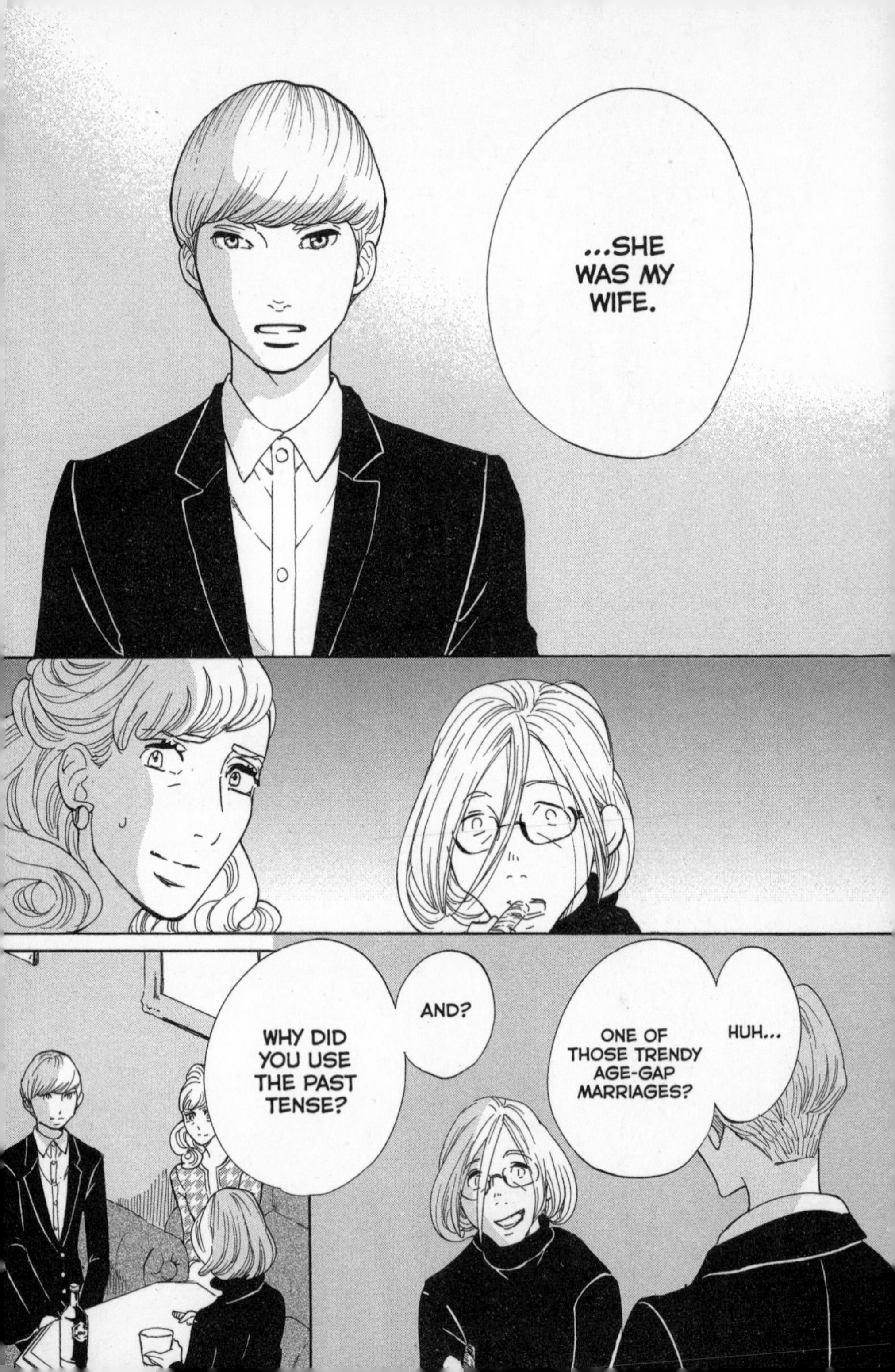
...SHE WAS MY WIFE.
HUH...
ONE OF THOSE TRENDY AGE-GAP MARRIAGES?
AND?
WHY DID YOU USE THE PAST TENSE?

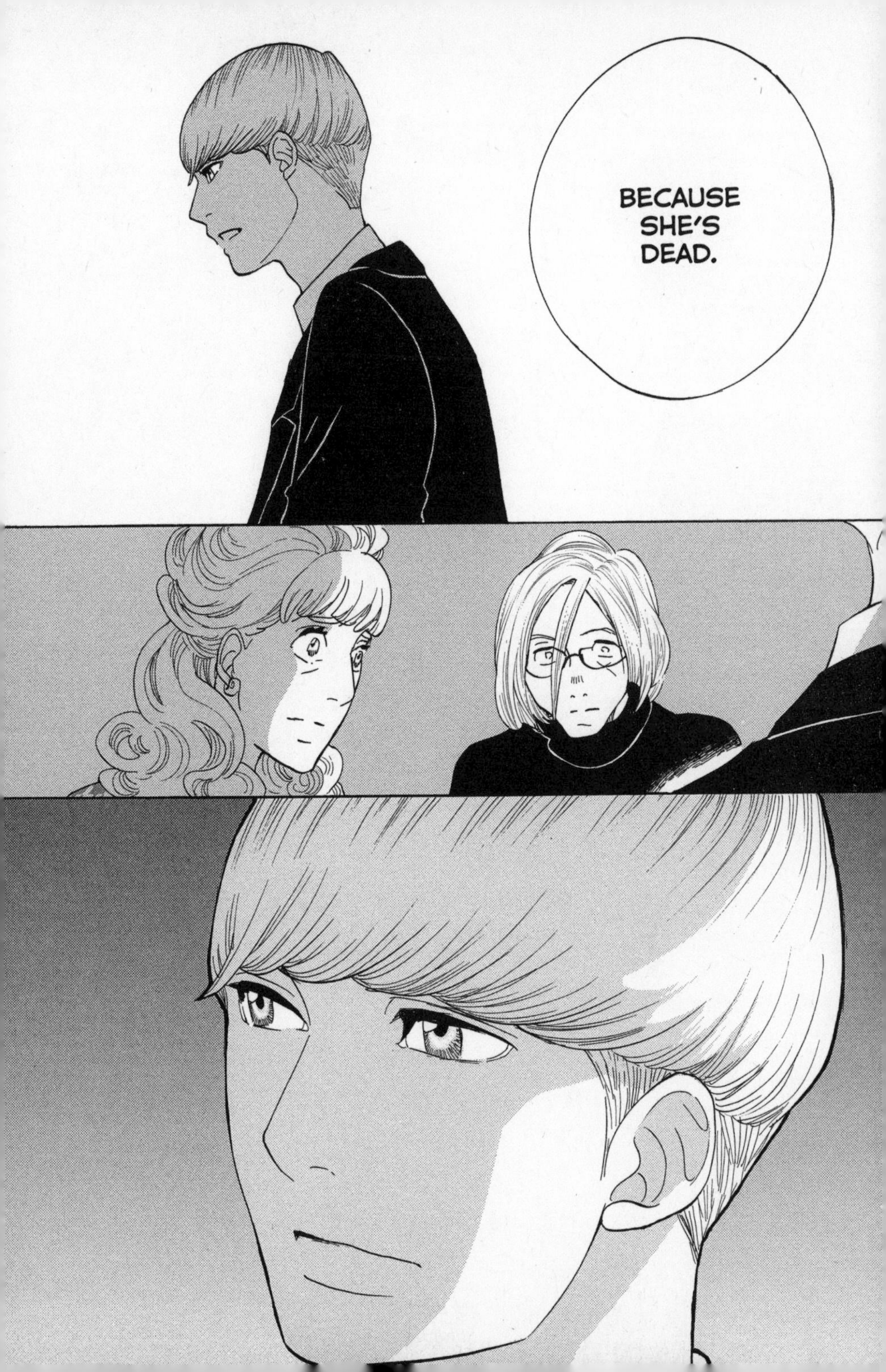
BECAUSE SHE'S DEAD.

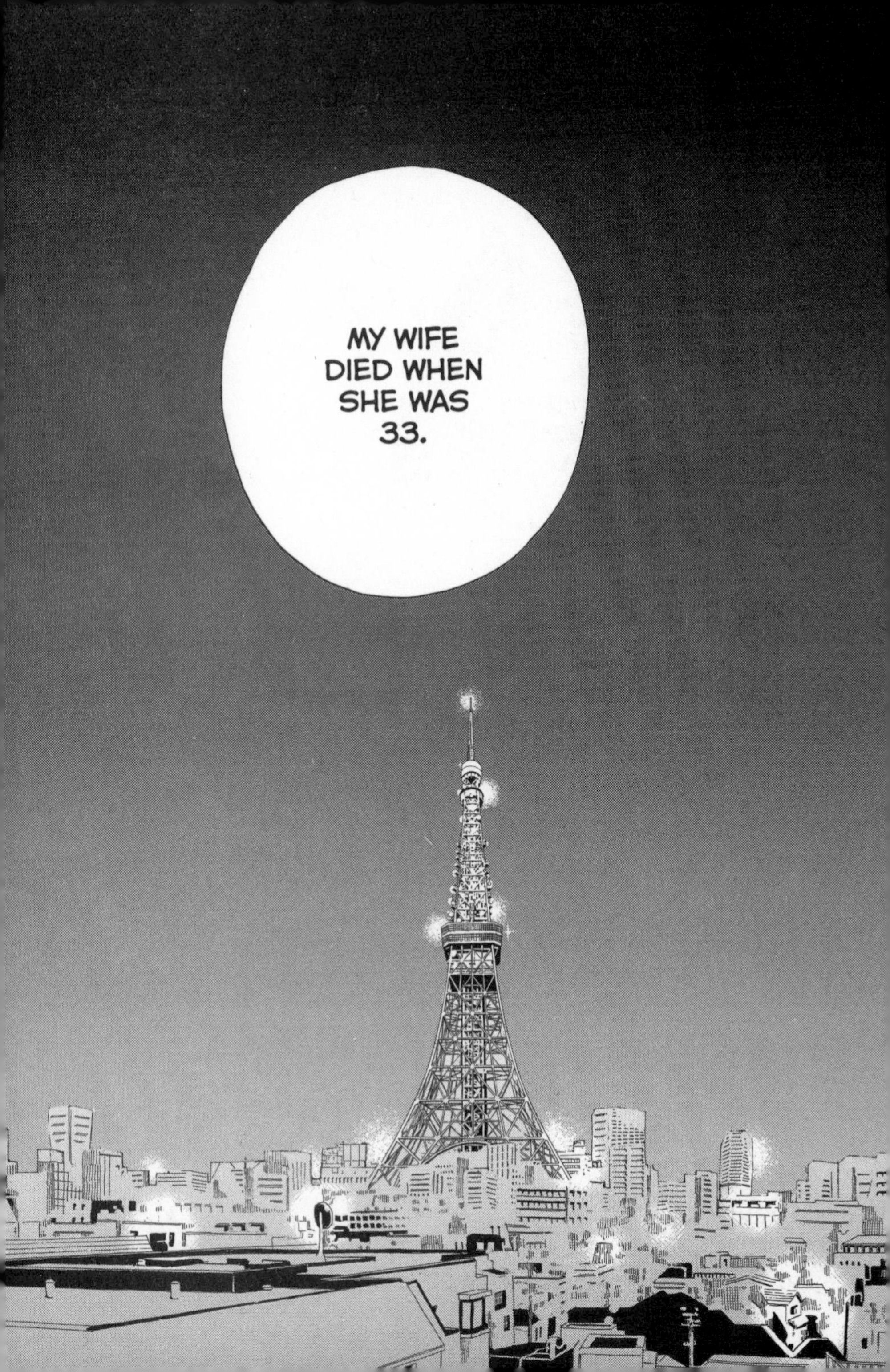
MY WIFE DIED WHEN SHE WAS 33.

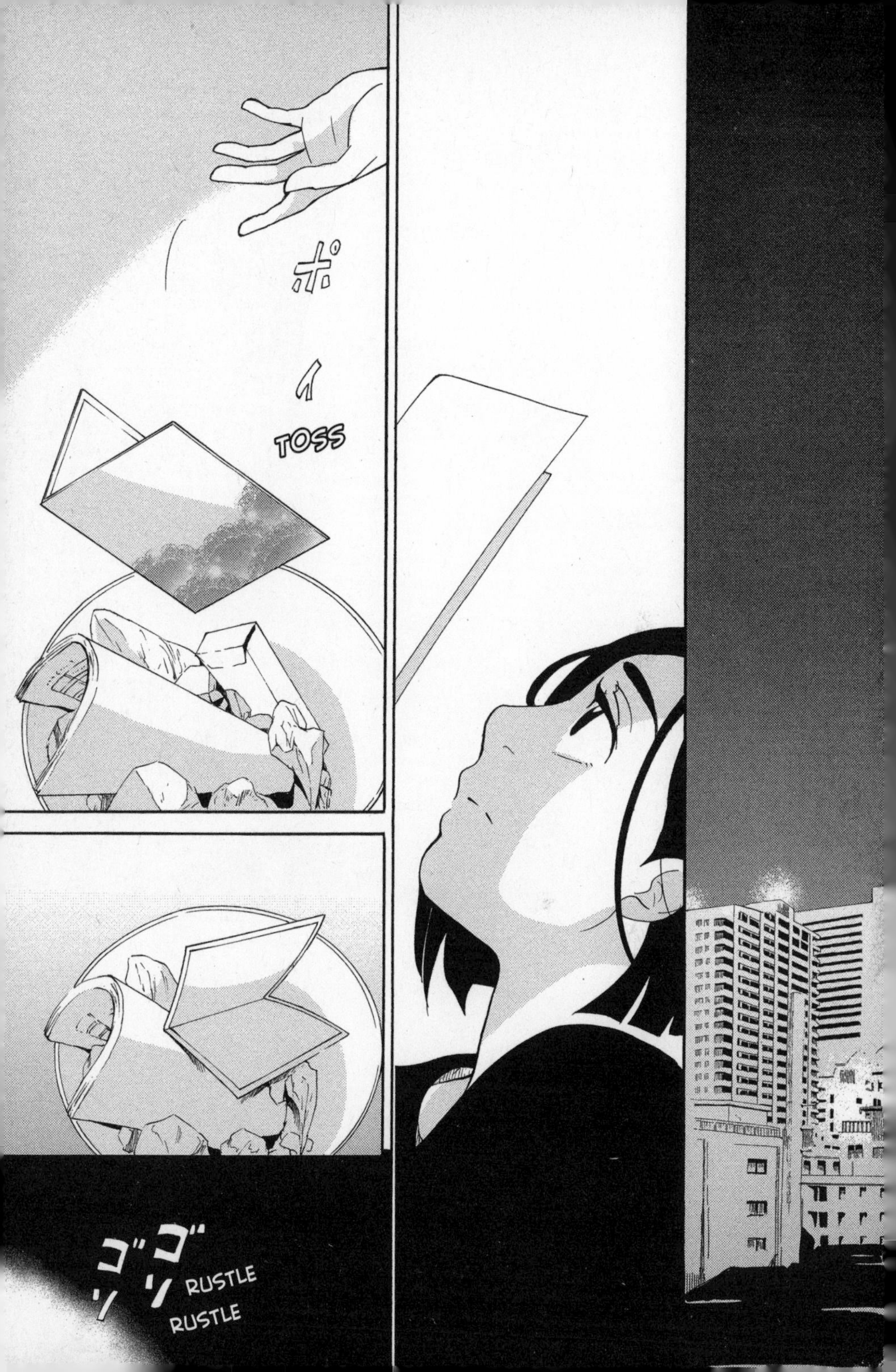
ポイ
TOSS
ゴソゴソ
RUSTLE
RUSTLE

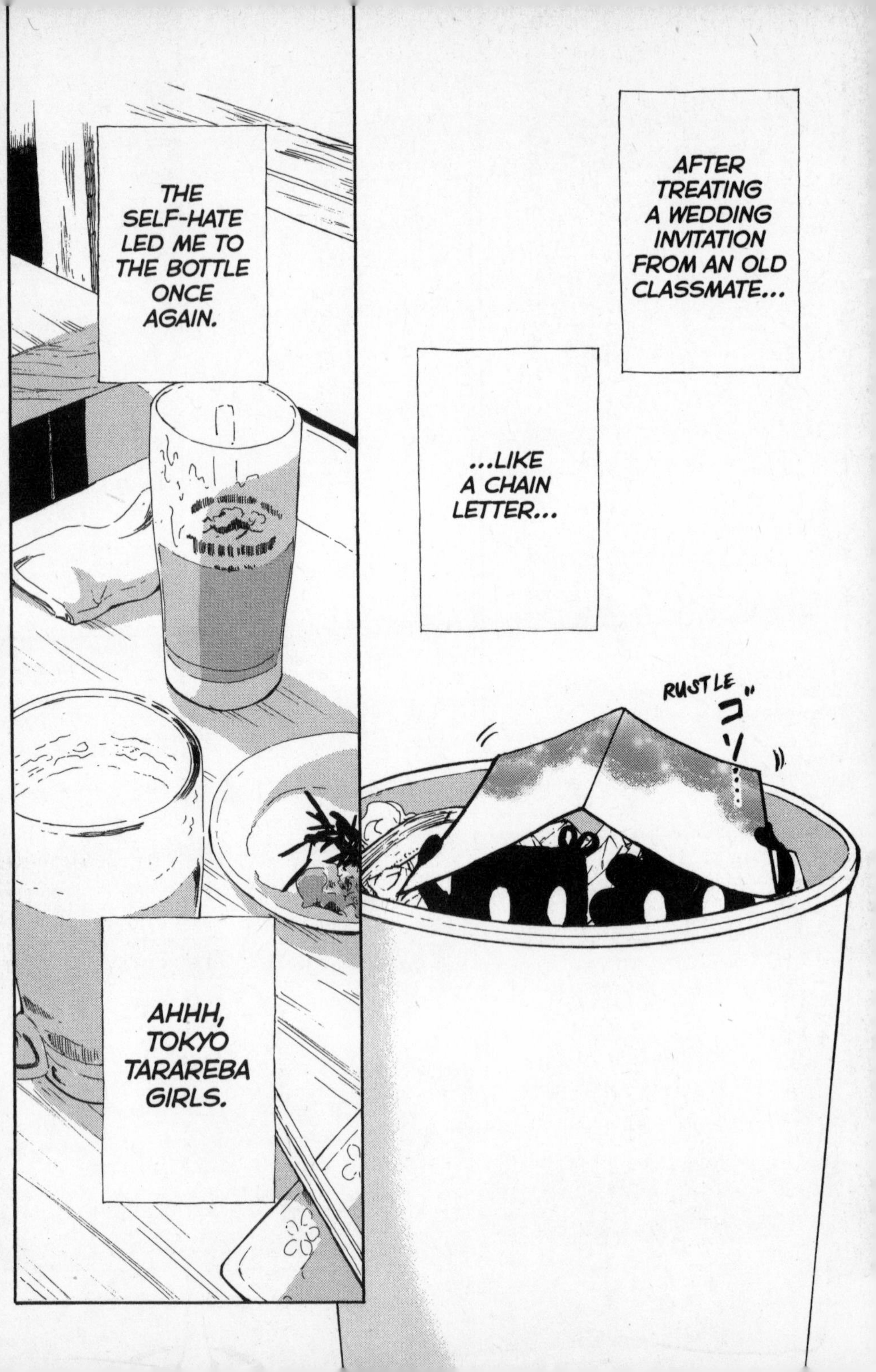
AFTER TREATING A WEDDING INVITATION FROM AN OLD CLASSMATE...
...LIKE A CHAIN LETTER...
RUSTLE
ゴソ
THE SELF-HATE LED ME TO THE BOTTLE ONCE AGAIN.
AHHH, TOKYO TARAREBA GIRLS.

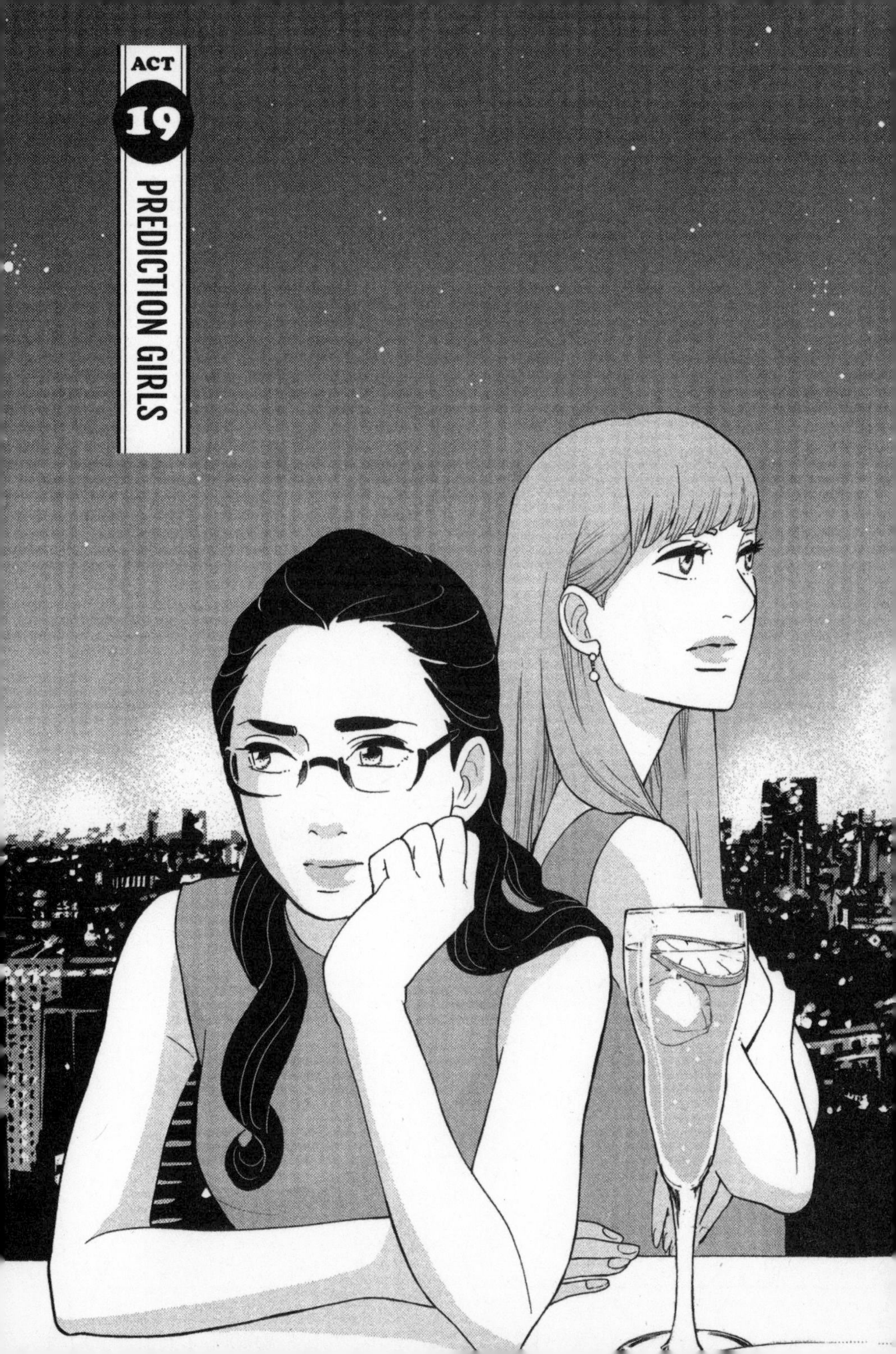
ACT
19
PREDICTION GIRLS

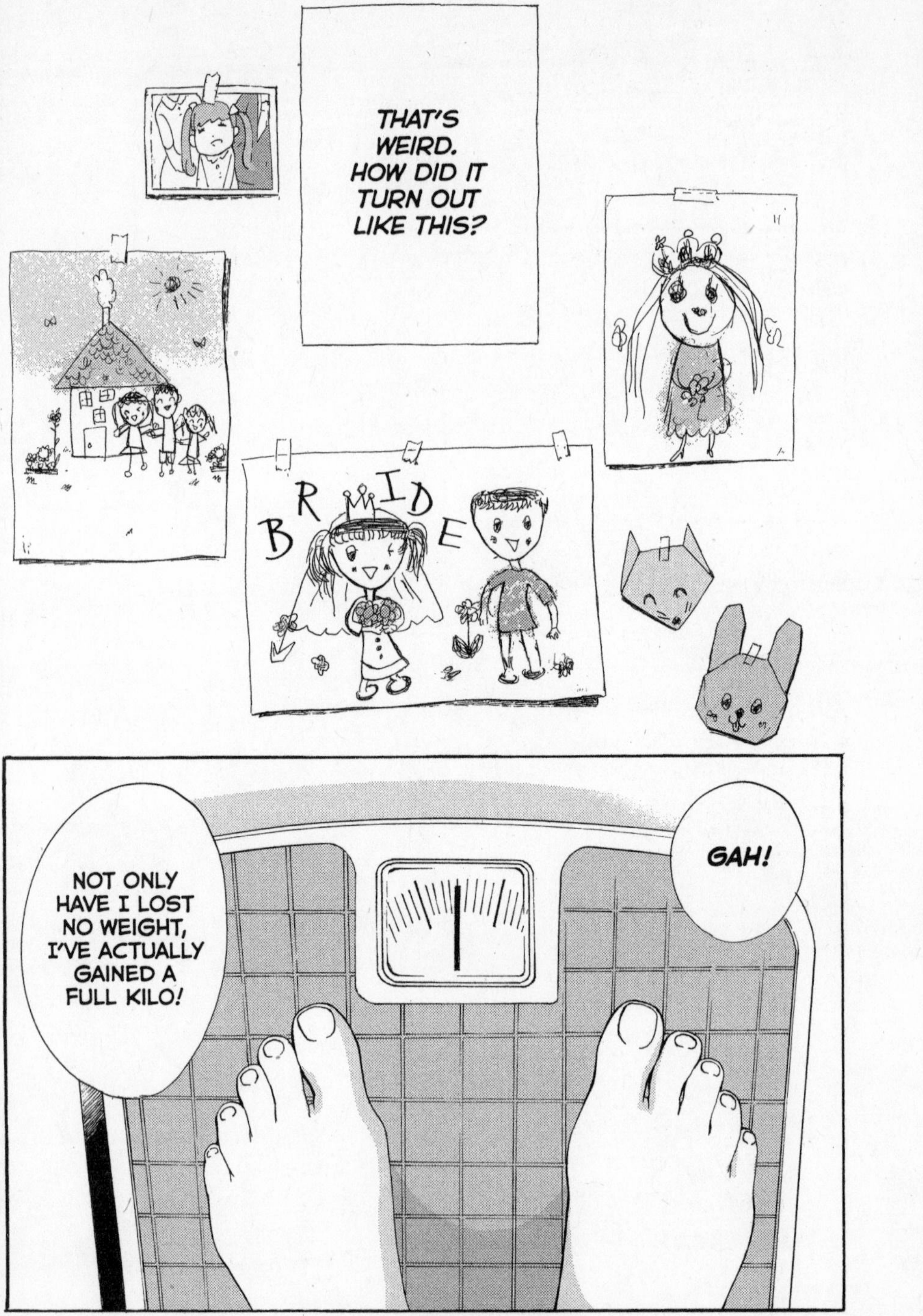
THAT'S WEIRD. HOW DID IT TURN OUT LIKE THIS?
BRIDE
GAH!
NOT ONLY HAVE I LOST NO WEIGHT, I'VE ACTUALLY GAINED A FULL KILO!

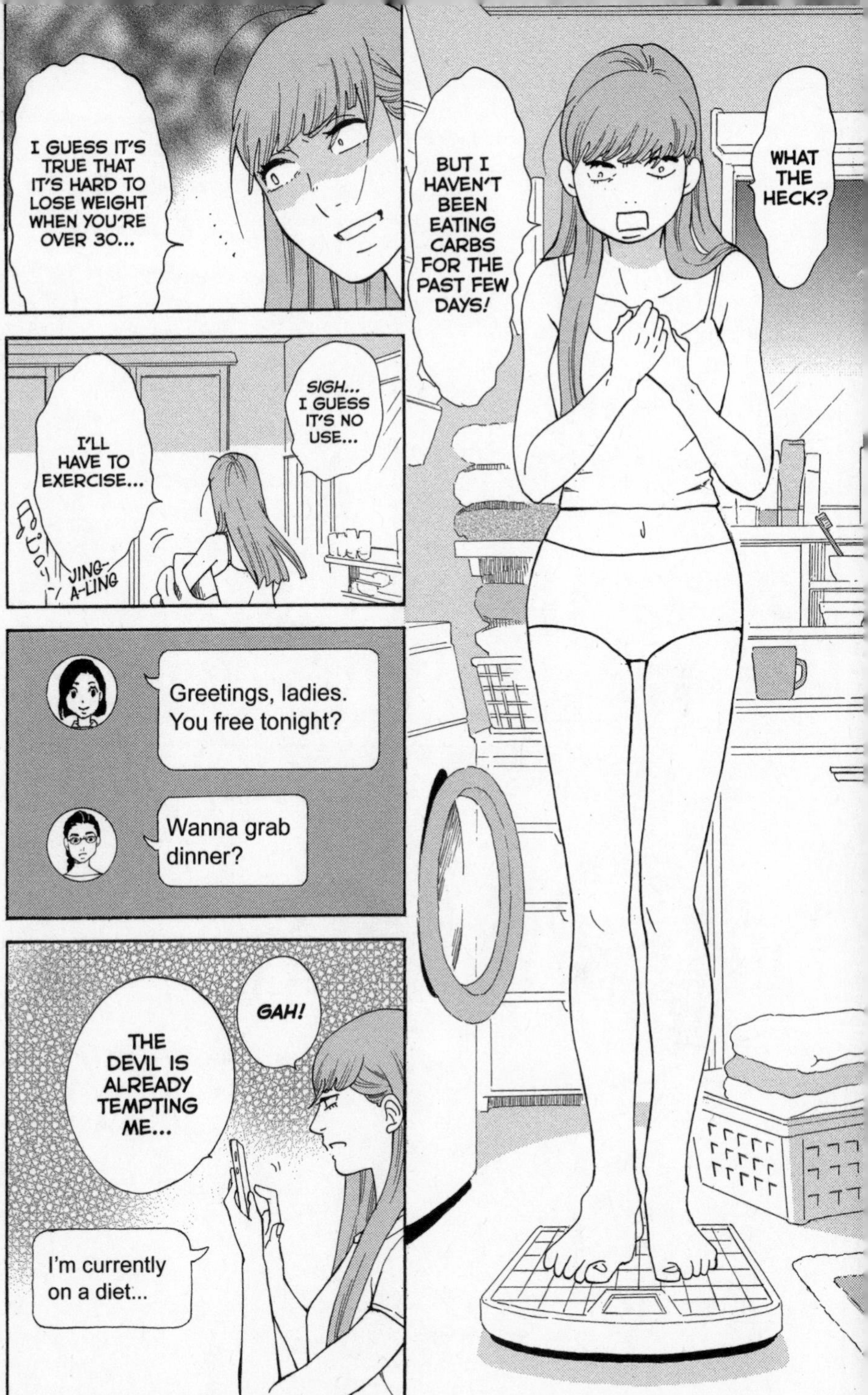
WHAT THE HECK?
BUT I HAVEN'T BEEN EATING CARBS FOR THE PAST FEW DAYS!
I GUESS IT'S TRUE THAT IT'S HARD TO LOSE WEIGHT WHEN YOU'RE OVER 30...
SIGH... I GUESS IT'S NO USE...
I'LL HAVE TO EXERCISE...
JING-A-LING
Greetings, ladies. You free tonight?
Wanna grab dinner?
GAH!
THE DEVIL IS ALREADY TEMPTING ME...
I'm currently on a diet...

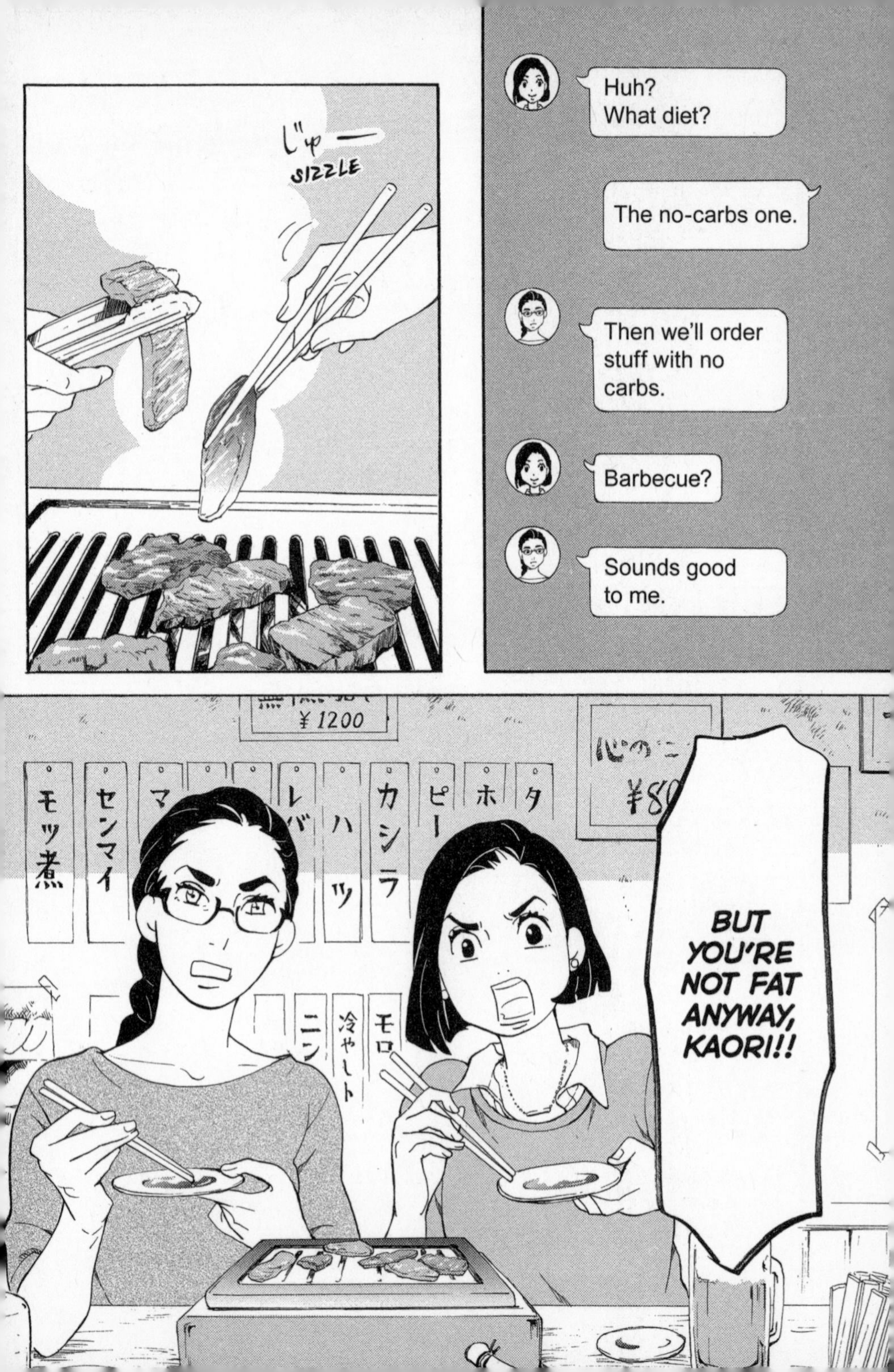
Huh?
What diet?
The no-carbs one.
Then we'll order stuff with no carbs.
Barbecue?
Sounds good to me.
じゅー
SIZZLE
¥1200
タ
ホ
ピー
カシラ
ハツ
レバ
センマイ
モツ煮
モロ
冷やしト
BUT YOU'RE NOT FAT ANYWAY, KAORI!!

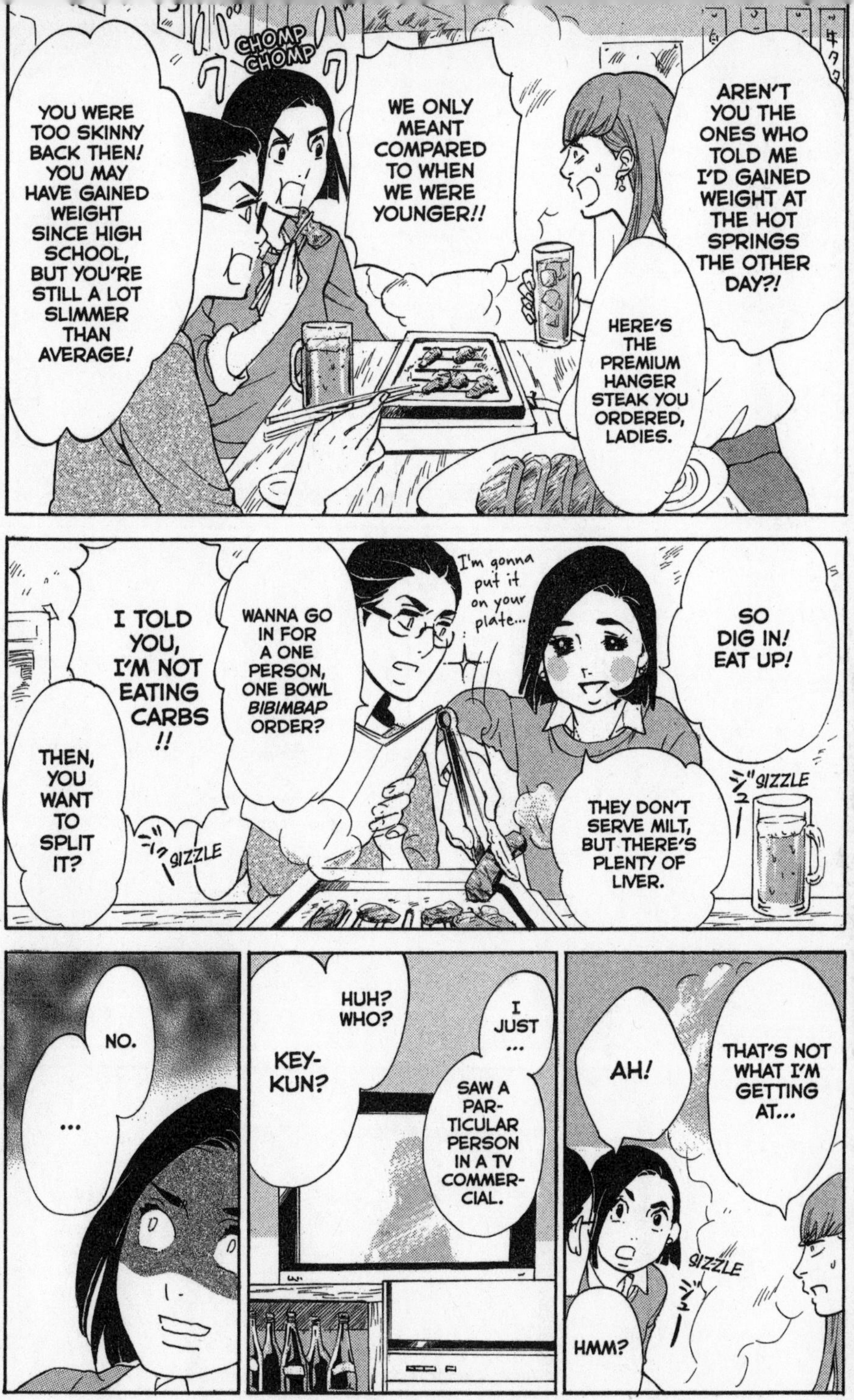
AREN'T YOU THE ONES WHO TOLD ME I'D GAINED WEIGHT AT THE HOT SPRINGS THE OTHER DAY?!
HERE'S THE PREMIUM HANGER STEAK YOU ORDERED, LADIES.
WE ONLY MEANT COMPARED TO WHEN WE WERE YOUNGER!!
CHOMP CHOMP
YOU WERE TOO SKINNY BACK THEN! YOU MAY HAVE GAINED WEIGHT SINCE HIGH SCHOOL, BUT YOU'RE STILL A LOT SLIMMER THAN AVERAGE!
SO DIG IN! EAT UP!
THEY DON'T SERVE MILT, BUT THERE'S PLENTY OF LIVER.
SIZZLE
I'm gonna put it on your plate...
WANNA GO IN FOR A ONE PERSON, ONE BOWL *BIBIMBAP* ORDER?
I TOLD YOU, I'M NOT EATING CARBS!!
THEN, YOU WANT TO SPLIT IT?
SIZZLE
THAT'S NOT WHAT I'M GETTING AT...
AH!
SIZZLE
HMM?
I JUST ...
SAW A PAR-TICULAR PERSON IN A TV COMMER-CIAL.
HUH? WHO?
KEY-KUN?
NO.
...

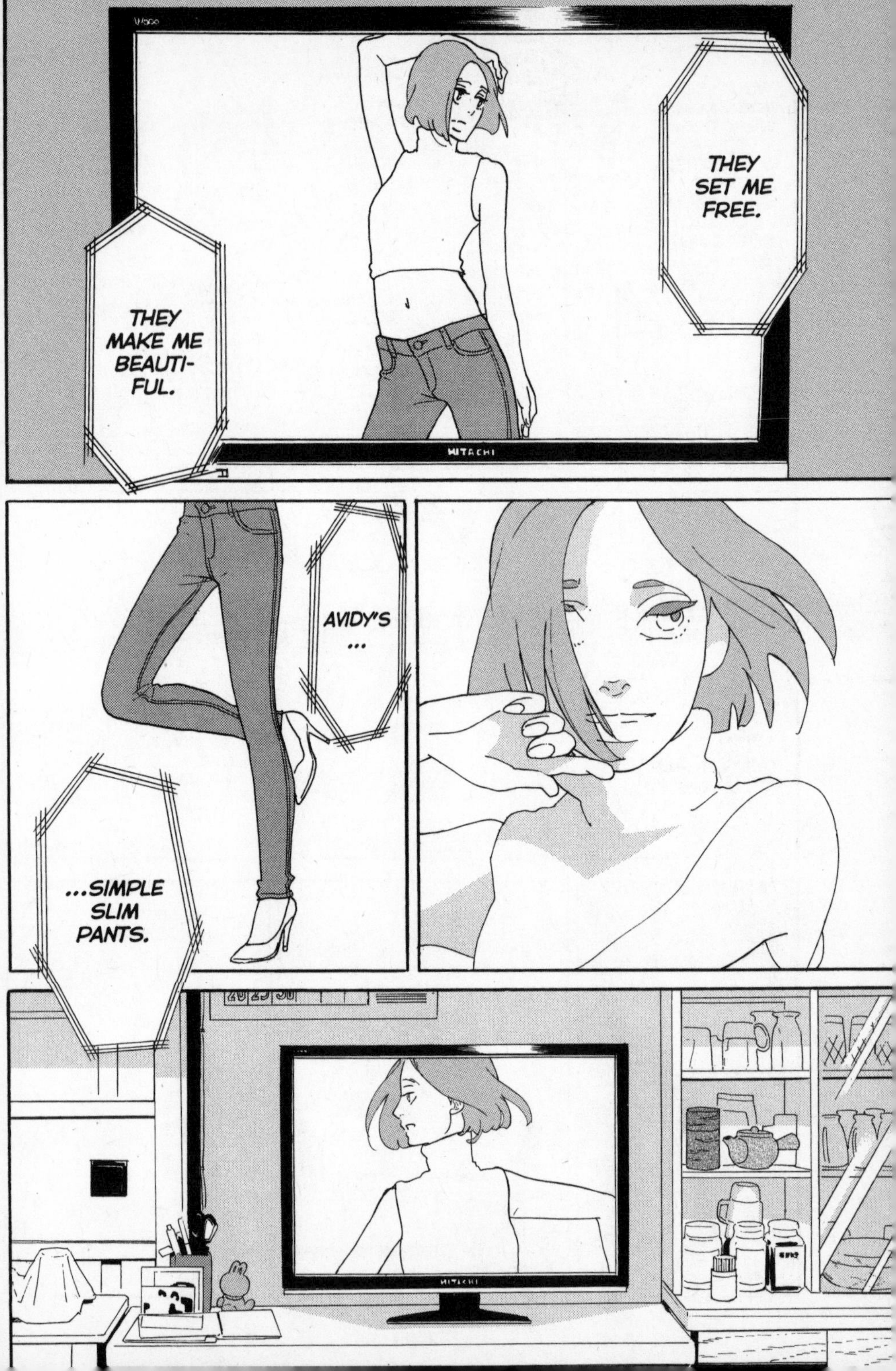
THEY SET ME FREE.
THEY MAKE ME BEAUTI-FUL.
HITACHI
AVIDY'S ...
...SIMPLE SLIM PANTS.
HITACHI

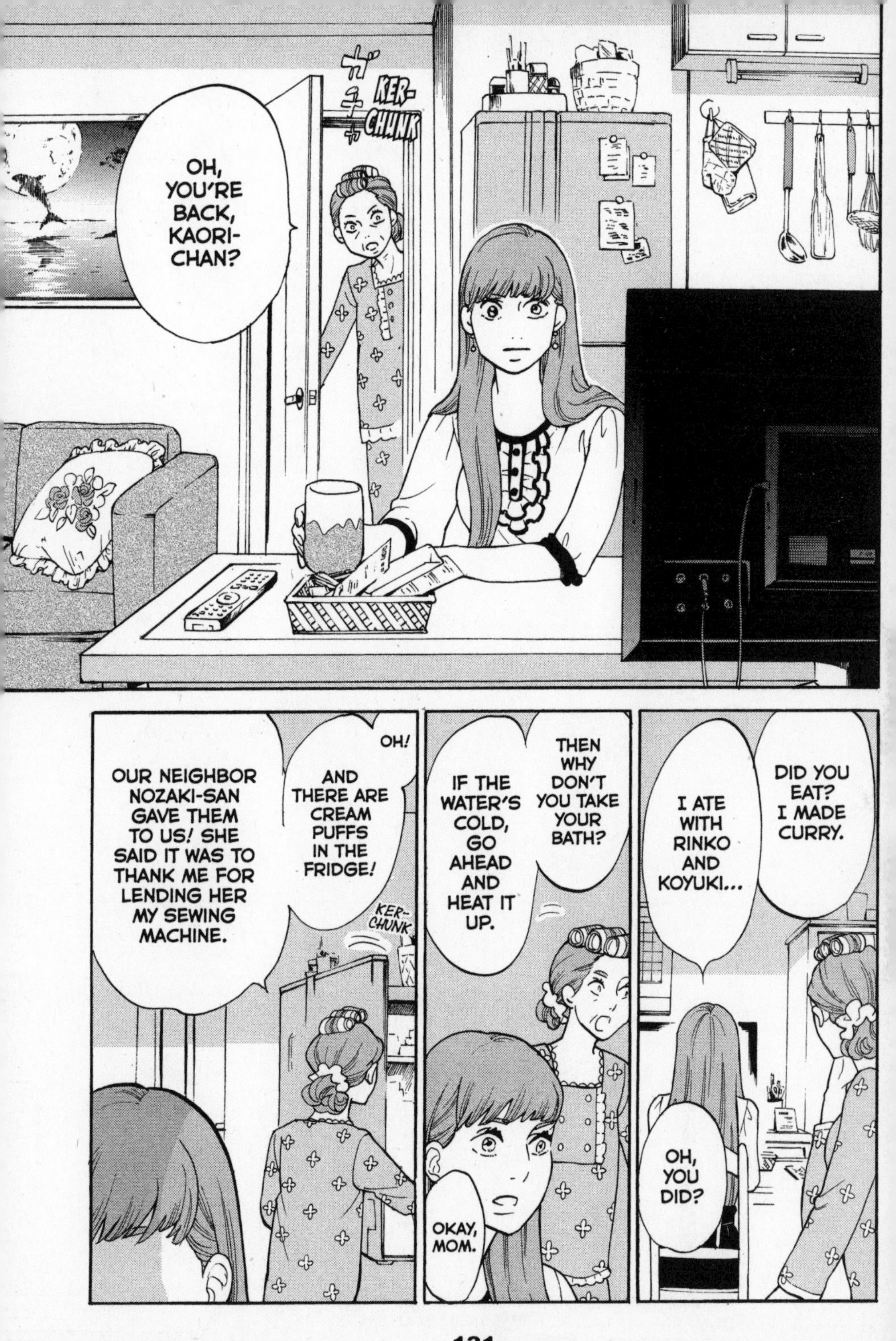
ガチャ
KER-CHUNK
OH, YOU'RE BACK, KAORI-CHAN?
DID YOU EAT? I MADE CURRY.
I ATE WITH RINKO AND KOYUKI...
OH, YOU DID?
THEN WHY DON'T YOU TAKE YOUR BATH?
IF THE WATER'S COLD, GO AHEAD AND HEAT IT UP.
OKAY, MOM.
OH!
AND THERE ARE CREAM PUFFS IN THE FRIDGE!
KER-CHUNK
OUR NEIGHBOR NOZAKI-SAN GAVE THEM TO US! SHE SAID IT WAS TO THANK ME FOR LENDING HER MY SEWING MACHINE.

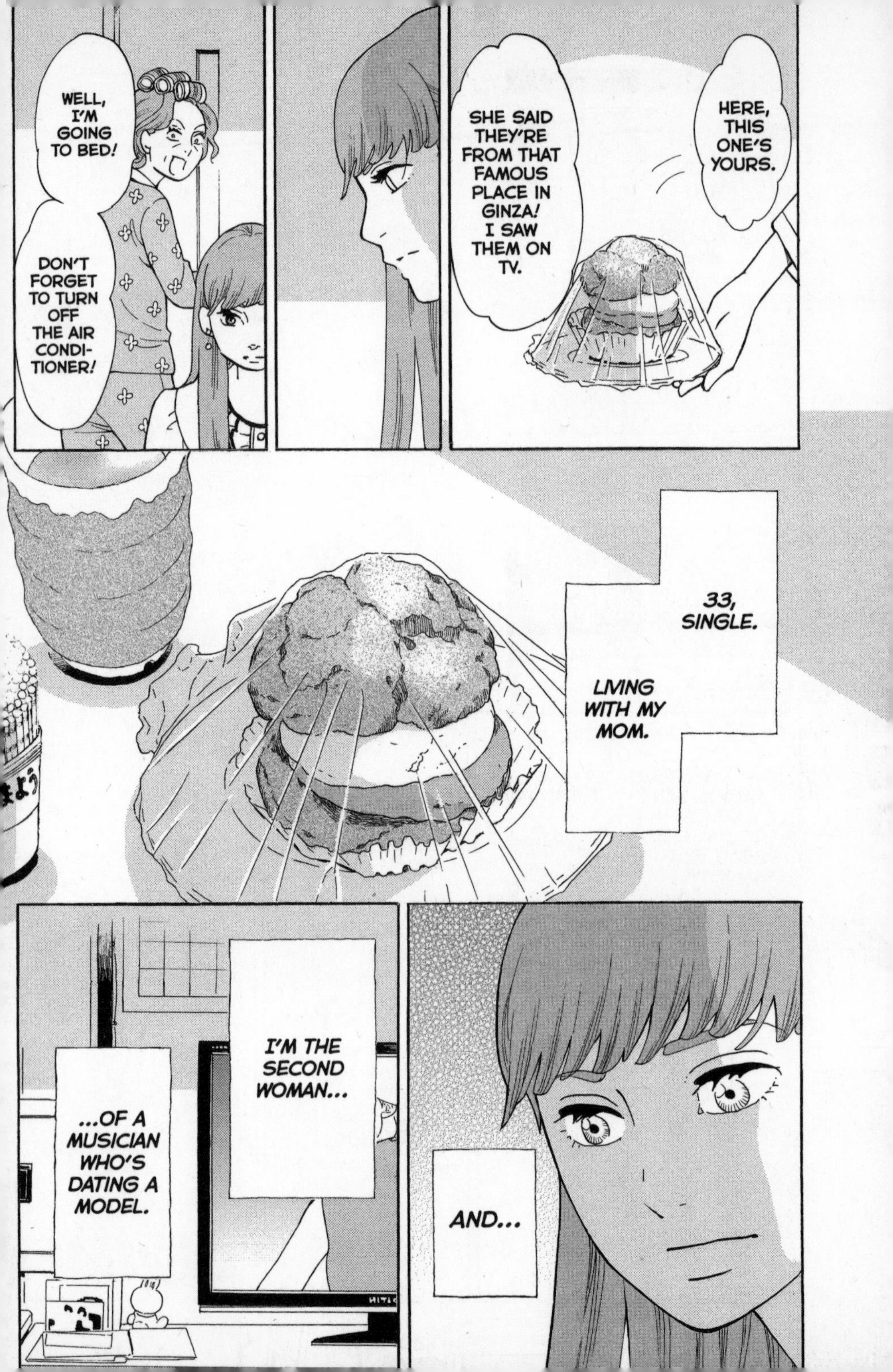
HERE, THIS ONE'S YOURS.
SHE SAID THEY'RE FROM THAT FAMOUS PLACE IN GINZA! I SAW THEM ON TV.
WELL, I'M GOING TO BED!
DON'T FORGET TO TURN OFF THE AIR CONDI-TIONER!
33, SINGLE.
LIVING WITH MY MOM.
AND...
I'M THE SECOND WOMAN...
...OF A MUSICIAN WHO'S DATING A MODEL.

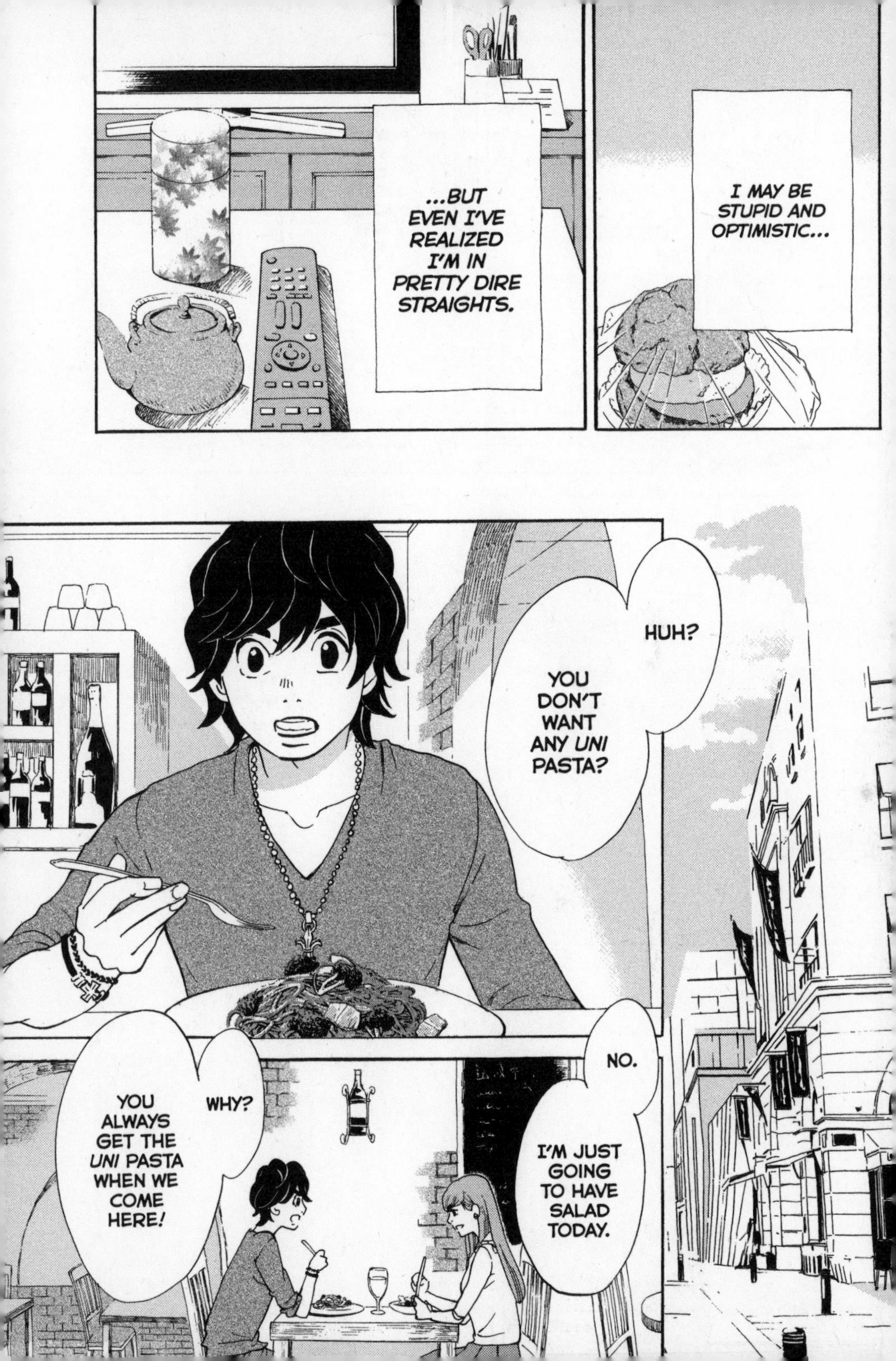

I MAY BE STUPID AND OPTIMISTIC...
...BUT EVEN I'VE REALIZED I'M IN PRETTY DIRE STRAIGHTS.
HUH?
YOU DON'T WANT ANY *UNI* PASTA?
NO.
I'M JUST GOING TO HAVE SALAD TODAY.
WHY?
YOU ALWAYS GET THE *UNI* PASTA WHEN WE COME HERE!

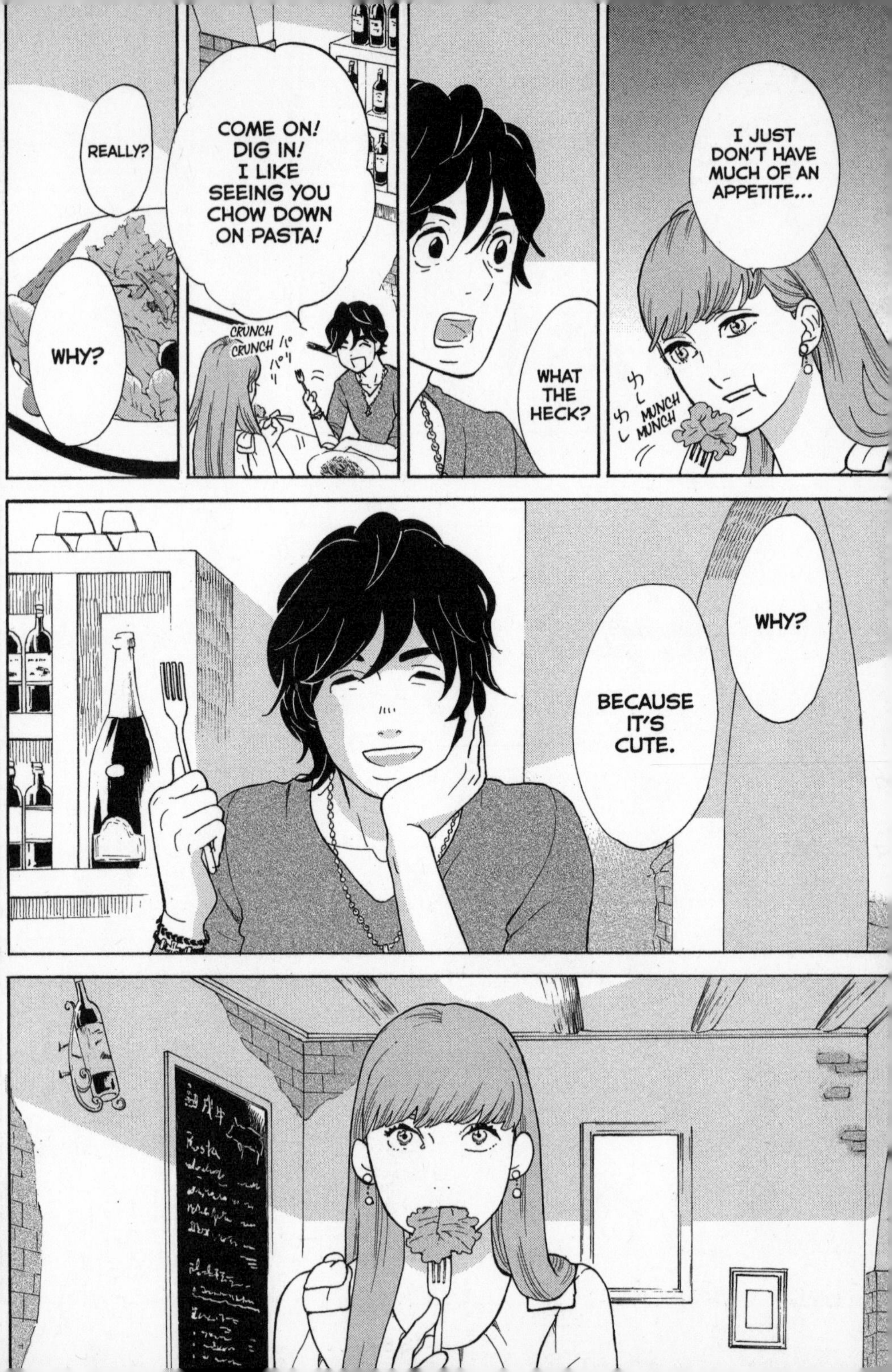
I JUST DON'T HAVE MUCH OF AN APPETITE...
MUNCH MUNCH
WHAT THE HECK?
COME ON! DIG IN! I LIKE SEEING YOU CHOW DOWN ON PASTA!
CRUNCH CRUNCH
パリパリ
REALLY?
WHY?
WHY?
BECAUSE IT'S CUTE.

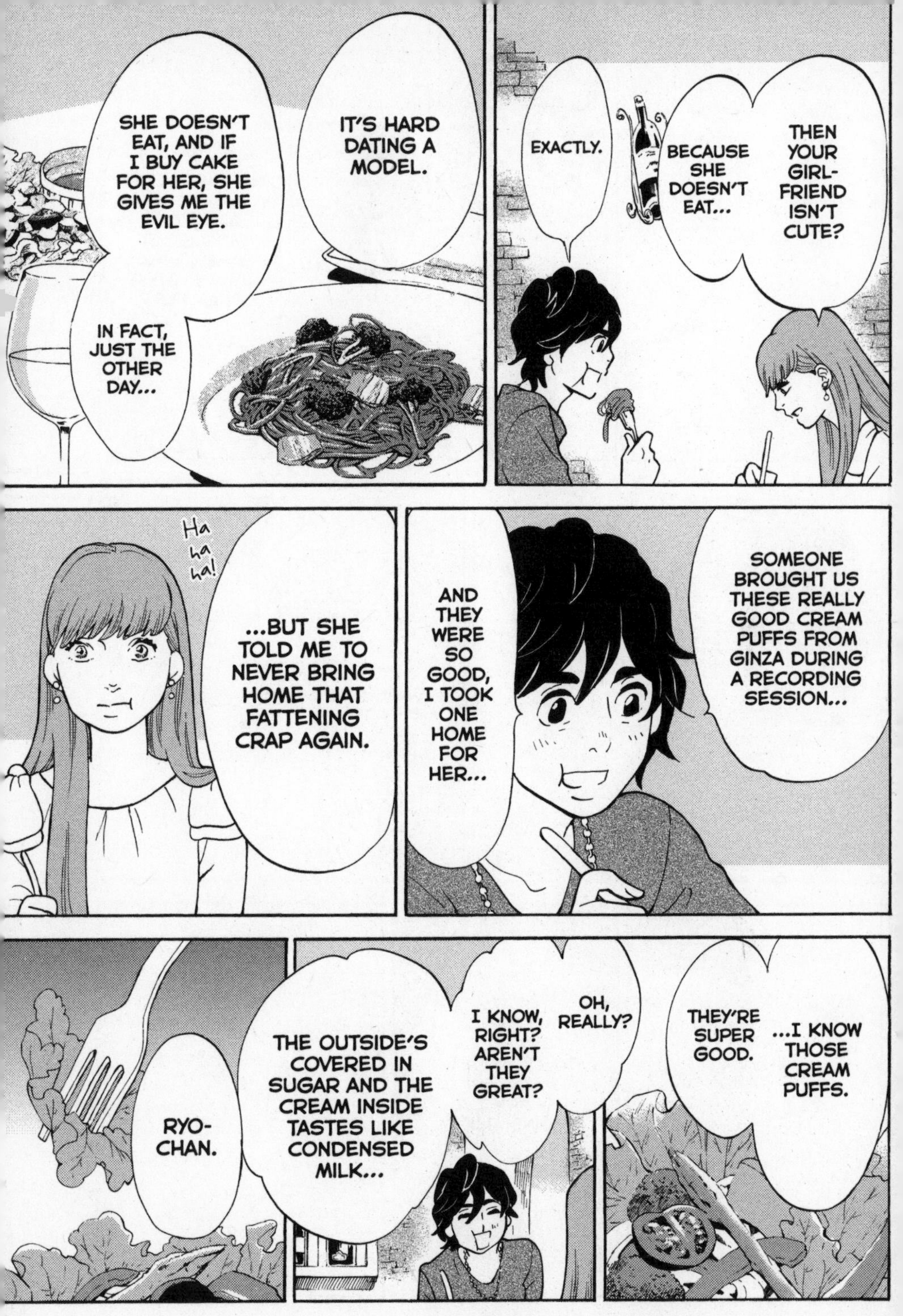
THEN YOUR GIRL-FRIEND ISN'T CUTE?
BECAUSE SHE DOESN'T EAT...
EXACTLY.
IT'S HARD DATING A MODEL.
SHE DOESN'T EAT, AND IF I BUY CAKE FOR HER, SHE GIVES ME THE EVIL EYE.
IN FACT, JUST THE OTHER DAY...
SOMEONE BROUGHT US THESE REALLY GOOD CREAM PUFFS FROM GINZA DURING A RECORDING SESSION...
AND THEY WERE SO GOOD, I TOOK ONE HOME FOR HER...
Ha ha ha!
...BUT SHE TOLD ME TO NEVER BRING HOME THAT FATTENING CRAP AGAIN.
...I KNOW THOSE CREAM PUFFS.
THEY'RE SUPER GOOD.
OH, REALLY?
I KNOW, RIGHT? AREN'T THEY GREAT?
THE OUTSIDE'S COVERED IN SUGAR AND THE CREAM INSIDE TASTES LIKE CONDENSED MILK...
RYO-CHAN.

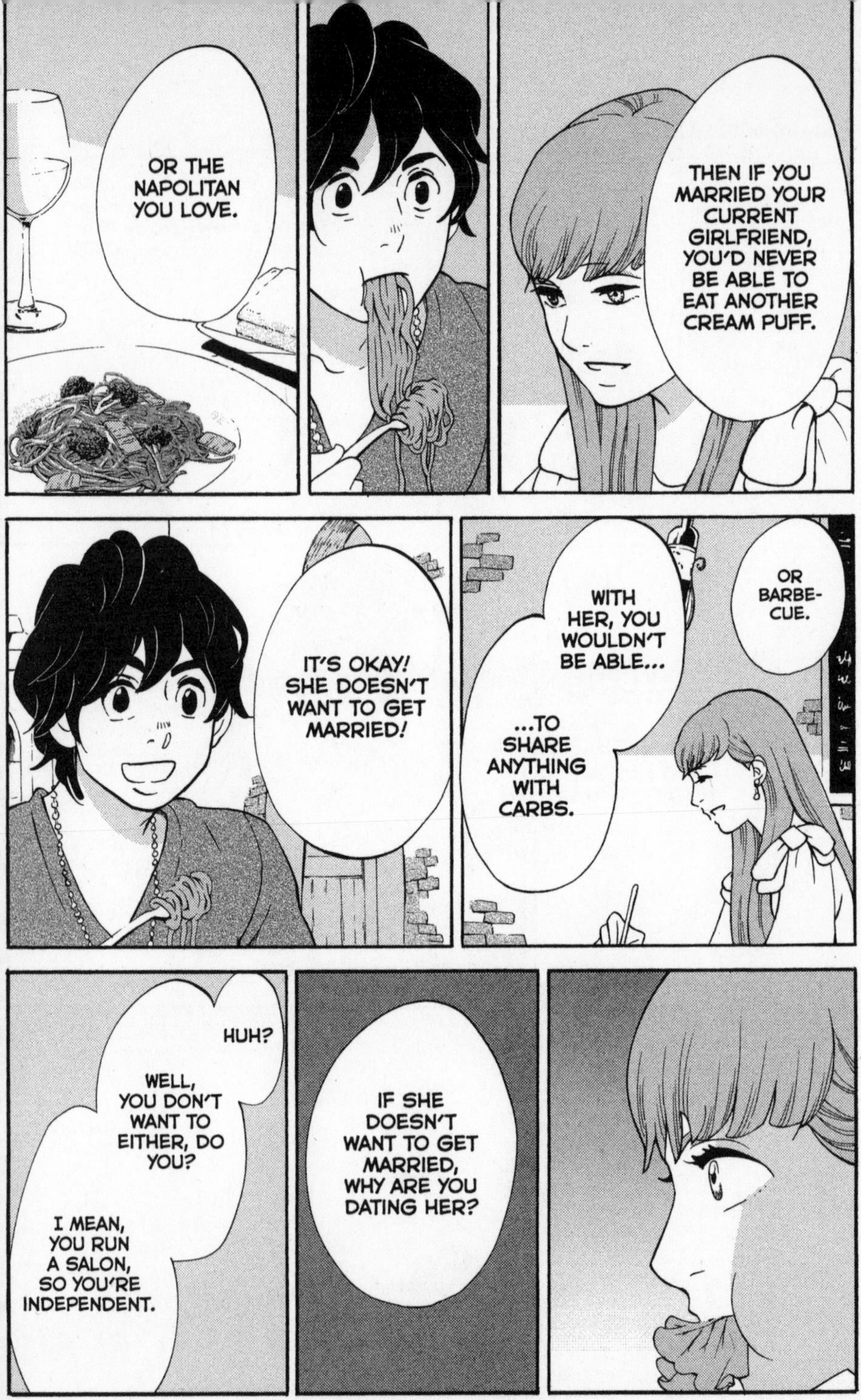
THEN IF YOU MARRIED YOUR CURRENT GIRLFRIEND, YOU'D NEVER BE ABLE TO EAT ANOTHER CREAM PUFF.
OR THE NAPOLITAN YOU LOVE.
WITH HER, YOU WOULDN'T BE ABLE...
...TO SHARE ANYTHING WITH CARBS.
OR BARBE-CUE.
IT'S OKAY! SHE DOESN'T WANT TO GET MARRIED!
IF SHE DOESN'T WANT TO GET MARRIED, WHY ARE YOU DATING HER?
HUH?
WELL, YOU DON'T WANT TO EITHER, DO YOU?
I MEAN, YOU RUN A SALON, SO YOU'RE INDEPENDENT.

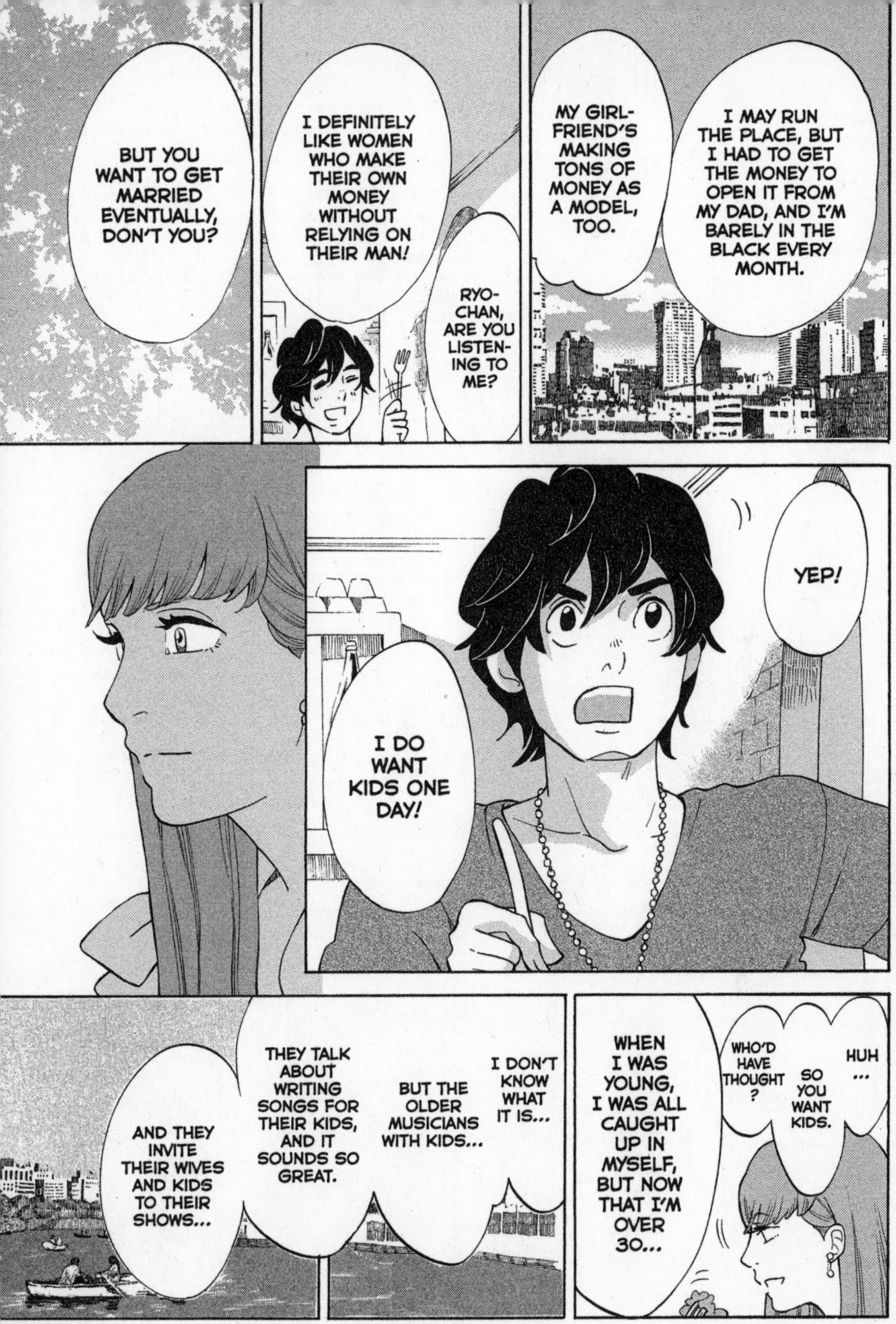
I MAY RUN THE PLACE, BUT I HAD TO GET THE MONEY TO OPEN IT FROM MY DAD, AND I'M BARELY IN THE BLACK EVERY MONTH.
MY GIRL-FRIEND'S MAKING TONS OF MONEY AS A MODEL, TOO.
I DEFINITELY LIKE WOMEN WHO MAKE THEIR OWN MONEY WITHOUT RELYING ON THEIR MAN!
RYO-CHAN, ARE YOU LISTEN-ING TO ME?
BUT YOU WANT TO GET MARRIED EVENTUALLY, DON'T YOU?
YEP!
I DO WANT KIDS ONE DAY!
HUH...
SO YOU WANT KIDS.
WHO'D HAVE THOUGHT?
WHEN I WAS YOUNG, I WAS ALL CAUGHT UP IN MYSELF, BUT NOW THAT I'M OVER 30...
I DON'T KNOW WHAT IT IS...
BUT THE OLDER MUSICIANS WITH KIDS...
THEY TALK ABOUT WRITING SONGS FOR THEIR KIDS, AND IT SOUNDS SO GREAT.
AND THEY INVITE THEIR WIVES AND KIDS TO THEIR SHOWS...

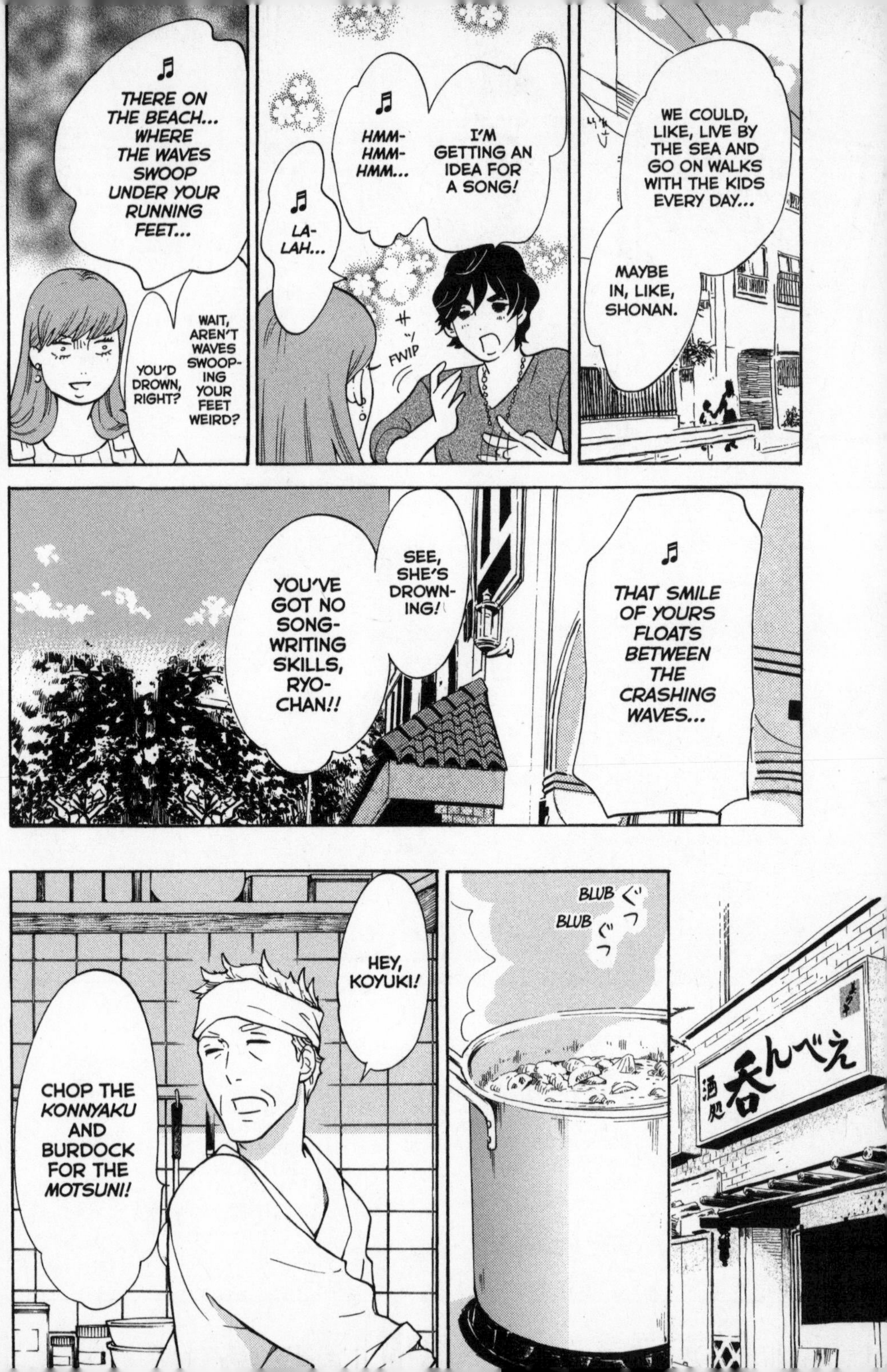
♫
WE COULD, LIKE, LIVE BY THE SEA AND GO ON WALKS WITH THE KIDS EVERY DAY...
MAYBE IN, LIKE, SHONAN.
♫
I'M GETTING AN IDEA FOR A SONG!
HMM-HMM-HMM...
♫
LA-LAH...
FWIP
♫
THERE ON THE BEACH... WHERE THE WAVES SWOOP UNDER YOUR RUNNING FEET...
WAIT, AREN'T WAVES SWOOPING YOUR FEET WEIRD?
YOU'D DROWN, RIGHT?
♫
THAT SMILE OF YOURS FLOATS BETWEEN THE CRASHING WAVES...
SEE, SHE'S DROWNING!
YOU'VE GOT NO SONGWRITING SKILLS, RYO-CHAN!!
BLUB ぐつ
BLUB ぐつ
酒処 呑んべえ
HEY, KOYUKI!
CHOP THE *KONNYAKU* AND BURDOCK FOR THE *MOTSUNI*!

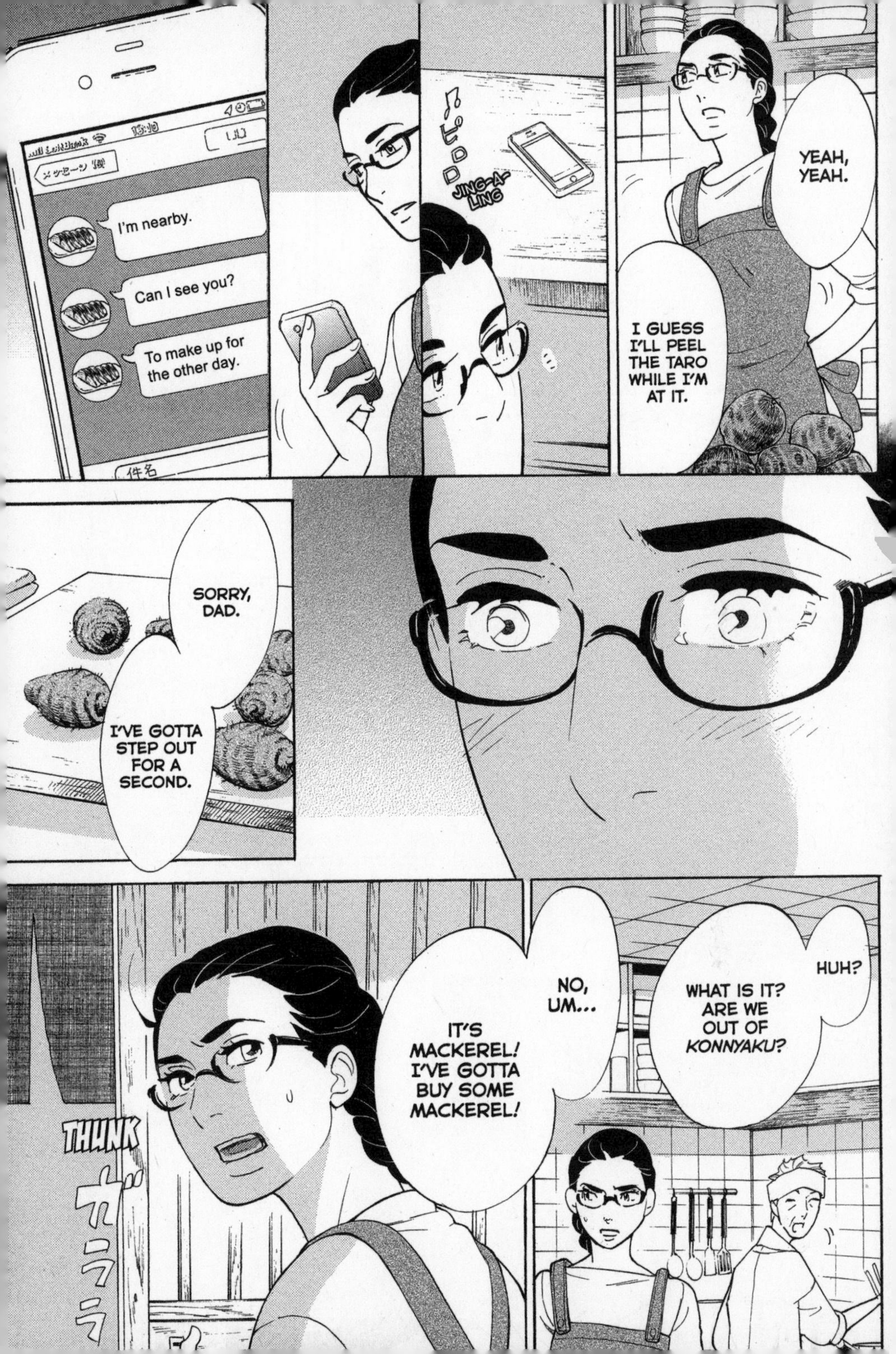
YEAH, YEAH.
I GUESS I'LL PEEL THE TARO WHILE I'M AT IT.
JING-A-LING
I'm nearby.
Can I see you?
To make up for the other day.
件名
SORRY, DAD.
I'VE GOTTA STEP OUT FOR A SECOND.
HUH?
WHAT IS IT? ARE WE OUT OF *KONNYAKU*?
NO, UM...
IT'S MACKEREL! I'VE GOTTA BUY SOME MACKEREL!
THUNK

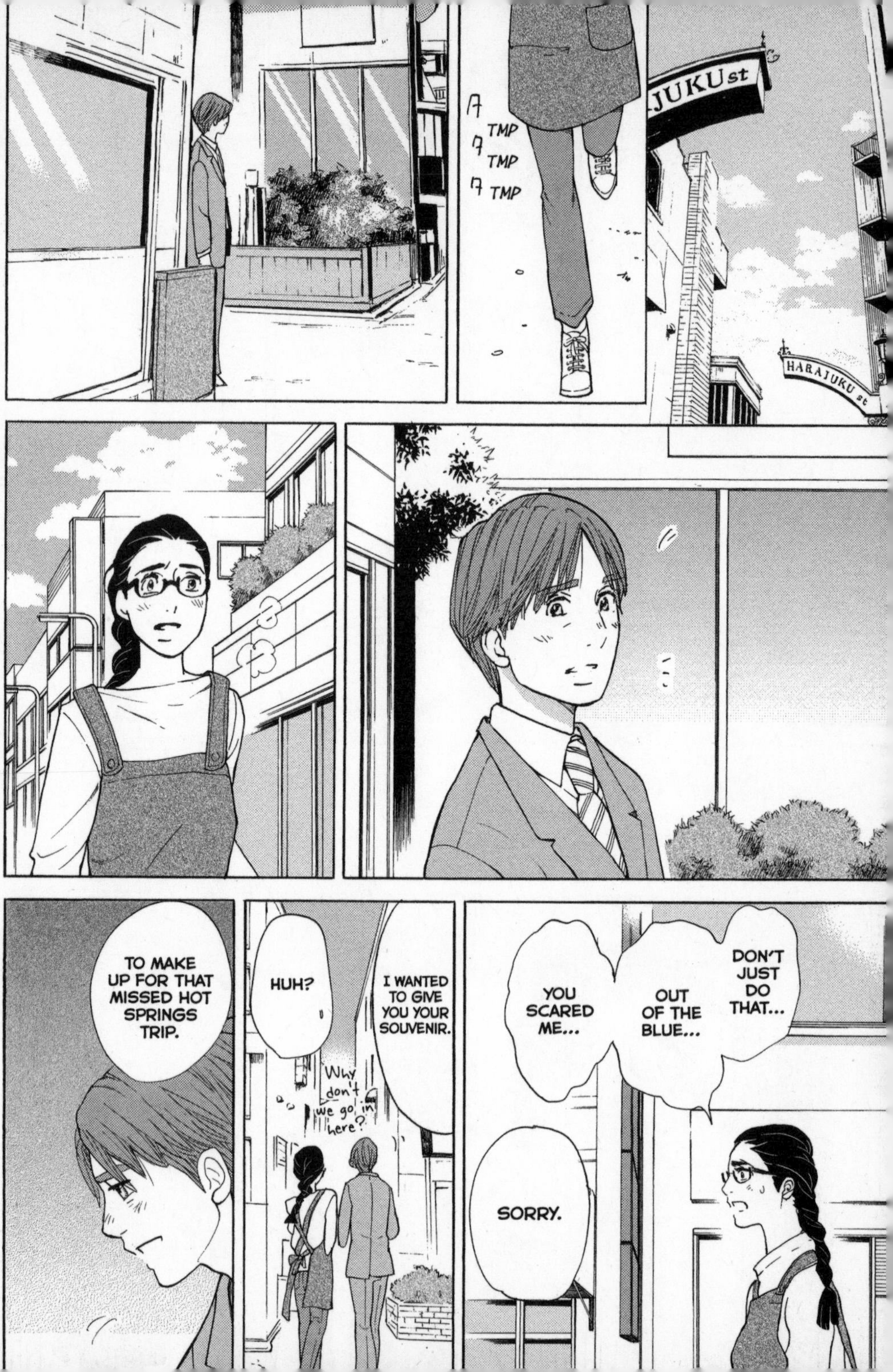
TMP
TMP
TMP
JUKU st
HARAJUKU st
DON'T JUST DO THAT...
OUT OF THE BLUE...
YOU SCARED ME...
SORRY.
I WANTED TO GIVE YOU YOUR SOUVENIR.
HUH?
Why don't we go in here?
TO MAKE UP FOR THAT MISSED HOT SPRINGS TRIP.

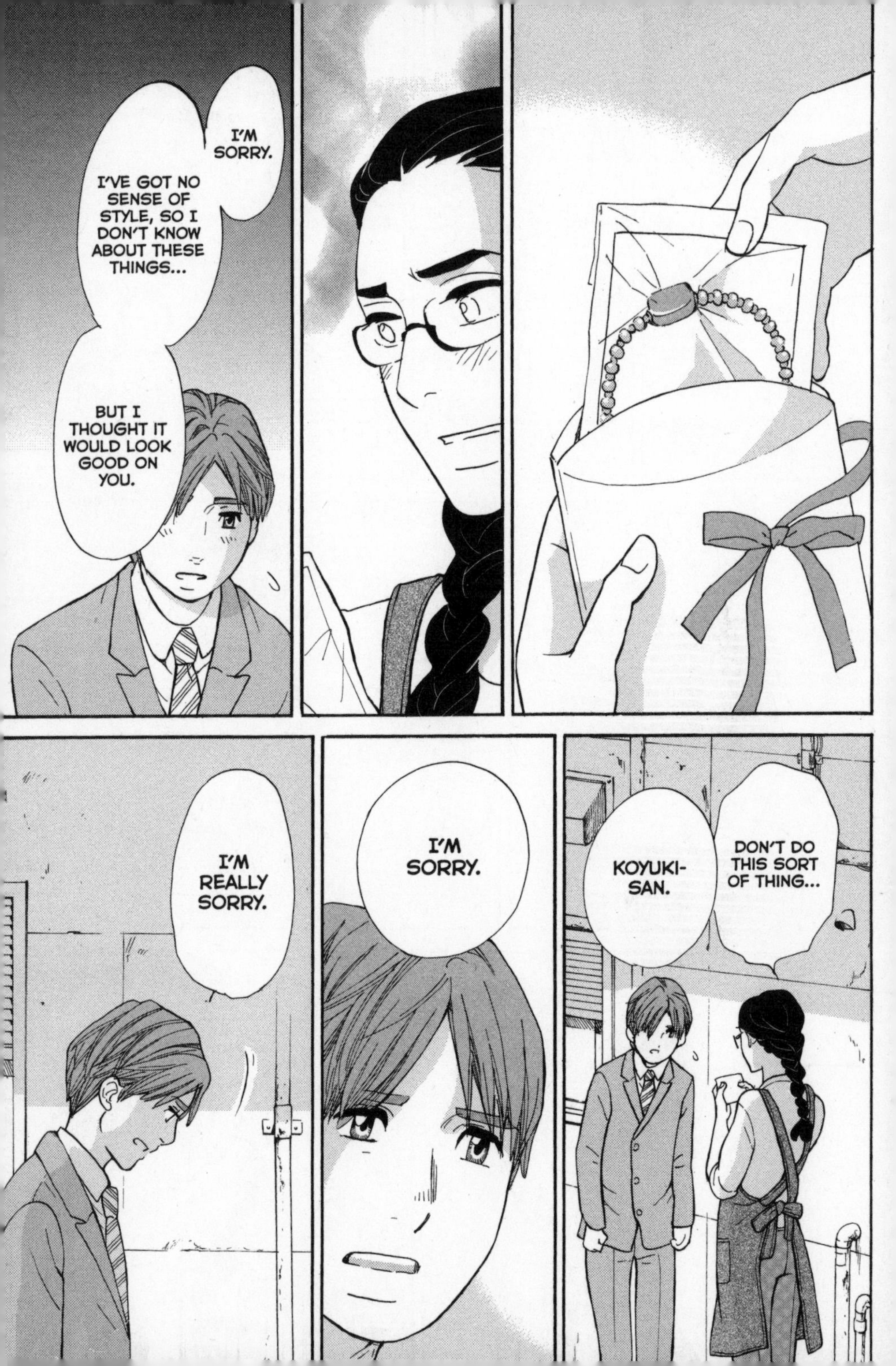
I'M SORRY.
I'VE GOT NO SENSE OF STYLE, SO I DON'T KNOW ABOUT THESE THINGS...
BUT I THOUGHT IT WOULD LOOK GOOD ON YOU.
DON'T DO THIS SORT OF THING...
KOYUKI-SAN.
I'M SORRY.
I'M REALLY SORRY.

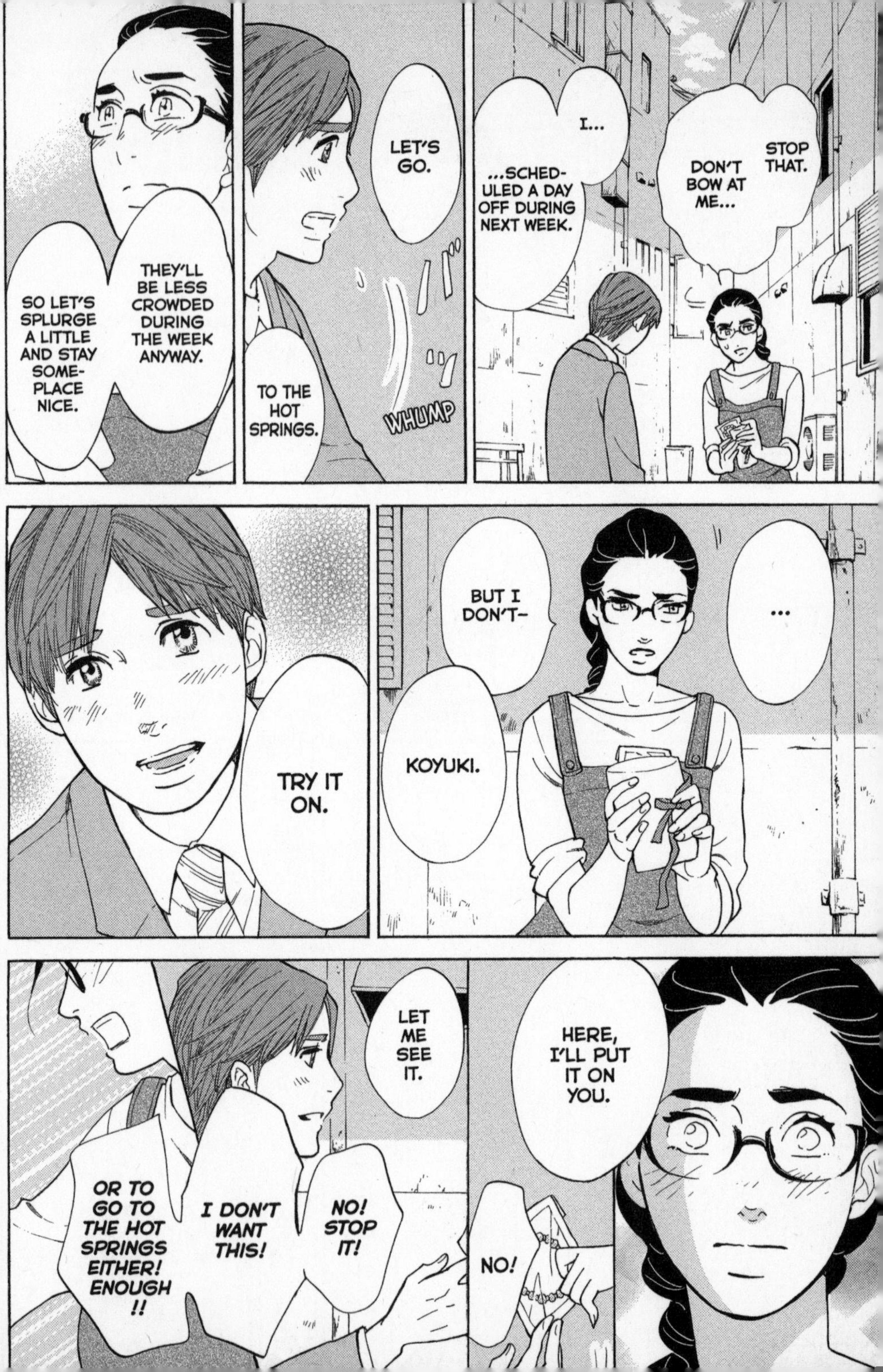
STOP THAT.
DON'T BOW AT ME...
I...
...SCHED-ULED A DAY OFF DURING NEXT WEEK.
LET'S GO.
TO THE HOT SPRINGS.
WHUMP
THEY'LL BE LESS CROWDED DURING THE WEEK ANYWAY.
SO LET'S SPLURGE A LITTLE AND STAY SOME-PLACE NICE.
...
BUT I DON'T-
KOYUKI.
TRY IT ON.
HERE, I'LL PUT IT ON YOU.
NO!
LET ME SEE IT.
NO! STOP IT!
I DON'T WANT THIS!
OR TO GO TO THE HOT SPRINGS EITHER! ENOUGH!!

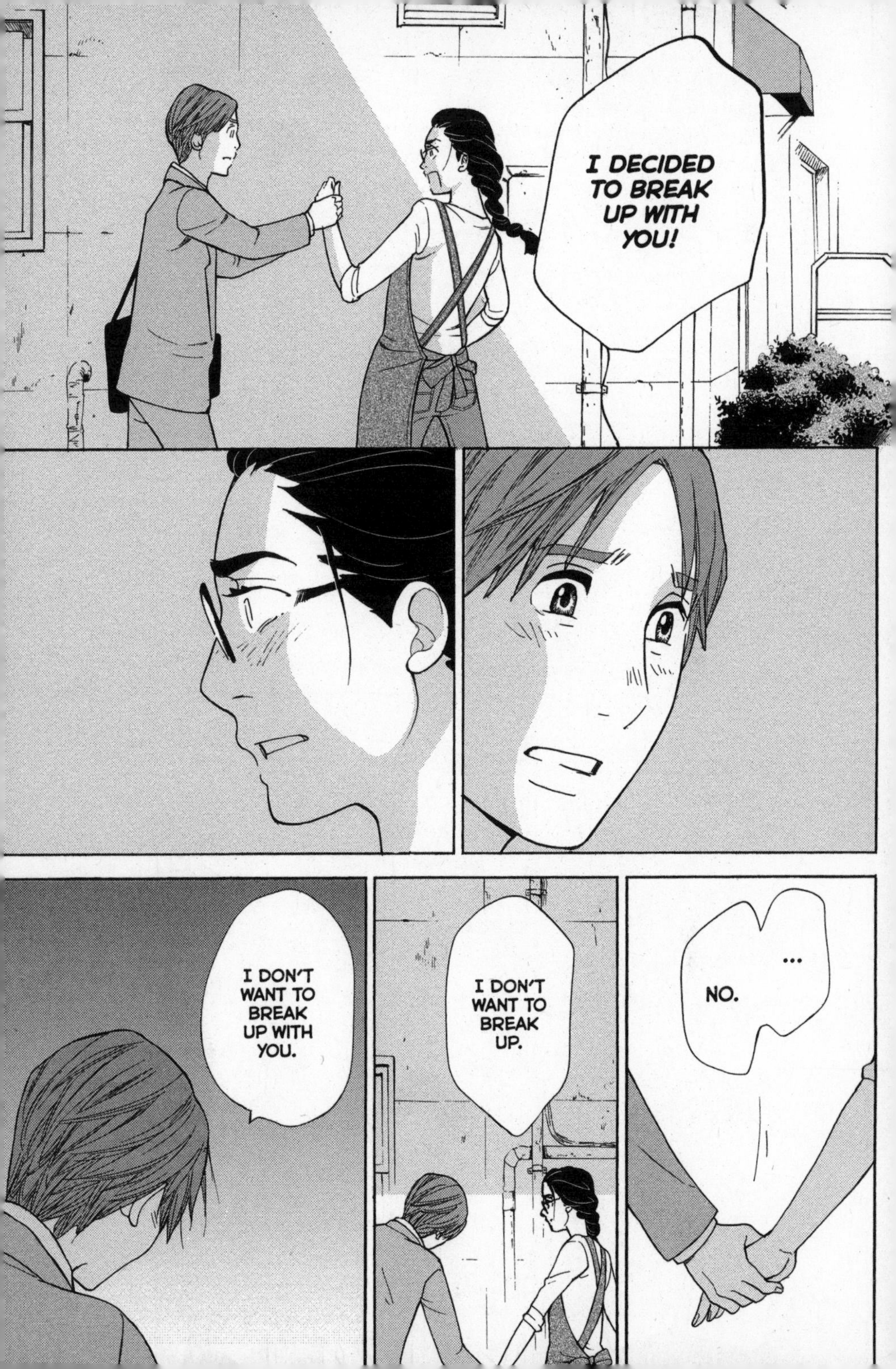
I DECIDED TO BREAK UP WITH YOU!
...
NO.
I DON'T WANT TO BREAK UP.
I DON'T WANT TO BREAK UP WITH YOU.

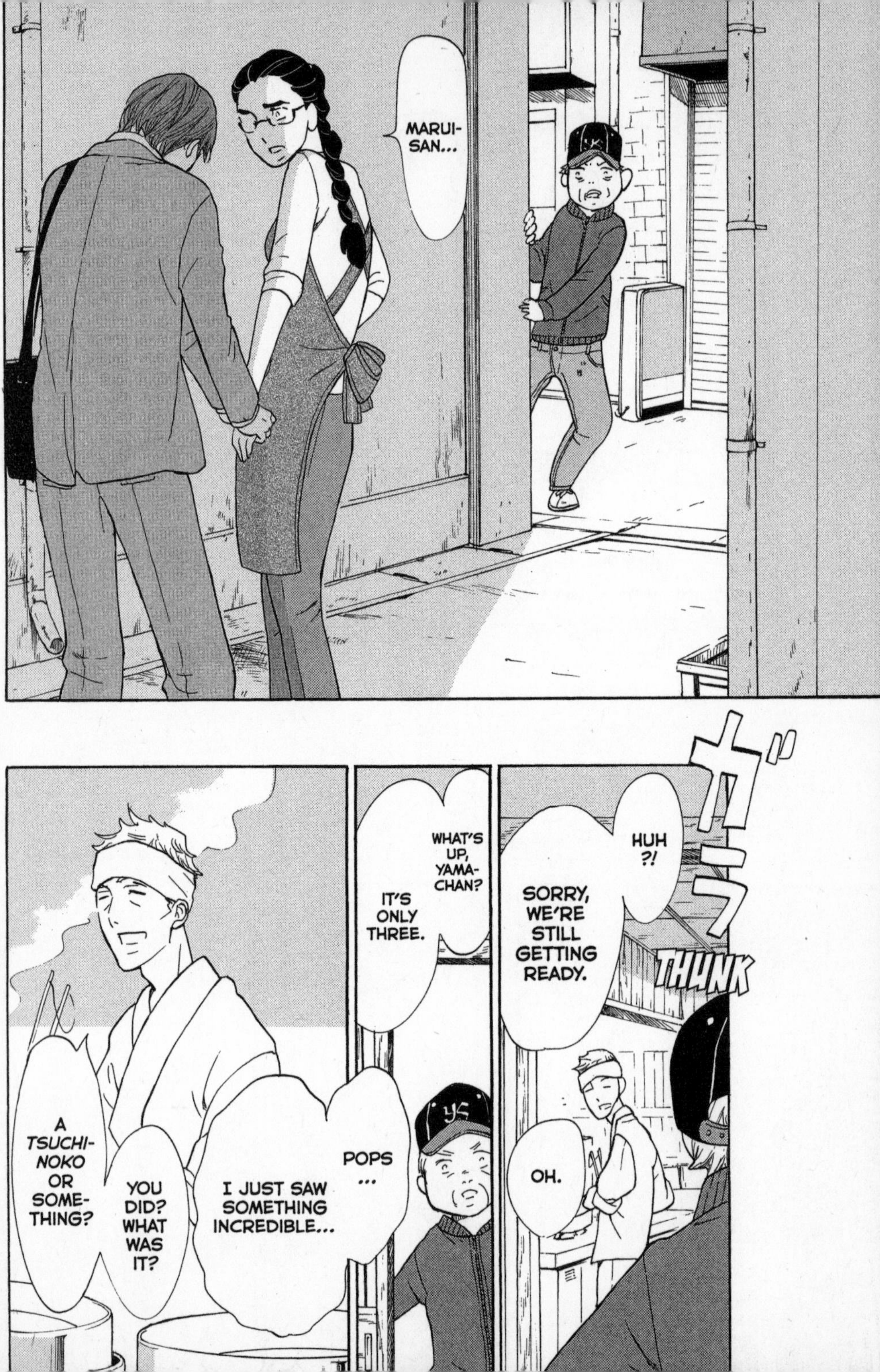
MARUI-SAN...
ガラ
THUNK
HUH ?!
SORRY, WE'RE STILL GETTING READY.
OH.
WHAT'S UP, YAMA-CHAN?
IT'S ONLY THREE.
POPS ...
I JUST SAW SOMETHING INCREDIBLE...
YOU DID? WHAT WAS IT?
A TSUCHI-NOKO OR SOME-THING?

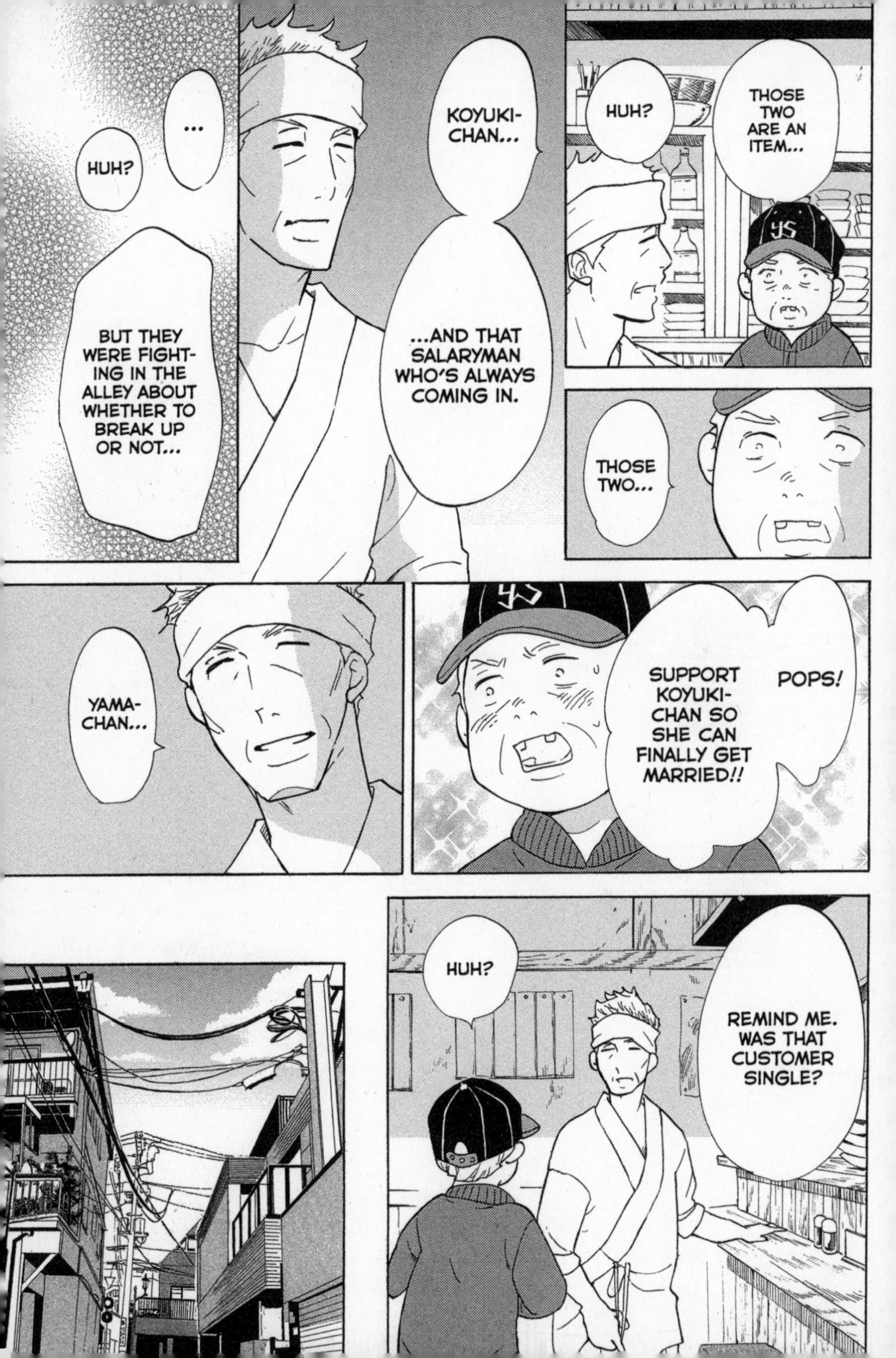
THOSE TWO ARE AN ITEM...
HUH?
THOSE TWO...
KOYUKI-CHAN...
...AND THAT SALARYMAN WHO'S ALWAYS COMING IN.
...
HUH?
BUT THEY WERE FIGHTING IN THE ALLEY ABOUT WHETHER TO BREAK UP OR NOT...
POPS!
SUPPORT KOYUKI-CHAN SO SHE CAN FINALLY GET MARRIED!!
YAMA-CHAN...
REMIND ME. WAS THAT CUSTOMER SINGLE?
HUH?

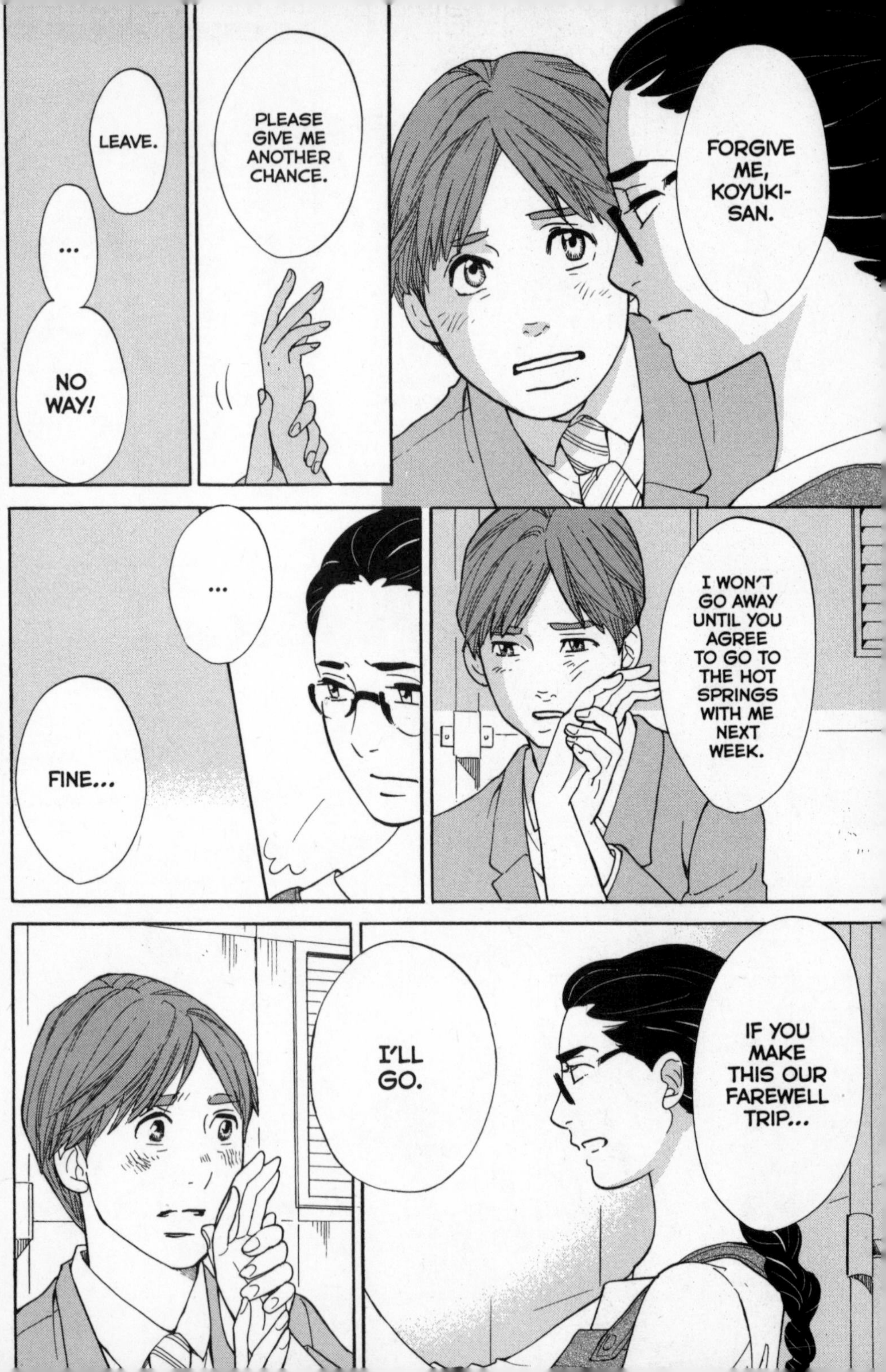
FORGIVE ME, KOYUKI-SAN.
PLEASE GIVE ME ANOTHER CHANCE.
LEAVE.
...
NO WAY!
I WON'T GO AWAY UNTIL YOU AGREE TO GO TO THE HOT SPRINGS WITH ME NEXT WEEK.
...
FINE...
IF YOU MAKE THIS OUR FAREWELL TRIP...
I'LL GO.

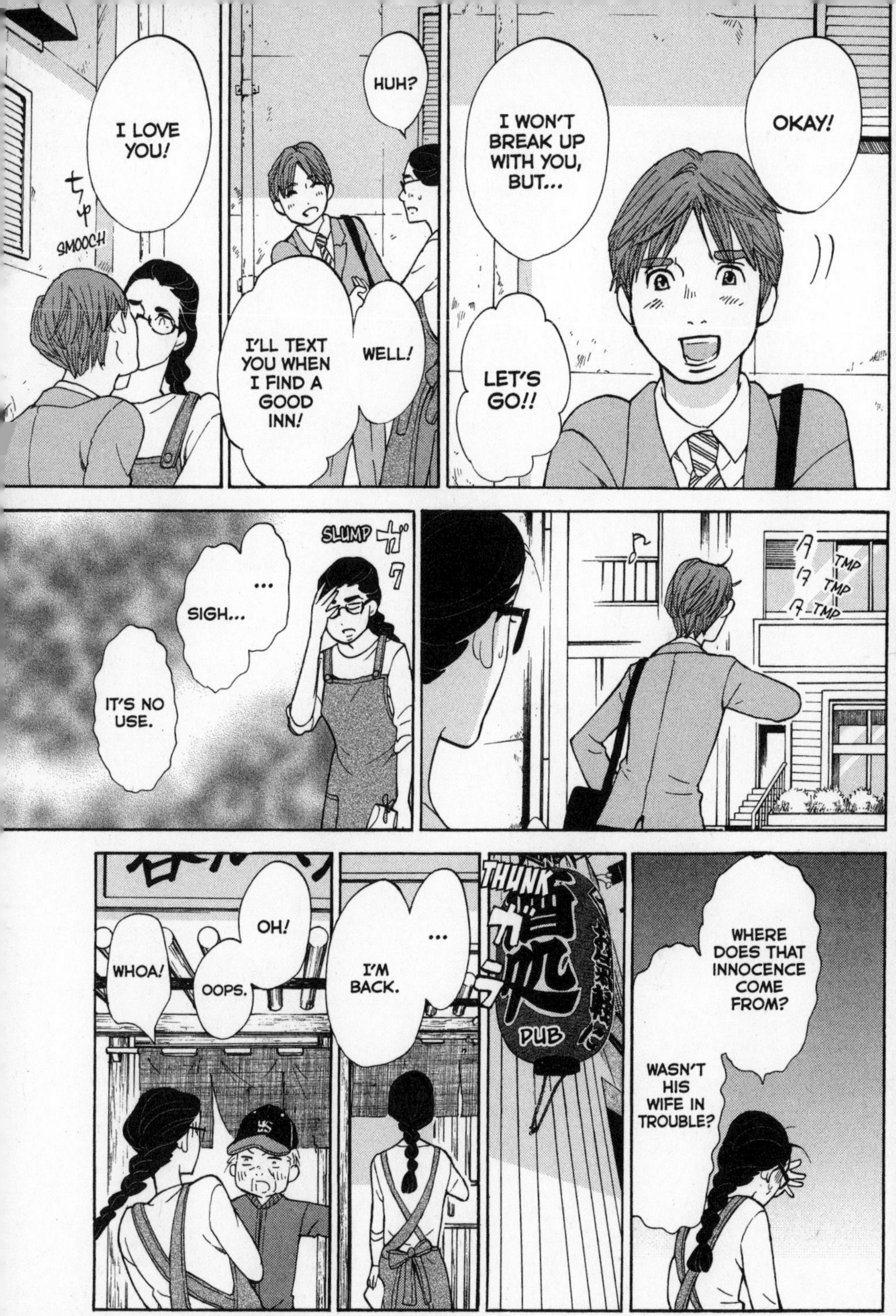
OKAY!
I WON'T BREAK UP WITH YOU, BUT...
LET'S GO!!
HUH?
WELL!
I'LL TEXT YOU WHEN I FIND A GOOD INN!
I LOVE YOU!
SMOOCH
TMP
TMP
TMP
SLUMP
...
SIGH...
IT'S NO USE.
WHERE DOES THAT INNOCENCE COME FROM?
WASN'T HIS WIFE IN TROUBLE?
THUNK
PUB
...
I'M BACK.
OH!
OOPS.
WHOA!

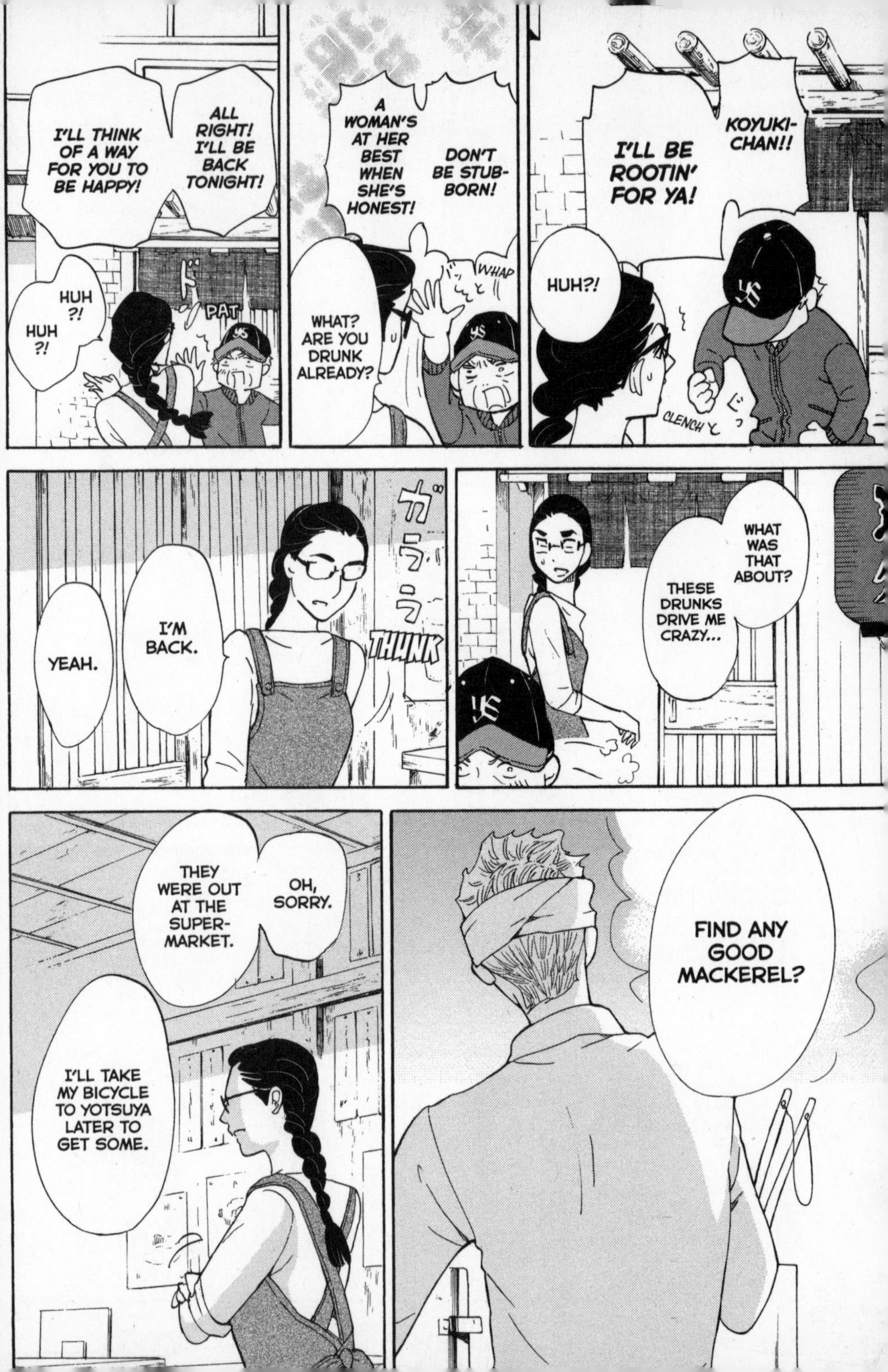
KOYUKI-CHAN!!
I'LL BE ROOTIN' FOR YA!
HUH?!
CLENCH
DON'T BE STUB-BORN!
A WOMAN'S AT HER BEST WHEN SHE'S HONEST!
WHAP
WHAT? ARE YOU DRUNK ALREADY?
ALL RIGHT! I'LL BE BACK TONIGHT!
I'LL THINK OF A WAY FOR YOU TO BE HAPPY!
PAT
HUH ?!
HUH ?!
WHAT WAS THAT ABOUT?
THESE DRUNKS DRIVE ME CRAZY...
THUNK
I'M BACK.
YEAH.
FIND ANY GOOD MACKEREL?
OH, SORRY.
THEY WERE OUT AT THE SUPER-MARKET.
I'LL TAKE MY BICYCLE TO YOTSUYA LATER TO GET SOME.

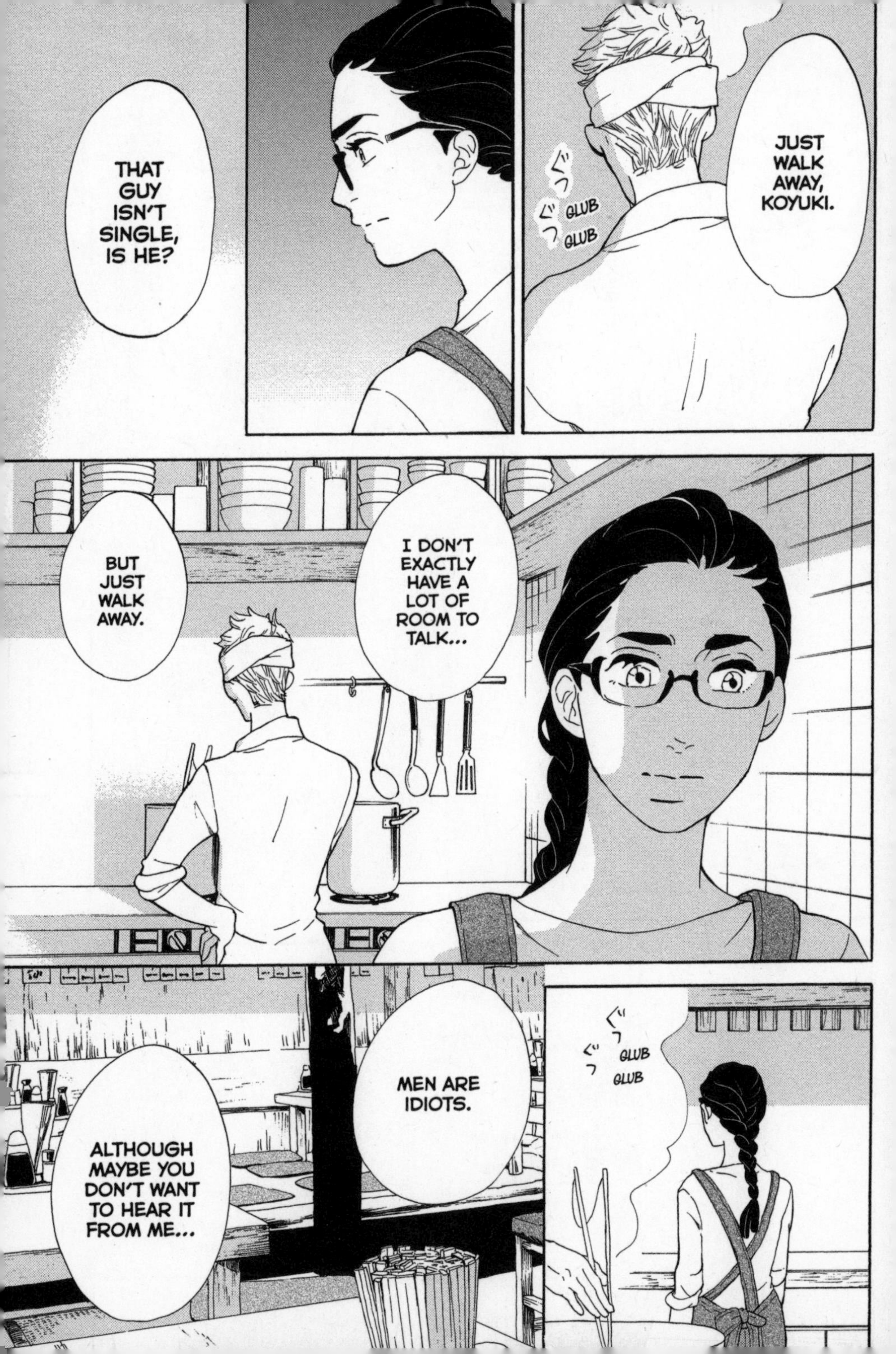
JUST WALK AWAY, KOYUKI.
ぐつぐつ
GLUB GLUB
THAT GUY ISN'T SINGLE, IS HE?
I DON'T EXACTLY HAVE A LOT OF ROOM TO TALK...
BUT JUST WALK AWAY.
ぐつぐつ
GLUB GLUB
MEN ARE IDIOTS.
ALTHOUGH MAYBE YOU DON'T WANT TO HEAR IT FROM ME...

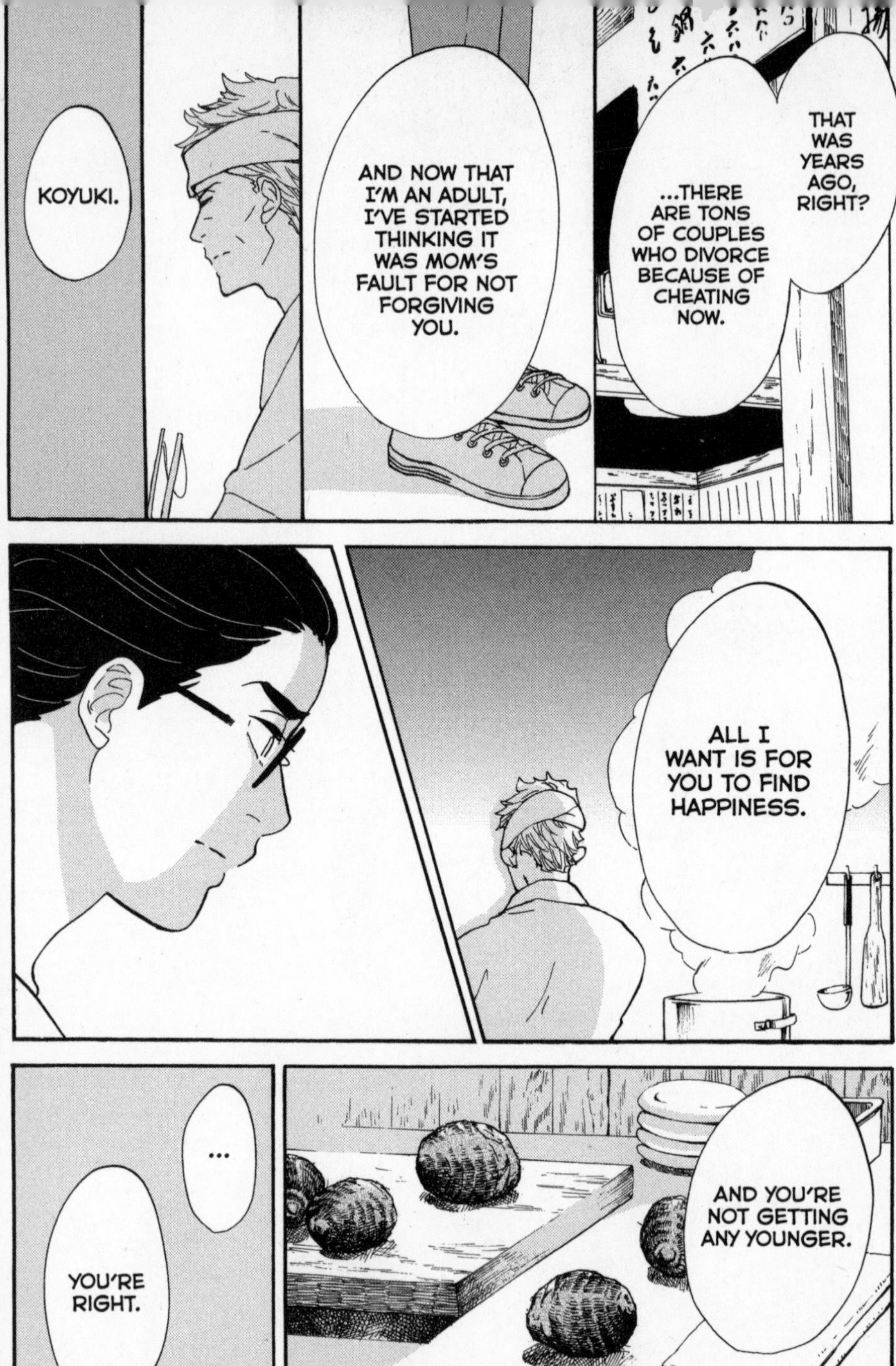
THAT WAS YEARS AGO, RIGHT?
...THERE ARE TONS OF COUPLES WHO DIVORCE BECAUSE OF CHEATING NOW.
AND NOW THAT I'M AN ADULT, I'VE STARTED THINKING IT WAS MOM'S FAULT FOR NOT FORGIVING YOU.
KOYUKI.
ALL I WANT IS FOR YOU TO FIND HAPPINESS.
AND YOU'RE NOT GETTING ANY YOUNGER.
...
YOU'RE RIGHT.

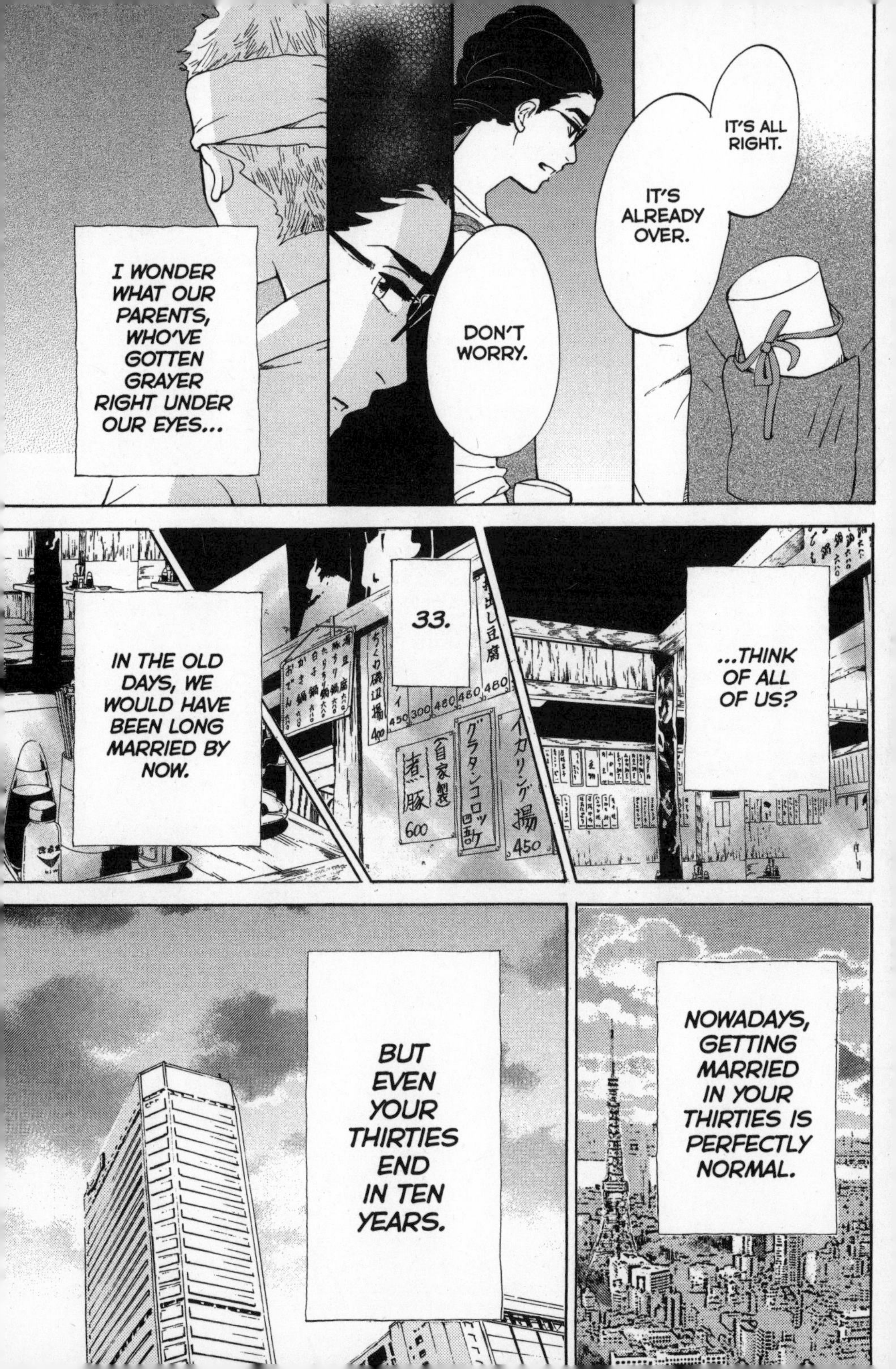
IT'S ALL RIGHT.
IT'S ALREADY OVER.
DON'T WORRY.
I WONDER WHAT OUR PARENTS, WHO'VE GOTTEN GRAYER RIGHT UNDER OUR EYES...
...THINK OF ALL OF US?
33.
揚出し豆腐
480
イカリング揚
450
(自家製)
煮豚
600
IN THE OLD DAYS, WE WOULD HAVE BEEN LONG MARRIED BY NOW.
NOWADAYS, GETTING MARRIED IN YOUR THIRTIES IS PERFECTLY NORMAL.
BUT EVEN YOUR THIRTIES END IN TEN YEARS.

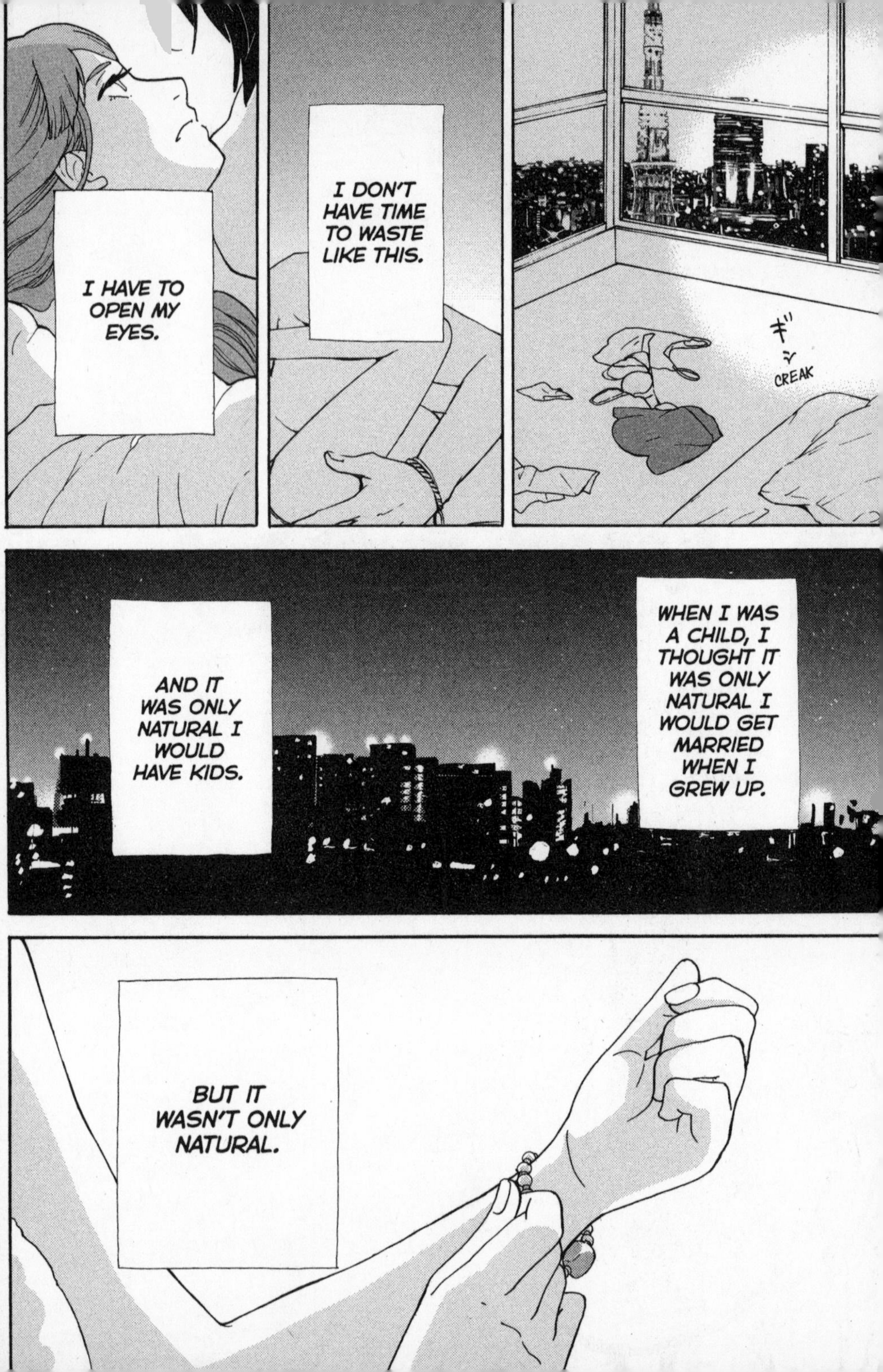
CREAK
I DON'T HAVE TIME TO WASTE LIKE THIS.
I HAVE TO OPEN MY EYES.
WHEN I WAS A CHILD, I THOUGHT IT WAS ONLY NATURAL I WOULD GET MARRIED WHEN I GREW UP.
AND IT WAS ONLY NATURAL I WOULD HAVE KIDS.
BUT IT WASN'T ONLY NATURAL.

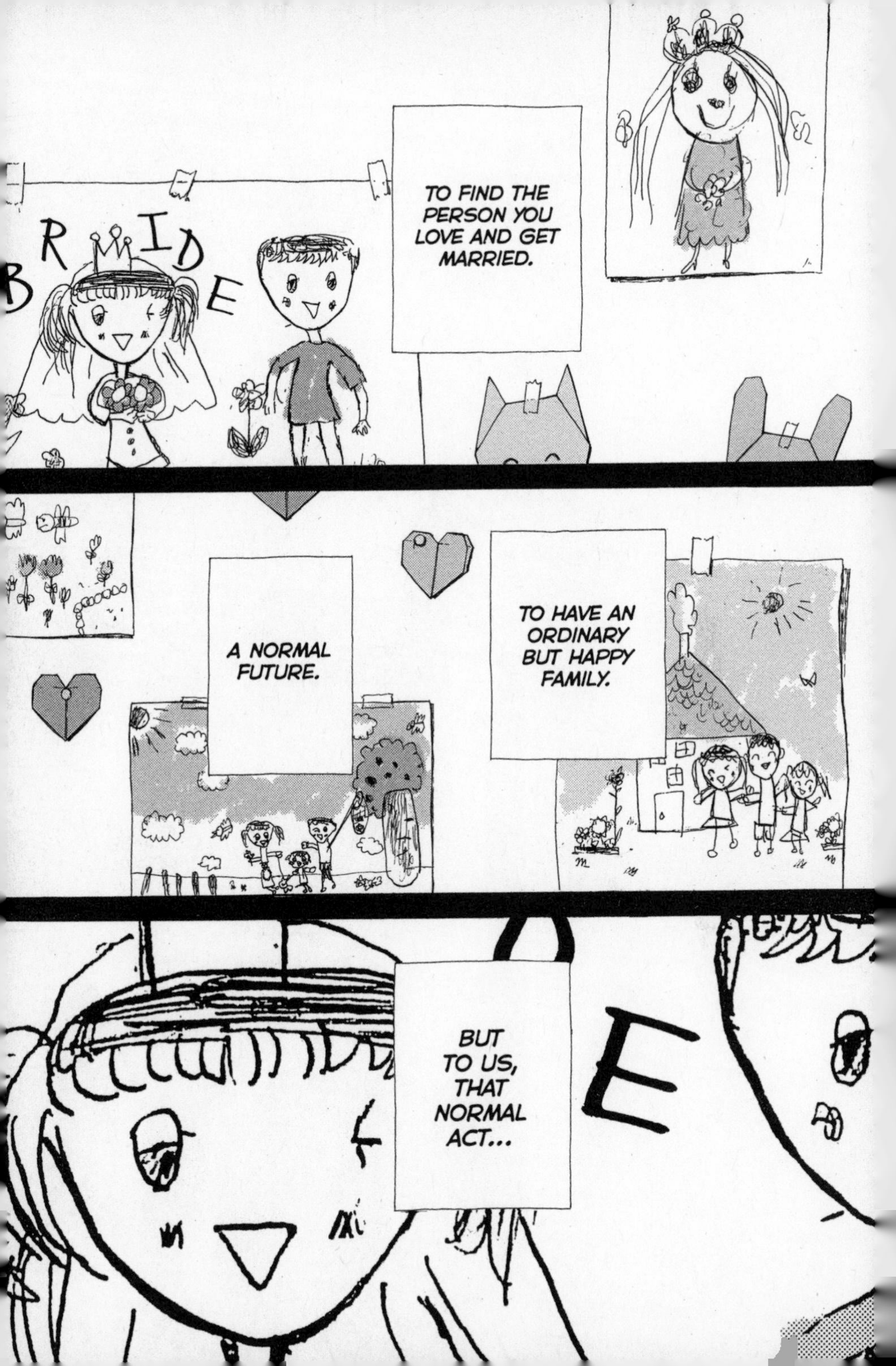
TO FIND THE PERSON YOU LOVE AND GET MARRIED.
BRIDE
TO HAVE AN ORDINARY BUT HAPPY FAMILY.
A NORMAL FUTURE.
BUT TO US, THAT NORMAL ACT...

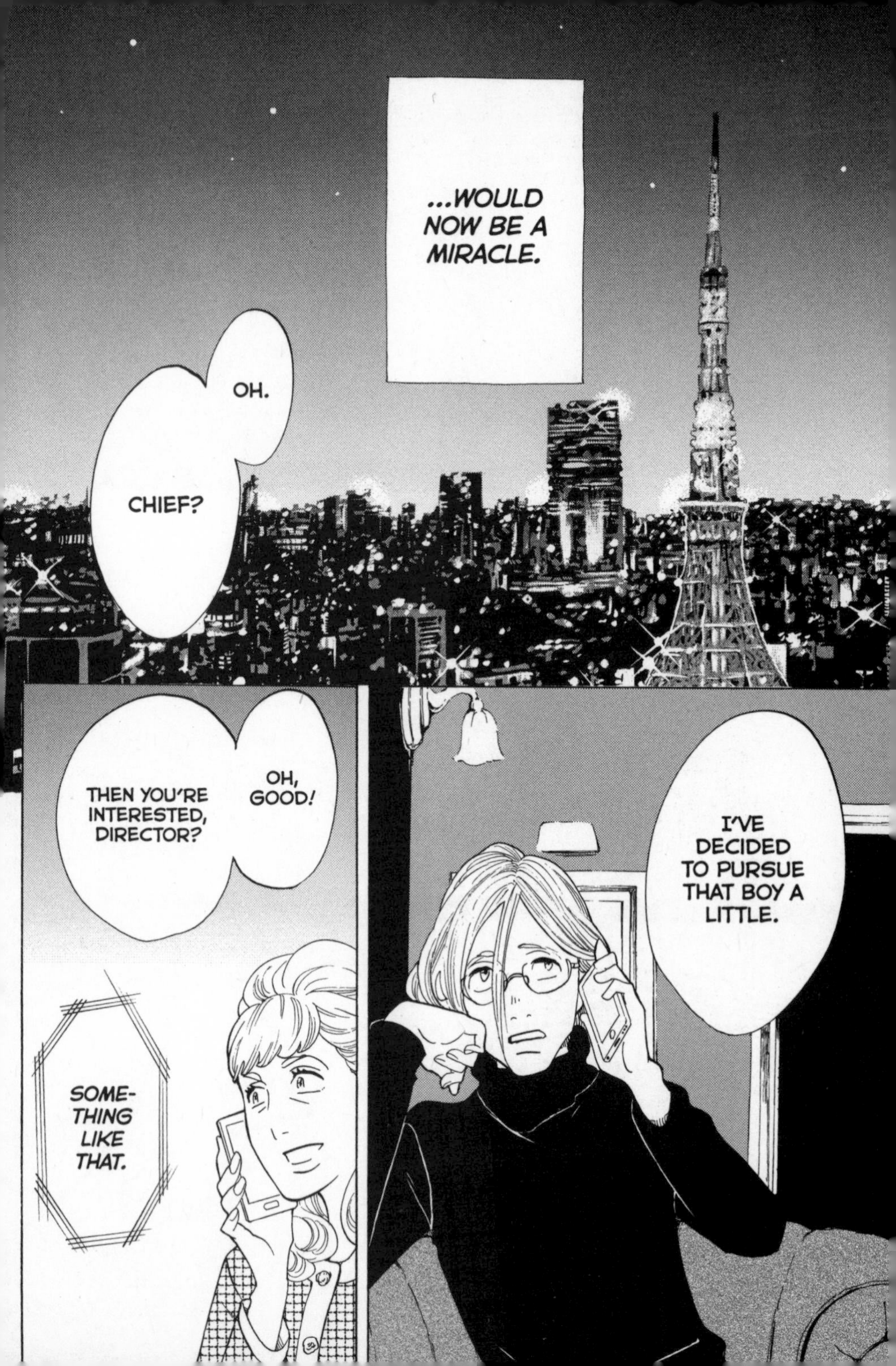
...WOULD NOW BE A MIRACLE.
OH.
CHIEF?
I'VE DECIDED TO PURSUE THAT BOY A LITTLE.
OH, GOOD!
THEN YOU'RE INTERESTED, DIRECTOR?
SOME-THING LIKE THAT.

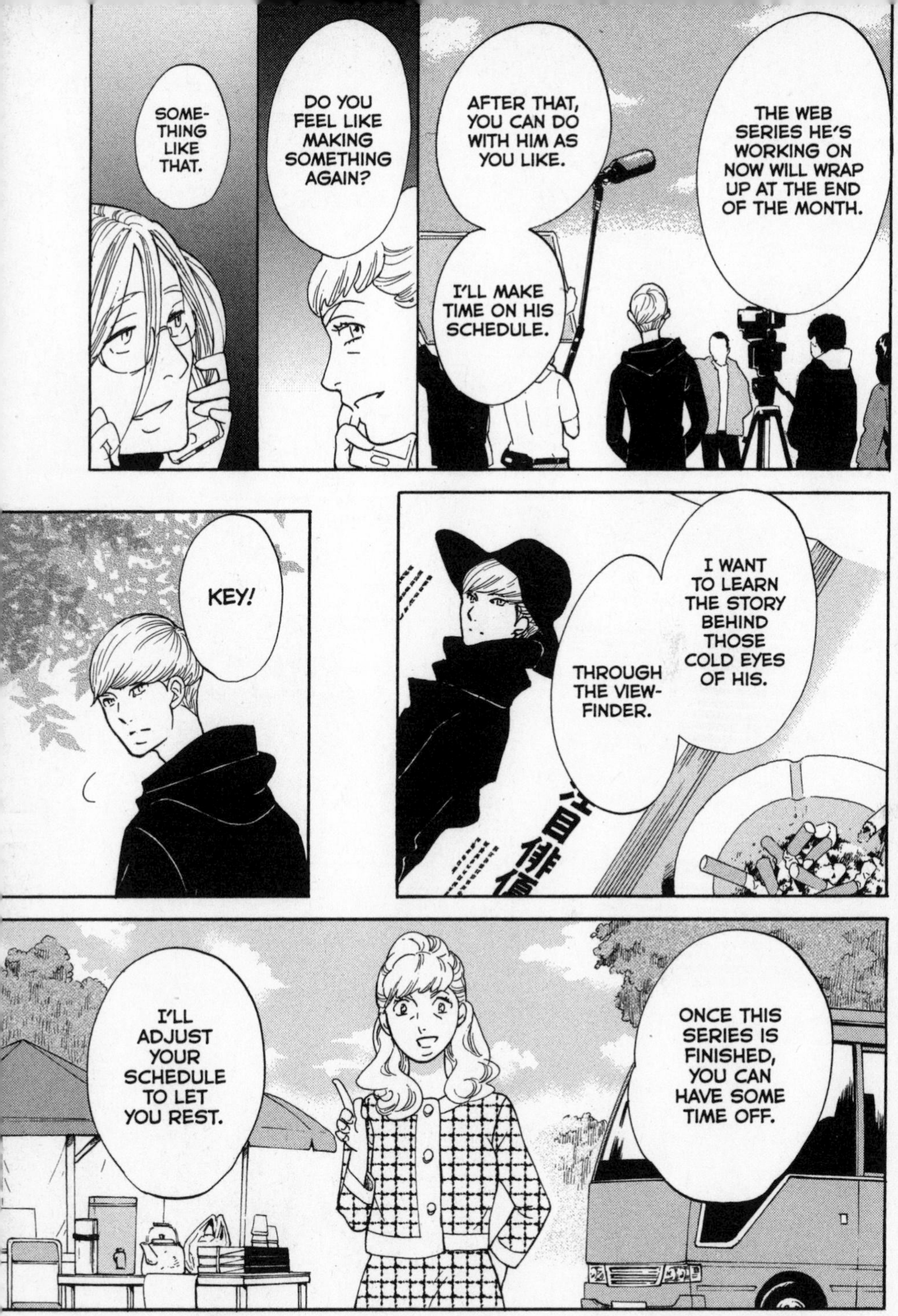
THE WEB SERIES HE'S WORKING ON NOW WILL WRAP UP AT THE END OF THE MONTH.
AFTER THAT, YOU CAN DO WITH HIM AS YOU LIKE.
I'LL MAKE TIME ON HIS SCHEDULE.
DO YOU FEEL LIKE MAKING SOMETHING AGAIN?
SOMETHING LIKE THAT.
I WANT TO LEARN THE STORY BEHIND THOSE COLD EYES OF HIS.
THROUGH THE VIEWFINDER.
KEY!
ONCE THIS SERIES IS FINISHED, YOU CAN HAVE SOME TIME OFF.
I'LL ADJUST YOUR SCHEDULE TO LET YOU REST.

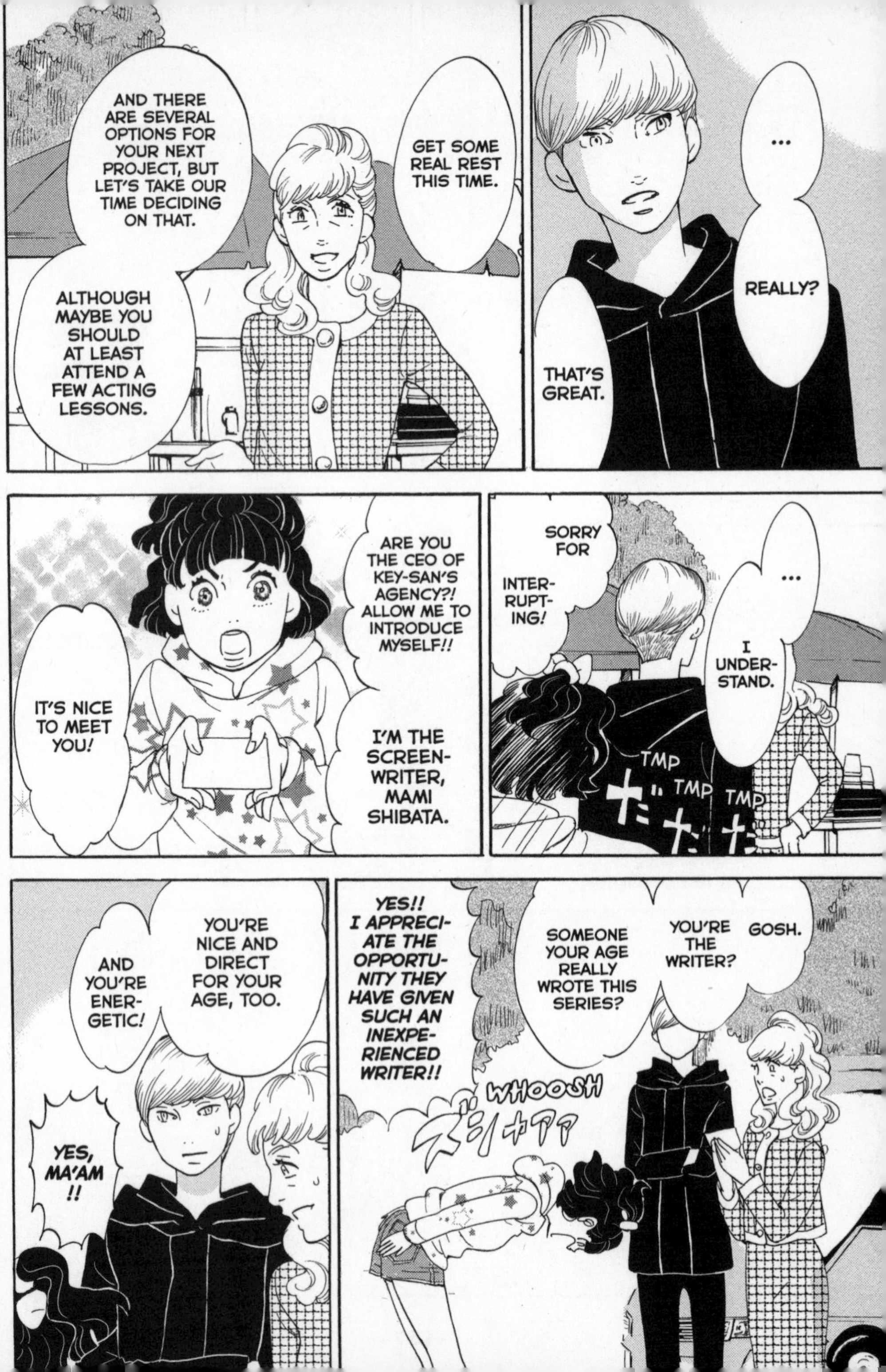
...
REALLY?
THAT'S GREAT.
GET SOME REAL REST THIS TIME.
AND THERE ARE SEVERAL OPTIONS FOR YOUR NEXT PROJECT, BUT LET'S TAKE OUR TIME DECIDING ON THAT.
ALTHOUGH MAYBE YOU SHOULD AT LEAST ATTEND A FEW ACTING LESSONS.
...
I UNDER-STAND.
SORRY FOR
INTER-RUPT-ING!
TMP TMP TMP
ARE YOU THE CEO OF KEY-SAN'S AGENCY?! ALLOW ME TO INTRODUCE MYSELF!!
I'M THE SCREEN-WRITER, MAMI SHIBATA.
IT'S NICE TO MEET YOU!
GOSH.
YOU'RE THE WRITER?
SOMEONE YOUR AGE REALLY WROTE THIS SERIES?
YES!! I APPRECI-ATE THE OPPORTU-NITY THEY HAVE GIVEN SUCH AN INEXPE-RIENCED WRITER!!
WHOOSH
YOU'RE NICE AND DIRECT FOR YOUR AGE, TOO.
AND YOU'RE ENER-GETIC!
YES, MA'AM !!

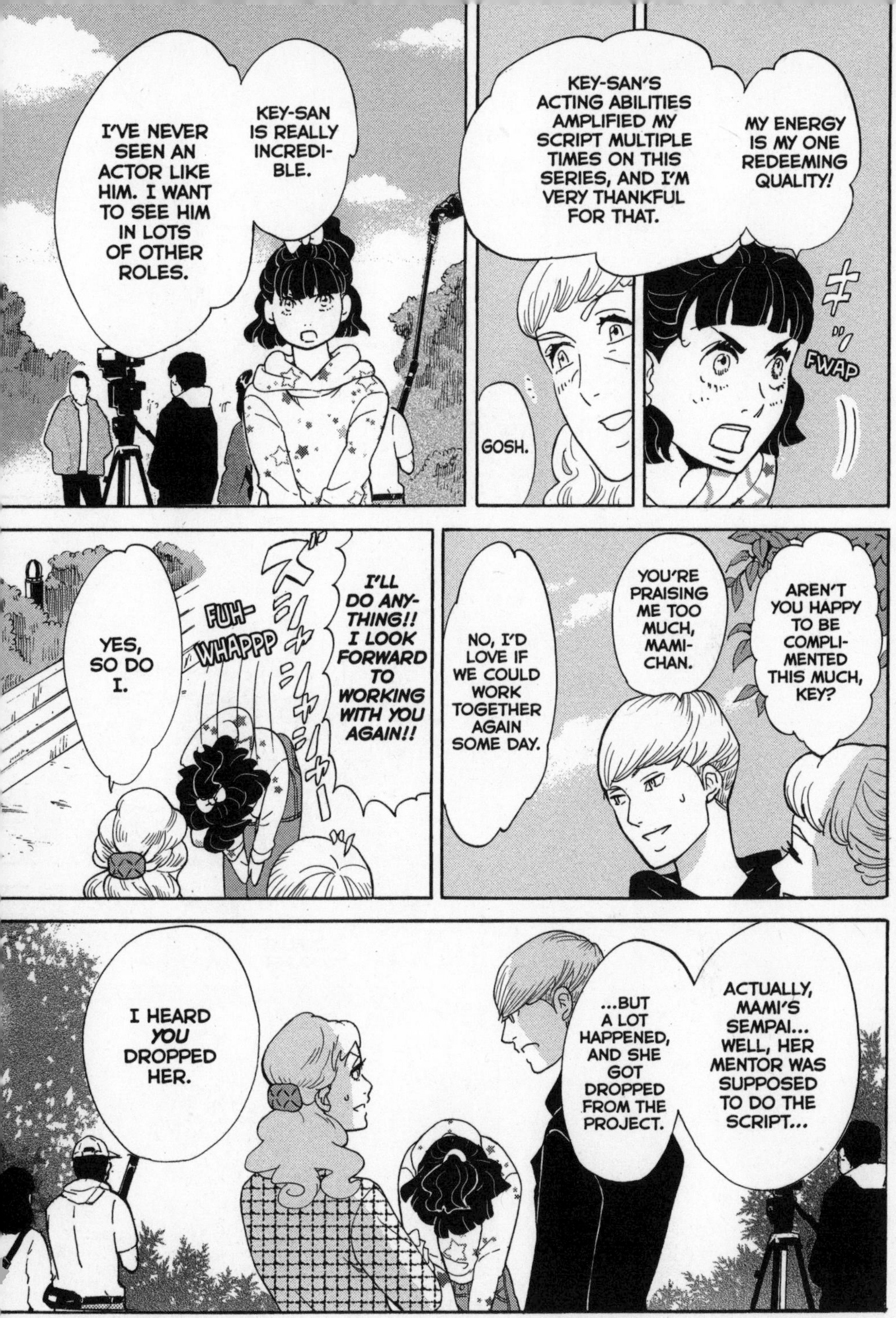

MY ENERGY IS MY ONE REDEEMING QUALITY!
FWAP
KEY-SAN'S ACTING ABILITIES AMPLIFIED MY SCRIPT MULTIPLE TIMES ON THIS SERIES, AND I'M VERY THANKFUL FOR THAT.
GOSH.
KEY-SAN IS REALLY INCREDIBLE.
I'VE NEVER SEEN AN ACTOR LIKE HIM. I WANT TO SEE HIM IN LOTS OF OTHER ROLES.
AREN'T YOU HAPPY TO BE COMPLIMENTED THIS MUCH, KEY?
YOU'RE PRAISING ME TOO MUCH, MAMI-CHAN.
NO, I'D LOVE IF WE COULD WORK TOGETHER AGAIN SOME DAY.
I'LL DO ANYTHING!! I LOOK FORWARD TO WORKING WITH YOU AGAIN!!
FUH-WHAPPP
YES, SO DO I.
ACTUALLY, MAMI'S SEMPAI... WELL, HER MENTOR WAS SUPPOSED TO DO THE SCRIPT...
...BUT A LOT HAPPENED, AND SHE GOT DROPPED FROM THE PROJECT.
I HEARD *YOU* DROPPED HER.

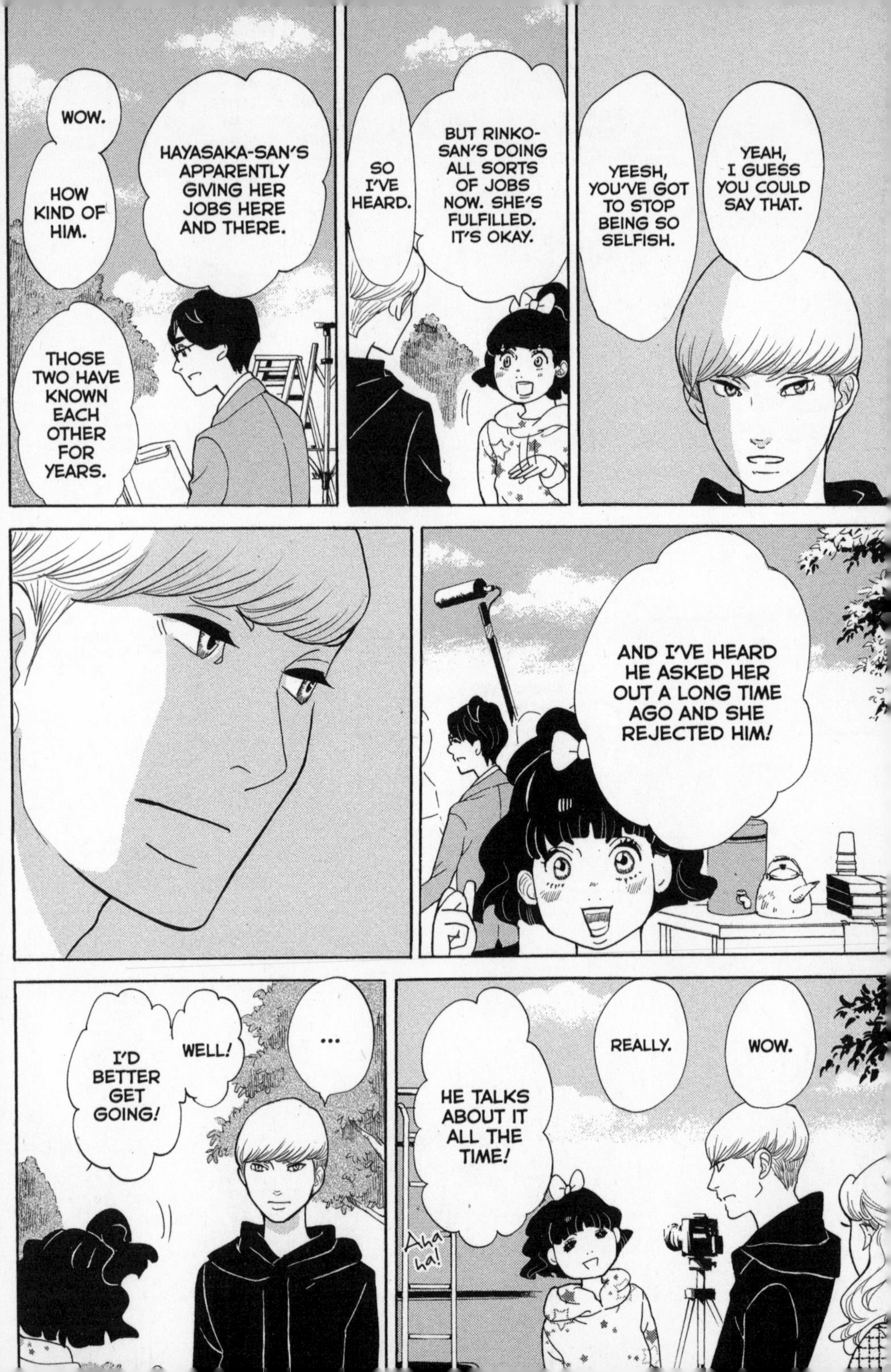
YEAH, I GUESS YOU COULD SAY THAT.
YEESH, YOU'VE GOT TO STOP BEING SO SELFISH.
BUT RINKO-SAN'S DOING ALL SORTS OF JOBS NOW. SHE'S FULFILLED. IT'S OKAY.
SO I'VE HEARD.
HAYASAKA-SAN'S APPARENTLY GIVING HER JOBS HERE AND THERE.
WOW.
HOW KIND OF HIM.
THOSE TWO HAVE KNOWN EACH OTHER FOR YEARS.
AND I'VE HEARD HE ASKED HER OUT A LONG TIME AGO AND SHE REJECTED HIM!
WOW.
REALLY.
HE TALKS ABOUT IT ALL THE TIME!
Aha ha!
...
WELL!
I'D BETTER GET GOING!

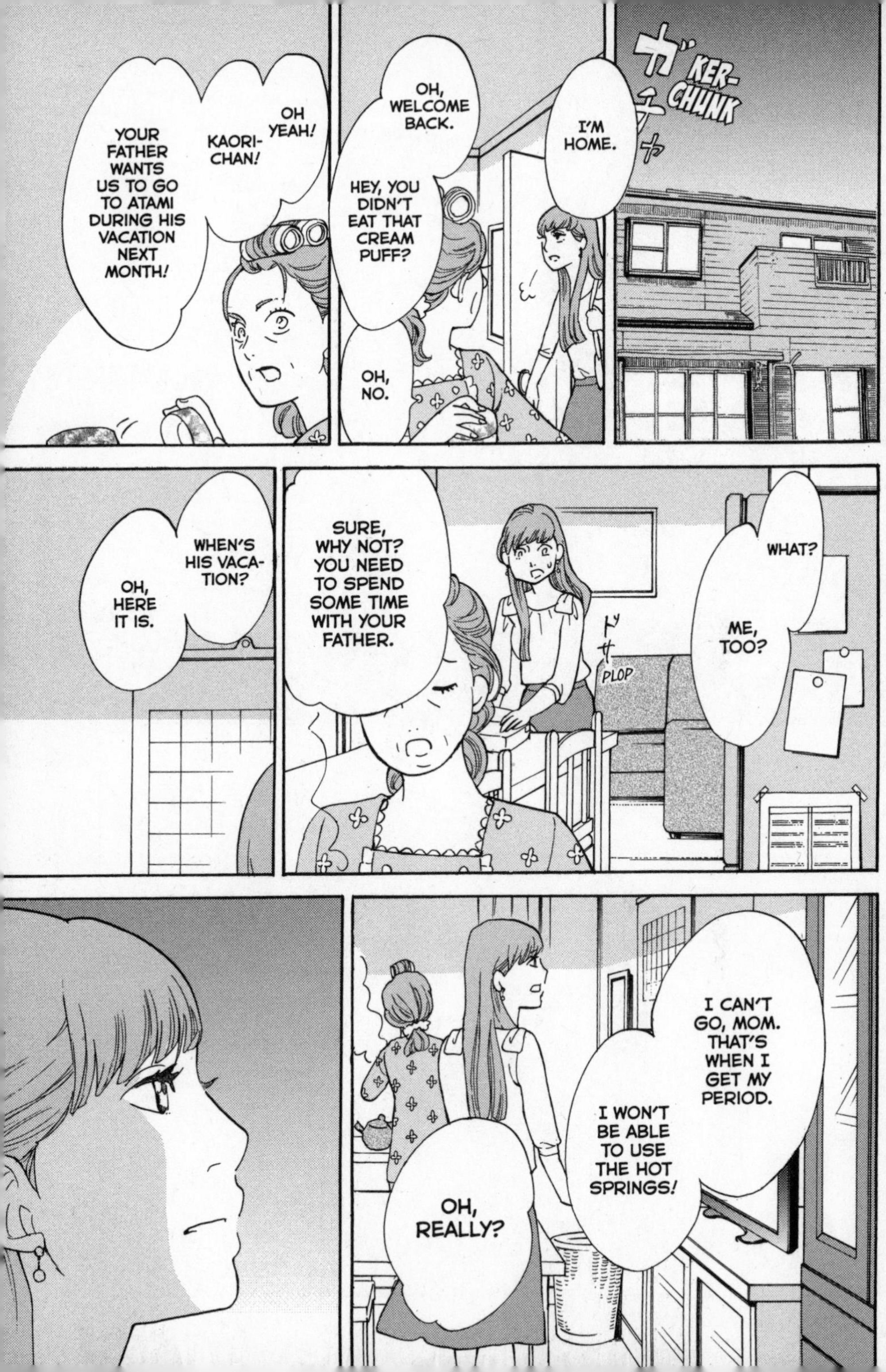
KER-CHUNK
I'M HOME.
OH, WELCOME BACK.
HEY, YOU DIDN'T EAT THAT CREAM PUFF?
OH, NO.
OH YEAH!
KAORI-CHAN!
YOUR FATHER WANTS US TO GO TO ATAMI DURING HIS VACATION NEXT MONTH!
WHAT?
ME, TOO?
PLOP
SURE, WHY NOT? YOU NEED TO SPEND SOME TIME WITH YOUR FATHER.
WHEN'S HIS VACA-TION?
OH, HERE IT IS.
I CAN'T GO, MOM. THAT'S WHEN I GET MY PERIOD.
I WON'T BE ABLE TO USE THE HOT SPRINGS!
OH, REALLY?

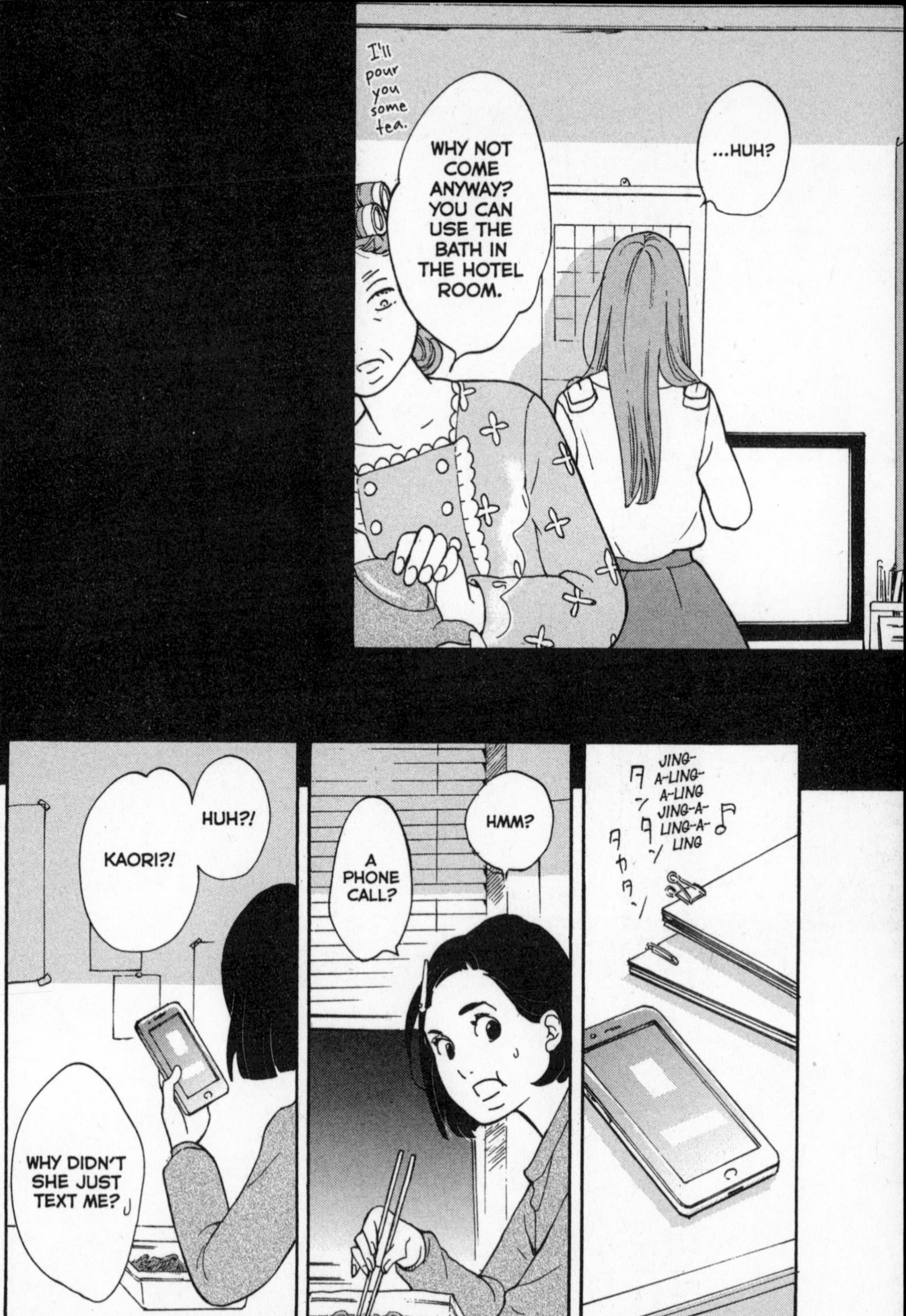
...HUH?
WHY NOT COME ANYWAY? YOU CAN USE THE BATH IN THE HOTEL ROOM.
I'll pour you some tea.
JING-A-LING A-LING JING-A-LING-A-LING
HMM?
A PHONE CALL?
HUH?!
KAORI?!
WHY DIDN'T SHE JUST TEXT ME?

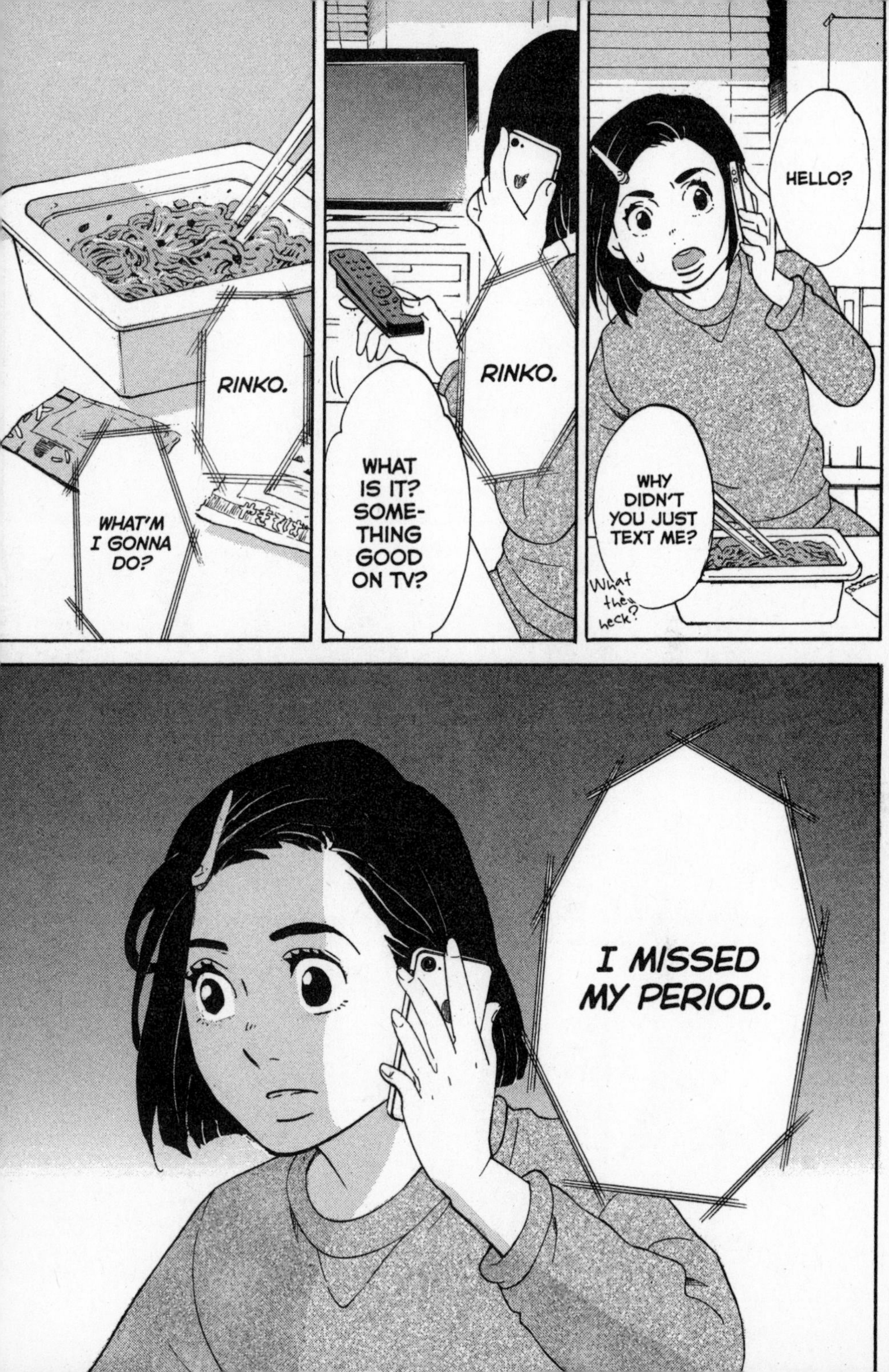
HELLO?
WHY DIDN'T YOU JUST TEXT ME?
What the heck?
RINKO.
WHAT IS IT? SOMETHING GOOD ON TV?
RINKO.
WHAT'M I GONNA DO?
I MISSED MY PERIOD.

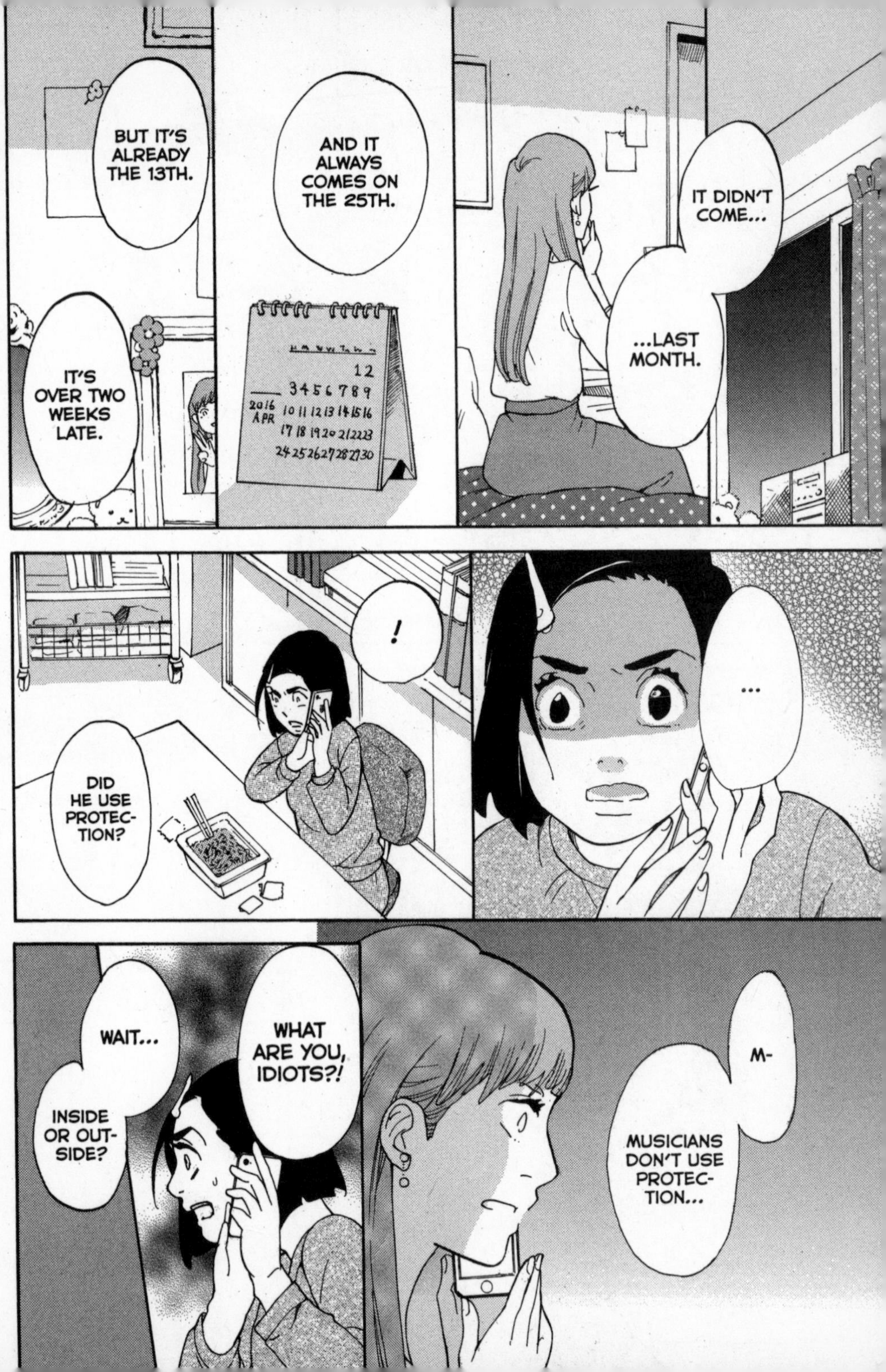
IT DIDN'T COME...
...LAST MONTH.
AND IT ALWAYS COMES ON THE 25TH.
BUT IT'S ALREADY THE 13TH.
IT'S OVER TWO WEEKS LATE.
...
!
DID HE USE PROTECTION?
M-
MUSICIANS DON'T USE PROTECTION...
WHAT ARE YOU, IDIOTS?!
WAIT...
INSIDE OR OUTSIDE?

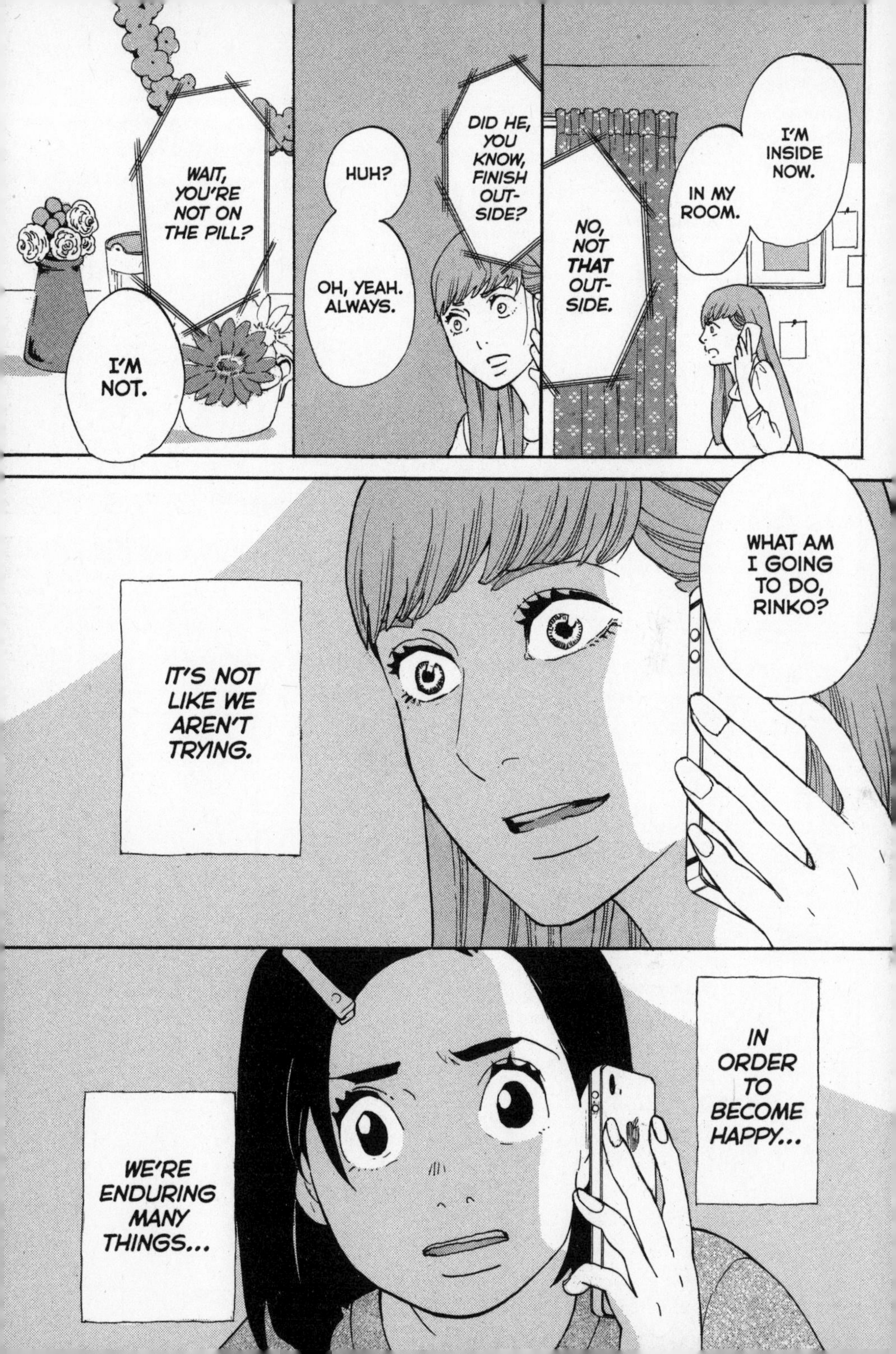
I'M INSIDE NOW.
IN MY ROOM.
DID HE, YOU KNOW, FINISH OUT-SIDE?
HUH?
NO, NOT THAT OUT-SIDE.
OH, YEAH. ALWAYS.
WAIT, YOU'RE NOT ON THE PILL?
I'M NOT.
WHAT AM I GOING TO DO, RINKO?
IT'S NOT LIKE WE AREN'T TRYING.
IN ORDER TO BECOME HAPPY...
WE'RE ENDURING MANY THINGS...

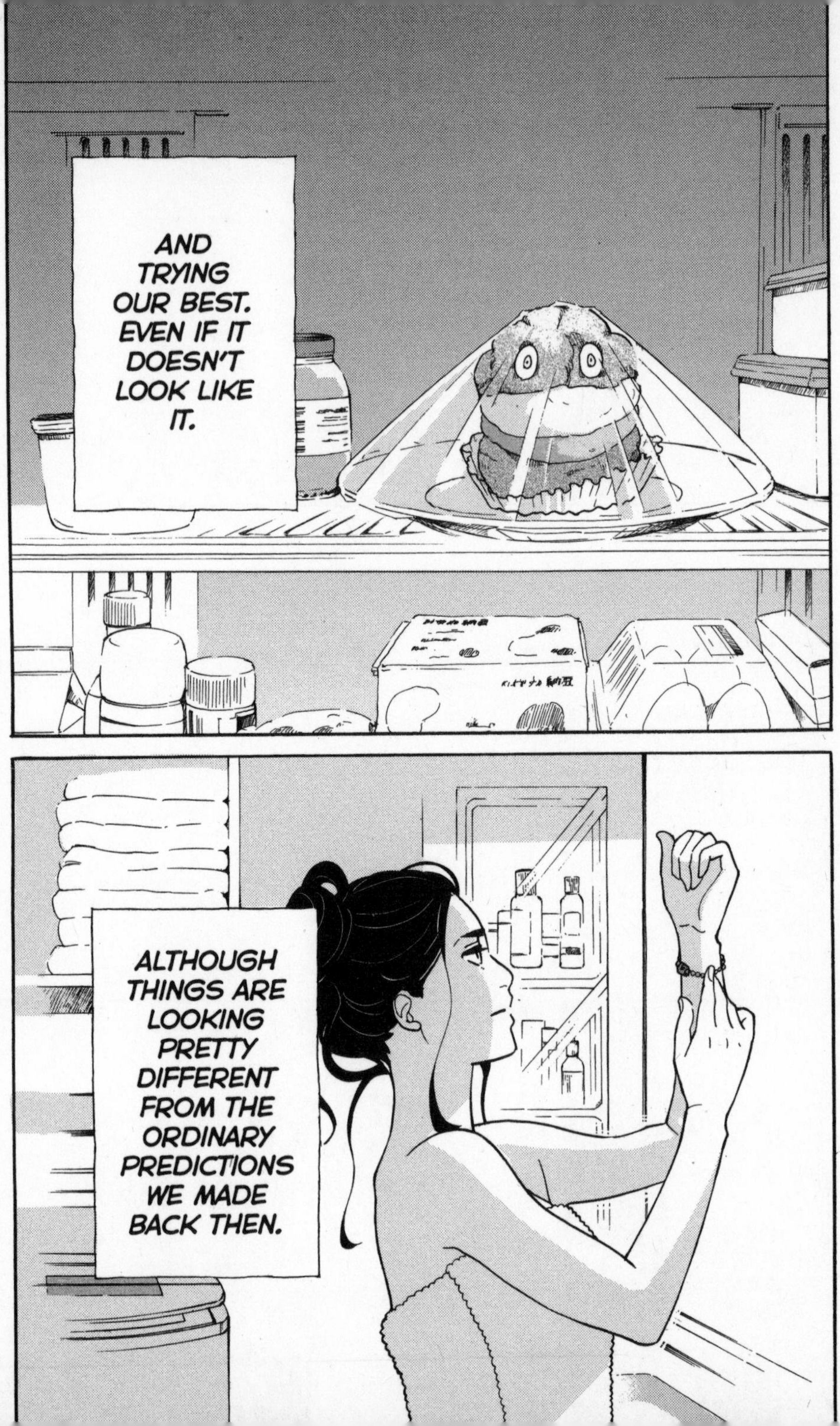
AND TRYING OUR BEST. EVEN IF IT DOESN'T LOOK LIKE IT.
ALTHOUGH THINGS ARE LOOKING PRETTY DIFFERENT FROM THE ORDINARY PREDICTIONS WE MADE BACK THEN.

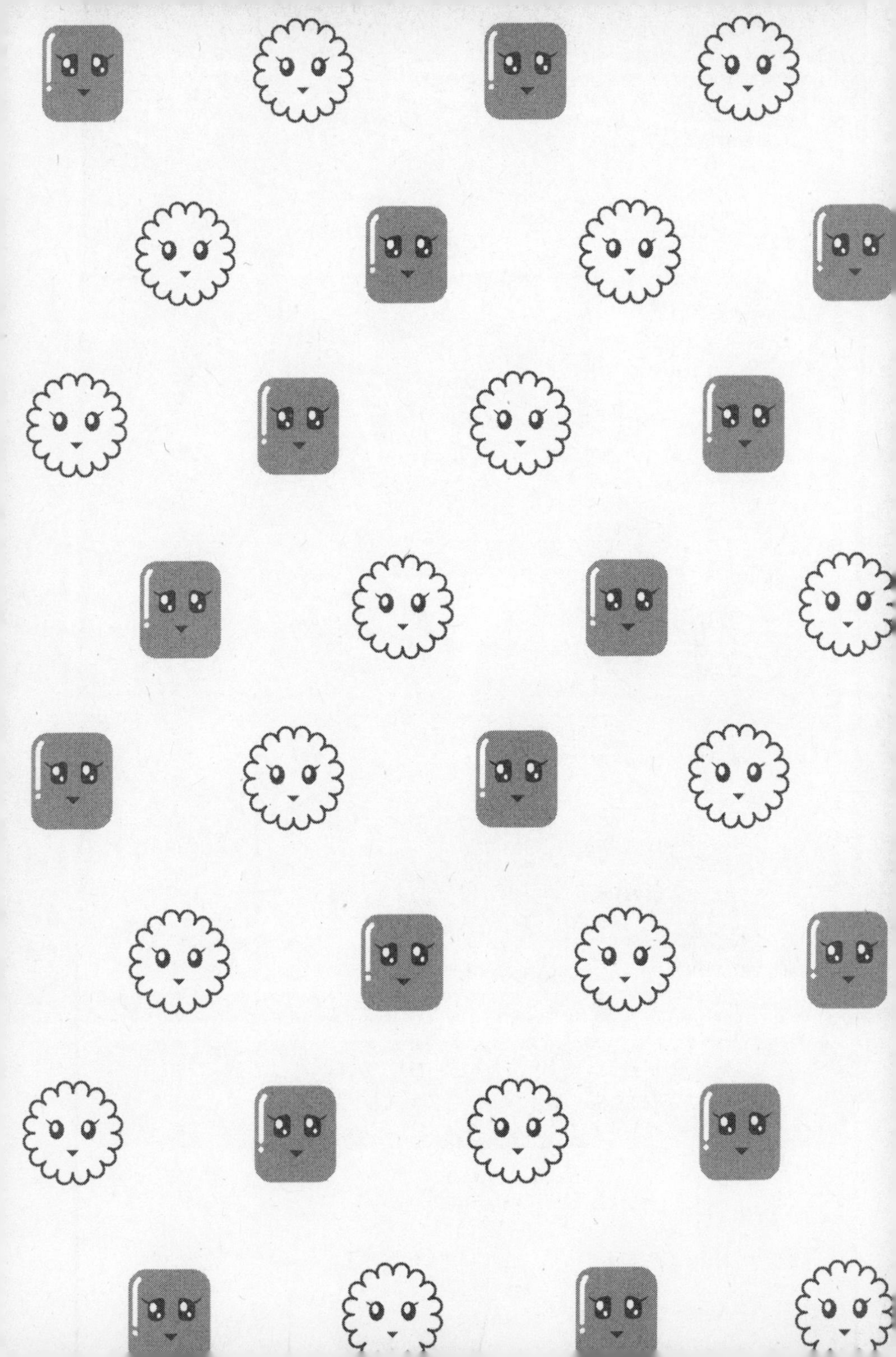

TOKYO TARAREBA GIRLS
(SIDE STORY)

Tarare-Bar

IN THE FOLLOWING SIDE STORY, "TARARE-BAR,"
WE PUBLISH PROBLEMS SUBMITTED BY READERS
FROM ACROSS JAPAN.

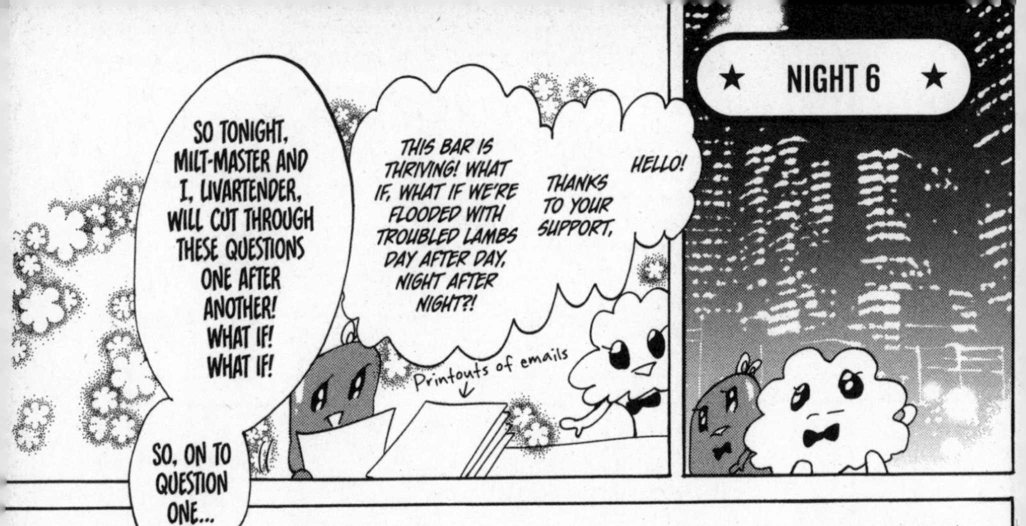
★ NIGHT 6 ★
HELLO!
THANKS TO YOUR SUPPORT,
THIS BAR IS THRIVING! WHAT IF, WHAT IF WE'RE FLOODED WITH TROUBLED LAMBS DAY AFTER DAY, NIGHT AFTER NIGHT?!
SO TONIGHT, MILT-MASTER AND I, LIVARTENDER, WILL CUT THROUGH THESE QUESTIONS ONE AFTER ANOTHER! WHAT IF! WHAT IF!
Printouts of emails
SO, ON TO QUESTION ONE...

PROBLEM: I DON'T KNOW HOW TO APPROACH THE PERSON I'M INTERESTED IN

THERE'S A MAN AT WORK I FIND VERY ATTRACTIVE. WE DON'T INTERACT AT WORK AT ALL, ONLY PASSING EACH OTHER IN THE HALLS AT MOST (I WANDER AROUND HIS DESK MEANINGLESSLY TIME AND TIME AGAIN). NATURALLY, I'VE NEVER SPOKEN TO HIM EITHER.
I LOOKED UP HIS NAME IN THE COMPANY REGISTER AND EMPLOYED MY SEARCH SKILLS TO FIND HIS INSTAGRAM PAGE, BUT NOW I DON'T KNOW HOW TO BRIDGE THE GAP BETWEEN US. PLUS, ON INSTAGRAM, HE DELVES INTO FASHION CRITICISM, REFERENCES GOING TO BLUE BOTTLE COFFEE, AND UPLOADS PHOTOS OF HIS GIRLFRIEND WHO WOULD LOOK GREAT IN COMME DES GARÇONS. HE'S SO AWARE. HE'S SO MUCH TRENDIER THAN ME, AND HIS GIRLFRIEND IS SO CUTE, THAT WHEN I WATCH HIM EVERY DAY ON INSTAGRAM, I FEEL LIKE I COULD BE HAPPY JUST STAYING A FAN CYBERSTALKING HIM FROM AFAR...
BUT AT WORK, I GO OUT OF MY WAY TO WANDER AROUND IN HIS VICINITY, MY HEART AFLUTTER. I'VE LOST SIGHT OF WHAT I WANT TO BE TO HIM. I MEAN, HE IS PHYSICALLY JUST MY TYPE, BUT IT LOOKS LIKE HE'S GOT THIS LONG-TERM GIRLFRIEND, SO I THINK I'D LIKE TO HAVE SEX WITH HIM JUST ONCE.

PEN NAME: KANO-P (23)

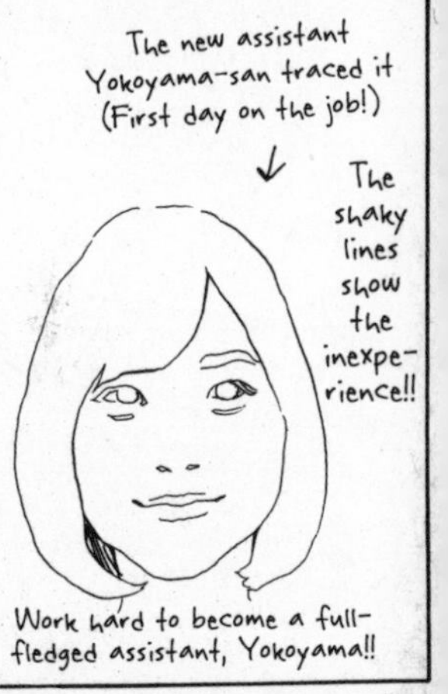
The new assistant Yokoyama-san traced it (First day on the job!)
The shaky lines show the inexperience!!
Work hard to become a full-fledged assistant, Yokoyama!!

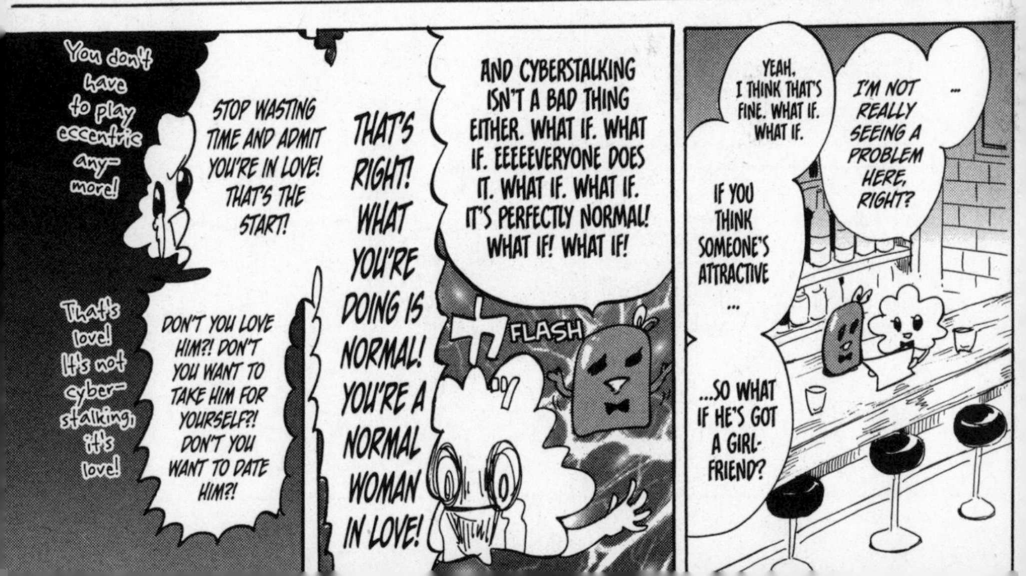
...
I'M NOT REALLY SEEING A PROBLEM HERE, RIGHT?
YEAH, I THINK THAT'S FINE. WHAT IF. WHAT IF.
IF YOU THINK SOMEONE'S ATTRACTIVE ...
...SO WHAT IF HE'S GOT A GIRLFRIEND?
AND CYBERSTALKING ISN'T A BAD THING EITHER. WHAT IF. WHAT IF. EEEEEVERYONE DOES IT. WHAT IF. WHAT IF. IT'S PERFECTLY NORMAL! WHAT IF! WHAT IF!
THAT'S RIGHT! WHAT YOU'RE DOING IS NORMAL! YOU'RE A NORMAL WOMAN IN LOVE!
STOP WASTING TIME AND ADMIT YOU'RE IN LOVE! THAT'S THE START!
You don't have to play eccentric anymore!
FLASH
DON'T YOU LOVE HIM?! DON'T YOU WANT TO TAKE HIM FOR YOURSELF?! DON'T YOU WANT TO DATE HIM?!
That's love! It's not cyberstalking, it's love!

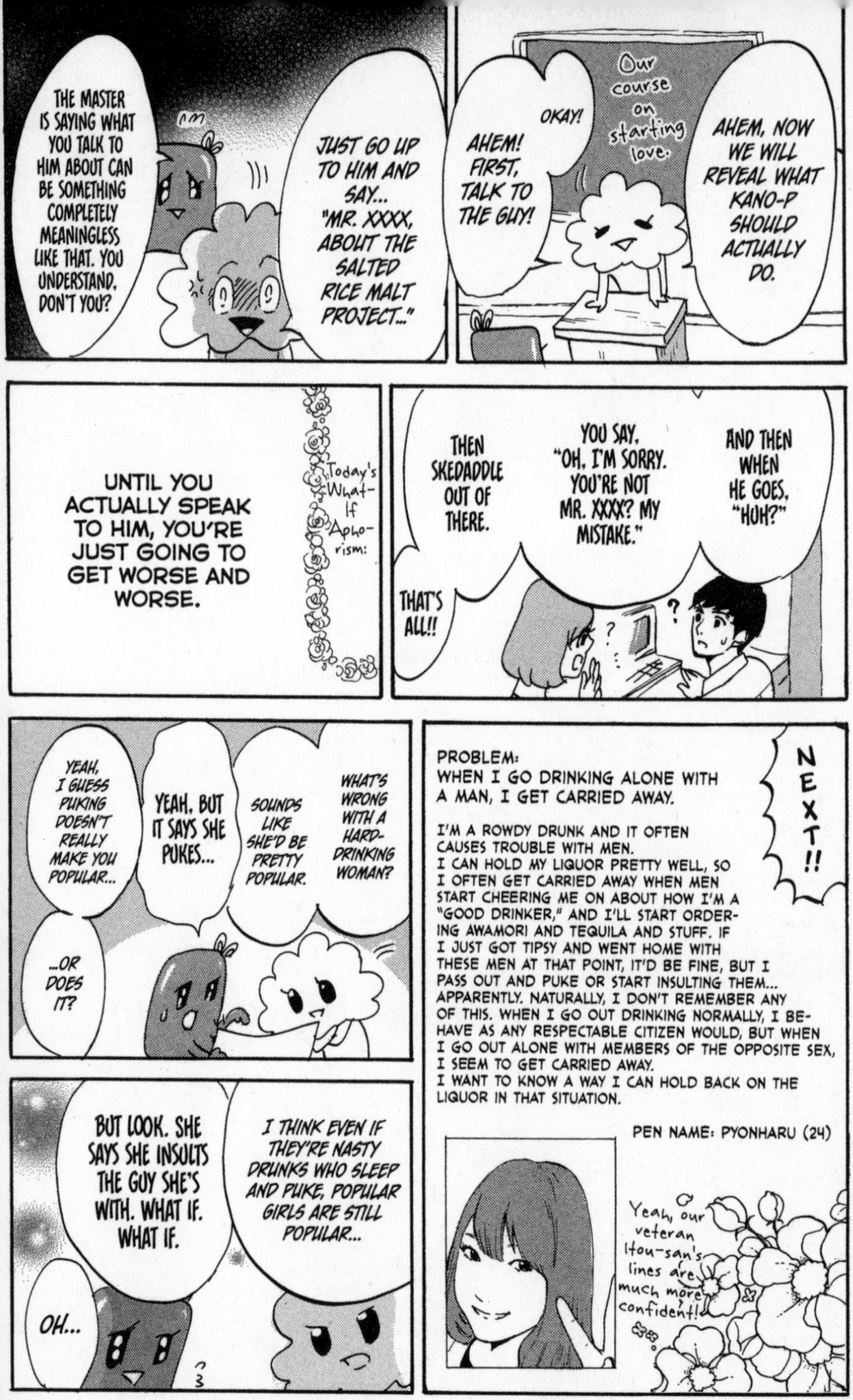
AHEM, NOW WE WILL REVEAL WHAT KANO-P SHOULD ACTUALLY DO.
Our course on starting love.
OKAY!
AHEM! FIRST, TALK TO THE GUY!
JUST GO UP TO HIM AND SAY... "MR. XXXX, ABOUT THE SALTED RICE MALT PROJECT..."
THE MASTER IS SAYING WHAT YOU TALK TO HIM ABOUT CAN BE SOMETHING COMPLETELY MEANINGLESS LIKE THAT. YOU UNDERSTAND, DON'T YOU?
AND THEN WHEN HE GOES, "HUH?"
YOU SAY, "OH, I'M SORRY. YOU'RE NOT MR. XXXX? MY MISTAKE."
THEN SKEDADDLE OUT OF THERE.
THAT'S ALL!!
Today's What-If Aphorism:
UNTIL YOU ACTUALLY SPEAK TO HIM, YOU'RE JUST GOING TO GET WORSE AND WORSE.
NEXT!!
PROBLEM:
WHEN I GO DRINKING ALONE WITH A MAN, I GET CARRIED AWAY.
I'M A ROWDY DRUNK AND IT OFTEN CAUSES TROUBLE WITH MEN.
I CAN HOLD MY LIQUOR PRETTY WELL, SO I OFTEN GET CARRIED AWAY WHEN MEN START CHEERING ME ON ABOUT HOW I'M A "GOOD DRINKER," AND I'LL START ORDERING AWAMORI AND TEQUILA AND STUFF. IF I JUST GOT TIPSY AND WENT HOME WITH THESE MEN AT THAT POINT, IT'D BE FINE, BUT I PASS OUT AND PUKE OR START INSULTING THEM... APPARENTLY. NATURALLY, I DON'T REMEMBER ANY OF THIS. WHEN I GO OUT DRINKING NORMALLY, I BEHAVE AS ANY RESPECTABLE CITIZEN WOULD, BUT WHEN I GO OUT ALONE WITH MEMBERS OF THE OPPOSITE SEX, I SEEM TO GET CARRIED AWAY.
I WANT TO KNOW A WAY I CAN HOLD BACK ON THE LIQUOR IN THAT SITUATION.
PEN NAME: PYONHARU (24)
Yeah, our veteran Itou-san's lines are much more confident!
WHAT'S WRONG WITH A HARD-DRINKING WOMAN?
SOUNDS LIKE SHE'D BE PRETTY POPULAR.
YEAH, BUT IT SAYS SHE PUKES...
YEAH, I GUESS PUKING DOESN'T REALLY MAKE YOU POPULAR...
...OR DOES IT?
I THINK EVEN IF THEY'RE NASTY DRUNKS WHO SLEEP AND PUKE, POPULAR GIRLS ARE STILL POPULAR...
BUT LOOK. SHE SAYS SHE INSULTS THE GUY SHE'S WITH. WHAT IF. WHAT IF.
OH...

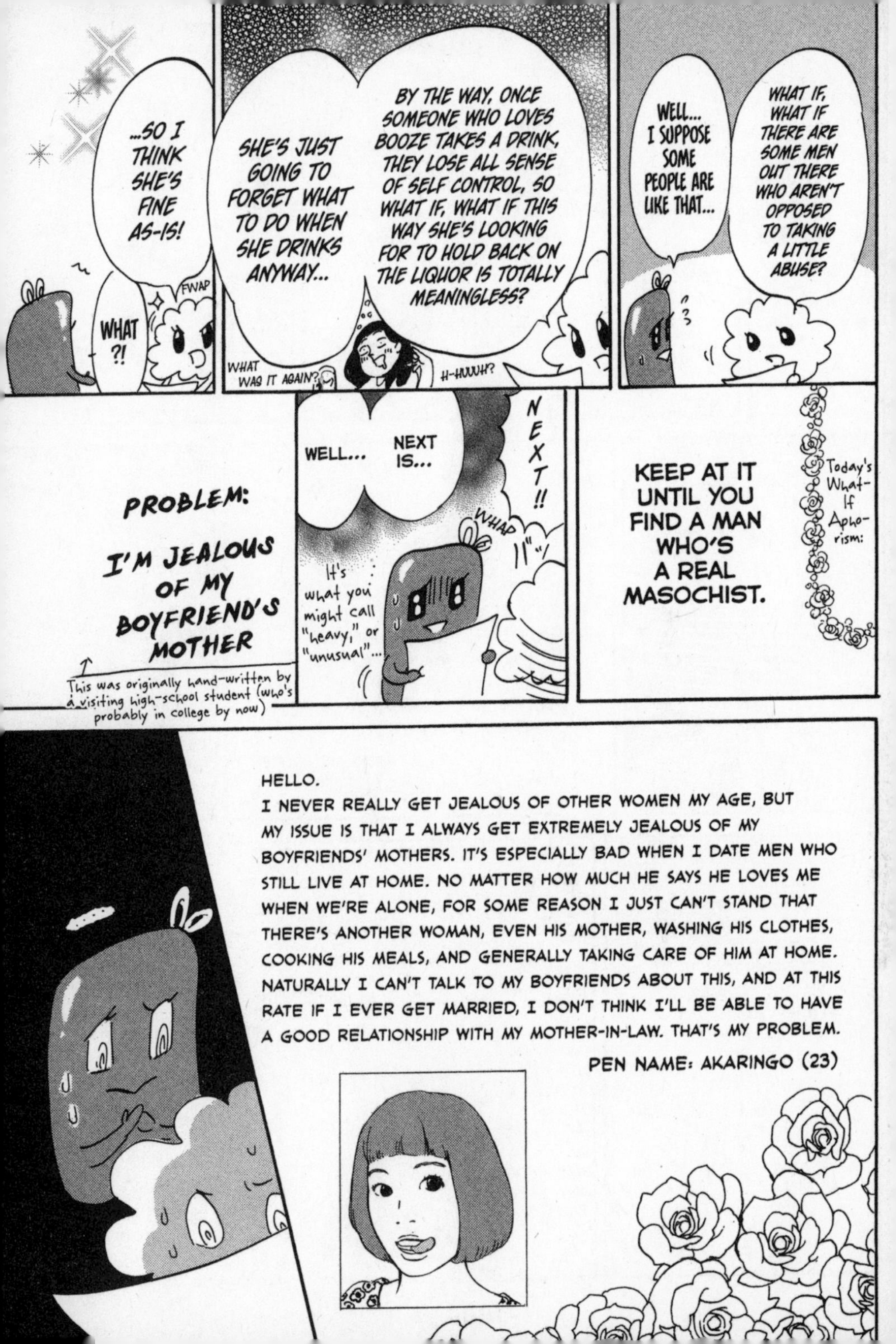
WHAT IF, WHAT IF THERE ARE SOME MEN OUT THERE WHO AREN'T OPPOSED TO TAKING A LITTLE ABUSE?
WELL... I SUPPOSE SOME PEOPLE ARE LIKE THAT...
BY THE WAY, ONCE SOMEONE WHO LOVES BOOZE TAKES A DRINK, THEY LOSE ALL SENSE OF SELF CONTROL, SO WHAT IF, WHAT IF THIS WAY SHE'S LOOKING FOR TO HOLD BACK ON THE LIQUOR IS TOTALLY MEANINGLESS?
SHE'S JUST GOING TO FORGET WHAT TO DO WHEN SHE DRINKS ANYWAY...
H-HUUUH?
WHAT WAS IT AGAIN?
...SO I THINK SHE'S FINE AS-IS!
FWAP
WHAT?!
Today's What-If Aphorism:
KEEP AT IT UNTIL YOU FIND A MAN WHO'S A REAL MASOCHIST.
NEXT!!
NEXT IS...
WELL...
WHAP
It's what you might call "heavy," or "unusual"...
PROBLEM:
I'M JEALOUS OF MY BOYFRIEND'S MOTHER
This was originally hand-written by a visiting high-school student (who's probably in college by now)
HELLO.
I NEVER REALLY GET JEALOUS OF OTHER WOMEN MY AGE, BUT MY ISSUE IS THAT I ALWAYS GET EXTREMELY JEALOUS OF MY BOYFRIENDS' MOTHERS. IT'S ESPECIALLY BAD WHEN I DATE MEN WHO STILL LIVE AT HOME. NO MATTER HOW MUCH HE SAYS HE LOVES ME WHEN WE'RE ALONE, FOR SOME REASON I JUST CAN'T STAND THAT THERE'S ANOTHER WOMAN, EVEN HIS MOTHER, WASHING HIS CLOTHES, COOKING HIS MEALS, AND GENERALLY TAKING CARE OF HIM AT HOME. NATURALLY I CAN'T TALK TO MY BOYFRIENDS ABOUT THIS, AND AT THIS RATE IF I EVER GET MARRIED, I DON'T THINK I'LL BE ABLE TO HAVE A GOOD RELATIONSHIP WITH MY MOTHER-IN-LAW. THAT'S MY PROBLEM.
PEN NAME: AKARINGO (23)

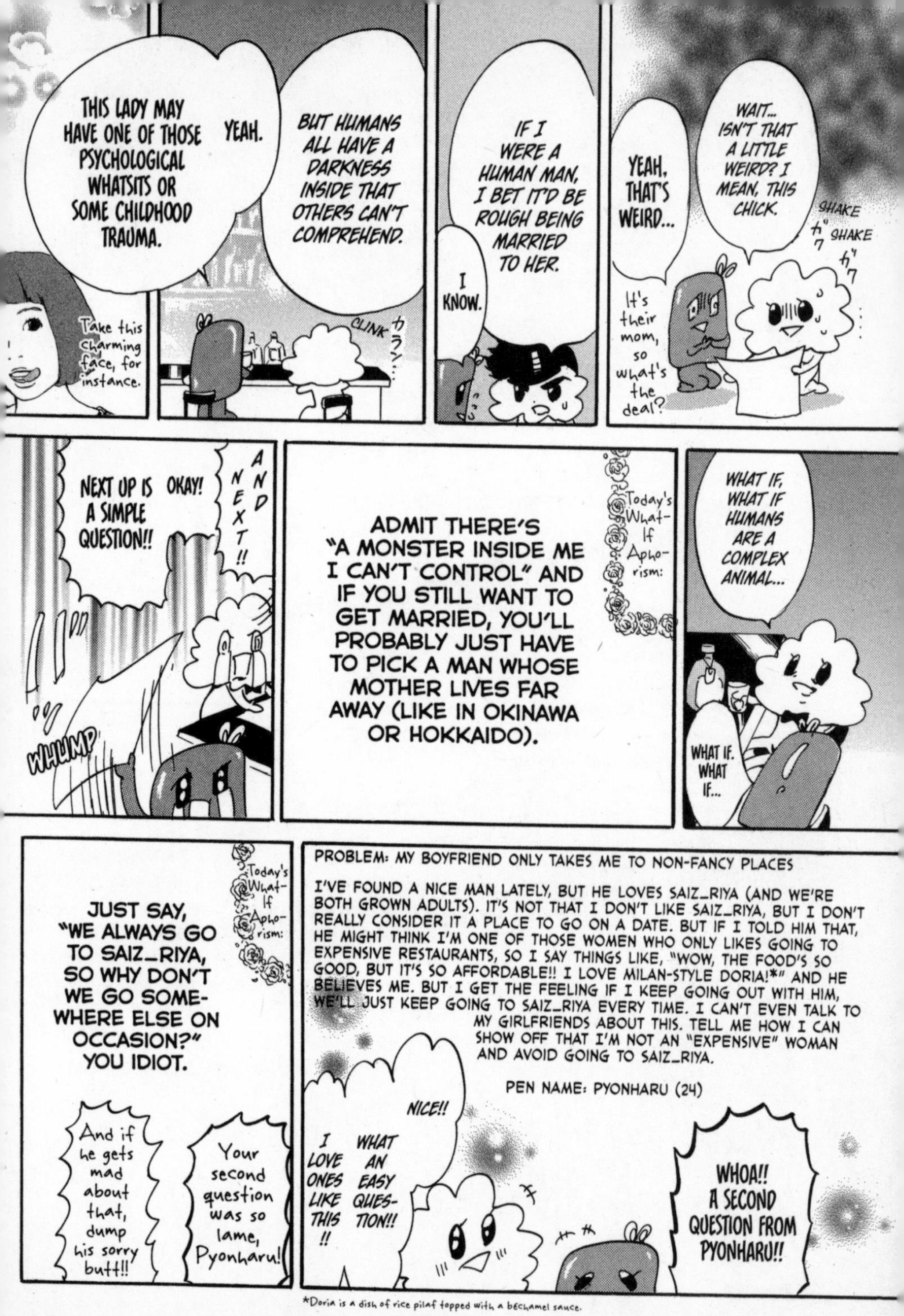
WAIT... ISN'T THAT A LITTLE WEIRD? I MEAN, THIS CHICK.
SHAKE SHAKE
YEAH, THAT'S WEIRD...
It's their mom, so what's the deal?
IF I WERE A HUMAN MAN, I BET IT'D BE ROUGH BEING MARRIED TO HER.
I KNOW.
BUT HUMANS ALL HAVE A DARKNESS INSIDE THAT OTHERS CAN'T COMPREHEND.
YEAH.
CLINK
THIS LADY MAY HAVE ONE OF THOSE PSYCHOLOGICAL WHATSITS OR SOME CHILDHOOD TRAUMA.
Take this charming face, for instance.
WHAT IF, WHAT IF HUMANS ARE A COMPLEX ANIMAL...
WHAT IF. WHAT IF...
Today's What-If Aphorism:
ADMIT THERE'S "A MONSTER INSIDE ME I CAN'T CONTROL" AND IF YOU STILL WANT TO GET MARRIED, YOU'LL PROBABLY JUST HAVE TO PICK A MAN WHOSE MOTHER LIVES FAR AWAY (LIKE IN OKINAWA OR HOKKAIDO).
AND NEXT!!
OKAY!
NEXT UP IS A SIMPLE QUESTION!!
WHUMP
PROBLEM: MY BOYFRIEND ONLY TAKES ME TO NON-FANCY PLACES
I'VE FOUND A NICE MAN LATELY, BUT HE LOVES SAIZ_RIYA (AND WE'RE BOTH GROWN ADULTS). IT'S NOT THAT I DON'T LIKE SAIZ_RIYA, BUT I DON'T REALLY CONSIDER IT A PLACE TO GO ON A DATE. BUT IF I TOLD HIM THAT, HE MIGHT THINK I'M ONE OF THOSE WOMEN WHO ONLY LIKES GOING TO EXPENSIVE RESTAURANTS, SO I SAY THINGS LIKE, "WOW, THE FOOD'S SO GOOD, BUT IT'S SO AFFORDABLE!! I LOVE MILAN-STYLE DORIA!*" AND HE BELIEVES ME. BUT I GET THE FEELING IF I KEEP GOING OUT WITH HIM, WE'LL JUST KEEP GOING TO SAIZ_RIYA EVERY TIME. I CAN'T EVEN TALK TO MY GIRLFRIENDS ABOUT THIS. TELL ME HOW I CAN SHOW OFF THAT I'M NOT AN "EXPENSIVE" WOMAN AND AVOID GOING TO SAIZ_RIYA.
PEN NAME: PYONHARU (24)
WHOA!! A SECOND QUESTION FROM PYONHARU!!
NICE!!
WHAT AN EASY QUESTION!!
I LOVE ONES LIKE THIS!!
Today's What-If Aphorism:
JUST SAY, "WE ALWAYS GO TO SAIZ_RIYA, SO WHY DON'T WE GO SOMEWHERE ELSE ON OCCASION?" YOU IDIOT.
Your second question was so lame, Pyonharu!
And if he gets mad about that, dump his sorry butt!!

*Doria is a dish of rice pilaf topped with a béchamel sauce.

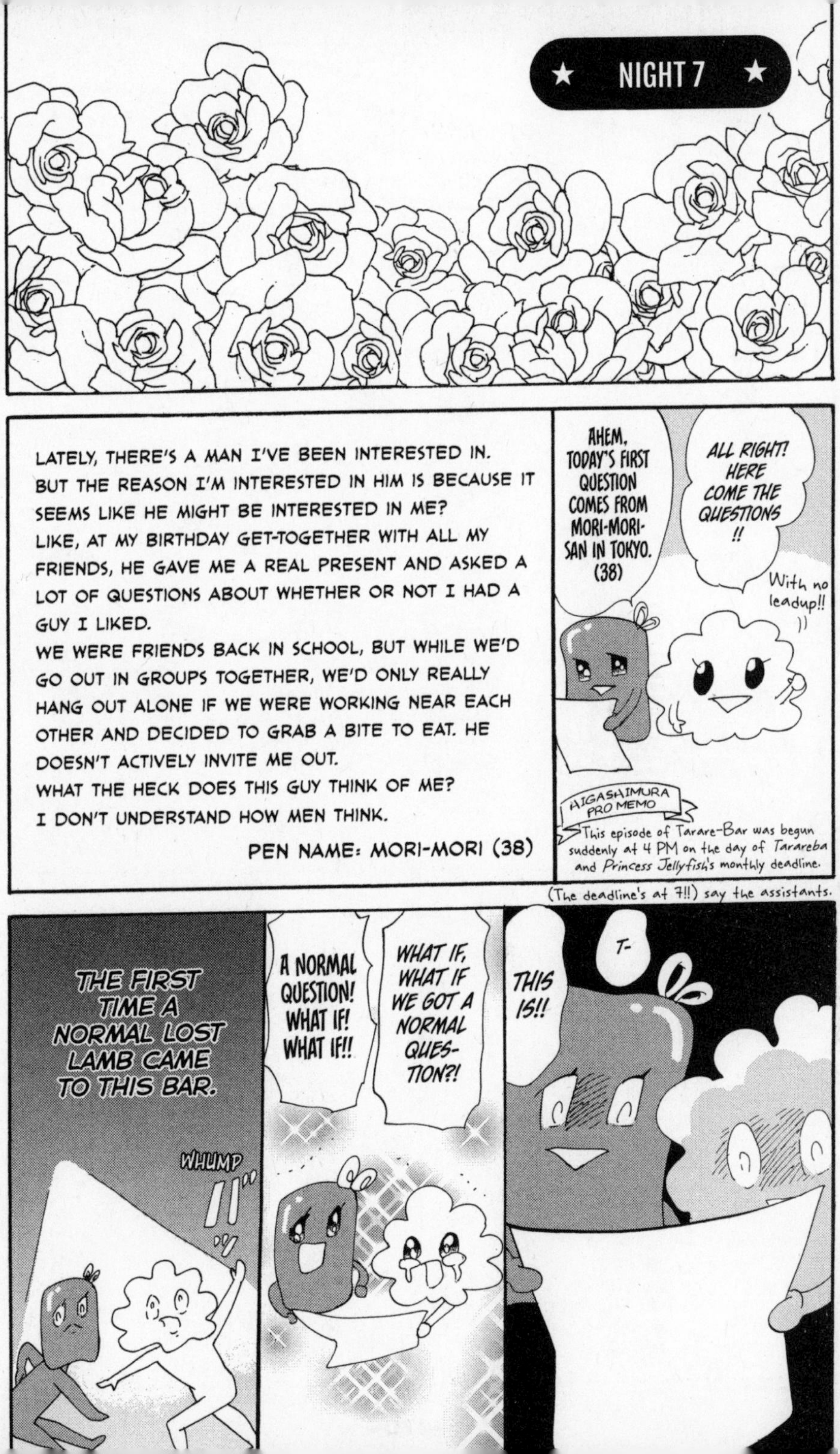
★ NIGHT 7 ★
ALL RIGHT! HERE COME THE QUESTIONS!!
AHEM, TODAY'S FIRST QUESTION COMES FROM MORI-MORI-SAN IN TOKYO. (38)
With no leadup!!
LATELY, THERE'S A MAN I'VE BEEN INTERESTED IN.
BUT THE REASON I'M INTERESTED IN HIM IS BECAUSE IT SEEMS LIKE HE MIGHT BE INTERESTED IN ME?
LIKE, AT MY BIRTHDAY GET-TOGETHER WITH ALL MY FRIENDS, HE GAVE ME A REAL PRESENT AND ASKED A LOT OF QUESTIONS ABOUT WHETHER OR NOT I HAD A GUY I LIKED.
WE WERE FRIENDS BACK IN SCHOOL, BUT WHILE WE'D GO OUT IN GROUPS TOGETHER, WE'D ONLY REALLY HANG OUT ALONE IF WE WERE WORKING NEAR EACH OTHER AND DECIDED TO GRAB A BITE TO EAT. HE DOESN'T ACTIVELY INVITE ME OUT.
WHAT THE HECK DOES THIS GUY THINK OF ME?
I DON'T UNDERSTAND HOW MEN THINK.
PEN NAME: MORI-MORI (38)
HIGASHIMURA PRO MEMO
This episode of Tarare-Bar was begun suddenly at 4 PM on the day of Tarareba and Princess Jellyfish's monthly deadline.
(The deadline's at 7!!) say the assistants.
T-
THIS IS!!
WHAT IF, WHAT IF WE GOT A NORMAL QUES-TION?!
A NORMAL QUESTION! WHAT IF! WHAT IF!!
THE FIRST TIME A NORMAL LOST LAMB CAME TO THIS BAR.
WHUMP

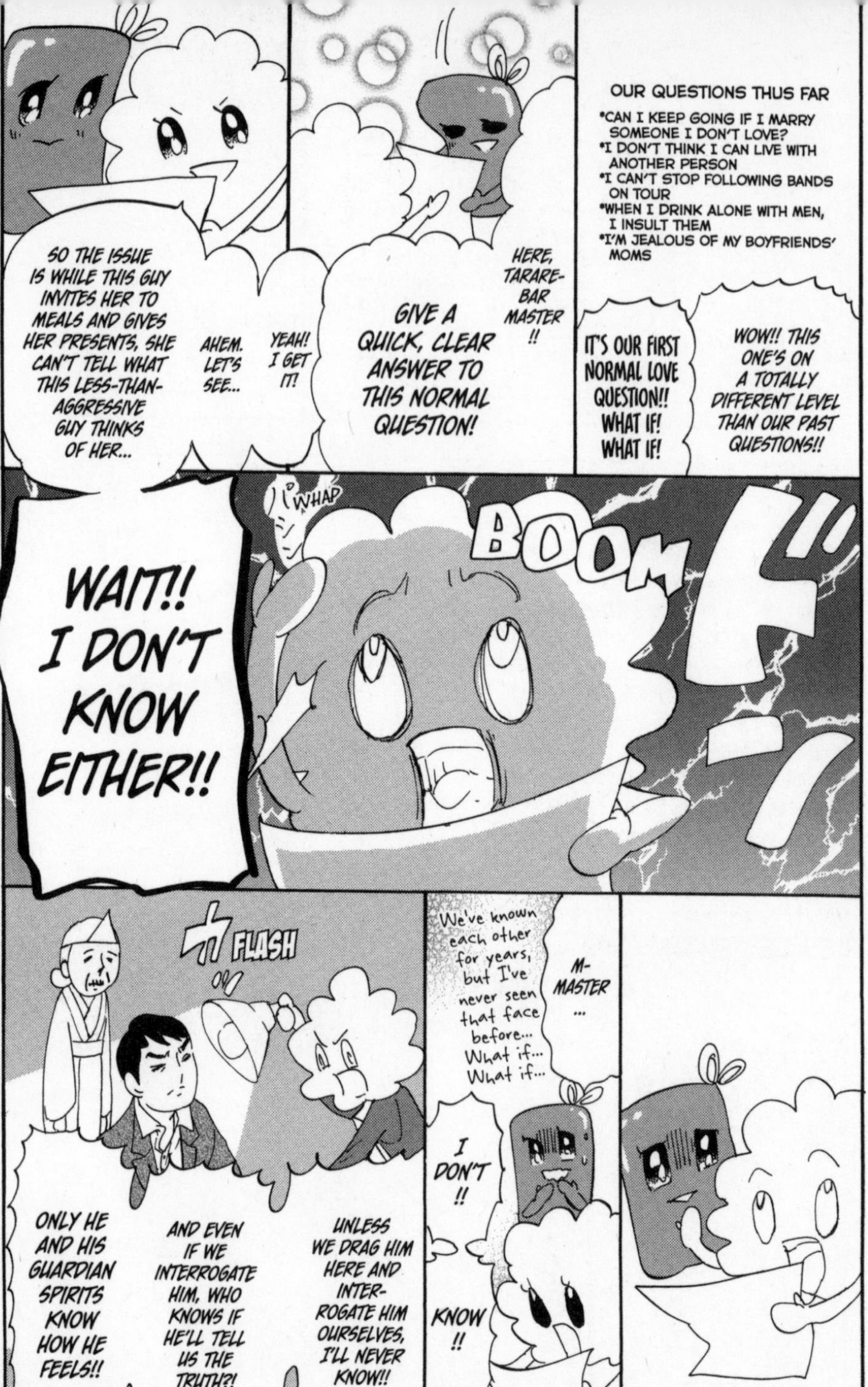

OUR QUESTIONS THUS FAR
*CAN I KEEP GOING IF I MARRY SOMEONE I DON'T LOVE?
*I DON'T THINK I CAN LIVE WITH ANOTHER PERSON
*I CAN'T STOP FOLLOWING BANDS ON TOUR
*WHEN I DRINK ALONE WITH MEN, I INSULT THEM
*I'M JEALOUS OF MY BOYFRIENDS' MOMS
WOW!! THIS ONE'S ON A TOTALLY DIFFERENT LEVEL THAN OUR PAST QUESTIONS!!
IT'S OUR FIRST NORMAL LOVE QUESTION!! WHAT IF! WHAT IF!
HERE, TARARE-BAR MASTER!!
GIVE A QUICK, CLEAR ANSWER TO THIS NORMAL QUESTION!
YEAH! I GET IT!
AHEM. LET'S SEE...
SO THE ISSUE IS WHILE THIS GUY INVITES HER TO MEALS AND GIVES HER PRESENTS, SHE CAN'T TELL WHAT THIS LESS-THAN-AGGRESSIVE GUY THINKS OF HER...
WHAP
BOOM
WAIT!! I DON'T KNOW EITHER!!
M-MASTER...
We've known each other for years, but I've never seen that face before... What if... What if...
I DON'T!!
KNOW!!
FLASH
UNLESS WE DRAG HIM HERE AND INTER-ROGATE HIM OURSELVES, I'LL NEVER KNOW!!
AND EVEN IF WE INTERROGATE HIM, WHO KNOWS IF HE'LL TELL US THE TRUTH?!
ONLY HE AND HIS GUARDIAN SPIRITS KNOW HOW HE FEELS!!

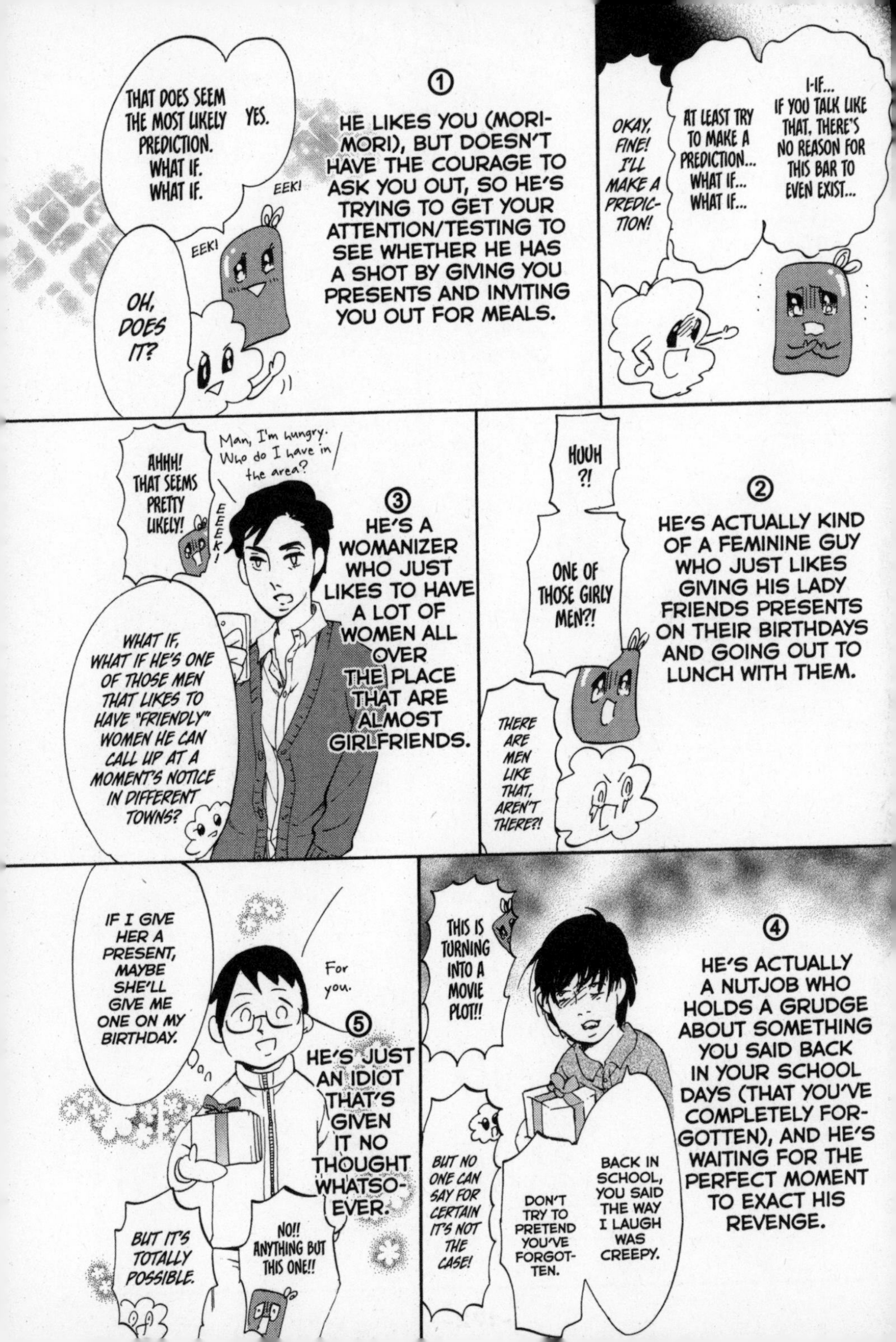
I-IF... IF YOU TALK LIKE THAT, THERE'S NO REASON FOR THIS BAR TO EVEN EXIST...
AT LEAST TRY TO MAKE A PREDICTION... WHAT IF... WHAT IF...
OKAY, FINE! I'LL MAKE A PREDICTION!
① HE LIKES YOU (MORI-MORI), BUT DOESN'T HAVE THE COURAGE TO ASK YOU OUT, SO HE'S TRYING TO GET YOUR ATTENTION/TESTING TO SEE WHETHER HE HAS A SHOT BY GIVING YOU PRESENTS AND INVITING YOU OUT FOR MEALS.
YES.
THAT DOES SEEM THE MOST LIKELY PREDICTION. WHAT IF. WHAT IF.
EEK!
EEK!
OH, DOES IT?
② HE'S ACTUALLY KIND OF A FEMININE GUY WHO JUST LIKES GIVING HIS LADY FRIENDS PRESENTS ON THEIR BIRTHDAYS AND GOING OUT TO LUNCH WITH THEM.
HUUH ?!
ONE OF THOSE GIRLY MEN?!
THERE ARE MEN LIKE THAT, AREN'T THERE?!
③ HE'S A WOMANIZER WHO JUST LIKES TO HAVE A LOT OF WOMEN ALL OVER THE PLACE THAT ARE ALMOST GIRLFRIENDS.
Man, I'm hungry. Who do I have in the area?
AHHH! THAT SEEMS PRETTY LIKELY!
EEEK!
WHAT IF, WHAT IF HE'S ONE OF THOSE MEN THAT LIKES TO HAVE "FRIENDLY" WOMEN HE CAN CALL UP AT A MOMENT'S NOTICE IN DIFFERENT TOWNS?
④ HE'S ACTUALLY A NUTJOB WHO HOLDS A GRUDGE ABOUT SOMETHING YOU SAID BACK IN YOUR SCHOOL DAYS (THAT YOU'VE COMPLETELY FOR-GOTTEN), AND HE'S WAITING FOR THE PERFECT MOMENT TO EXACT HIS REVENGE.
THIS IS TURNING INTO A MOVIE PLOT!!
BACK IN SCHOOL, YOU SAID THE WAY I LAUGH WAS CREEPY.
DON'T TRY TO PRETEND YOU'VE FORGOT-TEN.
BUT NO ONE CAN SAY FOR CERTAIN IT'S NOT THE CASE!
⑤ HE'S JUST AN IDIOT THAT'S GIVEN IT NO THOUGHT WHATSO-EVER.
For you.
IF I GIVE HER A PRESENT, MAYBE SHE'LL GIVE ME ONE ON MY BIRTHDAY.
NO!! ANYTHING BUT THIS ONE!!
BUT IT'S TOTALLY POSSIBLE.

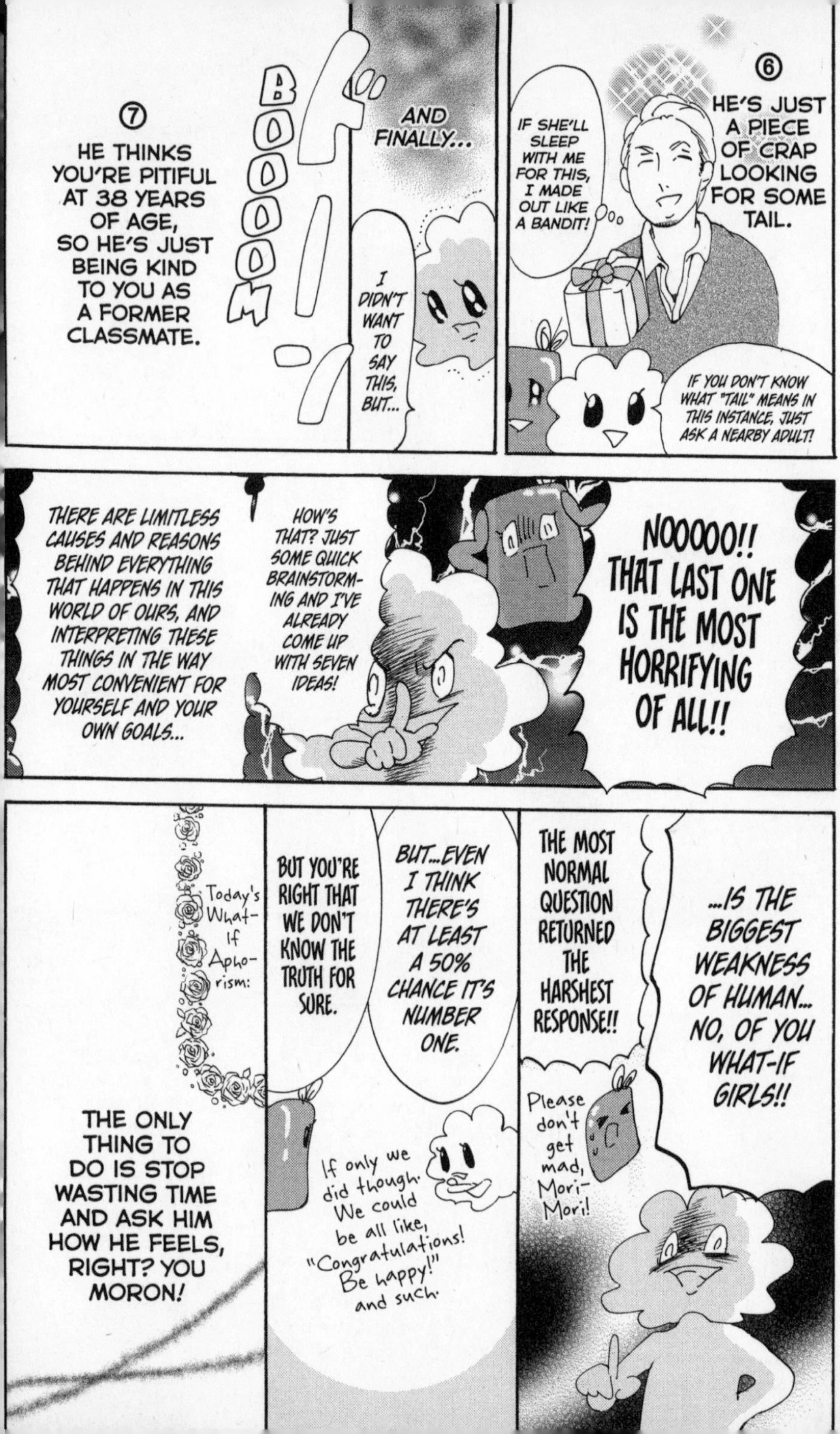
⑥
HE'S JUST A PIECE OF CRAP LOOKING FOR SOME TAIL.
IF SHE'LL SLEEP WITH ME FOR THIS, I MADE OUT LIKE A BANDIT!
IF YOU DON'T KNOW WHAT "TAIL" MEANS IN THIS INSTANCE, JUST ASK A NEARBY ADULT!
AND FINALLY...
I DIDN'T WANT TO SAY THIS, BUT...
BOOOOOM
⑦
HE THINKS YOU'RE PITIFUL AT 38 YEARS OF AGE, SO HE'S JUST BEING KIND TO YOU AS A FORMER CLASSMATE.
NOOOOO!! THAT LAST ONE IS THE MOST HORRIFYING OF ALL!!
HOW'S THAT? JUST SOME QUICK BRAINSTORMING AND I'VE ALREADY COME UP WITH SEVEN IDEAS!
THERE ARE LIMITLESS CAUSES AND REASONS BEHIND EVERYTHING THAT HAPPENS IN THIS WORLD OF OURS, AND INTERPRETING THESE THINGS IN THE WAY MOST CONVENIENT FOR YOURSELF AND YOUR OWN GOALS...
...IS THE BIGGEST WEAKNESS OF HUMAN... NO, OF YOU WHAT-IF GIRLS!!
THE MOST NORMAL QUESTION RETURNED THE HARSHEST RESPONSE!!
Please don't get mad, Mori-Mori!
BUT...EVEN I THINK THERE'S AT LEAST A 50% CHANCE IT'S NUMBER ONE.
BUT YOU'RE RIGHT THAT WE DON'T KNOW THE TRUTH FOR SURE.
If only we did though. We could be all like, "Congratulations! Be happy!" and such.
Today's What-If Aphorism:
THE ONLY THING TO DO IS STOP WASTING TIME AND ASK HIM HOW HE FEELS, RIGHT? YOU MORON!

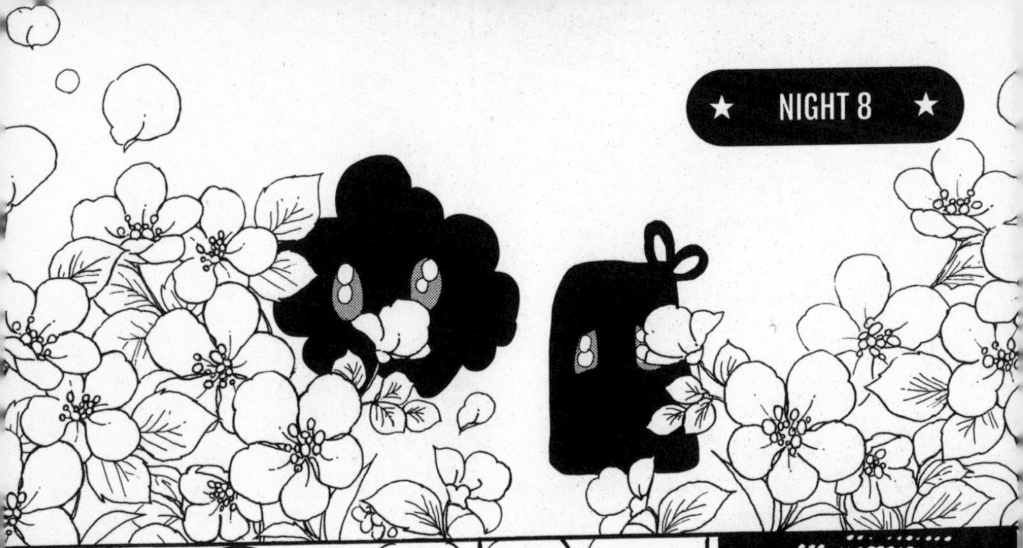
★ NIGHT 8 ★

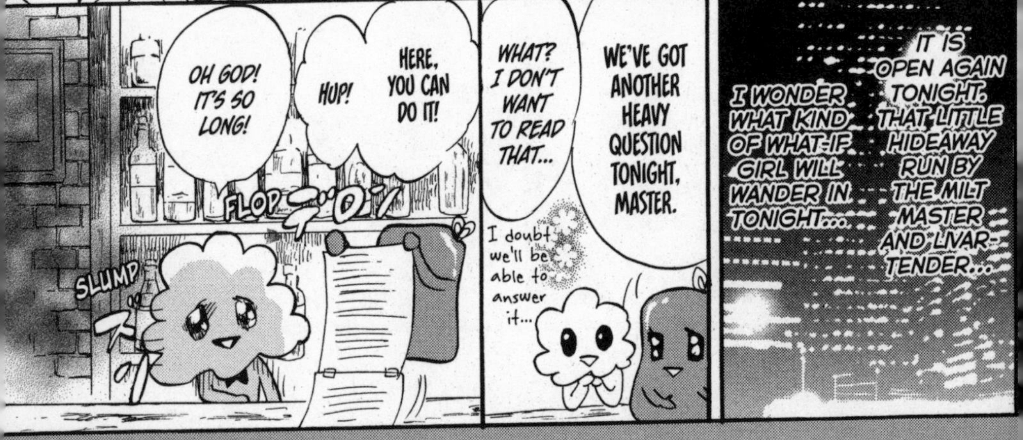
IT IS OPEN AGAIN TONIGHT. THAT LITTLE HIDEAWAY RUN BY THE MILT MASTER AND LIVAR-TENDER...
I WONDER WHAT KIND OF WHAT-IF GIRL WILL WANDER IN TONIGHT...
WE'VE GOT ANOTHER HEAVY QUESTION TONIGHT, MASTER.
WHAT? I DON'T WANT TO READ THAT...
I doubt we'll be able to answer it...
HERE, YOU CAN DO IT!
HUP!
OH GOD! IT'S SO LONG!
FLOP
SLUMP

PROBLEM: I CAN NEVER HAVE A RELATIONSHIP THAT ISN'T PURELY PHYSICAL...

I AM 32. I'VE NEVER HAD A REAL "BOYFRIEND." IN MY TWENTIES I HAD NO SELF CONFIDENCE, AND I GOT TO THINKING THAT I'D RATHER SPEND ONE NIGHT WITH THE BOY I LIKED THAN BE A VIRGIN FOR THE REST OF MY LIFE. SO, I JUST ASKED MY CRUSH TO HAVE SEX WITH ME. BUT THEN, CONTRARY TO MY ORIGINAL PLAN OF JUST MAKING DO WITH THAT MEMORY, I ENDED UP IN A FRIENDS-WITH-BENEFITS SITUATION INSTEAD.

THEN, EIGHT YEARS PASSED. ONCE THAT RELATIONSHIP BECAME TOO MUCH TO BEAR, I DECIDED TO FIND A NEW LOVE. THEN, I FELL FOR A "MODEL IN HIS THIRTIES" AND A "CUTE BOY SEVEN YEARS MY JUNIOR." BUT I DON'T KNOW ANYTHING ABOUT ROMANCE BESIDES SEX, SO BEFORE I KNEW IT I WAS IN A PURELY PHYSICAL RELATIONSHIP WITH THESE TWO WITH NO SIGNS OF ANY PROGRESS BEYOND THAT.

WHAT AM I DOING AT MY AGE? I'VE STARTED THINKING THAT IF I WAS JUST GOING TO BECOME A TOTAL EASY LAY, I SHOULD'VE JUST STAYED WITH MY LONG-TERM FRIEND WITH BENEFITS, SO I'M ON THE VERGE OF GOING BACK TO HIM. PLEASE GIVE ME SOME ADVICE.

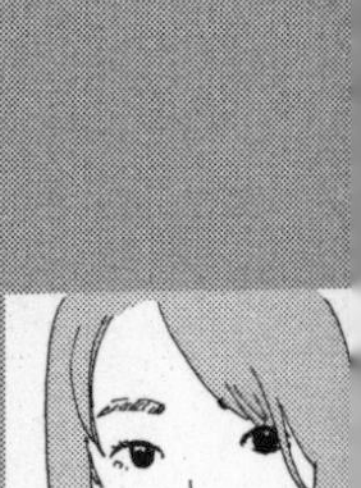

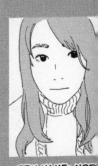

PEN NAME: NOR THE BEANPOLE (32)

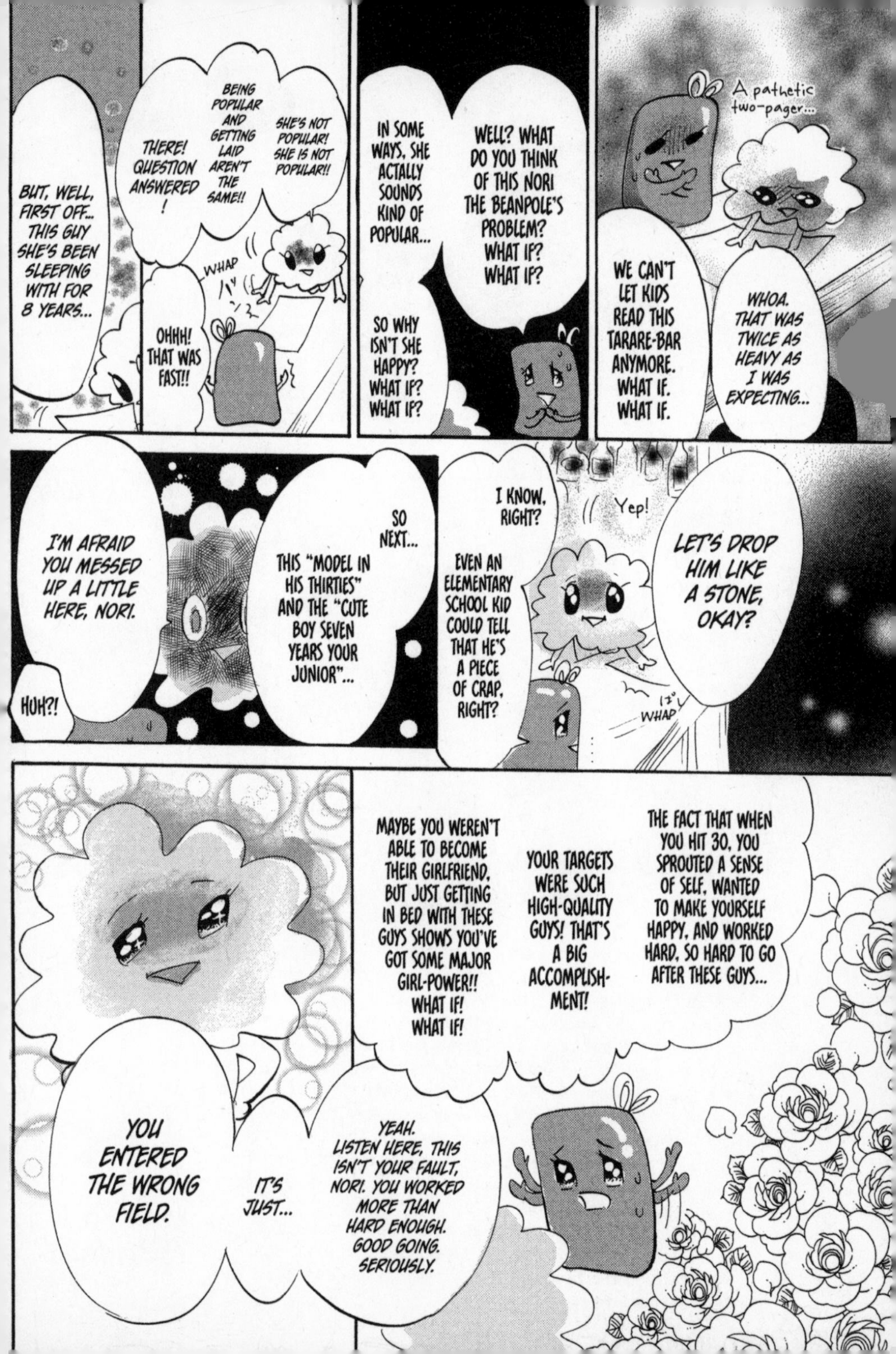
A pathetic two-pager...
WHOA. THAT WAS TWICE AS HEAVY AS I WAS EXPECTING...
WE CAN'T LET KIDS READ THIS TARARE-BAR ANYMORE. WHAT IF. WHAT IF.
WELL? WHAT DO YOU THINK OF THIS NORI THE BEANPOLE'S PROBLEM? WHAT IF? WHAT IF?
IN SOME WAYS, SHE ACTALLY SOUNDS KIND OF POPULAR...
SO WHY ISN'T SHE HAPPY? WHAT IF? WHAT IF?
SHE'S NOT POPULAR! SHE IS NOT POPULAR!!
BEING POPULAR AND GETTING LAID AREN'T THE SAME!!
THERE! QUESTION ANSWERED!
WHAP
OHHH! THAT WAS FAST!!
BUT, WELL, FIRST OFF... THIS GUY SHE'S BEEN SLEEPING WITH FOR 8 YEARS...
LET'S DROP HIM LIKE A STONE, OKAY?
Yep!
I KNOW, RIGHT?
EVEN AN ELEMENTARY SCHOOL KID COULD TELL THAT HE'S A PIECE OF CRAP, RIGHT?
WHAP
SO NEXT...
THIS "MODEL IN HIS THIRTIES" AND THE "CUTE BOY SEVEN YEARS YOUR JUNIOR"...
I'M AFRAID YOU MESSED UP A LITTLE HERE, NORI.
HUH?!
THE FACT THAT WHEN YOU HIT 30, YOU SPROUTED A SENSE OF SELF, WANTED TO MAKE YOURSELF HAPPY, AND WORKED HARD, SO HARD TO GO AFTER THESE GUYS...
YOUR TARGETS WERE SUCH HIGH-QUALITY GUYS! THAT'S A BIG ACCOMPLISH-MENT!
MAYBE YOU WEREN'T ABLE TO BECOME THEIR GIRLFRIEND, BUT JUST GETTING IN BED WITH THESE GUYS SHOWS YOU'VE GOT SOME MAJOR GIRL-POWER!! WHAT IF! WHAT IF!
YEAH. LISTEN HERE, THIS ISN'T YOUR FAULT, NORI. YOU WORKED MORE THAN HARD ENOUGH. GOOD GOING. SERIOUSLY.
IT'S JUST...
YOU ENTERED THE WRONG FIELD.

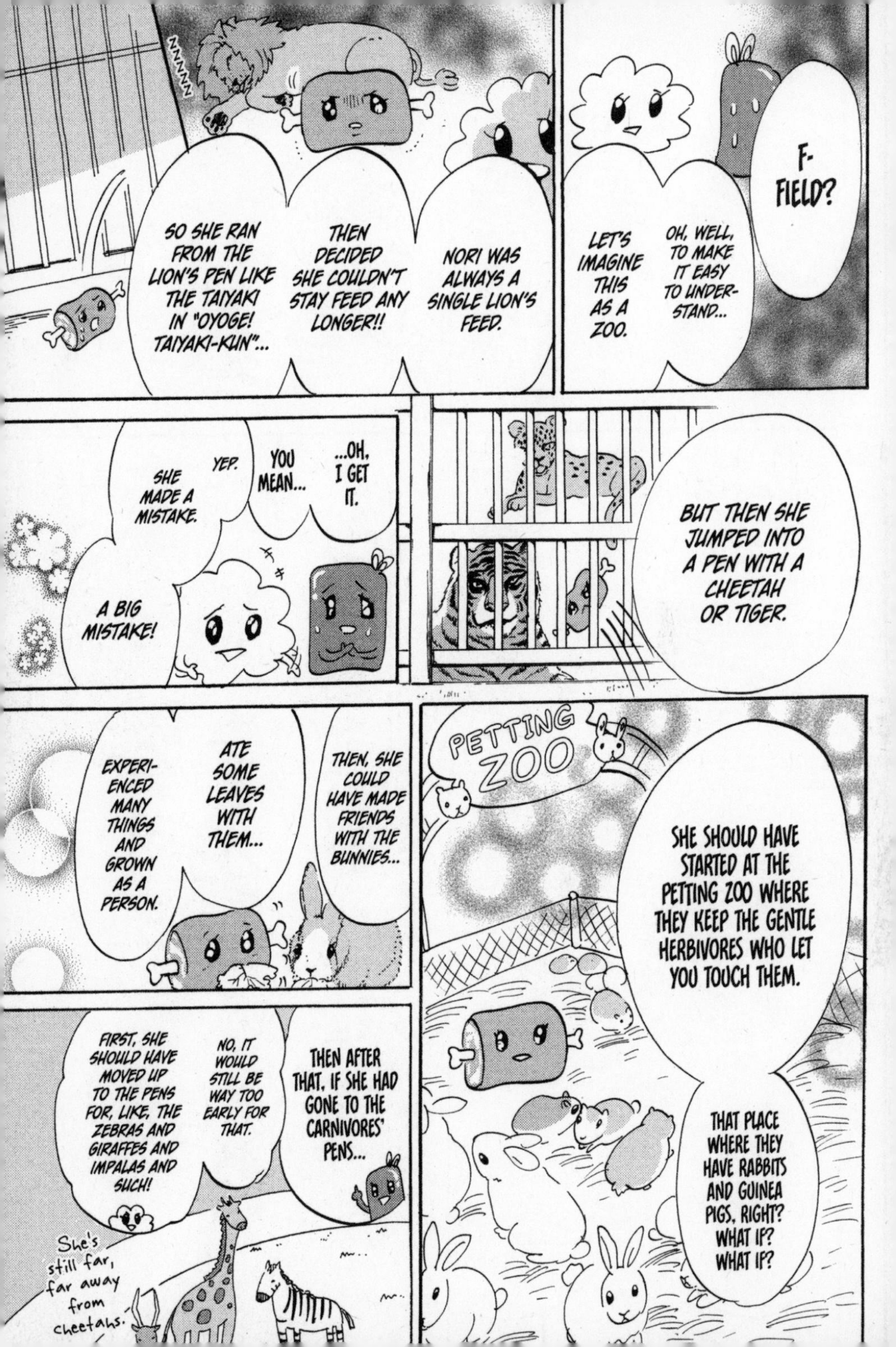
F-FIELD?
OH, WELL, TO MAKE IT EASY TO UNDERSTAND...
LET'S IMAGINE THIS AS A ZOO.
NORI WAS ALWAYS A SINGLE LION'S FEED.
THEN DECIDED SHE COULDN'T STAY FEED ANY LONGER!!
SO SHE RAN FROM THE LION'S PEN LIKE THE TAIYAKI IN "OYOGE! TAIYAKI-KUN"...
ZZZZZ
BUT THEN SHE JUMPED INTO A PEN WITH A CHEETAH OR TIGER.
...OH, I GET IT.
YOU MEAN...
YEP.
SHE MADE A MISTAKE.
A BIG MISTAKE!
PETTING ZOO
SHE SHOULD HAVE STARTED AT THE PETTING ZOO WHERE THEY KEEP THE GENTLE HERBIVORES WHO LET YOU TOUCH THEM.
THAT PLACE WHERE THEY HAVE RABBITS AND GUINEA PIGS, RIGHT? WHAT IF? WHAT IF?
THEN, SHE COULD HAVE MADE FRIENDS WITH THE BUNNIES...
ATE SOME LEAVES WITH THEM...
EXPERI-ENCED MANY THINGS AND GROWN AS A PERSON.
THEN AFTER THAT, IF SHE HAD GONE TO THE CARNIVORES' PENS...
NO, IT WOULD STILL BE WAY TOO EARLY FOR THAT.
FIRST, SHE SHOULD HAVE MOVED UP TO THE PENS FOR, LIKE, THE ZEBRAS AND GIRAFFES AND IMPALAS AND SUCH!
She's still far, far away from cheetahs.

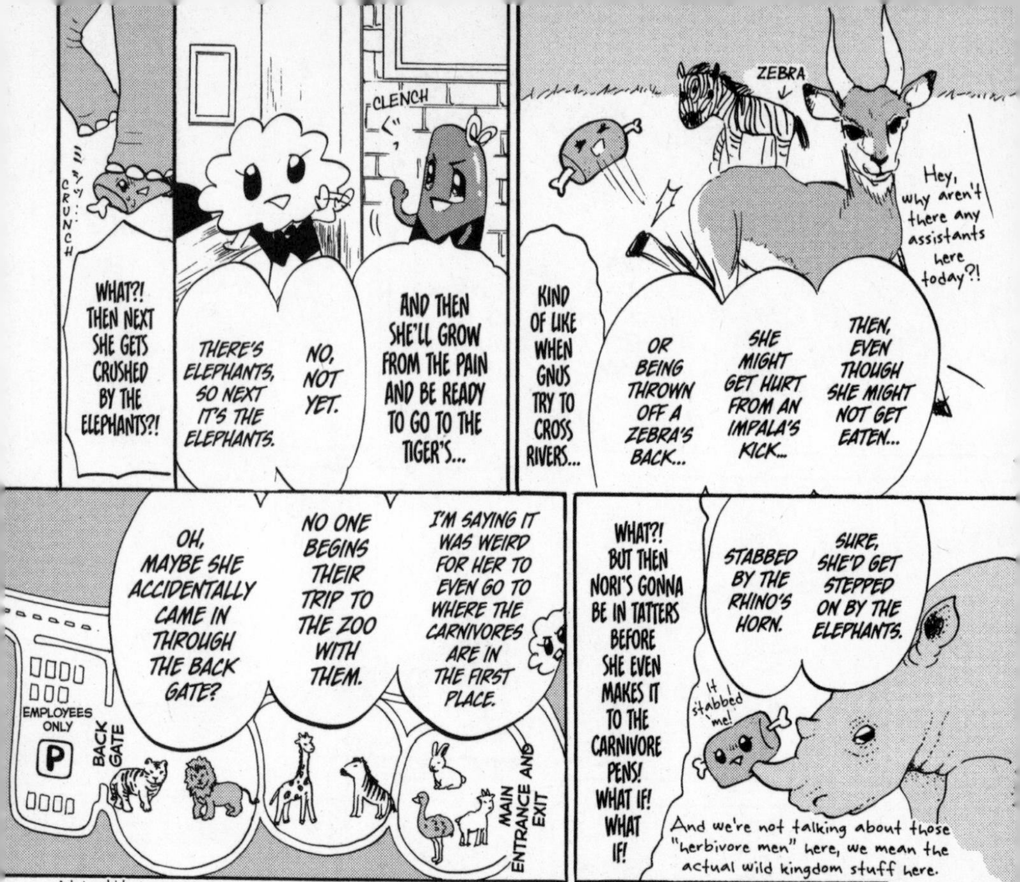
ZEBRA
Hey, why aren't there any assistants here today?!
THEN, EVEN THOUGH SHE MIGHT NOT GET EATEN...
SHE MIGHT GET HURT FROM AN IMPALA'S KICK...
OR BEING THROWN OFF A ZEBRA'S BACK...
KIND OF LIKE WHEN GNUS TRY TO CROSS RIVERS...
CLENCH
AND THEN SHE'LL GROW FROM THE PAIN AND BE READY TO GO TO THE TIGER'S...
NO, NOT YET.
THERE'S ELEPHANTS, SO NEXT IT'S THE ELEPHANTS.
CRUNCH
WHAT?! THEN NEXT SHE GETS CRUSHED BY THE ELEPHANTS?!
SURE, SHE'D GET STEPPED ON BY THE ELEPHANTS.
STABBED BY THE RHINO'S HORN.
WHAT?! BUT THEN NORI'S GONNA BE IN TATTERS BEFORE SHE EVEN MAKES IT TO THE CARNIVORE PENS! WHAT IF! WHAT IF!
It stabbed me!
And we're not talking about those "herbivore men" here, we mean the actual wild kingdom stuff here.
I'M SAYING IT WAS WEIRD FOR HER TO EVEN GO TO WHERE THE CARNIVORES ARE IN THE FIRST PLACE.
NO ONE BEGINS THEIR TRIP TO THE ZOO WITH THEM.
OH, MAYBE SHE ACCIDENTALLY CAME IN THROUGH THE BACK GATE?
MAIN ENTRANCE AND EXIT
EMPLOYEES ONLY
P
BACK GATE

Note: *Herbivore Men are men characterized b their disinterest in love, relationships, and sex (see full note in Volume 2).

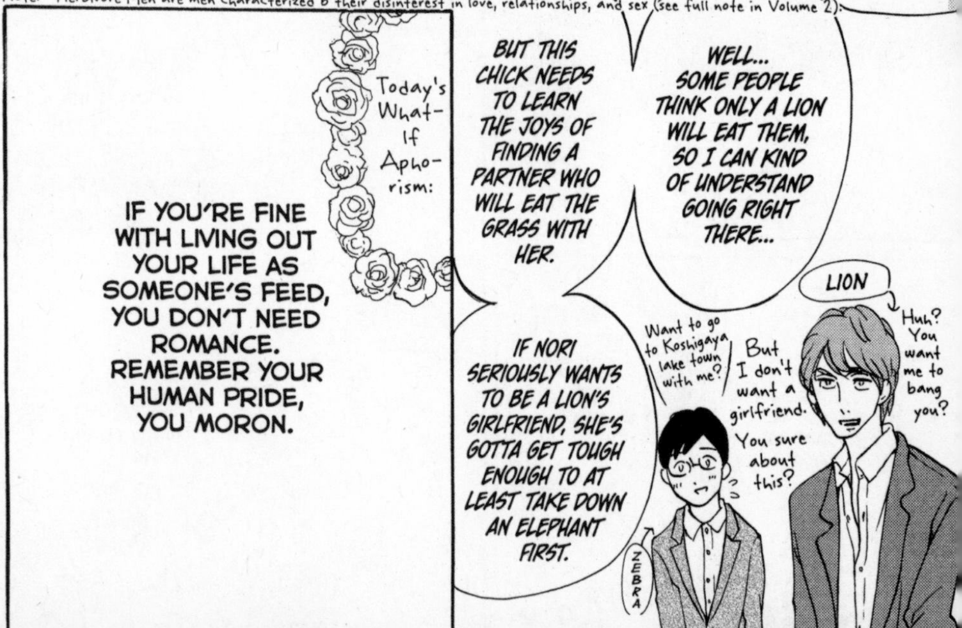
WELL... SOME PEOPLE THINK ONLY A LION WILL EAT THEM, SO I CAN KIND OF UNDERSTAND GOING RIGHT THERE...
BUT THIS CHICK NEEDS TO LEARN THE JOYS OF FINDING A PARTNER WHO WILL EAT THE GRASS WITH HER.
LION
Huh? You want me to bang you?
But I don't want a girlfriend.
Want to go to Koshigaya lake town with me?
You sure about this?
IF NORI SERIOUSLY WANTS TO BE A LION'S GIRLFRIEND, SHE'S GOTTA GET TOUGH ENOUGH TO AT LEAST TAKE DOWN AN ELEPHANT FIRST.
ZEBRA
Today's What-If Aphorism:
IF YOU'RE FINE WITH LIVING OUT YOUR LIFE AS SOMEONE'S FEED, YOU DON'T NEED ROMANCE. REMEMBER YOUR HUMAN PRIDE, YOU MORON.

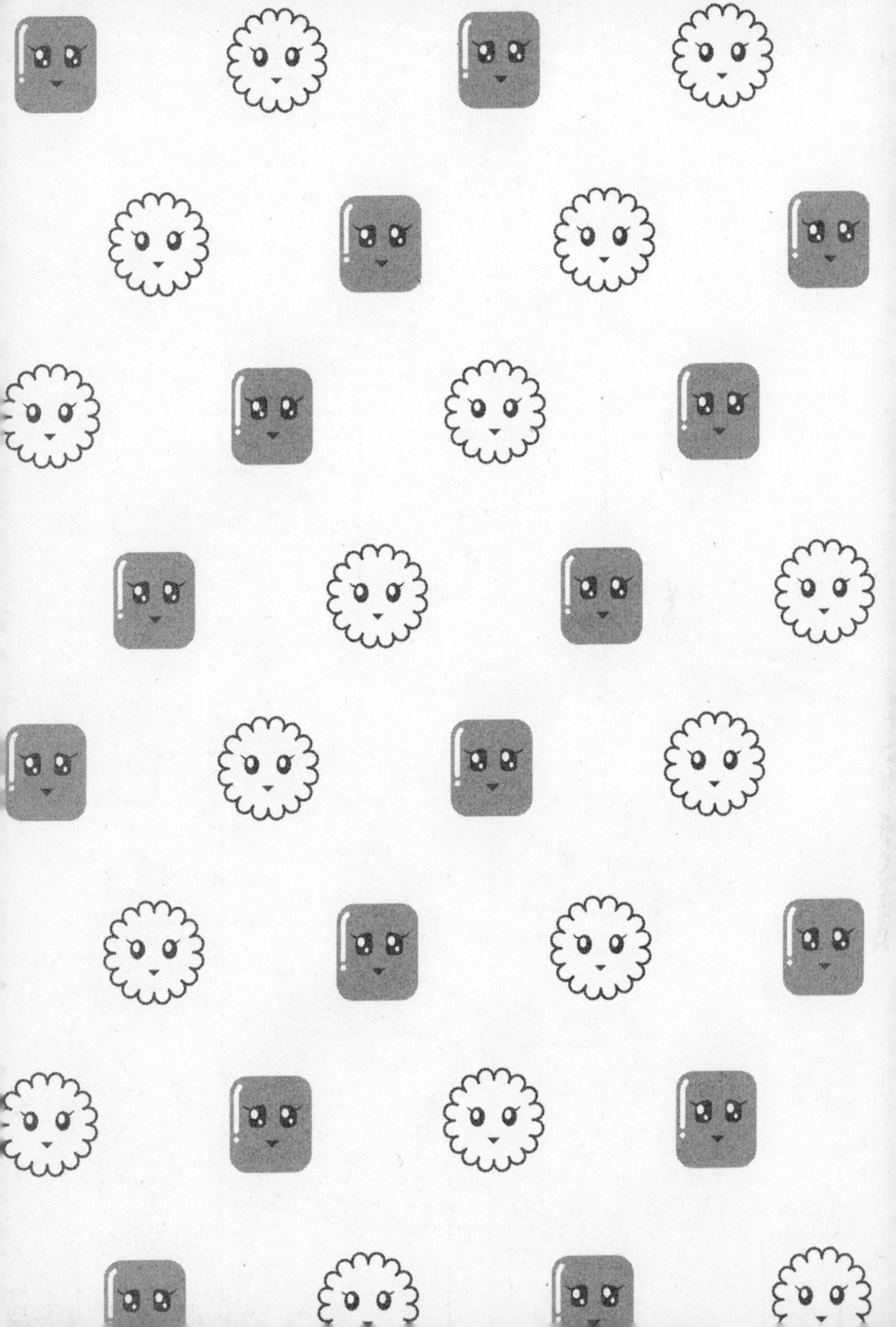

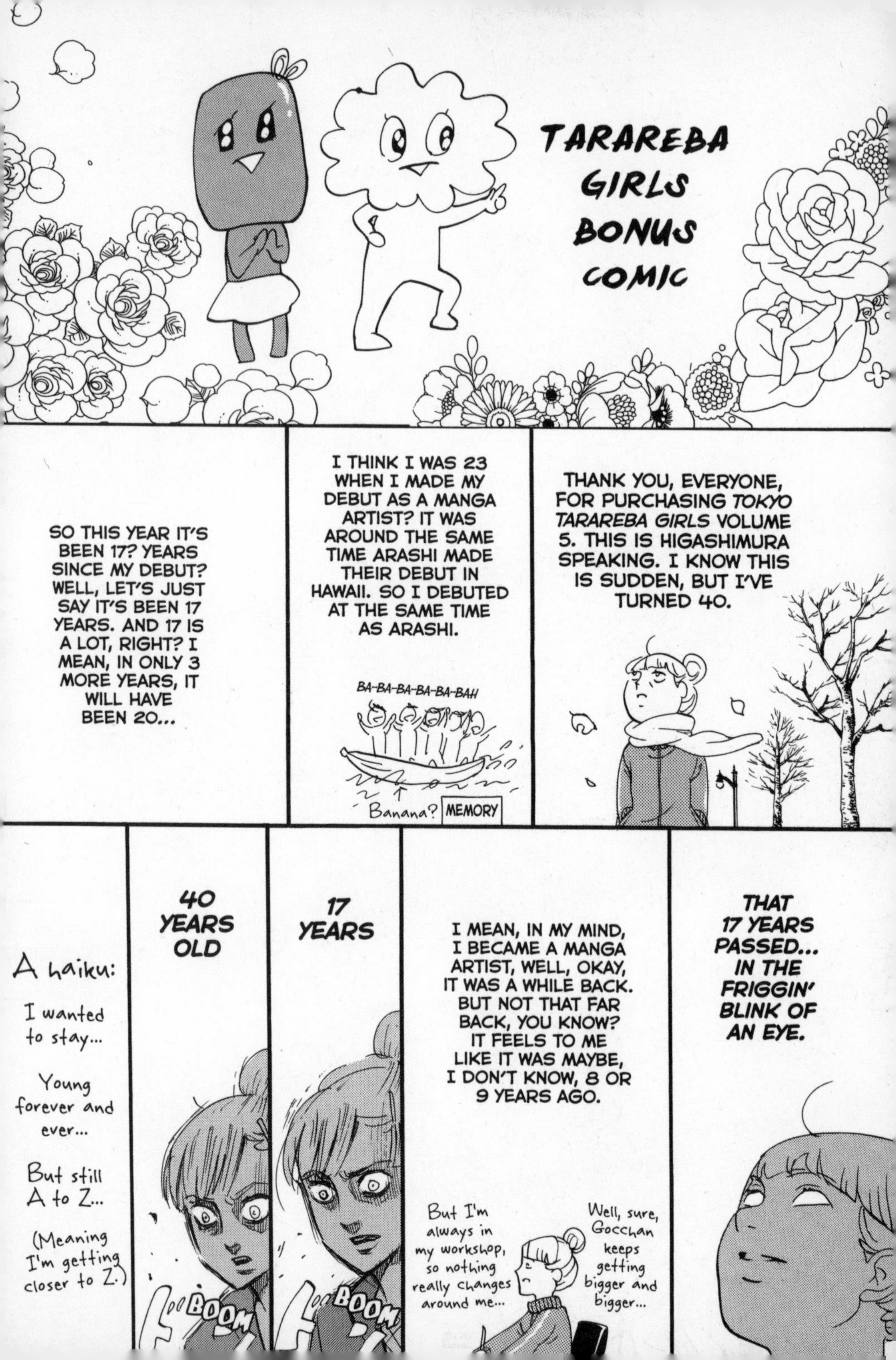
TARAREBA GIRLS BONUS COMIC
THANK YOU, EVERYONE, FOR PURCHASING *TOKYO TARAREBA GIRLS* VOLUME 5. THIS IS HIGASHIMURA SPEAKING. I KNOW THIS IS SUDDEN, BUT I'VE TURNED 40.
I THINK I WAS 23 WHEN I MADE MY DEBUT AS A MANGA ARTIST? IT WAS AROUND THE SAME TIME ARASHI MADE THEIR DEBUT IN HAWAII. SO I DEBUTED AT THE SAME TIME AS ARASHI.
BA-BA-BA-BA-BA-BAH
Banana?
MEMORY
SO THIS YEAR IT'S BEEN 17? YEARS SINCE MY DEBUT? WELL, LET'S JUST SAY IT'S BEEN 17 YEARS. AND 17 IS A LOT, RIGHT? I MEAN, IN ONLY 3 MORE YEARS, IT WILL HAVE BEEN 20...
THAT 17 YEARS PASSED... IN THE FRIGGIN' BLINK OF AN EYE.
I MEAN, IN MY MIND, I BECAME A MANGA ARTIST, WELL, OKAY, IT WAS A WHILE BACK. BUT NOT THAT FAR BACK, YOU KNOW? IT FEELS TO ME LIKE IT WAS MAYBE, I DON'T KNOW, 8 OR 9 YEARS AGO.
Well, sure, Gocchan keeps getting bigger and bigger...
But I'm always in my workshop, so nothing really changes around me...
17 YEARS
BOOM
40 YEARS OLD
BOOM
A haiku:
I wanted to stay...
Young forever and ever...
But still A to Z...
(Meaning I'm getting closer to Z.)

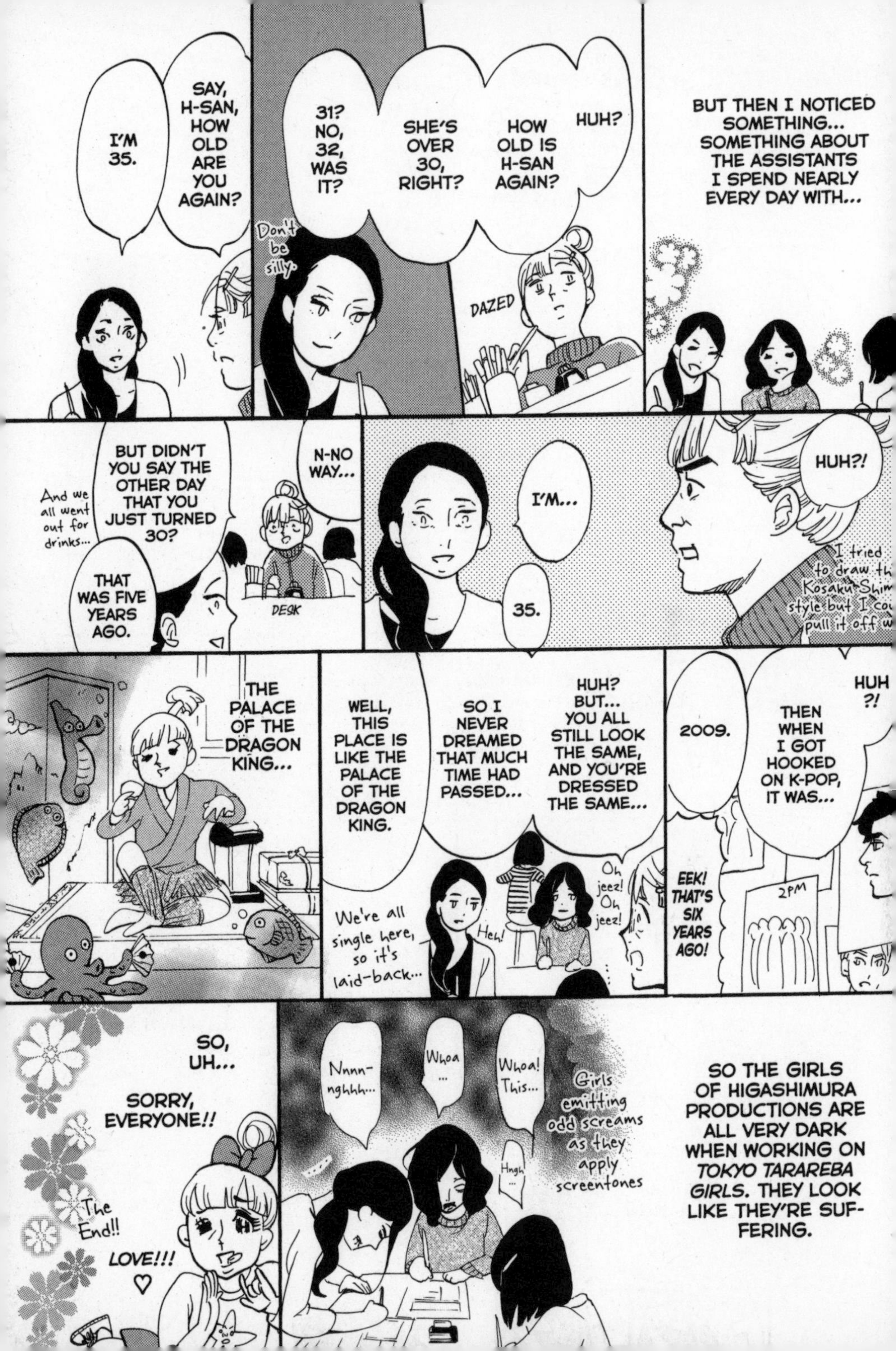
BUT THEN I NOTICED SOMETHING... SOMETHING ABOUT THE ASSISTANTS I SPEND NEARLY EVERY DAY WITH...
HUH?
HOW OLD IS H-SAN AGAIN?
SHE'S OVER 30, RIGHT?
31? NO, 32, WAS IT?
Don't be silly.
DAZED
SAY, H-SAN, HOW OLD ARE YOU AGAIN?
I'M 35.
HUH?!
I'M...
35.
N-NO WAY...
BUT DIDN'T YOU SAY THE OTHER DAY THAT YOU JUST TURNED 30?
And we all went out for drinks...
THAT WAS FIVE YEARS AGO.
DESK
HUH ?!
THEN WHEN I GOT HOOKED ON K-POP, IT WAS...
2009.
EEK! THAT'S SIX YEARS AGO!
2PM
HUH? BUT... YOU ALL STILL LOOK THE SAME, AND YOU'RE DRESSED THE SAME...
SO I NEVER DREAMED THAT MUCH TIME HAD PASSED...
WELL, THIS PLACE IS LIKE THE PALACE OF THE DRAGON KING.
Oh jeez! Oh jeez!
Heh!
We're all single here, so it's laid-back...
THE PALACE OF THE DRAGON KING...
SO THE GIRLS OF HIGASHIMURA PRODUCTIONS ARE ALL VERY DARK WHEN WORKING ON *TOKYO TARAREBA GIRLS*. THEY LOOK LIKE THEY'RE SUF-FERING.
Whoa! This...
Whoa...
Nnnn-nghhh...
Girls emitting odd screams as they apply screentones
Hngh...
SO, UH...
SORRY, EVERYONE!!
The End!!
LOVE!!! ♡

Tokyo Tarareba Girls Translation notes

Tokyo Tarareba Girls: *"Tarareba"* means "What-if," like the "What-if" stories you tell yourself about what could be or could have been. The name is also taken from the names of the two food characters in the series, *tara* (codfish milt) and *reba* (liver) who always say *"tara"* and *"reba"* respectively at the end of their sentences in Japanese, referencing the "what-if" meaning of *"tarareba."*

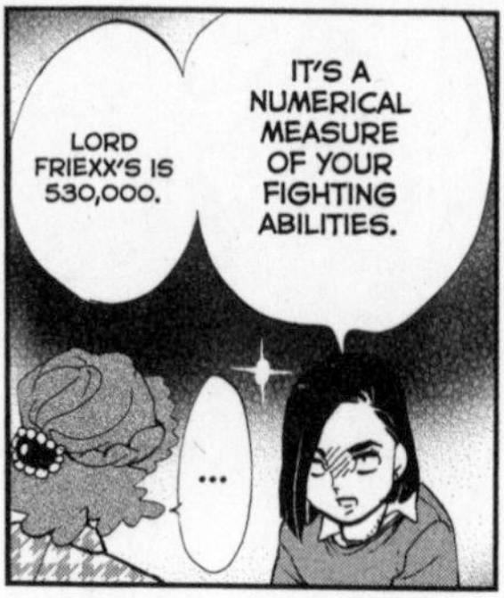
IT'S A NUMERICAL MEASURE OF YOUR FIGHTING ABILITIES.
LORD FRIEXX'S IS 530,000.
...

Lord Friexx, page 12
Lord Friexx is most likely a reference to the character Frieza, who is one of the most powerful recurring villains in the *Dragon Ball* franchise.

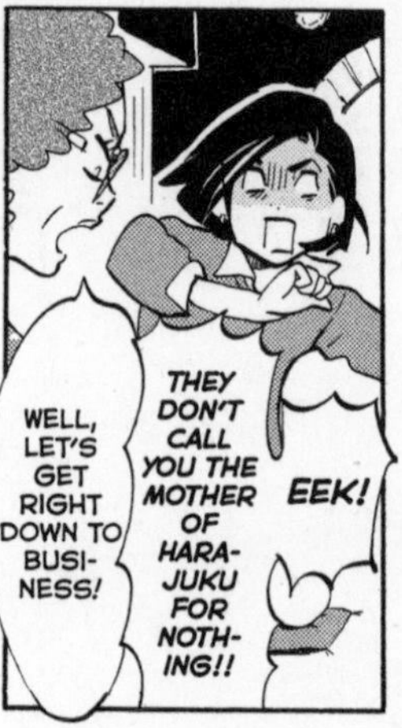
EEK!
THEY DON'T CALL YOU THE MOTHER OF HARA-JUKU FOR NOTH-ING!!
WELL, LET'S GET RIGHT DOWN TO BUSI-NESS!

Mother of Harajuku *(Harajuku No Haha)*, page 13
A famous real-life fortune-teller, based in Harajuku.

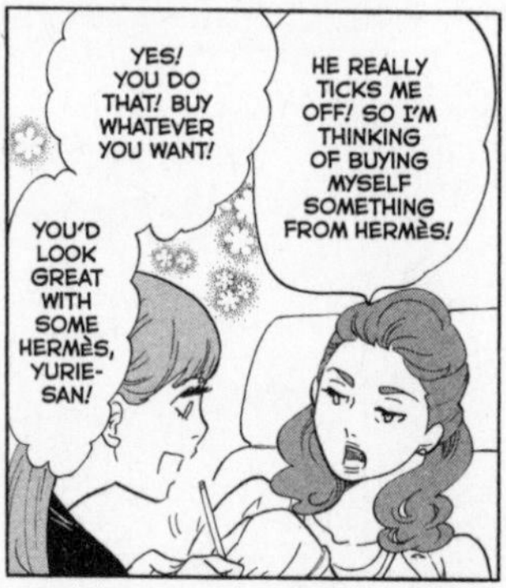
HE REALLY TICKS ME OFF! SO I'M THINKING OF BUYING MYSELF SOMETHING FROM HERMÈS!
YES! YOU DO THAT! BUY WHATEVER YOU WANT!
YOU'D LOOK GREAT WITH SOME HERMÈS, YURIE-SAN!

Hermès International S.A., page 17
A French luxury goods manufacturer. They have boutiques in Japan, including Tokyo.

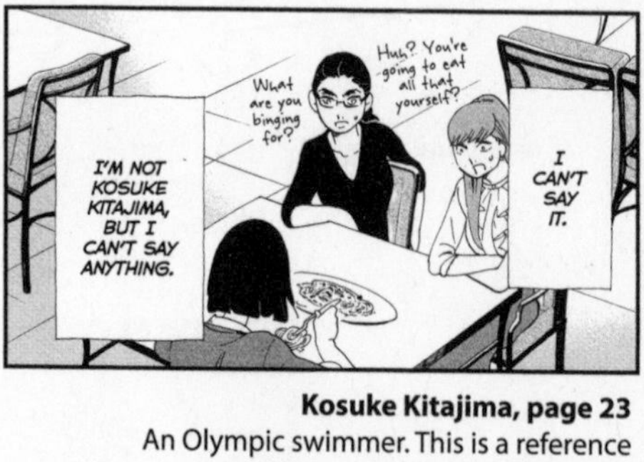
I CAN'T SAY IT.
Huh? You're going to eat all that yourself?
What are you binging for?
I'M NOT KOSUKE KITAJIMA, BUT I CAN'T SAY ANYTHING.

Kosuke Kitajima, page 23
An Olympic swimmer. This is a reference to a comment he made after a race.

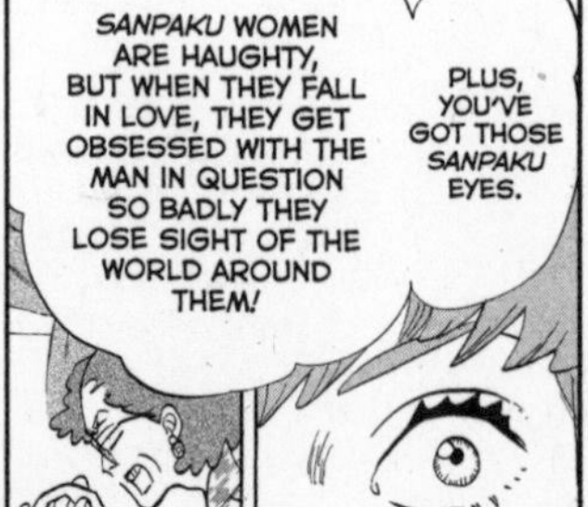
PLUS, YOU'VE GOT THOSE SANPAKU EYES.
SANPAKU WOMEN ARE HAUGHTY, BUT WHEN THEY FALL IN LOVE, THEY GET OBSESSED WITH THE MAN IN QUESTION SO BADLY THEY LOSE SIGHT OF THE WORLD AROUND THEM!

***Sanpaku* eyes, page 24**
Eyes in which the whites are visible above or below the iris (when the subject is looking straight ahead).

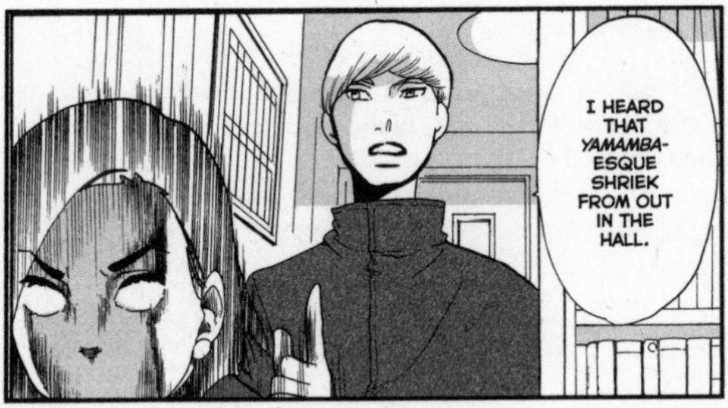
I HEARD THAT *YAMAMBA*-ESQUE SHRIEK FROM OUT IN THE HALL.

***Yamamba*, page 48**

Both the "mountain witch" from Japanese folklore and a more extreme offshoot of the *ganguro* fashion style named after her because of the presumed resemblance of its adherents to the witch.

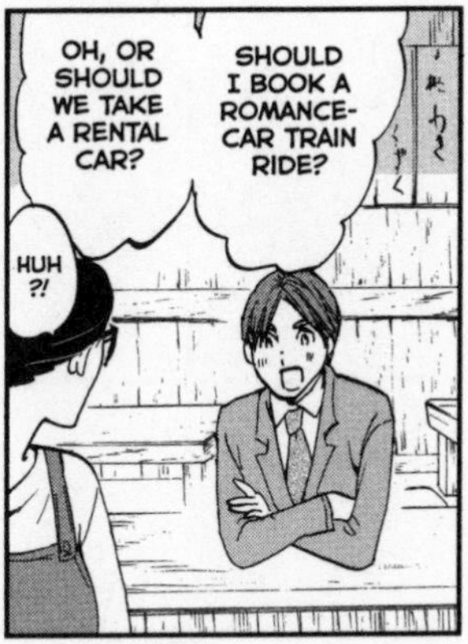
SHOULD I BOOK A ROMANCE-CAR TRAIN RIDE?
OH, OR SHOULD WE TAKE A RENTAL CAR?
HUH ?!

Romancecar, page 56

The Romancecar is a luxury Odakyu train line in Japan that services tourist destinations like Hakone. The name comes from the original "romance seats"—two-seaters built without an armrest in the middle.

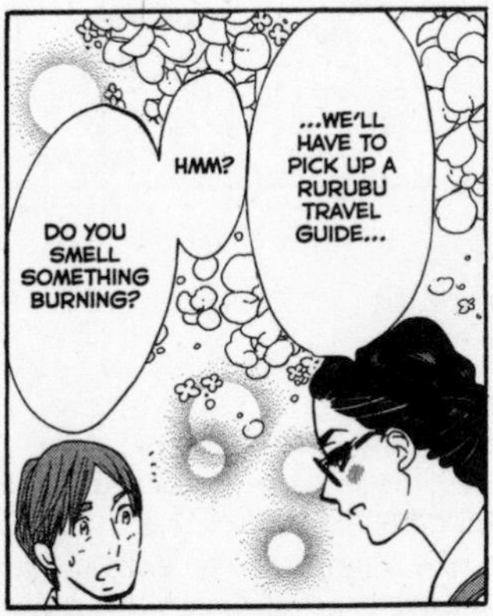
...WE'LL HAVE TO PICK UP A RURUBU TRAVEL GUIDE...
HMM?
DO YOU SMELL SOMETHING BURNING?

Rurubu, page 57

Refers to a series of travel guides published in Japan by JTB Publishing, Inc.

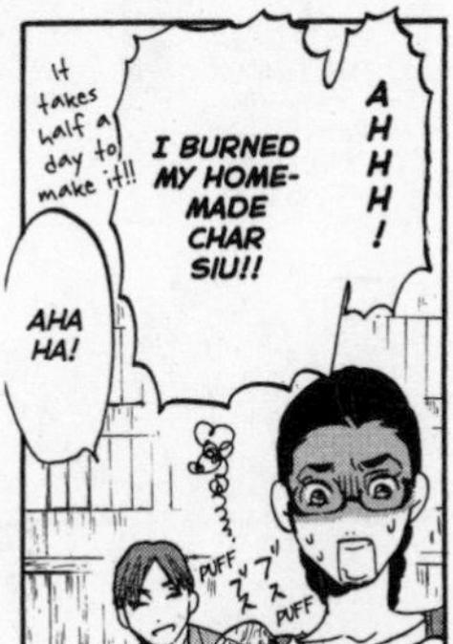
AHHH!
I BURNED MY HOME-MADE CHAR SIU!!
It takes half a day to make it!!
AHA HA!
PUFF
PUFF

Char Siu, page 57

A type of Cantonese barbecued pork.

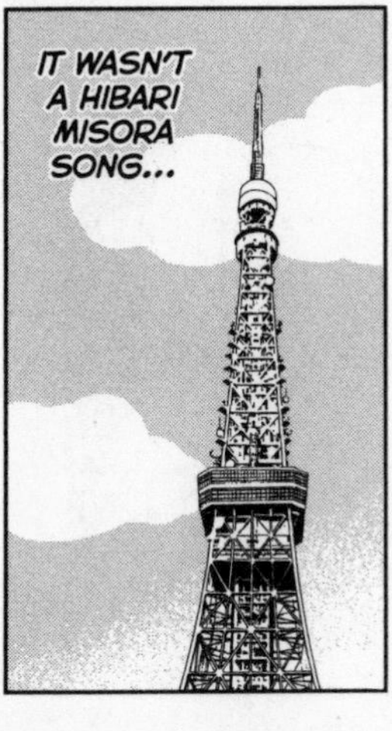
IT WASN'T A HIBARI MISORA SONG...

Hibari Misora, page 62

A singer and actress who began her career as a child in the 1940s, recording over 1000 songs and appearing in over 150 movies before dying in 1989 at only 52 years old. Rinko's narration in the following panels are modifications of a few lines from her song "Tokyo Kid."

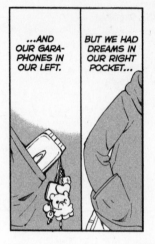

Gara-phones, page 62

Gara-phones, short for "Galapagos phones." These were highly specialized mobile phones popular in Japan that predated true smart phones. Because they were built on proprietary systems that only worked well within Japan, they failed to catch on in the wider world, and so, like many residents of the Galapagos Islands, they became specialized and outdated to the point of being unique.

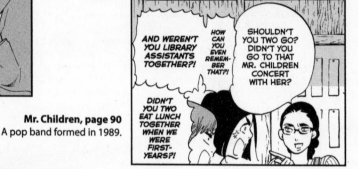

BUT WE HAD DREAMS IN OUR RIGHT POCKET...
...AND OUR GARA-PHONES IN OUR LEFT.

SHOULDN'T YOU TWO GO? DIDN'T YOU GO TO THAT MR. CHILDREN CONCERT WITH HER?
HOW CAN YOU EVEN REMEMBER THAT?!
AND WEREN'T YOU LIBRARY ASSISTANTS TOGETHER?!
DIDN'T YOU TWO EAT LUNCH TOGETHER WHEN WE WERE FIRST-YEARS?!

Mr. Children, page 90

A pop band formed in 1989.

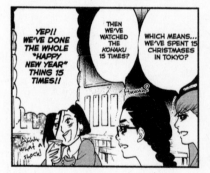

WHICH MEANS... WE'VE SPENT 15 CHRISTMASES IN TOKYO?
THEN WE'VE WATCHED THE KOHAKU 15 TIMES?
Huuuh?
YEP!! WE'VE DONE THE WHOLE "HAPPY NEW YEAR" THING 15 TIMES!!
Ahhh, what a shock!

Kohaku, page 90

Kohaku is short for *NHK Kohaku Uta Gassen (NHK Red and White Song Battle)*, which is a New Year's Eve invite-only singing "competition" between the most successful recording artists in Japan. The artists are split along gender lines, with female artists making up the red team, and male artists comprising the white team. At the end of the program, judges and the audience vote on which team performed the best. Performing on the show is seen as a highlight in an artist's career.

I'M FINE WITH ANYONE WHO ISN'T THE FIRSTBORN SON!!

Firstborn son, page 106

Firstborn sons in Japan are usually on the hook for caring for their parents as they age, and/or for taking over any sort of family enterprise or family property. Thus, Koyuki is looking for someone who won't ultimately end up with family duties, and who would likely be more able to live a life more on her terms.

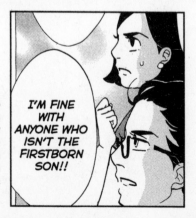

***Motsuni*, page 108**

A dish of stewed animal offal. It's generally beef offal, but pork and chicken are also popular.

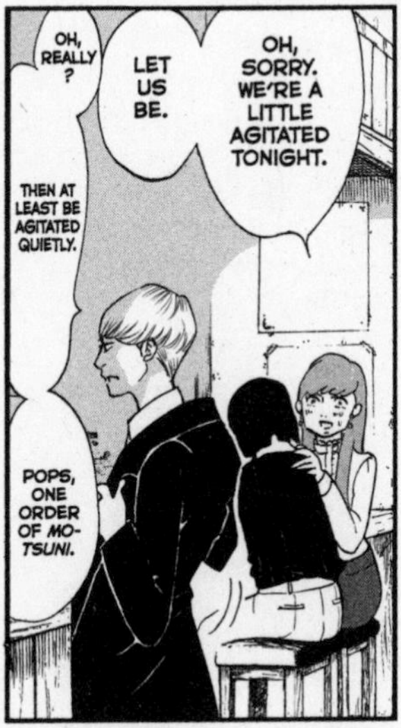
OH, SORRY. WE'RE A LITTLE AGITATED TONIGHT.
LET US BE.
OH, REALLY?
THEN AT LEAST BE AGITATED QUIETLY.
POPS, ONE ORDER OF *MOTSUNI*.

Sugako Hashida, page 111

A very successful TV screenwriter. She began writing in the 1960s and has had a long career since.

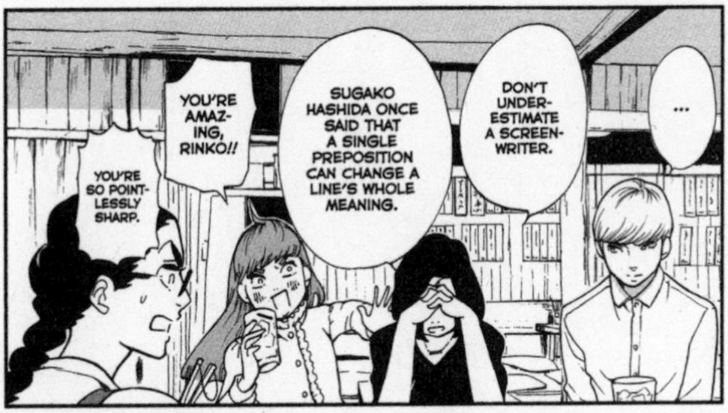
...
DON'T UNDERESTIMATE A SCREENWRITER.
SUGAKO HASHIDA ONCE SAID THAT A SINGLE PREPOSITION CAN CHANGE A LINE'S WHOLE MEANING.
YOU'RE AMAZING, RINKO!!
YOU'RE SO POINTLESSLY SHARP.

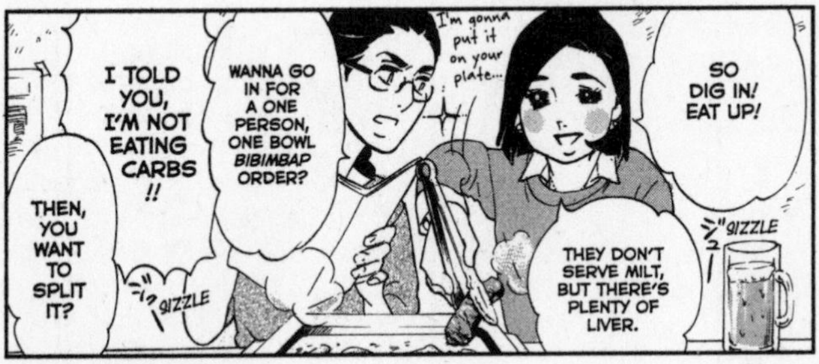
SO DIG IN! EAT UP!
I'm gonna put it on your plate...
THEY DON'T SERVE MILT, BUT THERE'S PLENTY OF LIVER.
SIZZLE
WANNA GO IN FOR A ONE PERSON, ONE BOWL *BIBIMBAP* ORDER?
I TOLD YOU, I'M NOT EATING CARBS!!
THEN, YOU WANT TO SPLIT IT?
SIZZLE

Bibimbap, page 129

A Korean dish made of rice mixed with meat, vegetables, and various sauces.

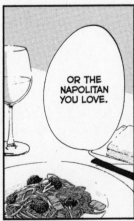

Napolitan, page 136

A Japanese spaghetti dish made with sausage, onions, peppers, and ketchup.

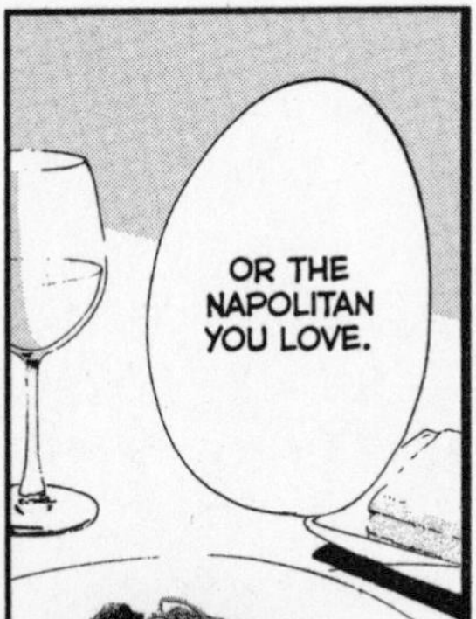
OR THE NAPOLITAN YOU LOVE.

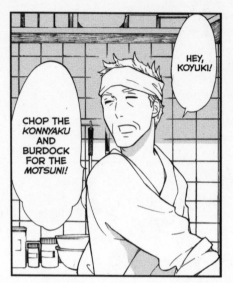

HEY, KOYUKI!
CHOP THE *KONNYAKU* AND BURDOCK FOR THE *MOTSUNI!*

***Konnyaku* and burdock, page 138**
Konnyaku is a firm gelatin made from the Konjac plant. Burdock is an edible root vegetable popular in Japanese cuisine.

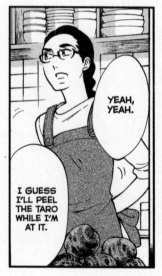

YEAH, YEAH.
I GUESS I'LL PEEL THE TARO WHILE I'M AT IT.

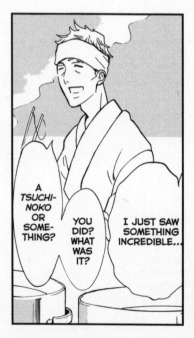

Taro, page 139
A type of edible tuber plant.

I JUST SAW SOMETHING INCREDIBLE...
YOU DID? WHAT WAS IT?
A *TSUCHI-NOKO* OR SOME-THING?

***Tsuchinoko*, page 144**
A creature from Japanese folklore resembling a fat snake.

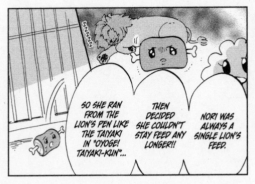

NORI WAS ALWAYS A SINGLE LION'S FEED.
THEN DECIDED SHE COULDN'T STAY FEED ANY LONGER!!
SO SHE RAN FROM THE LION'S PEN LIKE THE TAIYAKI IN "OYOGE! TAIYAKI-KUN"...

***Oyoge! Taiyaki-kun*, page 177**

A children's song released in 1975 after being featured in the children's show *Hirake Ponkikki.* The song is about a *taiyaki* (a fish-shaped sweet bun traditionally filled with red bean paste or cream) which manages to escape the bakery to swim freely in the sea.

Kosaku Shima, page 181

The protagonist of the manga series *Kacho Kosaku Shima*, about a salaryman named Kosaku Shima.

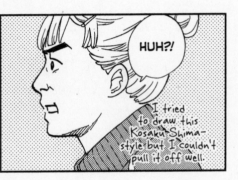

HUH?!
I tried to draw this Kosaku Shima-style but I couldn't pull it off well.

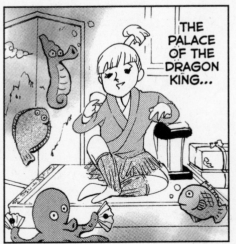

THE PALACE OF THE DRAGON KING...

The Palace of the Dragon King, page 181

The mythical dwelling of Ryujin, the undersea dragon king, featured in part of the Urashima Taro legend. Time flows differently in the palace, and what was a short while there could be equivalent to hundreds of years in the outside world.

Kinichiro Imamura isn't a bad guy, really, but on the first day of high school his narrow eyes and bleached blonde hair made him look so shifty that his classmates assumed the worst. Three years later, without any friends or fond memories, he isn't exactly feeling bittersweet about graduation. But after an accidental fall down a flight of stairs, Kinichiro wakes up three years in the past... on the first day of high school! School's starting again—but it's gonna be different this time around!

Vol. 1-3 now available in **PRINT** and **DIGITAL**!
Vol. 4 coming August 2018!
Find out **MORE** by visiting:
kodanshacomics.com/MitsurouKubo

ABOUT **MITSUROU KUBO**

Mitsurou Kubo is a manga artist born in Nagasaki prefecture. Her series *3.3.7 Byoshi!!* (2001-2003), *Tokkyu!!* (2004-2008), and *Again!!* (2011-2014) were published in *Weekly Shonen Magazine*, and *Moteki* (2008-2010) was published in the seinen comics magazine *Evening*. After the publication of *Again!!* concluded, she met Sayo Yamamoto, director of the global smash-hit anime *Yuri!!! on ICE*. Working with Yamamoto, Kubo contributed the original concept, original character designs, and initial script for *Yuri!!! on ICE*. *Again!!* is her first manga to be published in English.

KodanshaCOMICS

"*Complex Age* feels like an intimate look at women in fandom... I can't recommend it enough."
—*Manga Connection*

②

complex age
yui sakuma

26-year-old Nagisa Kataura has a secret. Transforming into her favorite anime and manga characters is her passion in life and she's earned great respect amongst her fellow cospayers. But to the rest of society, her hobby is a silly fantasy. As demands from both her office job and cosplaying begin to increase, she may one day have to make a tough choice— what's more important to her, cosplay or being "normal"?

Princess Jellyfish

Akiko Higashimura

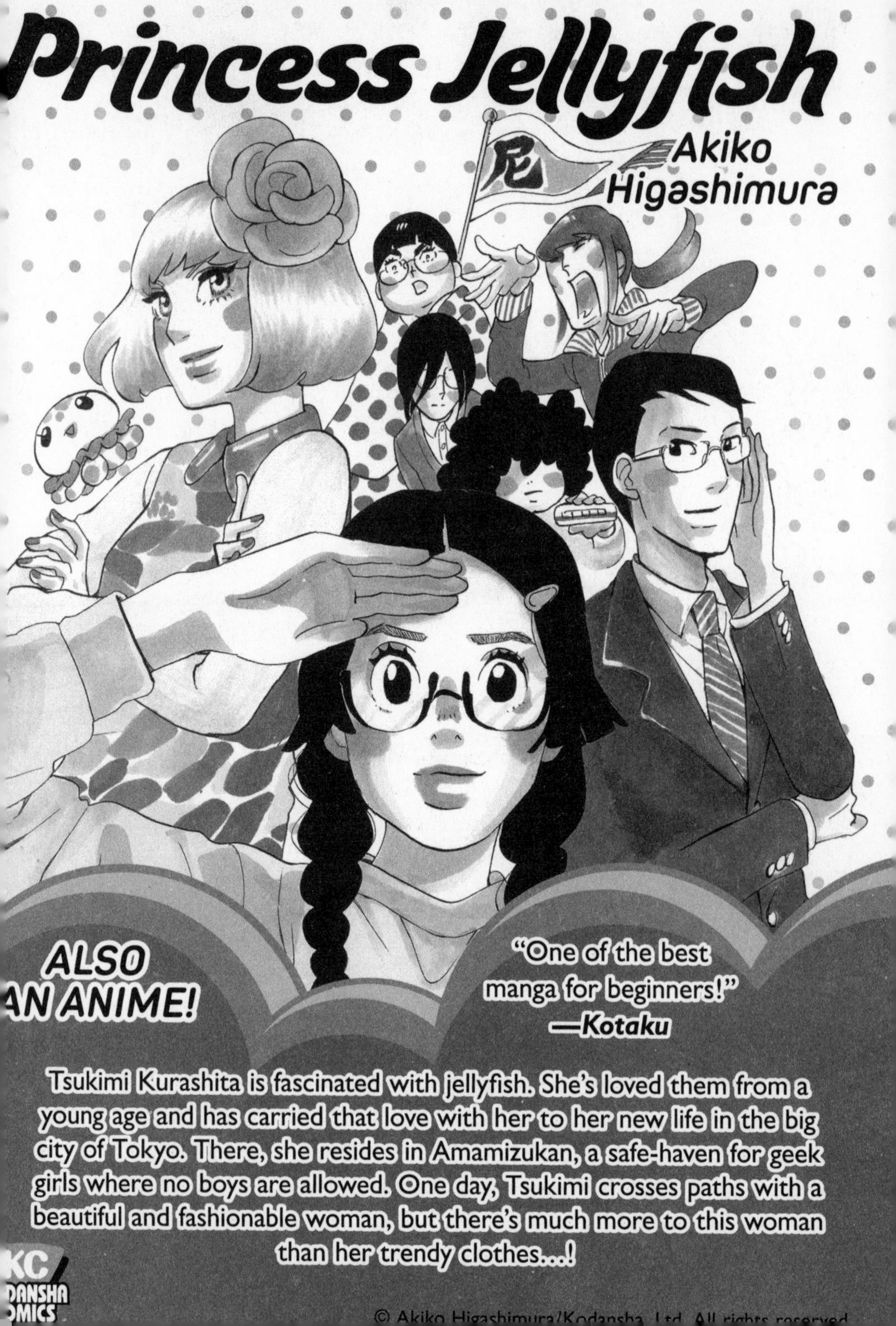
尼

ALSO AN ANIME!

"One of the best manga for beginners!"
—*Kotaku*

Tsukimi Kurashita is fascinated with jellyfish. She's loved them from a young age and has carried that love with her to her new life in the big city of Tokyo. There, she resides in Amamizukan, a safe-haven for geek girls where no boys are allowed. One day, Tsukimi crosses paths with a beautiful and fashionable woman, but there's much more to this woman than her trendy clothes...!

KC KODANSHA COMICS

In love, there are
no save points.

NOW AN
ANIME!

ヲタクに恋は難しい

WOTAKOI:
LOVE IS HARD FOR OTAKU
by FUJITA

Narumi has had it rough: Every boyfriend she's had dumped her
once they found out she was an otaku, so she's gone to great
lengths to hide it. At her new job, she bumps into Hirotaka, her
childhood friend and fellow otaku. When Hirotaka almost gets
her secret outed at work, she comes up with a plan to keep him
quiet. But he comes up with a counter-proposal:
Why doesn't she just date him instead?

Tokyo Tarareba Girls volume 5 is a work of fiction. Names, characters, places, and incidents are the products of the author's imagination or are used fictitiously. Any resemblance to actual events, locales, or persons, living or dead, is entirely coincidental.

A Kodansha Comics Trade Paperback Original.

Tokyo Tarareba Girls volume 5 copyright © 2016 Akiko Higashimura
English translation copyright © 2019 Akiko Higashimura

All rights reserved.

Published in the United States by Kodansha Comics,
an imprint of Kodansha USA Publishing, LLC, New York.

Publication rights for this English edition arranged through Kodansha Ltd.,
Tokyo.

First published in Japan in 2016 by Kodansha Ltd., Tokyo, as *Tokyo Tarareba Musume* volume 5.

ISBN 978-1-63236-735-8

Printed in the United States of America.

www.kodanshacomics.com

9 8 7 6 5 4 3 2 1

Translation: Steven LeCroy
Lettering: Thea Willis and Paige Pumphrey
Editing: Sarah Tilson and Lauren Scanlan
YKS Services LLC
Kodansha Comics